Artistic Luxury

Artistic Luxury

Fabergé Tiffany Lalique

Stephen Harrison, Emmanuel Ducamp, and Jeannine Falino

With contributions by Christie Mayer Lefkowith,
Pilar Vélez, Catherine Walworth, and Wilfried Zeisler

PUBLISHED BY THE CLEVELAND MUSEUM OF ART
IN ASSOCIATION WITH
YALE UNIVERSITY PRESS, NEW HAVEN AND LONDON

The Cleveland Museum of Art Board of Trustees

Artistic Luxury was organized by
the Cleveland Museum of Art. This
exhibition is presented through
the generous support of National
City. The Cleveland Museum of Art
gratefully acknowledges the Citizens
of Cuyahoga County for their support
through Cuyahoga Arts and Culture.
The Ohio Arts Council helped fund
this exhibition with state tax dollars
to encourage economic growth,
educational excellence, and cultural
enrichment for all Ohioans.

Generous support for the exhibition
catalogue has been provided by
a grant from The Tiffany & Co.
Foundation.

The Cleveland Museum of Art
19 October 2008–18 January 2009
Fine Arts Museums of San Francisco
7 February–31 May 2009
Library of Congress Control Number:
2008934163
Casebound, the Cleveland Museum
of Art, ISBN: 978-0-940717-98-5
Paperback, the Cleveland Museum of
Art, ISBN: 978-0-940717-99-2
Casebound, Yale University Press,
ISBN: 978-0-300-14224-2
Yale University Press
www.yalebooks.com

Produced by the Publications
Department of the Cleveland
Museum of Art

Editing: Barbara J. Bradley,
Kathleen Mills, Jane Takac Panza,
and Amy Sparks

Design: Laurence Channing

Production: Charles Szabla

Digital retouching: David Brichford
and Ellen Ferar

Rights and permissions: Bridget
Weber

Printing: Great Lakes Integrated,
Cleveland

Contents

Director's Foreword   VII

Acknowledgments   VIII

Artistic Luxury in the Belle Époque   1
Stephen Harrison

France: The Ascendancy of Lalique   74
Emmanuel Ducamp

Russia: Fabergé and His Competitors   152
Emmanuel Ducamp and Wilfried Ziesler

America: A Tale of Two Tiffanys   230
Jeannine Falino

Catalogue of the Exhibition   324

Select Bibliography   342

Comparative Illustrations   349

Photography Credits   353

Index   354

Director's Foreword

Fabergé, Tiffany, Lalique. Each of these legendary names conjures an era of opulence and innovation in the decorative arts, and each represents, in his own right, a peak of excellence in both craftsmanship and creativity that has rarely been equaled, either before or since. Born in the middle decades of the nineteenth century, these three designers came of age during a time of remarkable change both in the visual arts and in the market for (and marketing of) the luxury goods their work came to epitomize.

The accomplishments of each of these great artists and entrepreneurs—for they were both, and remarkably successful in establishing an international market for the jewelry and objets d'art their prolific and highly accomplished workshops produced—have been chronicled in numerous monographic studies and exhibitions. *Artistic Luxury,* however, offers the first comparative survey of the work of Peter Carl Fabergé, Louis Comfort Tiffany, and René Lalique during the decades just before and after the turn of the twentieth century. It was at this time that they came to dominate their field and into direct competition with one another. The centerpiece of this exhibition is a group of works each artist displayed at the 1900 Exposition Universelle in Paris, the only time they showed their wares together. That encounter fueled their rivalry and inspired them, as all spirited competitions do, to achieve something even greater.

Yet *Artistic Luxury* is more than this, for it also chronicles the rich context in which Fabergé, Tiffany, and Lalique worked and how they drew inspiration from and, in turn, influenced a great number of designers in the Europe and United States who are little known today but deserve greater recognition. As such, the exhibition offers a comprehensive account of one of the most fascinating periods in the history of modern design and the instrumental role that each of these great artists played in shaping it.

On behalf of the staff and Board of Trustees of the Cleveland Museum of Art, I would like to offer our deepest thanks to Stephen Harrison, curator of decorative art and design, and to the two scholars, Emmanuel Ducamp and Jeannine Falino, with whom he created *Artistic Luxury*. All three have labored on this project for many years, and the broad knowledge and exceptional care they brought to its development can be seen in every aspect of their work.

Special credit is due to several sponsors whose generous support has made the presentation of *Artistic Luxury* and the publication of this catalogue possible. First, I would like to express our gratitude to National City, which graciously agreed to serve as the lead sponsor of the exhibition. A substantial grant from Tiffany & Co. Foundation provided partial funding for the production of the catalogue, including the many hours of travel and research that went into it. A grant from Sotheby's provided much-needed support for programming and opening events. Finally, we are most grateful for the operating support provided by the residents of Cuyahoga County, through Cuyahoga Arts and Culture, and by the Ohio Arts Council.

Nymph and Butterfly Lamp Pendant (cat. 290). Alphonse Mucha for Tiffany & Co.

Timothy Rub
Director
The Cleveland Museum of Art

Acknowledgments

book and exhibition of the scope of *Artistic Luxury: Fabergé, Tiffany, Lalique*, encompassing the work of three major figures in design, as well as most of their peers, would not have
been possible without the support of many individuals and institutions. During the planning, research, and development phases over the course of the last five years, it was necessary to rely
on the expertise, generosity, and in some cases, the kind hospitality of others, and I thank them all on
behalf of the Cleveland Museum of Art.

My first debt of gratitude is owed to the many lenders to the exhibition, both institutions and
private individuals, whose enthusiasm for the project and willingness to participate in the exhibition
gave us a body of material unlike any assembled before for this period of study. Her Majesty Queen
Elizabeth II graciously agreed to lend to the exhibition, and I am grateful to Sir Hugh Roberts and
Caroline de Guitaut for their support and assistance at the Royal Collection. His Serene Highness
Prince Albert II of Monaco also kindly agreed to lend an important work from his collection as well
as serve as Honorary Grand Patron of the exhibition. Guy Oliver in London first encouraged and
facilitated our request, and Heather Acheson, Hervé Irien, John Jayet, and Carl de Lencquesaing in
Monaco, as well as Maggie Maccario-Doyle in New York, guided us with great charm and diplomatic
skill. Adrian Sassoon helped with two important collectors, and Katherine Purcell put us in touch
with several key lenders in addition to making available important loans from Wartski, London.

In America, Barbara Deisroth was an early and enthusiastic advocate who was unconditional in
her introductions to important collectors. She and Janet Zapata opened doors I never knew existed,
both giving freely of their time and vast knowledge of the period. In addition to her role as co-curator
and author, Jeannine Falino also facilitated visits to numerous collectors on both coasts and in between. Mark Waller introduced me to the major collectors of Lalique's circle. Mark Shaffer of A La
Vieille Russie in New York was quick to pledge his firm's support and agreed to approach several
key lenders on our behalf. Jocelyn Pickett provided valuable support with securing the loans from
Joan and Melissa Rivers. In addition, John Webster Keefe was the only person who could persuade a
certain collector to part with her treasure for so long, and Jack Becker at Cheekwood supported the
loan of crucial works from the Matilda Geddings Gray Foundation.

I am also grateful to those curators at institutions who made their collections available and were
powerful advocates for the project within their institutions: Cynthia Amnéus and Amy Miller Dehan
(Cincinnati Art Museum); David Bagnall (the Richard H. Driehaus Museum, Chicago); Karen Barlow
(Allentown Art Museum); David Barquist and Donna Corbin (Philadelphia Museum of Art); Martin
Chapman (Fine Arts Museums of San Francisco); Sarah Coffin (Cooper-Hewitt, National Design
Museum, Smithsonian Institution); Ulysses Dietz (the Newark Museum); Janet Dreiling (Spencer
Museum of Art, the University of Kansas); George Harlow (American Museum of Natural History);
Eleanor Jones Harvey (Smithsonian American Art Museum, Washington, D.C.); Barry Harwood
(Brooklyn Museum); Morrison Heckscher, Gary Tinterow, Alice Cooney Frelinghuysen, Jared Goss,
and Beth Carver Wees (the Metropolitan Museum of Art, New York); David Johnson, Lianna Paredes,
Karen Kettering, and Anne Odom (Hillwood Museum & Gardens); William Johnston (the Walters

Art Museum); Ron Labaco (High Museum of Art); Jütta Page (Toledo Museum of Art); Richard H. Saunders (Middlebury College Museum of Art); and Kevin Tucker (Dallas Museum of Art).

In Europe and Russia, those curators or directors who were particularly accommodating in loaning works from their collections include: Renate Eikelmann and Michael Koch (Bayerisches Nationalmuseum, Munich); Catherine Gendre (Musée Lambinet, Versailles); Cornelie Holzach (Schmuckmuseum Pforzheim); Florian Hufnagl (Die Neue Sammlung, Munich); Tamara Igumnova and Alexander Shkurko (State Historical Museum, Moscow); Nichola Johnson (Sainsbury Centre for Visual Arts, University of East Anglia, Norwich); Rudiger Joppien (Museum für Kunst und Gewerbe, Hamburg); Marjolaine Mourot (Musée Nationale de la Marine, Paris); Suzanne Netzer and Angela Schönberger (Kunstgewerbemuseum, Berlin); João Castel-Branco Pereira and Maria Fernanda Passos Leite (Calouste Gulbenkian Foundation/Calouste Gulbenkian Museum, Lisbon); Mikhail Piotrovsky, Georgi Vilinbakhov, Wladimir Matveiev, Natalia Kolomiets, Tamara Rappe, Olga Kostjuk, Ekaterina Abramova, Maria Khaltunen, and Elena Shlikevich (State Hermitage Museum, St. Petersburg); Evelyne Possémé and Jean-Luc Olivié (Musée des Arts Décoratifs, Paris); J. P. Sigmond (Rijksmuseum, Amsterdam); and Philippe Thiébaut and Olivier Gabet (Musée d'Orsay, Paris).

The works from private collections have given depth and fresh context to the material in museum collections, and the many owners who have graciously agreed to lend their works have made these associations possible. Many have chosen to remain anonymous, and some were also very helpful with their knowledge, deserving special recognition: Craig Castilla, Ralph Esmerian, Christopher Forbes, Audrey Friedman and Haim Manishevitz, Neil Lane, Christie Mayer Lefkowith, Joseph and Ruth Sataloff, Eric Streiner, and Robert Zehil.

In addition, several independent scholars have helped us freely and have added immeasurably to the quality of both the exhibition checklist and this manuscript. In America, Melissa Buchanan, Nicholas Dawes, Martin Eidelberg, Elise Zorn Karlin, Yvonne Markowitz, Nicholas Nicholson, and Joan Rosasco were especially helpful. Likewise, in Europe and Russia, Iraida Bott, Richard Comte, Anton Efimov, Tatiana Fabergé, Elisabeth Gagarine, Alice Ilitch, Elaine Vogel Keller, Martin Levy, Nina Lobanov-Rostovsky, Kieran McCarthy, Sergei Orekhov, Diana Scarisbrick, Josephine Shea, Valentin Skurlov, Alexander von Solodkoff, Ulla Tillander-Godenhielm, and Rita Vanhove all kindly assisted us in our research. I am especially grateful to Christie Mayer Lefkowith for her essay on Lalique's role in the fin-de-siècle perfume industry, Pilar Vélez for sharing her research on Lluís Masriera, and Wilfried Zeisler for his work with Emmanuel Ducamp on the subject of Franco-Russian ties. Their contributions to the catalogue added a rich texture to our story.

Certain individuals at research institutions and company archives around the world have been indulgent and helpful with our many queries and requests, particularly the staffs at the Archives Nationale in Paris, the National Archives of the Russian Federation in Moscow, and the State Russian Historical Archive in St. Petersburg; Joan Oliveras Bagués, Maribel Puigvert, and Judit Nadal (Bagués-Masriera, Barcelona); Laurent Baty and Diane-Sophie de Raigniac (Mellerio dits Meller, Paris); Pamela Eyerdam (Cleveland Public Library); Russell Feather (National Museum of Natural History, Smithsonian Institution, Washington, D.C.); Anne Gros (Christofle, Paris); Spruill Harder (Fine Arts Library of Harvard College, Cambridge); Edward Kasinec (New York Public Library); Michaela Lerch (Baccarat, Paris); Claudine Sablier Paquet and Odile Emanuelli (Archives Boucheron, Paris); Béatrice de Plinval and Mélanie Sallois (Chaumet, Paris); David Saja and Carole Camillo (Cleveland Museum of Natural History); Annamarie Sandecki, Meghan Magee, and Louisa Bann (Tiffany & Co. Archives, Parsippany, N.J.); Ann Sindelar (Western Reserve Historical Society,

Cleveland); Timothy Stevens (Gilbert Collection, London); and Eric Turner (Victoria and Albert Museum, London).

At the Cleveland Museum of Art this project had the good fortune to be stewarded by many talented people, and a few colleagues deserve special mention. Former director Katharine Lee Reid enthusiastically supported the endeavor from its beginnings, as did Timothy Rub from his first days as her successor. Heidi Strean shepherded the project from start to finish with a sense of humor and remarkable patience; Mary Suzor oversaw every logistic of shipping and installation with incredible accuracy and creativity; Catherine Walworth assisted with all aspects of the exhibition in addition to writing many lively vignettes for this book; Howard Agriesti spent the better part of two years looking through the lens of a camera to produce much of the photography for the catalogue; Laurence Channing laid out the design with impeccable taste and high standards; and Carol Ciulla kept the decorative arts department and its curator from running amok during the entire project—no easy task. To each of them, I am personally, as well as professionally, grateful.

A core group of CMA staff members contributed enormous time and energy to bring our ideas to fruition: Morena Carter and Sheri Walter in the exhibitions office; Bridget Weber in collections management; editors Barbara Bradley, Jane Takac Panza, and Amy Sparks; graphic designers Tom Barnard and Steven Probert, and production manager Charles Szabla; Betsy Lantz and Ingalls Library staff members Lou Adrean, Becky Bristol, Chris Edmonson, Jennie Delvaney, and Erin Robinson; Marjorie Williams and education division staff members Shannon Masterson, Seema Rao, and Michael Starinsky; Cindy Fink and marketing and communications staff members Laura Andrews, James Kopniske, and Susan Watiker; David Brichford, Adam LaPorta, Gary Kirchenbauer, and Bruce Shewitz in photography; Karen Carr, Jack Stinedurf, and Hunter Walter in development; Jeffrey Strean and exhibition design and production staff members Jeremiah Boncha, Philip Brutz, Rusty Culp, Jim Engleman, Mark Gamiere, Andrew Gutierrez, Lizzy Lee, and Dante Rodriguez; and art handlers Barry Austin, Arthur Beukemann, John Beukemann, Joe Blaser, Todd Hoak, and Mike Marks. Michael Cale, Stefanie Hilles, and Christina Larson graciously volunteered their time to assist with the catalogue and research. Former CMA deputy director Charles Venable first encouraged the idea then supported its development. Former staff members Lynn Cameron, Bruce Christman, Joanie O'Brien, Rachel Rozensweig, and Larry Sisson all contributed to the project early on. In addition, outside support from conservators Paula Hobart and Adam Jenkins, photographers Jean Chénel and David Schlegel, and mountmaker Bob Fuglestadt is greatly appreciated. Krista Brugnara, head of exhibitions, and Martin Chapman, curator of decorative arts, were willing partners at the Fine Arts Museums of San Francisco.

Finally, I would like to thank Emmanuel Ducamp and Jeannine Falino for working with me on this project, bringing their valuable expertise to bear on such a dynamic subject. All three of us are grateful to our families and friends for patiently waiting until we finished to resume our normal lives.

Stephen Harrison

Pendant Brooch (cat. 214). Potter & Mellen.

Lenders to the Exhibition

Her Majesty Queen Elizabeth II

His Serene Highness Prince Albert II of Monaco

Private collections (6)

Mr. and Mrs. Craig Castilla

J. Randolph Hiller

Neil Lane

Christie Mayer Lefkowith

Clare and Harold Sam Minoff

Joan and Melissa Rivers

Mr. and Mrs. Robert Sage

Dr. Joseph and Ruth Sataloff

Michael and Judy Steinhardt

Eric Streiner

Diane B. Wilsey

Robert A. Zehil

A La Vieille Russie, New York

Allentown Art Museum

American Museum of Natural History, New York

Anderson Collection of Art Nouveau, University of East Anglia, Norwich

Bagués-Masriera, Barcelona

Bayerisches Nationalmuseum, Munich

Boucheron, Paris

Brooklyn Museum

Calouste Gulbenkian Foundation/Museum, Lisbon

Cheekwood Botanical Garden & Museum of Art, Nashville, on loan from the Matilda Geddings Gray Foundation

Cincinnati Art Museum

The Cleveland Museum of Art

Cleveland Museum of Natural History

Cooper-Hewitt, National Design Museum, Smithsonian Institution, New York

Dallas Museum of Art

Die Neue Sammlung, Munich

Faerber Collection, Geneva

Fine Arts Museums of San Francisco

The Forbes Collection, New York

Gallery Moderne–Le Style Lalique, Ltd., Piermont, N.Y.

High Museum of Art, Atlanta

Hillwood Estate, Museum & Gardens, Washington, D.C.

Kunstgewerbemuseum, Berlin

Fred Leighton, New York

The Metropolitan Museum of Art, New York

Middlebury College Museum of Art

Musée des Arts Décoratifs, Paris

Musée d'Orsay, Paris

Musée Lambinet, Versailles

Musée National de la Marine, Paris

Museum für Kunst und Gewerbe, Hamburg

The Newark Museum

Philadelphia Museum of Art

Primavera Gallery, New York

R. Esmerian, Inc., New York

The Richard H. Driehaus Museum, Chicago

Rijksmuseum, Amsterdam

Rookwood Pottery Co., Cincinnati

Schmuckmuseum Pforzheim

Siegelson, New York

Smithsonian American Art Museum, Washington, D.C.

Spencer Museum of Art, the University of Kansas, Lawrence

The State Hermitage Museum, St. Petersburg

State Historical Museum, Moscow

Tiffany & Co., Archives, Parsippany, N.J.

Toledo Museum of Art

The Walters Art Museum, Baltimore

Wartski, London

Artistic Luxury in the Belle Époque

Stephen Harrison

The impulse ... toward the luxury of taste as distinguished from the luxury of costliness, will doubtless advance beyond our conceptions of today, creating sound economic and social conditions, leaving in its wake loveliness and pleasure."
—Irene Sargent, "A Recent Arts and Crafts Exhibition" (1903)

This prediction, voiced by the prominent American design critic of her day, foreshadowed the mission of several generations of artists, designers, theorists, and critics to reverse what they viewed as the dangerous and detrimental disconnect between art and design that had come as the result of industrial production and commercialization.

This same debate, in an expanded form, played out across Europe at the turn of the century. Some have argued that this fundamental call for reform in design and, more specifically, in the method of production emanated chiefly from William Morris in England. While the driving force of his influence cannot be diminished, more recent assessments of the Arts and Crafts movement have stressed that these principles developed independently in parallel in most Western locales at the end of the nineteenth century.[1] In Europe as in America the proponents of handicraft sought reform in the production of consumer goods and, by extension, the reintroduction of human hands in the process of both design and production. It was only by doing so, according to contemporary theorists, that art could once again be present in unique objects—a relative transubstantiation deemed impossible to achieve in mass-produced, machine-made goods. Of course, there was an entire world of manufacturers who disagreed with them and stepped up to the arena of critical opinion time and again by exhibiting in international exhibitions in an attempt to prove these critics wrong.

The world of jewelry and luxury goods provided a logical arena for this struggle between art and commercial success. The nature of the business was ideal for considering the question of hand work versus machine work as it encompassed all strata of production—from individual artisans working alone or in small studios, such as René Lalique in France; to larger firms of many craftsmen presided over by a single, often celebrated, master designer such as Peter Carl Fabergé or Louis Comfort Tiffany; to the machine-dominated jewelry factories of towns such as Birmingham in England or Newark in America that produced large quantities of adornments in the style of the celebrated masters. Such a broad spectrum of production methods made it possible to debate the actual presence of "art" in the works produced and afforded the critics an ample vehicle for discussion of which firm or craftsman was more artistic or mundane, enlightened by pure inspiration or debased by the demands of commerce.

Reflecting on the role of art in design, one author wrote in 1902 that "commercialism in art commenced when art lost touch with commerce." He went on to observe, "When art ceased to answer the legitimate demands of the age in which it existed, decadence set in. Art degenerated into an aristocratic adjunct and was viewed with distrust by the people."[2] For that critic, art had become an elitist notion that should never have been separated from the commerce of making objects for people to use, be it by hand or machine. The idea that commercialism could or should be divorced from art or that the two had to be mutually exclusive stood in contrast to the perceived need of people to have access to art in their daily lives.

Centerpiece from the Nereid Service (detail, cat. 110). Goldsmiths' & Silversmiths' Company Ltd.

The Belle Époque

For those whose lives had been enriched by the enormously far-reaching and unprecedented industrial advances of the nineteenth century, the approaching new century presented an opportunity to enjoy the fruits of their labors. Known variously as the Gay Nineties, the Gilded Age, or the Belle Époque, this era of optimism, frivolity, and conspicuous consumption presented a window on the world for which no rose-colored glasses were needed. Eventually, the winds of war and revolution would blow back in their faces, but for the last decade of the nineteenth century and the first years of the twentieth, life was beautiful for a privileged few. Art historian John Russell Taylor describes the Belle Époque as the era in which the highest of society delighted in flirting with the lowest—a time of decadence, or "the moment when the ripe slips over toward the rotten."[3] He also notes that this was the last great age of the painted portrait, an apt metaphor for the vanity and ego described by the era's greatest observer of the psyche, Sigmund Freud.

Image was paramount in the lives of society mavens, and portraits became the perfect symbol of status and rank, reminding at once of ancestry and breeding, taste and ability. Taylor asserts that portraits were the best way to record the accomplishments of the recent past and the promise of future generations, even more so than photography, since photographs were not grand or traditional enough, or for that matter flattering enough for posterity.[4] He wryly observes that "from the paintings of Sargent and Boldini . . . [one] can get a vivid impression of a carefree world in which the beautiful people of the day never had to worry where their next string of pearls or diamond tiara was coming from."[5] Both John Singer Sargent and Giovanni Boldini, the two most celebrated portrait painters of their day, reveled in the stratification of society and idealized their subjects, taking delight in their self-indulgent attitudes toward the necessities of life as well as their adornments—the dark, rich interiors or large jewels seemingly omnipresent in society portraits.[6]

The hanging of portraits was not a difficult choice to make for the wealthy. Grand renderings of society scions were easily understood by the viewer, requiring no more effort than an impressionable mind. Far more vexing was the choice of other art to adorn the walls. In the capitals of Europe, wealthy Americans and Russian aristocrats sought both social recognition and refuge from the seemingly less relevant life in their own cities. Academies and societies of artists formed and began exhibiting contemporary trends in painting and sculpture at seasonal salons to appeal to these potential patrons. It was at those salons that serious art perplexed the feeble minds of its "admirers," who inevitably passed over the murky landscapes of the Impressionists, the garish colors of the Fauvists, and the dark brooding canvases of the Symbolists. Religion or social realism did not sell either, though a quaintly placed peasant tending sheep was acceptable if not too overtly rendered. What sold best were depictions of society itself—the rituals of dining, visiting, going to the opera or theater, and the pursuit of leisure, which

Fig. 1. Elegant portraits, such as this one of heiress Lisa Colt Curtis by American painter John Singer Sargent, played an important role in establishing an image of wealth and lineage among society grandees during the Belle Époque.

Demantoid garnets in varying shades of green cover the surface of this dragonfly brooch by an unknown French or German maker, drawing more attention to the stones than to the artistry of the jewel (cat. 312).

Fig. 2. Opening nights at the opera were sometimes called "tiara nights" in the press because of the many glittering hairpieces worn by ladies of society.

Opera glasses were an elegant accessory for the theater or concert hall. This pair in enameled ivory was designed by Georges le Saché and possibly retailed by Tiffany & Co. (cat. 261).

was just as regulated by rules as what clothes were to be worn when and where.[7] These subjects were more than just accessible; they reinforced and even validated the glittering life that the social rich fiercely fought to maintain.

It is no wonder then that the decorative arts, when introduced to the salons in Paris and the exhibition halls in London in the 1890s, provided both an avenue to the consumer for the appreciation of art in accessible terms and an opportunity for studio craftsmen to exhibit their work at the same level of recognition as fine art, thereby building reputations as "artists." Emmanuel Ducamp in his chapters here on the Russian and French luxury trades and Jeannine Falino in hers on America discuss the role and significance of salons and exhibitions for the rehabilitation of the craft tradition at a time when most critics decried the debasement of art by machine methods. The development of communities and cooperatives of artists such as Darmstadt in Germany; Mir Iskusstva in Russia; Guild of Handicraft in England; the Roycrofters in America; and the two influential cooperatives in Paris, Siegfried Bing's L'Art Nouveau and Julius Meier-Graefe's La Maison Moderne, all resulted from the agitation in the craft community for an outlet to educate and pass along the traditions of handmade production that many feared were in danger of extinction.

Art or Artistic

The great irony of this revival of craft tradition is that it had the unintended consequence of thrusting all decorative work—be it made by hand or with the aid of machines, by a craftsman at his bench or by many hands in a large firm, and, perhaps most significant, in one of the new styles or a traditional historicist revival—into the realm of what was considered "artistic." Indeed, while critics carefully reviewed every salon and exhibition to determine the extent to which the exhibited works were imbued with "art" or the intangible and subjective intentions of the artist (the definition of which varied from critic to critic), patrons and consumers merely looked for extraordinary technique, rare and varied materials, and above all uniqueness (or at least the perception of it). As Nancy Troy and others have observed, artistic luxury was not defined by style but rather by production.[8] In the eyes of the consumer, a work did not need to look modern, derived from nature, or even symbolic to be artistic. Certainly these stylistic markers were often associated with artistic work, but objects in more conventional and often historically based motifs were equally, if not more so, regarded as works of art, at least by the consumer, who in the end was the one who mattered most.

Indeed, Troy asserts that Bing and other Art Nouveau proponents relied heavily on historical styles for inspiration, at least in part, precisely because of past production methods that derived from an apprenticeship tradition propagated by early craft guilds in France.[9] The principles of William Morris and the Arts and Crafts movement, with their heavy debt to medieval methods and aesthetics of production, effected the same result in England and around the Western world. Never mind that handwork was impractical for large-scale production; the more unique an object, or the more unique its appearance, the more artistic it was considered. And the more artistic it was, the quicker it sold whether it was costly or inexpensive.

One contemporary critic in 1898, reviewing an exhibition of decorative art in Paris, observed that the principal aim of the participants "is to create articles of everyday utility, which shall be works of art, not by reason of their cost, or the value of the material of which they are made, but by virtue of the actual work put into them."[10] Along these same lines, an English critic writing in 1903 observed, "'Art manufacture' is a phrase now often encountered, though the two linked words many be held to be mutually contradictory, since 'manufacture' generally implies the multiplication of an idea and 'art' the production of an unique object."[11] He further explained that the designer of a unique object must consider the material, the process of realization, and its use before creating it. But equally important, the critic asserted, was the need "to produce something which shall be fresh and beautiful or quaint, so as to attract the eye which is jaded with too much novelty."[12] These observers were merely explaining the limitations that commerce inevitably placed on the creative process.

Therein lies the heart of the debate that arose as soon as the decorative arts were allowed into the realm of the fine arts: commercialism versus true art—art produced for a purpose and to sell as opposed to art made purely for creative expression. For some, the very notion that works might be made to appeal to a consumer's taste was anathema. Writing about an exhibition in 1904 of Lalique's work in Berlin, a critic expended most of his energy praising Lalique's artistic abilities but hastened to add that not every work was "worthy of admiration" since "together with

Preparatory clay model for an enameled dish made by Lalique around 1900 (cat. 189).

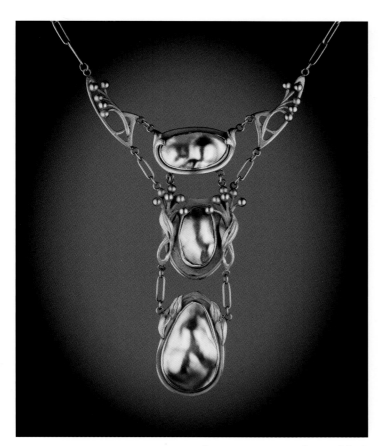

The Kalo Shop of Chicago produced handcrafted jewelry, such as this necklace of gold and "blister" pearls, in the Arts and Crafts tradition (cat. 119).

Overleaf left: Tiffany & Co. sold all manner of luxurious goods, including this parasol handle of carved jade with gold sycamore seedpods, sapphires, and solid gold tips (cat. 263).

Overleaf right: Snugly fitting necklaces, often with wide bands of pearls, were commonly referred to as "dog collars." Queen Alexandra of England allegedly wore them to disguise a blemish on her neck. This one was likely made by Falize Frères (cat. 99).

the costly pearls of intuitive genius, there exist commercial wares" in Lalique's work.[13] This perceived contradiction in the quality of Lalique's creative output, at least to the critic, signaled a recognition that some objects were meant to entice and others to sell. The same was the case with almost every other celebrated designer of the period, certainly Tiffany and Fabergé, who used the same tactic of displaying singular, extraordinary creations to cast a favorable light on their more accessible inventory. It was important that their works be seen as artistic but equally important that they be seen as luxurious and available.

If a work had to be of unique character to be thought of as artistic, exploiting the limits of its materials in a clever and creative way, then to be considered luxurious it also had to be rare and costly, secondary to the notion of usefulness. Luxury always symbolizes social power, linking ostentatious practice with the cult of aristocratic appearances. The nineteenth-century economist Thorstein Veblein, writing in his 1899 treatise *The Theory of the Leisure Class*, identified the desire to distinguish oneself from others and asserted that this urge was so commonplace that it extended to all levels of society.[14] Certainly the realm of fashion, which was just beginning to coalesce around the European style center of Paris at this same time, encouraged a self-indulgence that reinforced this theory. Yet luxury was as much a stable force of taste and tradition as it was a marker of trend and fashion.

For luxury firms such as the House of Fabergé, Tiffany & Co., Cartier, Boucheron, and others that specialized in traditional jewelry forms composed of diamonds and pearls, the ephemeral world (*l'empire de l'éphémère*) increasingly dictated by fashion houses engendered a need to compete in the arena of new trends while, perhaps more important, maintaining their reputations as arbiters of conservative good taste.[15] The result was a diversity of styles and motifs in their inventories that ran the gamut from eighteenth-century revivals to the developed aestheticism of Art Nouveau to the first stirrings of modernism. Still, luxury that derived from the past, accessible if not banal, contrasted with luxury emanating from the hand of a "true artist," hence the emergence of celebrated master designers such as Félix Bracquemond, Henri Vever, René Lalique, Lucien Falize, Georges Fouquet, Lucien Gaillard, Christopher Dresser, Archibald Knox, Paulding Farnham, Louis Comfort Tiffany, Edward Colonna, and Peter Carl Fabergé, to name but a few.[16]

Their names became synonymous with artistic luxury, partly from concerted efforts to market their designs as the creations of artists, not mere jewelers or craftsmen, and partly from the careful promotion of their work in fashionable new cooperative boutiques such as Bing's L'Art Nouveau and Meier-Graefe's La Maison Moderne.[17] Both promoted the work of individual designers by name and cultivated a certain exclusivity that inevitably became imbued in the works procured through their boutiques. Louis Comfort Tiffany, for example, presented his creations in his own booth at the 1900 Exposition Universelle in Paris, while at the same time his work was sold in Bing's pavilion outside the exposition.

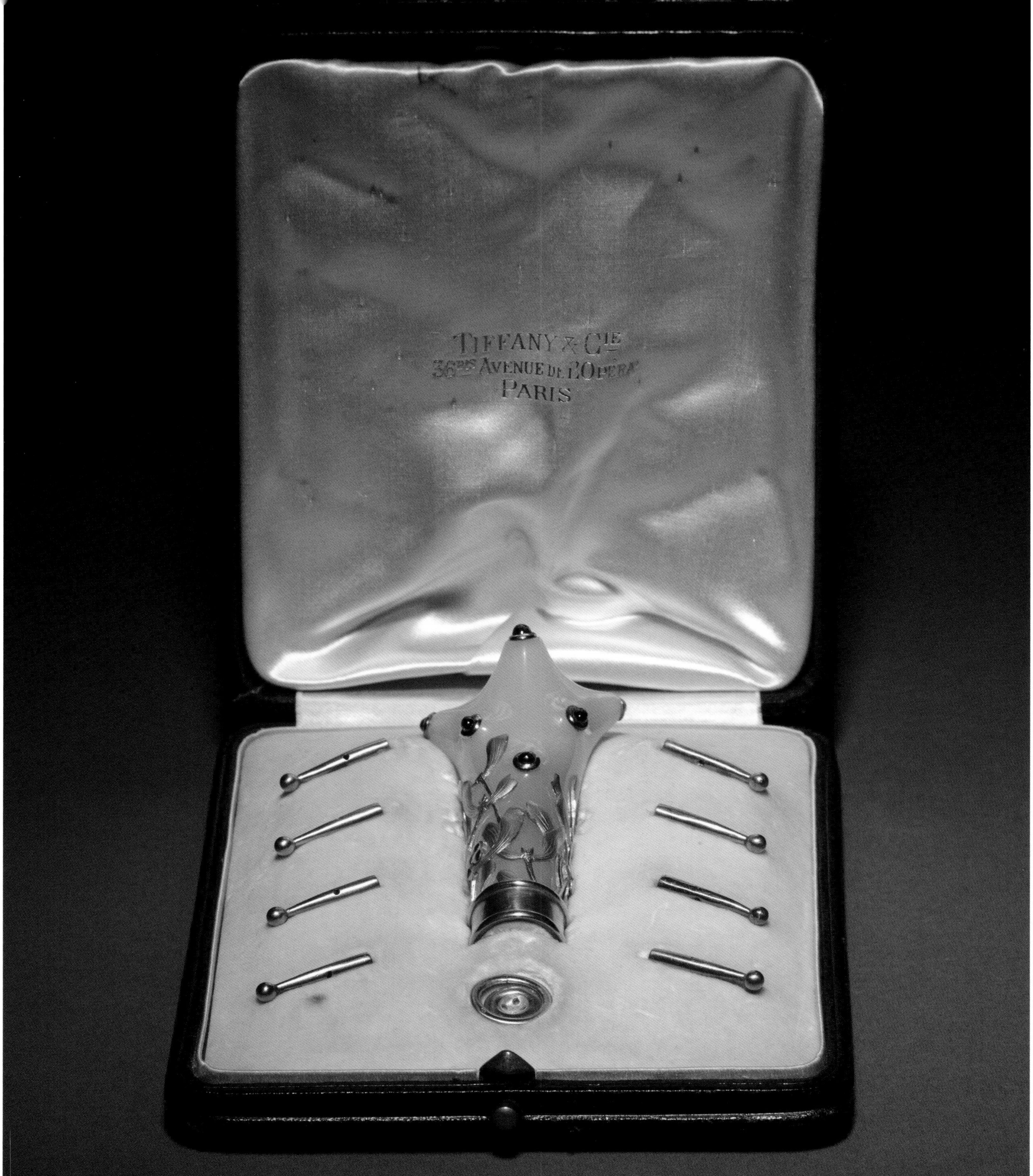

TIFFANY & Cie
36bis AVENUE DE L'OPERA
PARIS

Bing was particularly enamored of Tiffany's work, perhaps because it represented such a departure from mainstream glass production at the time, which was dominated by many houses producing miles and miles of cut glass for the rich and not-so-rich alike. Cut glass sparkled in almost any light and felt heavy and substantial in the hand. By contrast, Tiffany's Favrile glass glowed with iridescence and instantly seemed like a work of art, rather than just a luxurious, though practical and useful, object.

Such "new art" was exactly what Bing sought, and he found a willing and eager talent in Louis Comfort Tiffany. Largely through Bing's promotion, Tiffany's name became synonymous with artistic glass in Europe. In an early use of a designer's reputation to attract customers, Tiffany was the only artist mentioned in an advertisement for Bing's Paris showroom in an 1898 issue of the magazine *Dekorative Kunst*. The fact that Bing expected Germans to know Tiffany by name and to look to his shop for exclusive sales indicates the high level of recognition Tiffany had achieved in Europe by this point. This early marketing would eventually play a larger role in maintaining sales for Tiffany's studio works, even after his association with Tiffany & Co., the most conservative luxury firm in America, became official when he finally joined the firm as design director after his father's death in 1902.

Marketing Artistic Luxury

Left above: Louis Comfort Tiffany quickly found a receptive audience for his hand-blown glass known as Favrile (cats. 306, 289, 300, 280, 277). The wide range of forms and decorative surfaces made each vase a unique work of art in the eyes of his customers.

Left: Fig. 3. As owner of the gallery L'Art Nouveau in Paris, Siegfried Bing promoted Tiffany's glass through advertisements in leading art journals such as the German magazine *Dekorative Kunst.*

Right: Fig. 4. Unlike the commercial display at the Tiffany booth at the 1900 Exposition Universelle in Paris, Bing's pavilion at the fair featured Tiffany's glass in Art Nouveau interiors such as this boudoir designed by Georges de Feure.

No matter how energtically the critics expounded on the state of art at the turn of the century—art versus artistic, handmade or machine-made, or the advancement of society through art—the fact remained that the work they discussed was made to sell, or if not to sell then to enhance the reputation of the maker whose works were for sale. Even though commercialism was debated, its presence in the world of art would always be pervasive. Makers of luxurious goods, especially Fabergé, Tiffany, and Lalique, consciously sought recognition for their work on the world stage so that these objects would be seen as art, but the ultimate goal was the sale of their stock in trade. While they hoped their "artistic" work was admired and not denounced in the art world, back home in New York or St. Petersburg or down the street in Paris there were still large workrooms of craftsmen piecing together mosaics and windows, churning out wedding rings and bracelets, collar studs and compacts—all for sale by their respective firms.

By the turn of the nineteenth century, the principal vehicle for name recognition in just about every arena of art and industry had become the large, international exposition. These mammoth, audacious events were unparalleled in their ability to draw legions of wide-eyed consumers walking perhaps aimlessly but dutifully from one exhibit to the next. Billed as international, they were never truly democratic in their allocation of space or percentage of representation, though pains were made to appear as such through ever more elaborate committee bureaucracies and categories of competition with each successive fair. The first so-called international exposition was the Great Exhibition in

London in 1851. The brainchild of Prince Albert, Queen Victoria's consort, one half of the mammoth Crystal Palace was reserved for Great Britain and her empire, while the rest of the world was regulated to the other half.

As the century wore on, Western countries each vied for the attention of the world's consumers through more and more expositions (some forty-five so-called international or universal events took place between 1851 and 1904),[18] which became increasingly concentrated on commercial prowess and national pride. These events were expensive to mount, so each exhibitor carefully considered which expositions were worthy of participation. The decision to put their wares on display was a calculated business move designed to maximize exposure at given strategic points in the exhibitors' careers.

As his professional path began to develop, Louis Comfort Tiffany first revealed his artistic proclivities in small showings in art leagues and clubs in New York City. Later, a selection of his paintings was shown through the auspices of his father, Charles Lewis Tiffany, at the 1876 Centennial Exhibition in Philadelphia. The first major world's fair in which Louis Comfort Tiffany exhibited as his own firm was the 1893 World's Columbian Exposition in Chicago just a year after his Tiffany Glass & Decorating Co. was established on Long Island and the production of his signature ware, Favrile glass, had begun.[19] Even though Louis maintained his own separate company, he nevertheless benefited from the association with his father's firm and always situated his booth adjacent to that of Tiffany & Co. at all major expositions where both were participants. While it may seem logical that father and son would naturally foster such camaraderie, it should not be underestimated just how mutually beneficial this arrangement was. For Louis Comfort Tiffany, the association with Tiffany & Co. was a giant leg up, a chance to bask in the light of the firm's reputation for quality and rarefied

Fig. 5. Louis Comfort Tiffany and his father, Charles Lewis Tiffany, always exhibited in separate but neighboring booths at world's fairs and expositions, as in this photograph of the 1900 Paris Exposition Universelle.

Right: Fig. 6. René Lalique in his studio, around 1900.

works. For Tiffany & Co., Louis's works lent an artistic dimension to the firm's production in the mind's eye of the consumer even though the two were truly separate entities. Both Tiffany and his father exploited these opportunities to boost each other's glory, and their strategy was crucial to the success of both not only in maintaining their reputations but in continuing to develop them as well.

Not quite a generation younger than Louis Comfort Tiffany, René Lalique similarly studied drawing and developed professionally as an artist. He received his first break at the hands of a relative, M. Vuilleret, a jeweler who hired Lalique as an apprentice draftsman.[20] While Tiffany's and Lalique's careers were not exactly comparable in terms of development, given Tiffany's continual association with his father's large established firm, their creative paths offer an interesting contrast. Louis Tiffany first achieved fame with glass then moved into jewelry design after his father's death. Conversely, Lalique established his reputation first in jewelry then moved exclusively into glass production after the death of his wife.

Like Tiffany in New York, Lalique began showing in the 1880s at exhibitions in Paris, the center of the art world at the time, and later at the prestigious salons formerly dedicated exclusively to painting and sculpture. These showings were crucial to his exposure among Paris's watchful and influential design set, who held many of the cards for a young designer seeking to establish his own reputation and career. Writing of Lalique's first major exhibition of drawings for jewelry in 1884, the great French jeweler Alphonse Fouquet remarked, "I knew of no designer of jewelry [before], but finally I have found one."[21] Lalique had been supplying designs for a number of Parisian jewelers, but it was not until the following year, at the age of twenty-five, that Lalique first opened a shop in place Gaillon in Paris.

While Fouquet's favorable notice and others like it did little to help Lalique sell his works, such recognition gave him an imprimatur that was not unlike that of Tiffany & Co. for Louis Comfort Tiffany. As a result, Lalique was eventually asked to design jewelry for two of the most venerable French jewelry firms, Henri Vever and Boucheron, in preparation for the 1889 Exposition Universelle in Paris. Although his designs for that fair were unknown to the public, Lalique was then supplying a much more influential group of firms than when he first started. His emergence as a jeweler in his own right at the Salon de la Société des Artistes Français in 1894 became, like the 1893 Chicago world's fair for Tiffany, a watershed moment for Lalique's reputation among both critics and Parisians alike. He soon attracted the notice of famed actress Sarah Bernhardt, beginning a long association with the stage icon that would gain him much public attention.

Similar to Tiffany's progress after 1893, Lalique's works began to be shown by Siegfried Bing in his first Salon de l'Art Nouveau, the precursor to his Parisian shop L'Art Nouveau. For the next five years, Tiffany and Lalique would cross paths as participants in gallery showings and small exhibitions around Europe at the organization of Bing. This exposure was a tremendous boon for both. Tiffany's glass became so popular in Germany that any generic artistic glass became known as Tiffany

Left: Early in his career Lalique designed jewels for several well-known Parisian firms, especially that of master jeweler Henri Vever, the maker of this brooch marked by both Vever and Lalique (cat. 320).

Above: Fig. 7. Siegfried Bing promoted Tiffany's glass in gallery exhibitions all over Europe, including the Grafton Galleries in London just before his showing at the 1900 Paris exposition.

glass, whether it was made by him or not. The firms of Loetz and Moser both produced iridescent glass in imitation of Tiffany's Favrile, much to his consternation. Lalique's jewelry also began to influence more and more European designers, and his name became synonymous with the most succinct and sublime expression of the Art Nouveau. His following extended from London to Barcelona and eastward to Russia. Lalique would eventually capitalize on this exposure by exhibiting at international expositions in Turin (1902 and 1911) and St. Louis (1904), as well as solo exhibitions in London (1903), St. Petersburg, Russia (1903), and New York (1912). As Lalique's reputation for artistic creations grew in Paris, his work began to find favor with those who looked to Paris as a style center, those who traveled long distances to revel in the latest fashions for entertainment and adornment. Well-heeled Americans were chief among them, only to be outdone by the immensely wealthy Russian aristocracy.

Strong political friendship had long existed between France and Russia, which only strengthened social and economic ties present by the end of the nineteenth century. To demonstrate this bond in a highly publicized and visible way, Tsar Nicholas II and Tsarina Alexandra Feodorovna traveled to Paris in 1896 to inaugurate the construction of the Pont Alexandre III across the Seine. While the imperial couple was in Paris, President Félix Faure presented the tsar with a gift of an ornamental chalice in silver and molded glass made by Lalique.[22] The tsar and tsarina were due to return in 1900 for the official opening of the bridge before the exposition of that year, but they abruptly canceled their plans allegedly due to assassination fears on the part of the empress.[23] Russia was nonetheless represented at the exposition with displays ranging from traditional Russian architecture and folk art to symbols of imperial power and majesty such as vestments and costumes worn at the coronation of Nicholas II, replete with a miniature replica of the crown jewels by the House of Fabergé.

The traditional Russian arts and crafts at the 1900 exposition garnered much notice among reviewers of the fair, and to a somewhat lesser extent, so too did the display of Peter Carl Fabergé, the Russian court jeweler from St. Petersburg. Fabergé's career up to that point had more closely resembled that of Louis Comfort Tiffany than that of Lalique. Almost Tiffany's same age, Fabergé had long before (in 1870) taken over the running of the House of Fabergé, his father's jewelry business, so he was much more established as a master jeweler and purveyor of luxury goods than either Tiffany or Lalique, who were still regarded as artisans, though their fame was beginning to demand ever more commercial focus. Fabergé also sought the recognition that Tiffany and Lalique achieved by exhibiting their wares around Europe. He participated in regional expositions, though mostly in northern Europe and Russia, such as the All-Russian Exhibition in Moscow in 1882 where the firm was given a gold medal, and then again in Nuremberg in 1885. Later he took the firm's display to exhibitions in Stockholm (1887), Copenhagen (1888), and Nizhni Novgorod (1896).[24]

Fabergé had also been making special commissions, namely his famous Easter egg creations, for the imperial family since 1884, and so his reputation as the premier firm for rich, traditional jewelry

and luxury goods was well established in St. Petersburg. His participation in exhibitions was most helpful in enhancing his reputation throughout the rest of Russia, and he opened branches in Moscow (1887) and Odessa (1890). Fabergé's reputation as a court jeweler also meant he was well known in Paris prior to 1900. The many gold and bejeweled snuffboxes, cigarette cases, jewelry, and works of silver that were handed out by Russian diplomats and the tsar on official visits to Paris helped establish his position among traditionalists in Paris. In particular, the 1896 visit by Nicholas II and Alexandra Feodorovna resulted in a plethora of Fabergé objects in the hands of influential Parisians just as the preparations for the 1900 Exposition Universelle were getting under way. All three—Fabergé, Tiffany, Lalique—were poised at this point in their careers to show the world, at the dawn of a new century, their best work, and seemingly all the world awaited.

Paris 1900

For the better part of 1900 much of the Western world's attention focused on Paris, which became known as the "City of Light," both literally and figuratively. Ablaze with electric illumination—no better an example of industrial progress—the city glowed with optimism for the future.[25] In great anticipation, countries appointed commissioners, formed selection committees, and began appropriating funds to participate in what was generally agreed would be the most elaborate and comprehensive world's fair up to that point. Paris was transformed. Using as an anchor the space surrounding the Eiffel Tower, which had been built for the 1889 exposition, the fair encompassed a 277-acre (112-hectare) area extending to the Champs de Mars, the Champs Elysées, the esplanade of the Invalides, and along the banks of the Seine. Some of the buildings remaining today in the area include the Gare (now Musée) d'Orsay, the Grand Palais and Petit Palais, as well as the Pont Alexandre III across the Seine.[26] The first line of the Paris Métro was laid to facilitate the arrival of the throngs of visitors to the fair. There was also a moving sidewalk, constructed to aid the expected crowds in their perambulations.

Against a backdrop of legendary dance, theatrical, operatic, and musical performances by such leading lights as Sarah Bernhardt and Löie Fuller, more than 50 million visitors watched an aesthetic

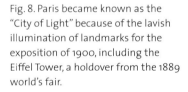

Fig. 8. Paris became known as the "City of Light" because of the lavish illumination of landmarks for the exposition of 1900, including the Eiffel Tower, a holdover from the 1889 world's fair.

Fig. 9. Each country built its own pavilion at the 1900 world's fair along the banks of the river Seine to reflect the style of its native folk architecture.

drama of a different kind within the confines of the exposition. Grand display halls contrasted with the idiosyncratic collection of international pavilions in every conceivable folk architectural tradition. Nearly 85,000 exhibits from almost sixty countries were arranged for maximum density: stacked high on the walls were paintings of all genres and composition, and the booths of the exhibitors were filled with display cases equally cluttered with objects, giving the look of an enormous exotic bazaar. Within the areas set aside for jewelry and luxurious objects, two distinctly opposing camps emerged: the traditionalists, who favored both historical and nationalistic styles, and the early modernists, who championed the organic and symbolic forms and motifs of the Art Nouveau.[27] Often these two schools of thought were juxtaposed next to each other, as in the case of the two Tiffany displays, Tiffany & Co. and Tiffany Glass & Decorating Co., or even within the same exhibit such as the House of Fabergé.

The divide could be seen in the architecture of the booths themselves, such as that of Lalique situated next to his mentor, Vever. Lalique's presentation embraced and proclaimed the symbolism of the Art Nouveau with sinewy cabinets and bronze figures of women metamorphosing into the grille that repeated as a backdrop around the display cases.[28] Vever, whose work was not strictly traditional but also absorbed some of the tenets of Art Nouveau design such as naturalistic and native folk motifs, nonetheless constructed a booth that was completely traditional in its architecture. In the American pavilion, the commissioners dictated the design of the exhibit stalls, requiring each exhibitor to conform to a largely neoclassical facade, with the interior layout the only discretion in design. Fabergé also exhibited in a classically inspired pavilion, well suited to the many neoclassical objects he brought to the fair. For the proponents of the Art Nouveau, such as Lalique, this approach to display was not effective, and Lalique sought a more integrated approach to the design of his boutique that reflected the spirit of the works within. The same held true for Bing's private pavilion adjacent to the fair itself, which was a veritable swamp of vinelike forms and motifs.

Of course, the works themselves were more telling of this aesthetic struggle that gripped designers and critics. The fervor with which contemporary critics lauded their favorite designers and derided the work of others was sometimes rooted in nationalist pride and rivalry. Wide-sweeping denouncement of an entire country's output was commonplace while at the same time individuals might be praised for their sublime treatment of this or that aspect of their designs. One particularly outspoken reviewer made quick work of most jewelry entries at the fair, save one:

> German jewellery cannot compete either with French or with American. But the Germans move in Lalique's direction. England, the Northern countries, and Austria, have shown absolutely nothing. The exhibits of Italy, Russia, and of the semi-civilized countries are not worth mentioning. . . . The imitators in all countries will seize the forms of Lalique and of his co-workers, and the Continent will soon be flooded with false copies of this style. But perhaps some clever observer will appropriate Lalique's idea, that decorative beauty, and not external value, is the main factor in the designing of jewellery. In that case the Exhibition will have served a good purpose.[29]

This last comment about beauty versus value seems to have been the most frequent criticism leveled at American firms, particularly the most prominent, Tiffany

Left: Wilhelm Lucas von Cranach, the most celebrated of Germany's jewelers working around 1900 in the Art Nouveau style, was most often compared to Lalique (cat. 22).

Fabergé often set very large indigenous stones, such as this Siberian aquamarine purchased in 1894 as a gift by the young tsarevich Nicholas shortly before his wedding to the future tsarina Alexandra (cat. 29).

& Co. The firm's association with the celebrated gemologist George Frederick Kunz distinguished its jewelry from the others in the sheer size and variety of the stones employed. Where others might have used a more subtle treatment of colored stones to highlight an overall palette or focus on a single stone, Paulding Farnham, Tiffany's chief designer at the time, virtually painted with gemstones that Kunz supplied.

This technique had been employed by Farnham in jewelry shown in 1893 at the Chicago world's fair. Although many critics then dismissed the practice as banal, the popular press and Tiffany's clientele were transfixed. The same critic as before went so far as to compare Tiffany's clients to island natives who wear necklaces of coins around their necks: "The rich customers of Tiffany and these aborigines have one thing in common—their view of ornament as a symbol of wealth."[30] Fabergé, Boucheron, and many other European jewelers of the day also used gemstones to bring color to their ornaments, in some cases presenting a single large amethyst or aquamarine or some other gemstone in a sumptuous but simple setting. So, too, did Lalique, Vever, Lucien Gaillard, Philippe Wolfers, and others, the difference being that the stones were incorporated as integral parts of the composition—a cockerel holding an amethyst or a pearl in its beak, an angel gazing upon a sapphire, or dragonflies clinging to a citrine—rather than just a gemstone in a conventional setting or a flower or insect paved in colored stones.

The use of more humble materials worked in a clever and beautiful way produced nearly the same interest and intrigue. A print by Félix Vallotton from this period depicts people crowded around Lalique's booth at the fair, presumably ogling the horn and tortoiseshell hair ornaments or the delicate surfaces of his various pendants and brooches in carved ivory or *plique-à-jour* (translucent enamel). These types of materials required lots of natural light to enliven their translucence, which precluded wearing such ornaments in the evening. Indeed, the main frustration leveled at Lalique was that his works were dull when worn at night.

This criticism meant little to Lalique, who knew about the power of producing ornaments that resembled small sculptures from the experience of exhibiting in the salons. These works, untouchable to many because of their price, led those same ogling visitors straight to Lalique's shop in the

Tiffany & Co. was admonished by the French critics for creating works that were, in their opinions, too lavishly paved in precious jewels (cat. 250).

Fig. 10. Parisian artist Félix Vallotton depicted the mobs of people who crowded around Lalique's booth at the 1900 world's fair in his print *La Vitrine de Lalique* (1901).

Overleaf: Fig. 11. Lalique's Art Nouveau–styled booth at the 1900 world's fair was situated adjacent to the more traditionally designed stand of his old master Henri Vever.

rue Varenne, where smaller, less costly versions were available. There one might buy a pendant without the rich enamel and costly baroque pearl of the more expensive version. Many of his works also employ a very subtle use of diamonds either as trim or a slight highlight, which made them more adaptable to evening, but Lalique knew well the French distinction between ornaments worn during the day (*bijoux*) and those worn at night (*joaillier*): precious stones should not be worn before evening. In this way, Lalique's works were different from the ornaments of Tiffany & Co. and the House of Fabergé.[31]

If Lalique was the quintessential Art Nouveau designer at the 1900 exposition, Fabergé represented the traditionalist side of the aesthetic debate. His command of eighteenth-century styles, honed by years of studying objets d'art belonging to Catherine the Great in the Hermitage, enabled him to achieve, through his workmasters, the same incomparable *guilloché* (machine-engraved) enamelwork found on period examples. Similarly, he demanded from his goldsmiths the highest standard of technique in order to proximate the intricate chasing he observed on early imperial treasures. His aesthetic sensibilities fit squarely in such an historicist mode, yet Fabergé was well aware of the trend toward Art Nouveau in the late

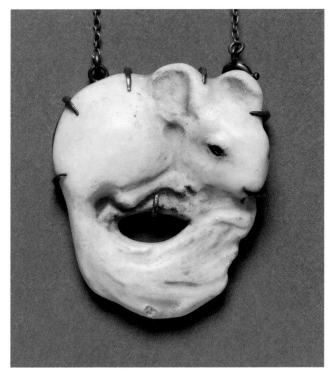

A charming dormouse pendant from the workshop of French ceramicist Raoul Lachenal reflects the subtly decorated sculptural forms of jewelry intended to be worn during the day (*bijoux*) (cat. 121).

1890s as the imperial family became increasingly enamored of the style. Two of the Easter eggs that Fabergé borrowed back from the imperial family to exhibit in Paris at the exposition were his most Art Nouveau creations to date, the *Imperial Lilies of the Valley Egg* (1898) and *Imperial Pansy Egg* (1899), both sinuous creations with fluid lines and floral motifs.

Largely because of his stature as the court jeweler in Russia, and the strong political ties that

Two versions of the same brooch show the range of decoration available to clients from Lalique's more commercial stock-in-trade (left, cat. 128; right, cat. 129).

The influence of historical gold-smithing, especially the work of the eighteenth-century English jeweler James Cox, the maker of this clock (fig. 12), can be seen in Fabergé's little novelty in the form of a shoe with gold Rococo revival ornament (cat. 76).

Fig. 13. The neoclassical-style architecture of Fabergé's booth at the 1900 Paris Exposition Universelle echoed the traditional forms of most of his designs.

existed between France and Russia at the time, Fabergé was appointed to the committee of jurors for the jewelry section of the fair. This accolade meant that he could not sell anything in that category, but so as not to miss out on sales, he also exhibited works in the related goldsmith's category. Despite his role as a juror, or perhaps to justify it, Fabergé exhibited his greatest masterworks for the Parisian critics and the rest of the world to see. As most of these had been commissioned by the imperial family, Fabergé borrowed them back for the duration of the fair. One recently discovered account of his display reveals just how lavish it turned out to be:

> The show case of Mr. Fabergé, of St. Petersburg, jeweler of the court, attracts great attention at the Paris Exposition. It contains the collection of Easter eggs, loaned by the present Empress and the dowager Empress of Russia. There are 40 of them, each recalling some event of the year worthy of remembrance. It is a charming fancy.[32]

This article is the first to be discovered that actually reveals the number of eggs Fabergé brought to Paris. Unless other Easter commissions for the tsars prior to 1900 remain unknown, this number must have included eggs belonging to other members of the family or court since only twenty-two imperial Easter eggs are recorded before that date. Nonetheless, this observation seems to indicate that all the imperial eggs up to that point were most likely included in his booth, revealing a much more lavish display by Fabergé in Paris than has ever been known before. The correspondent goes on to describe several works of note, including the *Imperial Azova Egg* (1890), *Imperial Danish Palaces Egg* (1890), *Imperial Lilies of the Valley Basket* (1896), the collection of flower studies owned by Grand Duchess Vladimir, *Imperial Coronation Egg* (1897), *Imperial Lilies of the Valley Egg* (1898), *Imperial Pansy Egg* (1899), and the little cabinet clock in the Louis XV style, modeled after an eighteenth-century version by James Cox.[33]

According to other accounts, Fabergé displayed these objects of great technical ability alongside objects of more simple design, such as his floral studies and hardstone animals, charming but not impressive in the eyes of the critics.[34] Of course, like so many others, Fabergé showed lavish formal jewelry in the form of tiaras, stomachers, and large brooches of diamonds and pearls, with the greatest curiosity in his booth perhaps being the tiny replica in diamonds of the imperial crown jewels. A diadem in the form of a traditional Russian hair ornament (*kokoshnik*) was singled out by the critic René Chanteclair as artistic merely because of its ethnic connotation: "It is regrettable that such specimens are not to be found in all countries, which are unfortunately losing all their originality."[35]

Preceding four pages: Fig. 14. The *Imperial Lilies of the Valley Egg* was thought to be among the most Art Nouveau of Fabergé's works presented in Paris at the world's fair of 1900.

Critics marveled at the extraordinary surprise contained in the *Imperial Pansy Egg,* a miniature heart-shaped frame containing tiny portraits of the family of Tsar Nicholas II under little red enamel hinged covers (cat. 61).

The *Imperial Danish Palaces Egg* reveals a folding screen depicting all the homes and yachts associated with the family of Tsarina Maria Feodorovna, who was born a Danish princess (cat. 58). Her son Nicholas became tsar in 1894.

Left: A recently discovered firsthand description of the Paris exposition of 1900 notes that this small desk clock was among the works lent by Dowager Empress Maria Feodorovna for Fabergé's display (cat. 42).

Like his contemporaries in other countries Fabergé made use of superb gemstones found throughout his homeland of Russia, such as the deeply colored Siberian amethysts of the necklace at right (cat. 78).

Critics praised the traditional Russian forms of Fabergé's jewelry, particularly kokoshnik-shaped tiaras similar to this one, that he displayed at the 1900 world's fair in Paris (cat. 93).

Demonstrating the popularity of national styles, the ornamental comb below was created by Georg Jensen in the Skønvirke aesthetic, the Danish equivalent to decorative folk traditions in Russia and across Europe (cat. 118).

This theme of national styles and native traditions loomed large at the turn of the century. As a major theoretical component of the international Arts and Crafts movement, indigenous motifs presented a solution for what to make by hand that would be honest in composition and not derivative of other historical styles. Theorists encouraged the revival of regional forms and motifs of decoration beginning in the 1890s, and as a result, cooperatives of designers sprang up across Europe encouraging and training village craftspeople in the skills needed to make the handiwork of their ancestors. Interest in early Russian folk art was high in the West, judging from the number of published articles on the subject and the enthusiasm of the authors during the period.[36] The two main arts and crafts communities that developed in Russia, Abramtsevo and Talashkino, were much heralded in the period press perhaps because they were the chosen causes for two aristocratic patrons, the Mamontov railway family and Princess Maria Tenishiva, respectively. But the influence of early Russian art extended to all sectors of society, particularly the production of enameled objects in the neo-Russian taste. Fabergé's workmaster in Moscow, Mikhail Perkhin, was most adept at this work and therefore much of what was sold in that style came from the Moscow shop.

Fabergé's work in the neo-Russian taste with his large assortment of traditional ladle-shaped cups (*kovsh*), tiaras (kokoshniks), and tea urns (samovars) was not unlike that presented by Tiffany & Co. at the 1900 exposition in Native American motifs. Tiffany & Co. first displayed a bowl in this theme for the 1893 Chicago world's fair, but it was not until 1900 that Paulding Farnham completed a fully developed group of bowls replicating the craft traditions of the American Indian.[37] This emphasis on a purely American aesthetic of native Western motifs could also be found in the work of other metalwork firms, most notably Jos. Heinrichs, who produced work mainly for hotels and restaurants. A line of large punchbowls and tankards with actual Indian arrowheads attached to the copper body were perhaps the most realistic of this genre.[38] The Rookwood Pottery

Company in Cincinnati also exhibited a line of ceramic vases with portraits of great chiefs and warriors. These native motifs helped draw attention to America as an exotic country, full of adventure and wild frontiers, and probably contributed to the impression that America was at the same time still untamed yet aware of its heritage. It is no coincidence that genuine Native American as well as African American exhibits were shown at the 1900 Exposition Universelle in a special section devoted to "comparative social conditions of the races" by the Bureau of Indian Affairs of the U.S. government.[39]

Similarly, Lalique and Vever presented work depicting Breton peasants and figures from the French Middle Ages just as Fabergé created Cossacks out of hardstone. One of the most striking examples shown at the 1900 exposition of folklore in precious metal and enamel was the elaborate centerpiece designed by the German artist Anton Seder and realized by Theodor Heiden in Munich. Depicting the quest for the Holy Grail, the work is a tour-de-force of German metalwork and enameling, artistic but nonetheless historic and nationalistic in style. Likewise, an enormous silver service exhibited at the fair by the Goldsmiths' & Silversmiths' Company in London, the *Nereid Service*, featured a massive centerpiece of nautical themes representing the triumph of Great Britain on the high seas.[40]

By contrast, the 1900 exposition also represented the triumph of Art Nouveau and the launch of early modernism. René Lalique was heralded as the finest jeweler working in France, a country the commissioners of the fair unabashedly proclaimed superior to all others in the world of art and a fact

Depicting the search for the Holy Grail, Anton Seder's jeweled and enameled centerpiece above reflects German artistic achievement and the impact of historicism at the 1900 world's fair (cat. 218).

Despite its overtly historicist overtones, the massive silver centerpiece at right by the Goldsmiths' & Silversmiths' Company Ltd. of London was still viewed as artistic when it was shown at the 1900 world's fair in Paris (cat. 110).

Overleaf: Fabergé's Moscow branch specialized in elaborate silver and gold work in traditional Russian motifs derived from seventeenth-century enamels (cat. 91).

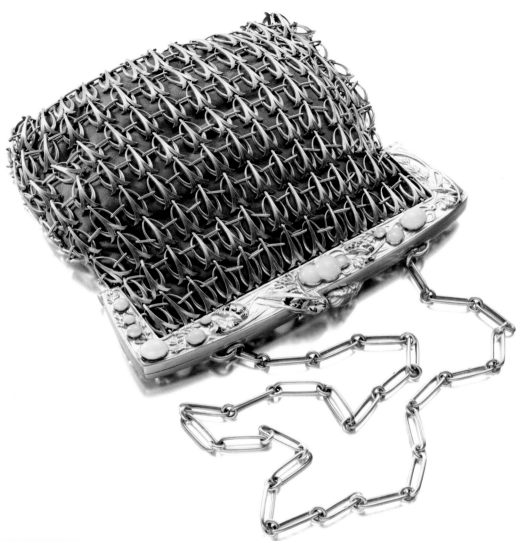

Symbols of the night, bats were a common grotesque motif in Art Nouveau jewelry as seen in the necklace at left probably by Lucien Janvier, retailed by Parisian jeweler Gustave Sandoz and presented as a formal jewel in its original elaborately fitted case (cat. 117).

The unsettling presence of wasps (in the handbag at right, cat. 157) and spiders (in the drawing below, fig. 15) can be seen in the work of René Lalique.

actually conceded in print by the American committee.[41] From architecture to individual exhibits, modern sensibilities could be found in every quarter of the fair, contrasted as always with more traditional architecture and design.[42] What tended to cause notice, and therefore garner medals, were those works that showed a creative application of Art Nouveau principles of organic form and either naturalistic or Symbolist decoration. Sometimes such works took the shape of fantastical creatures, insects, or flora and fauna. In other incarnations, the idealized figure of woman was often shown in metamorphosis either emerging from or returning to nature itself.

How an object was made also mattered. Works finished by hand were considered artistic while those produced by machine were not. Thus, the American silver company Gorham Mfg. Co. was lauded for Martelé, its line of hand-hammered silver in the Art Nouveau style, just as Louis Comfort Tiffany was praised for Favrile glass. The critics considered both to be highly innovative and artistic, and each won a grand prize. In addition to individual firms on the gallery floor, emporiums Bing's L'Art Nouveau and Meier-Graefe's La Maison Moderne offered a comprehensive look at the most fashionable modern creations of the time.

The Gorham Mfg. Co. was Tiffany & Co.'s fiercest American competitor in metalwork. Gorham's handwrought line, called Martelé, debuted at the 1900 Paris world's fair; the solid silver dressing table at left won a grand prix (cat. 111).

This sleek modernist pitcher by Keller Frères stood in stark contrast to more traditional silver forms seen at the 1900 exposition in Paris (cat. 120).

Perhaps more significant than the Art Nouveau at the 1900 Exposition Universelle, which was billed as a "Summation of the Century," was the emergence of other modes of modernity in design. Keller Frères exhibited a range of silver pitchers in abstract geometric shapes unlike anything seen before. Carlo Bugatti from Italy showed his expressive line of furniture reminiscent of Near Eastern decorative arts, and though his work was in the same vein as other more overtly Art Nouveau material, it was known as the Stile Floreale and would reflect more affinity with the Vienna Secession and Glasgow school than with French or Belgian Art Nouveau in the years to come.

International exhibitions after the 1900 exposition in Paris remained important vehicles for marketing the artistic qualities of a firm's production until World War I. For Tiffany and Lalique, these gatherings of the world's best design continued to beckon their participation. In addition to taking part in the Pan-American Exposition a year later in Buffalo, Louis Comfort Tiffany, spurred on by the interest in his glass from the many Russians who came to the Paris exposition, traveled to St. Petersburg to show at an exhibition there in 1902. As ever, his glass remained highly popular along with that of Émile Gallé, and many examples of both were purchased by wealthy aristocratic Russians such as Baron Alexander Stieglitz, who had founded an art academy in St. Petersburg.[43] That same year, Tiffany exhibited at the Esposizione Internationale in Turin as did Lalique, who also participated in the 1904 Louisiana Purchase Exposition (St. Louis world's fair). That particular event put Lalique into direct contact once again with one of his most loyal American clients, namely Henry Walters of Baltimore. Lalique also participated in two small showings in London in 1903, one at the Grafton Galleries in June and another at the South Kensington Museum (now the Victoria and Albert Museum) in November; then he showed once again in London at Thos. Agnew & Sons.[44] During the same period Lalique participated in a solo exhibition in St. Petersburg (1903), boosting his reputation in both cities by exhibiting briefly in small, exclusive galleries. Lalique exhibited once more at Turin (1911), as did Tiffany in San Francisco (1915), before World War I brought this method of marketing artistic luxury to an abrupt halt, not to be revived until the first great exhibition after the war in Paris in 1925.

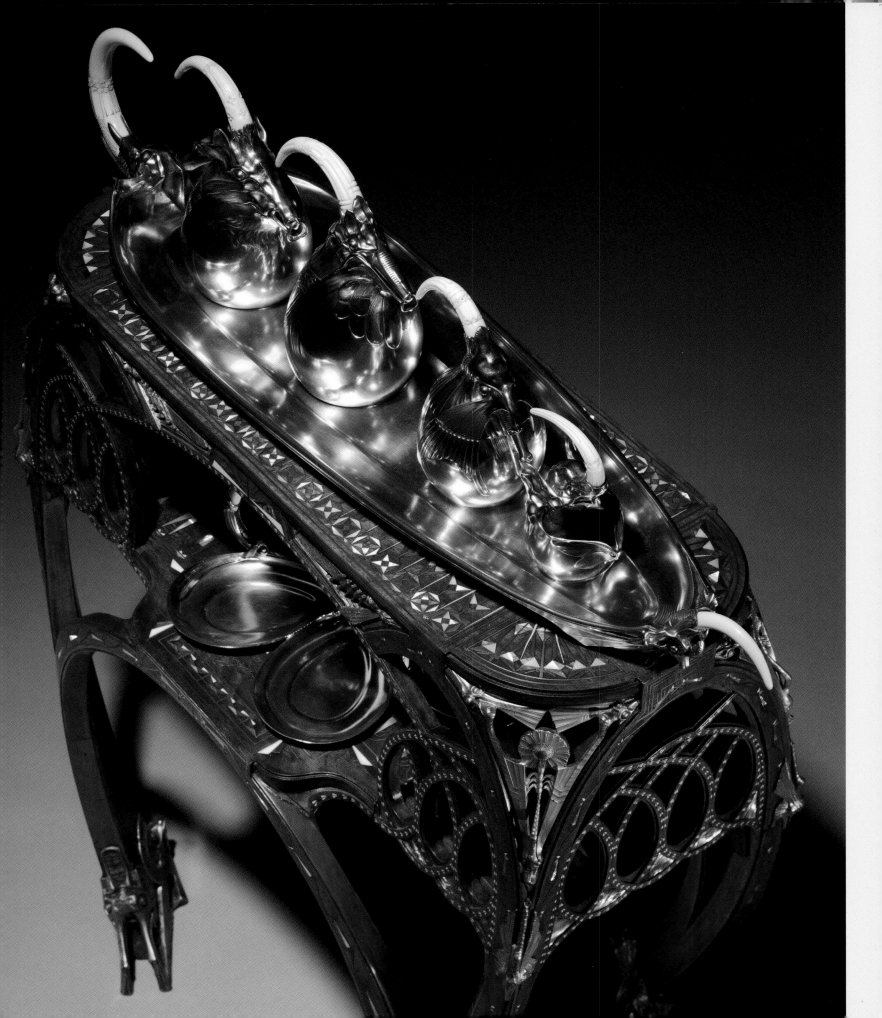

Modernism in Artistic Luxury

Left: *Tea and Coffee Service with Salver and Table* by Carlo Bugatti (detail, cats. 9, 10).

Right: Fig. 16. An illustration from *The Wood Beyond the World* (1894), published by theorist William Morris, captures the romantic spirit in England when Lalique studied there.

The asymmetrical treatment of hawthorn blossoms in this hair ornament by Lalique's contemporary Lucien Gaillard reflects a Japanese sensibility often found in works with floral motifs (cat. 106).

Design at the dawn of the twentieth century embraced a dichotomy of reform-minded trends and historical revivals. In Europe, as in America, architects and designers sought a new direction, a new language and vocabulary of design that would be more relevant in the lives of a changing society racked by political, social, and economic upheaval. A half-century of international expositions, a more widely disseminated press, and more efficient transportation resulted in design movements that were informed by their counterparts in other countries. For example, Austrian Max Peinlich, who achieved success at the Louisiana Purchase Exposition (St. Louis world's fair) in 1904, trained under Lucien Gaillard in France. René Lalique studied in England from 1878 to 1880, where the Pre-Raphaelite movement may have influenced

his lyrical interpretation of flowers and wraith-like women with sinuous tresses.[1]

The long-anticipated Exposition Universelle of 1900 in Paris brought together these shared influences and varied interpretations of what direction design should take in a new century. Besides being the ultimate spectacle where the newest in razors could be seen next to stationery and leather goods, the Paris exposition created a forum where it was possible to compare international design trends, both solidly rooted in the motifs of the previous century and those that began to look forward. Critic Gabriel Mourey saw the work of Germany as slavishly historicist and more interested in gloomy displays of authority than fresh ideas, while in the same breath he

praised the Darmstadt colony's display as a revelation: "Among the Darmstadt artists, everything is bright and joyous, full of happy fancy and true elegance."[2] In 1897, Ernst Ludwig, Grand Duke of Hesse-Darmstadt, invited this group of artists and designers, who were led by Scottish artist Mackay Hugh Baillie Scott and other members of the British Guild of Handicraft artists, to renovate the entire ducal palace in Darmstadt.[3] As a result, a neighborhood of nearby buildings designed by Peter Behrens and Hans Olbrich grew into a state-sponsored artist colony that reflected the philosophy of British revivalism.

The aesthetic sensibilities of William Morris and John Ruskin, their belief in a guild system based on medieval traditions, and a strong emphasis on historical motifs grounded Arts and Crafts theory. In 1903, Mourey weighed British handicraft style against France's Art Nouveau and said that, for a Lalique customer, the work would be slightly barbaric, but no less artistic.[4] The minimalist influence found in British design foreshadowed the aesthetics of wartime austerity and, ultimately, the streamlined design that followed.

Austria's central display at the 1900 exposition appeared radically modern.[5] Led by painter Gustav Klimt and expressed through the avant-garde periodical *Ver Sacrum,* the Viennese Secessionists had broken away from the mainstream academic art salons that favored historicism. Seeking to reform the fine and decorative arts, they founded their own society in 1897. The following year, they built an exhibition building and engraved the dictum "to every age its art and to art its freedom" above the entryway. Secessionists were allied with various designers and architects from Darmstadt and openly indebted to the Glasgow school,[6] particularly to Charles Rennie Mackintosh and his wife, Margaret MacDonald. As a result, Mackintosh's rectilinear designs, white-painted furniture, and tall proportions are reflected in the interiors designed by Josef Hoffmann, Kolomon Moser, and other Secessionist architects.[7] The gold-foil, abstract effect produced by Secessionist interior design, including mural paintings by Klimt, was described as a sort of chic Byzantium—"the very essence of elegance and luxury."[8]

The maker of the brooch at left, Austrian designer Ferdinand Hauser, was a member of the Viennese Secessionist movement, which declared itself outside the mainstream of design (cat. 114).

The sleek architectural lines of this desk clock by Fabergé highlight the rich beauty of the hardstones (lapis lazuli and jade) he used to create a contrast between simple, planar surfaces and more richly carved ornament (cat. 48).

Fig. 17. Russian artists were aware of European avant-garde movements, such as that of Charles Rennie Mackintosh in Glasgow, through the pages of the influential art journal *Mir Iskusstva*.

These small clocks convey Fabergé's knowledge of Austro-German design reform from centers such as Vienna and Darmstadt, where the tsarina's brother had developed an artist colony (left, cat. 50; right, cat. 49).

Feodorovna was an important cultural bridge. A German from Hesse, she was the sister of the grand duke, patron of the Darmstadt art colony. His wife, Victoria Melita, lent Fabergé silverwork to the 1899 Arts and Crafts exhibition in Munich's Glaspalast (Glass Palace), where Lalique jewelry was also on display.[9]

The Mir Iskusstva (World of Art) movement emerged in Russia at nearly the same time as the Vienna Secession and, like the Austrian group, developed its ideas through a self-named magazine. Mir Iskusstniki, as its members were known, were responsible for many exchanges between Russia and its artistic counterparts elsewhere. Konstantin Korovin, Mikhail Vrubel, and Valentin Serov each participated in Darmstadt exhibitions.[10] The magazine *Mir Iskusstva* also covered modernist exhibitions in Berlin, Dresden, and Darmstadt and reproduced modern design illustrations from other European journals.[11] The influence of designs emanating from this part of Europe, especially Vienna, can be seen even in the work of Fabergé, who specialized in traditional historicist-based motifs but

At the same time, Russia was considered so far afield, both culturally and geographically, that it was included in the Asian section of the Paris exposition. In reality its artistic community was more closely aligned with European avant-garde art movements in the West. Tsarina Alexandra

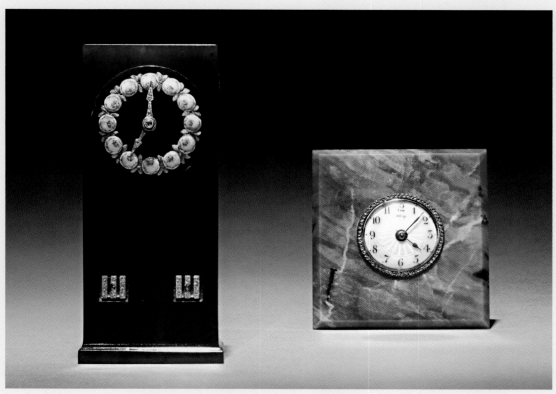

nonetheless responded to these emerging modernist aesthetics.

Italian designers had not kept apace in creating a modern industrial style, but in 1902 they boldly hosted in Turin the first ever international exposition dedicated solely to modern decorative art. Into this mix appeared Carlo Bugatti and his unique brand of modernism, which borrowed North African motifs and rich materials, making it a precursor to early Art Deco. Although he won a grand prize and achieved a measure of critical success, he was probably also one of the fringe artists accused of misusing costly materials in "extravagant bad taste."[12] In 1911, on the occasion of another Turin art fair, the French journal *L'Art Décoratif* dedicated an article to Bugatti and illustrated the insect-footed tea set now in the Cleveland Museum of Art. Its isometric form and the grisly use of insects on a tea table reveal an interest in macabre juxtapositions not unlike those of Lalique and his French peers.

In France, Siegfried Bing's gallery L'Art Nouveau and Julius Meier-Graefe's enterprise La Maison Moderne won over many critics to their philosophy of artistic handcrafted production. Bing's retail gallery gave its name to a movement that announced a modern, independent spirit. In 1901, when London's South Kensington Museum (now the Victoria and Albert Museum) accepted a donation of Art Nouveau furniture purchased largely from the 1900 Paris exposition, a storm of disapproval appeared in art periodicals.[13] Critics castigated the objects as degenerate work bred on the Continent. One British reviewer called these pieces "the rinsings of the dish, the aftereffects of the fantastic malady."[14] It was derided as anarchist art without regard for history, though it was heavily based on eighteenth-century designs.[15] Art Nouveau grew from a controversial experiment into a popular style between 1895 and 1905 before quickly fading by decade's end.

Afterward, nostalgia arose in some corners for the exuberance of 1900. In reviewing the 1913 Paris Salon, Émile Sedeyn protested:

It seems that applied art is missing a little too much the young and daring innovators, sometimes giddy, always adventurous, making their name in Fashion. Eight or nine years ago one complained, especially about jewelry, of a torrent of truly excessive fantasy. Today one deplores the nearly complete absence of creative imagination.[16]

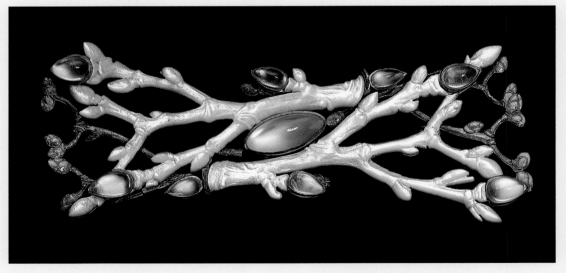

Lalique experimented with glass in his jewelry long before he became exclusively a glass artist, creating luminous effects such as the twigs of this pussy-willow brooch by backing them with silver foil (cat. 130).

As Lalique moved into glass production around 1910, he embraced the modern aesthetic of starkly simple forms and constrained decoration (cats. 154, 153, 186, and 160 [below]).

Overleaf: In these two early designs for glass carafes, Lalique references their use as containers of liquid by decorating them with frogs, mermaids, and water nymphs (cats. 185 and 191).

The new sense of restraint was compounded by the fact that one of the young, daring innovators of whom Sedeyn speaks, René Lalique, had moved on to a more classical approach to decoration and was by then a fulltime glass artist. In 1911 critic Henry Havard took a different view of Lalique's work:

> In the end, the surprise consisted of very interesting glassworks shown by M. Lalique. Lalique, you say?—Yes. The incontrovertible master of modern jewelry has made himself a glass artist; and for his first effort presents us with vases of indisputable originality and unique beauty.[17]

The year before, however, Havard had said that Lalique and Lucien Gaillard seemed to be losing themselves more and more in monochromes, where the public seemed little disposed

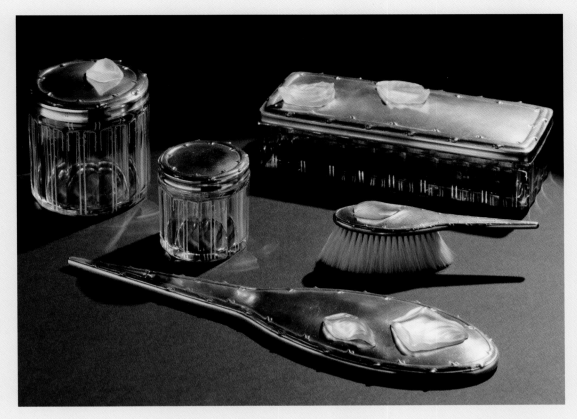

Between 1909 and 1912 Lalique experimented with glass making on a much larger scale than ever before. His *Frogs and Lilypads Vase* at left combines applied, cast, and molded techniques (cat. 151).

The delicate rose-colored glass randomly placed on the tops of some but not all the pieces of the dressing set above look as if rose petals had just fallen from the hair (cat. 146).

to follow.[18] The new work was not entirely unannounced, however. Lalique had been experimenting with glass for several years, at times mimicking the cloudy effects of translucent horn, the use of which he pioneered.

Lalique's glasswork engendered harsh criticism he had not experienced since his debut as an avant-garde jeweler in the mid 1890s. Reviewing the Paris Salon of 1909, M. P. Verneuil decreed that Lalique's silver vanity set with glass rose petals lacked the artist's usual good taste and accused him of misplacing his focus from jewelry to *bibelots* (objects made for display).[19] Within a very short time, however, the critics adapted favorably to the simplicity of Lalique's glass. American reviewers were responsive following an exhibit of his newest work in 1912 at the showrooms of china purveyor Haviland & Co. in New York. In 1914, Handon Thompson remarked on the utilitarian spirit of Lalique glass and the particular beauty of the vase decorated with frogs and lily pads, "set in bold relief upon the surface of the vase, which, catching the light, glow with

a resplendence that seems to come from an inner light."[20]

Aligning design with broader art trends, Gustave Kahn noted just before World War I that while Art Nouveau artists had drawn from the nineteenth-century art historical movements Japonisme and Impressionism, more modern designers drew on classical and provincial models while working alongside "cézanniens" and Cubist painters.[21] Paul Follot, for example, helped bridge the transition by interpreting popular Art Nouveau motifs such as insects and flowers in nonliteral configurations. By 1912, Lalique was exhibiting at the Salon d'Automne alongside the Cubist salon led by André Mare.[22] Although Lalique's jewelry remained heavily classical, his brooch with fractals representing rose petals is a geometric abstraction.

While World War I may have limited Lalique's interaction with America, he maintained both promotion and sales in New York. His suite of poppy-themed windows for the Coty Building on Fifth Avenue was installed in 1912, and by the following year Haviland & Co. advertised Lalique glass for sale.[23] In 1919, the Brooklyn Museum held an exhibition of twenty-eight Lalique glass pieces. Glass had become his dominant medium, although a reviewer for *International Studio* claimed it was all but unknown in America before the San Francisco exposition of 1915.[24]

Paul Haviland, who represented his father's New York store at the time it began carrying Lalique glass, was intimately connected with Alfred Stieglitz's avant-garde circle. During World War I, Haviland returned to France where he met and married Lalique's daughter Suzanne in 1917. Well connected to both luxury retail and the avant-garde, Haviland may have been a valuable son-in-law at the crucial moment when Lalique was expanding his glass production and advancing his modern style with new plastic forms. Lalique's second career in glass would eventually triumph at the 1925 Paris Exposition Universelle des Arts Décoratifs et Industriels Moderne, from which the Art Deco style got its name.

While Lalique reinvented himself through glass, the master of Art Nouveau glass Louis Comfort Tiffany was less embracing of the currents of change evident at the landmark exhibition of modern art, the 1913 Armory Show in New York. His earlier Middle and Far Eastern experiences made him aware of more exotic motifs, which were nothing like the traditional conservative design of his father's firm. Much of the work Louis Tiffany produced reflected his knowledge of international trends in early modernism, especially the tenets of the Arts

Fig. 18. Paul Haviland met and married Suzanne Lalique, the artist's daughter, during World War I. He was likely responsible for the introduction of Lalique glass at the New York store of Haviland & Co. after the war.

Left: Lalique embraced the shifting tide of design after 1900 from overtly naturalistic decoration to increasingly abstract and geometric forms, as in this brooch (cat. 179).

Right: After 1900, designers began to interpret natural motifs in the abstract, as Paul Follot achieved in this pendant necklace, which takes the form of a dragonfly (cat. 103).

Overleaf: Lalique's final designs in jewelry incorporated glass as the major element in repeating patterns of abstracted forms such as locusts and frogs (cats. 144, 152).

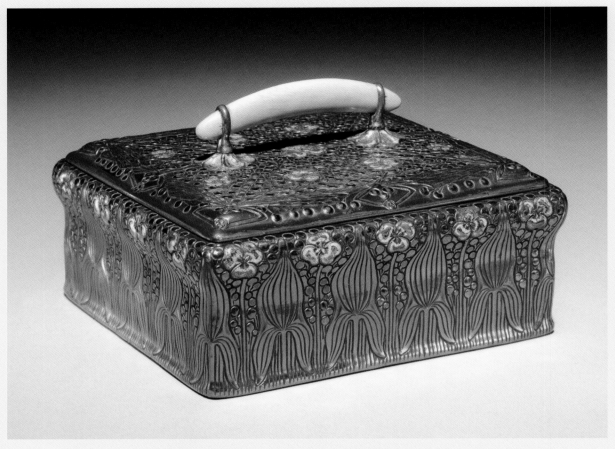

The stylized floral patterning found on this Tiffany Studios cigarette box references both the Glasgow school and the Vienna Secession, two closely allied movements in early modernism (cat. 281).

The resemblance of Louis Tiffany's globe table lamp (cat. 279) to the dome of the Vienna Secessionist's pavilion shown below may reflect Tiffany's admiration for the more abstracted treatment of naturalistic design in Viennese early modernism. The pavilion was designed by Austrian architect Josef Maria Olbrich in 1897 to house exhibitions of art and design by the Vienna Secessionists (fig. 19).

and Crafts movement, the Glasgow school, and the Vienna Secession. A Tiffany Studios patinated brass box with bone handle and a rhythmic stylized arrangement of flowers and leaves resembles a Morris textile design. The dragonflies along the edges of the lid also echo Art Nouveau motifs.

When Louis Tiffany took over as creative director of Tiffany & Co. after his father's death in 1902, he began working with designers such as Julia Munson at his Tiffany Studios to adapt both organic and geometric forms to his jewelry. This work was produced to sell through Tiffany & Co., always maintaining, however, a balance between avant-garde trends and conservative good taste. Even as Tiffany drew inspiration from his counterparts in Europe, he also strongly influenced artisans there, including those of the Darmstadt colony. Many German artists, as well as museum directors Wilhelm Bode and Julius Lessing, visited Chicago to see the 1893 World's Columbian Exposition, where Tiffany's Byzantine-inspired chapel interior embodied integrated design.[25] Art historians have suggested that even Josef Hoffmann's jewelry, including gold spiral settings for semi-precious stones in both jewels and interior design, might be directly inspired by Louis Comfort Tiffany's work.[26]

After 1900, Art Nouveau diminished considerably in the eyes of most critics, as well as the public. By 1910 the movement was almost completely outmoded, damaged irreparably by a host of imitators who parlayed the movement's signature elements into a manufactured style. Its greatest American proponent, Louis Comfort Tiffany, saw a decline in the interest of his work, particularly his most

significant contribution to the period, Favrile glass. Museums that had eagerly purchased his glass around the turn of the century began taking it off view. Tiffany, however, enshrined his own legacy at Laurelton Hall, his home in Oyster Bay, New York, where he established a foundation that began training artists in 1918.[27]

World War I had a dramatic effect on modern art, including the conscription of many of its young designers and innovators. Several of C. R. Ashbee's Guild of Handicraft members were at the front, including an artist Ashbee simply refers to as "the best enameler in England" making ammunition cartridges.[28] At home, women supported Red Cross fundraisers, including one

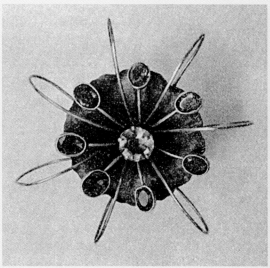

Top: Julia Munson likely designed the geometric moonstone and sapphire brooch in Tiffany Studios for sale at Tiffany & Co. (cat. 232).

Tiffany may have drawn inspiration for his jewelry from European work such as the brooch above from the English Guild of Handicraft (fig. 20) or the cup at left by German designer Otto Stüber (cat. 219).

The enameled brooch at right is marked by Louis Comfort Tiffany although the design is attributed in the period to Britain's C. R. Ashbee (cat. 282).

that called for them to take a pearl out of their best strands and donate it. The collected pearls were then strung into a Red Cross necklace and auctioned off in 1918. According to the popular press, pearls could be sent to London firms such as Tiffany & Co. and Boucheron in Paris.[29]

In Russia, Tsarina Alexandra Feodorovna and her daughters donned Red Cross uniforms and turned Tsarskoe Selo palace into an infirmary for wounded soldiers. The imperial family's charity work failed to neutralize the oncoming revolution that resulted in the tsar's abdication in 1917. A "luxury epidemic" in the face of the wartime privations fueled the people's resentment and became a topic of political debate.[30] Leon Trotsky reported on these conditions:

> The lack of bread and fuel in the capital did not prevent the court jeweler, Fabergé, from boasting that he had never before done such flourishing business. Lady-in-Waiting [Anna] Vyrubova says that in no other season were such gowns to be seen as in the winter of 1915–16, and never before were so many diamonds purchased.[31]

Former manager of Fabergé's London branch, H. C. Bainbridge, recalled that the workshops provided more and more soldiering materials as the war went on, including small arms, copper and aluminum weapons parts, and medical supplies.[32] It is perhaps the greatest irony that Fabergé's skilled workmen turned from intricately jeweled eggs to hand grenades.[33]

Fabergé, Tiffany, and Lalique had each flirted with modernism before a varying set of wartime hardships pushed their designs even further. Not only did war affect the availability of precious materials, but it also separated the era from the past and called historical ornament into question. Access to workshops and artisans was limited, and their clientele dramatically altered, transforming each artist's place in the market for better or for worse. After decades of creating work for the flush pockets of their Gilded Age patrons, it may have seemed counterintuitive to strip away ornamental decoration, yet the rich materials and gleaming, reductive surfaces of the 1920s were imagined in the dawn of World War I.

Catherine Walworth

Fig. 21. Grand Duchesses Olga and Tatiana, daughters of Nicholas II and Alexandra Feodorovna, in their Red Cross uniforms at Tsarskoe Selo, 1915.

Fig. 22. Fabergé's workmen were conscripted to produce wartime goods. The small copper pot below, fabricated in the first year of World War I, was made to be taken into the field.

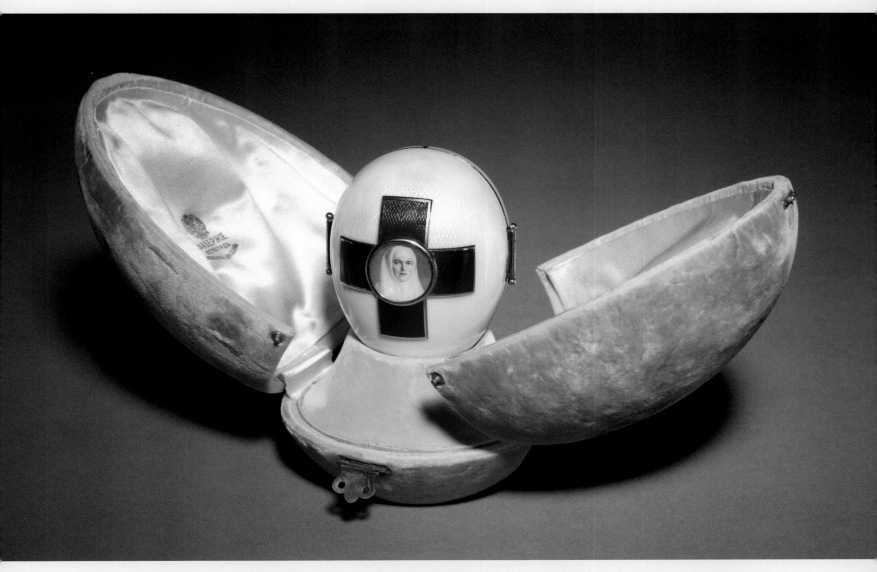

As World War I took hold, Fabergé's annual Easter presentation eggs for Nicholas II were designed with relative wartime austerity. The *Imperial Red Cross Egg* features portraits of two of the tsar's daughters in their Red Cross uniforms (cat. 62). The opened egg becomes an icon (see p. 177).

1. Philippe Garner, "The Jeweller Who Loved Glass: The Work of René Lalique," *Country Life* (6 June 1974): 1438.

2. Gabriel Mourey, "Round the Exhibition III: German Decorative Art," *Studio* (London) 12, no. 45 (November 1900): 50.

3. W. Fred, "The Artists' Colony at Darmstadt," *International Studio* 15 (November 1901–February 1902): 26. Olbrich believed, like the followers of British Arts and Crafts, that handicraft and artistic interiors could educate.

4. Gabriel Mourey, "L'Exposition des 'Arts and Crafts'," *Art et Décoration* 13 (January–June 1903): 96.

5. Gabriel Mourey, "Round the Exhibition IV: Austrian Decorative Art," *Studio* (London) 12, no. 45 (November 1900): 113.

6. According to Roger Billcliffe and Peter Vergo, the Secessionists may have searched illustrations in the *Studio* (London) for examples of Glasgow school work to include in their eighth exhibition in 1900: "There can be no doubt that, at the time of the 1900 exhibition, it was Mackintosh and the Scots who were the leaders, Hoffmann, Moser, and the Viennese artists the admiring followers." Roger Billcliffe and Peter Vergo, "Charles Rennie Mackintosh and the Austrian Art Revival," *Burlington Magazine* 119, no. 896 (November 1977): 740. The authors also compare the previous, somewhat cluttered Secessionist exhibitions like that in 1898 to the starker, whiter Scottish gallery of 1900. For more on this subject, see ibid., 739–46.

7. Ibid., 743.

8. Fernand Khnopff, "Josef Hoffmann: Architect and Decorator," *Studio* (London) 13, no. 49 (March 1901): 264–65.

9. Michael Koch, "The Rediscovery of Lalique's Jewelry," trans. Rosemary FitzGibbon, *Journal of Decorative and Propaganda Arts* 10 (Autumn 1988): 29.

10. See Alexander Koch, ed., "Deutsche und Russische Malerei auf der Darmstädter Ausstellung," *Deutsche Kunst und Dekoration* 9 (October 1901–March 1902): 124–28.

11. For more on this link between Russian and western European design, see Sergei Diaghilev, "Les Expositions de Berlin, de Dresde, et de Darmstadt," *Mir Iskusstva* 8–9 (1901): 142–52. For a more detailed examination of Russian modern style and European influences, see William Brumfield, "The Decorative Arts in Russian Architecture: 1900–1907," *Journal of Decorative and Propaganda Arts* 5 (Summer 1987): 12–27.

12. W. Fred, "The International Exhibition of Decorative Art at Turin: The Italian Section," *Studio* (London) 18, no. 69 (November 1902): 274.

13. George Donaldson donated the work as a spur to the commercial interests of British craftsmen. After acting as vice president of the jury of awards for furniture at the 1900 Paris exposition, he feared England was missing out on Art Nouveau as a popular design form that had swept other European countries. In the face of criticism he argued that England's mercantile strength could suffer if he did not place these objects in front of local craftsmen. See "The Victoria and Albert Museum: Gift of 'New Art' Furniture for Circulation," *Magazine of Art* 25 (1901): 466–71.

14. Pillory, "L'Art Nouveau at South Kensington," as cited in Judith A. Neiswander, "'Fantastic Malady' or Competitive Edge? English Outrage at Art Nouveau in 1901," *Apollo* 123 (November 1988): 311.

15. F. Hamilton Jackson, "'The New Art' as seen at the Paris Exhibition," as cited in Neiswander, "'Fantastic Malady' or Competitive Edge?" 310–13.

16. Émile Sedeyn, "L'Art Appliqué," *Art et Décoration* 33 (January–June 1913): 203.

17. Henry Havard, "Les Salons de 1911: Les Arts Décoratifs," *La Revue de L'Art Ancien et Moderne* 30 (July–December 1911): 20.

18. Henry Havard, "Les Salons de 1910: Les Arts Décoratifs," *La Revue de L'Art Ancien et Moderne* 28 (July–December 1910): 28.

19. M. P. Verneuil, "Les Objects d'Art au Salon," *Art et Décoration* 26 (July–December 1909): 60.

20. Handon Thompson, "The Glass of René Lalique," *House Beautiful* 35 (May 1914): 186.

21. Gustave Kahn, "La Réalisation d'un Ensemble d'Architecture et de Décoration," *L'Art Décoratif* 29 (January–June 1913): 92.

22. For a comprehensive discussion of salons in this era and the French transition to modern interior design, see Nancy J. Troy, *Modernism and the Decorative Arts in France: Art Nouveau to Le Corbusier* (New Haven: Yale University Press, 1991).

23. Advertisement, *New York Times*, 18 April 1913, 6. The Coty windows are still visible in the façade of the building, now housing the shop of Henri Bendel.

24. *International Studio* 67, no. 268 (June 1919): 126. The same reference to Lalique's displays at the 1915 Panama-Pacific Exhibition was mentioned in an earlier New York review: "Lalique Glass in Brooklyn," in "Notes on Current Art," *New York Times*, 4 May 1919, 40.

25. For a discussion of Tiffany's popularity with Austro-German artists, see Rüdiger Joppien, "Tiffany in Europe," in Marilynn A. Johnson, *Louis Comfort Tiffany: Artist for the Ages*, exh. cat., Seattle Art Museum and tour (London: Scala, 2005), 78–97.

26. Herwin Schaefer, "Tiffany's Fame in Europe," *Art Bulletin* 64, no. 1 (March 1962): 325.

27. See Alice Cooney Frelinghuysen, ed., *Louis Comfort Tiffany and Laurelton Hall: An Artist's Country Estate*, exh. cat. (New York/New Haven/London: Metropolitan Museum of Art/Yale University Press, 2005).

28. "Industrial Arts and the War," *Craftsman* 28, no. 5 (August 1915): 519.

29. "A Pearl from the Queen: Gift to the Red Cross Necklace," *London Times*, 4 March 1918, 11.

30. Wendy R. Salmond, *Arts and Crafts in Late Imperial Russia: Reviving the Kustar Art Industries, 1870–1917* (New York: Cambridge Univeristy Press, 1996), 178.

31. As quoted in ibid.

32. H. C. Bainbridge, *Peter Carl Fabergé, Goldsmith and Jeweller to the Russian Imperial Court and the Principal Crowned Heads of Europe* (New York: Batsford, 1949), 34–35.

33. Géza von Habsburg, *Fabergé: Then and Now* (Munich: Hirmer, 2004), 65.

Museums and Collecting

The key to the development of prestige and reputation for quality and artistic expression in the work of Fabergé, Tiffany, and Lalique was their continual push to link their works to those in museums. This idea manifested itself in the way they organized their shops, their displays at international expositions, their participation in small gallery exhibitions, the sale of objects to collectors (as objets d'art, not pieces to be worn), and ultimately placing objects in museums. For all three, this method of marketing not just their objects but their whole identity to the buying clientele was crucial, for their customers had the means and the desire to collect, and to collect meant that they would be coming back for more.

Carlo Bugatti was a controversial modernist figure in Italy, creating elaborate works in the Stile Floreale, as the Art Nouveau was called there, such as this tea and coffee set, salver, and table ornamented with exotic materials and forms (cats. 9, 10).

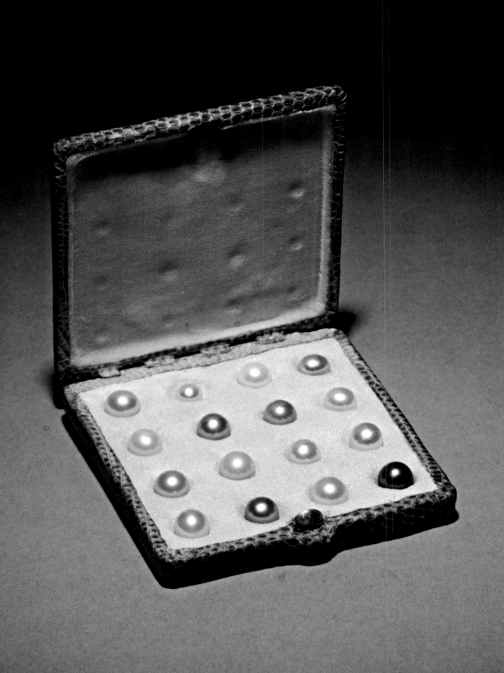

Cleveland industrialist Jeptha H. Wade II was encouraged to collect exotic stones by the celebrated gemologist George F. Kunz, who worked for Tiffany & Co., the likely supplier of this little box of rare pearls (cat. 264).

Right: Fig. 23. Tiffany & Co.'s marketing approach was always conservative and elegant, often in the manner of an engraved announcement or formal invitation to shop.

Below: Fig. 24. With showrooms in London and Paris, Tiffany & Co. welcomed visiting Americans to Europe.

Through museumlike exhibitions of exotic works in jade and metalwork, Tiffany reinforced the notion that its wares were works of art. The jade frog at the bottom right was likely made in Russia and retailed by the firm (cat. 247).

Tiffany & Co., in particular, worked hard to be seen as a purveyor of quality works worthy of a museum collection. These efforts included seeking publicity, whenever possible, for the magnificent precious and semi-precious stones the company was able to acquire. By exhibiting the raw stones, not just selling them, Tiffany was able to establish a level of exclusivity and, more important, exclusive access that elicited in his customers a desire to pay whatever it cost to own the same thing. George Kunz was, in effect, loaned out to Tiffany's wealthiest clients to help them build rare collections of stones or pearls, which would inevitably be given to the local natural history museum. J. P. Morgan in New York was perhaps the most well-known collector who benefited from Kunz's advice. Kunz also helped Cleveland industrialist Jeptha H. Wade II acquire unpolished as well as polished stones and even a small collection of rare pearls, which Wade allegedly carried around in his pocket for safekeeping.[45] Both Morgan and Wade were major clients of Tiffany & Co., and this sort of behind-the-scenes activity only served to keep them returning for more.

There was also a regular exhibition of some form or another in the Tiffany showroom. A large notice in the popular magazine the *Collector* taken out by the firm announced:

TIFFANY & CO.

SILVERWARE
MADE BY TIFFANY & CO.
IS SOLD ONLY BY TIFFANY & CO.

MAIL INQUIRIES GIVEN PROMPT ATTENTION

FIFTH AVENUE & 37TH STREET
NEW YORK

Messrs. Tiffany & Co. call the attention of collectors to the fact that in their Establishment may be found a great variety of rare, unique and interesting objects of art, vertu and high curiosity, which may be examined at all times by persons interested. These objects, collected from various sources, throughout the world, and in every case with a view to artistic quality and the most positive authenticity, are of a character so varied that they will be recognized as holding elements of interest for collectors upon the most widely divergent lines.[46]

The announcement continued by describing the assortment of "modern bronzes, faience and glass, Russian enamels, antique jewelry, miscellaneous art objects, a historical relic [sword], numismatical objects, and a unique gem [an engraved diamond]."[47] Magazines such as the *Collector* catered to the wealthiest and perhaps even the newest scions of society, who pursued the collecting of anything from rocks to snuffboxes to insects (all discussed within the pages of the popular serial) as fervently as they did companies and real estate. The brilliance of Tiffany's marketing strategy was to give the impression that the firm could even do the collecting for you. Tiffany & Co. documented an exhibition of jade and rock crystal with a catalogue in 1899 that was organized as any museum would, with a brief essay and label-like entries for each object.[48] Such activities further enhanced the firm's reputation and blurred the lines between art for exhibit and art for sale. Yet the public did not discern the distinction, and the Tiffany strategy worked, drawing an ever more exclusive crowd to their shops in New York, London, and Paris. Remarking about the rival Gorham display in a review of the 1900 Exposition Universelle, one trade journal proclaimed it the most beautiful at the fair, precisely because "the

Tiffany & Co.

Visitors to Europe

are cordially invited to visit the establishments of Tiffany & Co. at Avenue de l'Opera, 36 bis, Paris, and 221 and 221A Regent Street, W., London, where objects of interest may be viewed with the same freedom as in a museum.

By Special Appointment Gold and Silversmiths to H. M. King Edward VII and H. M. Queen Alexandra.

UNION SQUARE
NEW YORK

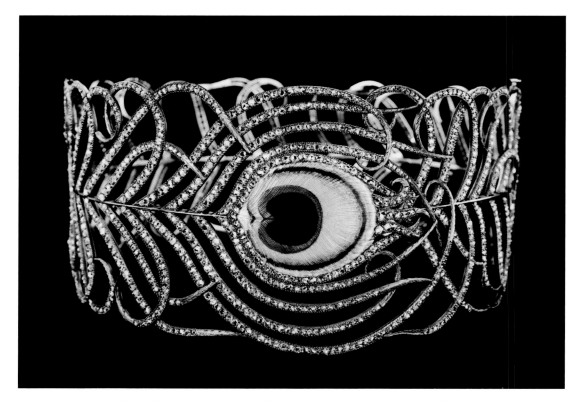

governing motive of the designers of this pavilion has been to present the exhibit as that of a private collection or museum, rather than to give it the appearance of a shop."[49]

René Lalique pursued a more direct approach to linking his objects with museum quality. Rather than exhibit antique or exotic works to associate his shop with a museum atmosphere, Lalique pitched his own works as museum-quality objects from the start. First through Bing, then on his own, he carefully targeted many of the works that he took to exhibitions and presented at the salons to specific clients, securing important commissions for works that could never really be worn because of their fragility and proportion. Early collectors of Lalique's work included Calouste Gulbenkian and Henry Walters, both of whom bought works that were extraordinary in their conception and craftsmanship and went straight into their collections as art objects, not jewelry. Lalique took the anti-marketing approach never to publicize or advertise, and in so doing, he attracted exactly the type of sophisticated collector who could pay his extremely high prices. Similarly, both Tiffany & Co. and the House of Fabergé rarely gave more than a brief notice about their address and opening hours, and fashioned the graphics to resemble a wedding invitation, formal and engraved.

Fabergé took this concept of exclusive access and museum quality one step further. He traded regularly on his status as court jeweler to the imperial family of Russia, mentioning his royal warrants on all his trade materials. He also used this strategy in London to garner the attention of the nobility, who sought the favor of the stylish and social new king and queen. A trade card from 1907 is elegantly engraved on one side with the imperial arms and a very brief message in script: "Mr. Fabergé has the honour to inform you that he has sent from St. Petersburg a new choice. An opportunity to show you this he would esteem."[50] On the reverse is simply a plain listing of some forty-five different types of everyday luxurious items from buttons to bellpushes.

The notoriety stemming from the association with royalty for Fabergé, famous actresses in the case of Lalique, and presidents and industrialists with Tiffany cannot be overestimated in the success

International exhibitions were designed to entice clients to buy. American heiress Alice Pike Barney commissioned this necklace from Mellerio dits Meller in Paris after seeing an identical one in the firm's showroom during the 1900 Paris Exposition Universelle (cat. 211).

Fig. 25. Mrs. George Jay Gould was the matriarch of one of America's leading industrial families. Her husband collected Tiffany & Co.'s orchid brooches.

of first their reputations and then their trade. Although Lalique favored a more demure approach to his growing fame, choosing instead to revel only in the press surrounding his associations, Fabergé and Tiffany openly trumpeted their connections, which often directly led to further commissions and sales. Fabergé, for example, found willing clients in the fashionable Duchess of Marlborough (the former Consuelo Vanderbilt) and Russian heiress Barbara Kelch, both of whom admired his imperial Easter eggs. Soon these fashionable ladies began to commission their own versions of his much-heralded creations. Others like them, particularly in England, purchased whatever Fabergé supplied in his stores. Because going to Moscow and St. Petersburg was not especially convenient for London ladies, Fabergé brought the store to them, first through visits with merchandise beginning in 1903, then by maintaining a branch of the store there from 1906 to 1911.[51] At the same time, Tiffany & Co. advertised that the firm's "Paris and London Houses always extend to visitors the same welcome and attention that is offered at the New York establishment."[52] Their ad went on to list the addresses and the fact that they sold by "special appointment" to King Edward VII and Queen Alexandra. It cannot be denied that the associative value of status and the allure of exclusivity helped propel the work of all three to a level of success that was as much the result of their genius for marketing as their intrinsic talent as artists.

Financial Royalty: Consuelo Vanderbilt, Barbara Kelch, and the House of Fabergé

Fashion correspondent Elsie Bee wrote in 1901, "Royalty and diamonds have ever been associated, and it is, therefore, not strange that in a country of uncrowned kings and queens this stone should lead all others."[1] In America, nineteenth-century captains of industry created their own dynastic lineages of wealth and power, and their children shopped alongside Europe's royalty in the grand houses of jewelry and luxury. The House of Fabergé became one of the most exclusive purveyors to Europe's extended royal family, mainly because of the association of their primary client, the Russian imperial family, with the other aristocratic houses across the continent. Just about all of them were related in some way to England's Queen Victoria. Following the lead of so many royal personages, an international caste of wealthy elite grew bold in its orders from the Fabergé firm, culminating in rare commissions for Fabergé eggs, the grandest imperial toy that money could buy.

For a wealthy New Yorker such as divorcée Alva Vanderbilt, who was denied a place on Mrs. Astor's famously exclusive list of society's 400, the best revenge was to marry off her daughter, Consuelo, to a husband among the European titled set. Alva crafted an impressive marriage agreement between her daughter and the ninth Duke of Marlborough that would instantly gain Consuelo, and by extension her mother, royal status. Consuelo Vanderbilt was already famous when she arrived in England as the new Duchess of Marlborough in March 1896. As a granddaughter of Cornelius "Commodore" Vanderbilt, who owned the New York Central Railroad, she was a popular figure in the American press, which reported on her social whirl in great detail. With the prospect of Vanderbilt millions filling his family's dwindling coffers, Marlborough stayed away from his own wedding rehearsal and spent the day in New York shopping.[2] This telling behavior signaled that their marriage was made, not in heaven, but in a Fifth Avenue drawing room and foreshadowed a trend in their unhappy union.

The *Jewelers' Circular*, the chief trade journal of the industry, credited Consuelo's 1895 wedding to "Sunny," Duke of Marlborough, with bolstering the jewelry trade.[3] Despite the traditional lack of showier jewels at morning weddings, Consuelo's

Fig. 26. In 1900, society portraitist Paul Helleu captured the lithe beauty of Consuelo Vanderbilt, who had recently joined the British aristocracy through her marriage to the Duke of Marlborough.

Right: Fig. 27. *Vanity Fair* caricaturist "Spy" (Leslie Ward) depicted the dandyism of Charles Spencer-Churchill, the ninth Duke of Marlborough in 1898.

Fig. 28. Queen Victoria, the mater-familias of Europe, is pictured here on New Year's day, 1896, with her granddaughter Tsarina Alexandra Feodorovna, Tsar Nicholas II, and the Prince of Wales (the future Edward VII).

marriage day was anything but plain. Her brides-maids wore blue velvet bands with pearls around their necks, turquoise brooches given by the duke, and diamond butterflies from the soon-to-be duchess.[4] As was the practice for stylish weddings, the fantastic jewels and silver that poured in as gifts were listed individually by the press along with the givers' names, a tradition that encouraged sensational generosity in the face of potential embarrassment. It was also fitting that the nuptials took place at St. Thomas Church on New York's grand Fifth Avenue at 53rd Street, just uptown from Tiffany & Co.

The British papers described the new duchess as something of a blank slate with no progressive political opinions and no indication of being a suffragette. She was deemed traditional in manner and dress, preferring a Victorian hairstyle and simple tailored clothing.[5] In fact, the young heiress found her new husband's love of ostentation distasteful. In America,

one must compete with the fabled "Joneses," but because of his status in England her husband felt the compulsion to keep up with the very real Prince and Princess of Wales—a much more lavish undertaking. Edward, Prince of Wales, kept a showy court separate from that of his mother, Queen Victoria, who remained in mourning after the death of her husband, Prince Albert, in 1861. As high-ranking members of the British aristocracy, the Marlboroughs were expected to attend many occasions at court, where the jewels were legendary. On their European honeymoon, Sunny quickly outfitted his bride with costly jewels and Worth gowns to augment the already astonishing jewels she had received at their wedding.[6]

Alexandra, the Princess of Wales, led the fashion for forehead and neck jewels in England along with the elegant young duchess who quickly joined the royal circle.[7] At the opera, Consuelo sparkled among her aristocratic companions on "tiara nights."[8] But there was a danger in being luxurious to the point of excess, and Americans were known for buying extravagantly.[9] Parisian luxury trades benefited from Americans shopping in their stores and mercilessly scoffed at them afterward. Chic Parisians knew not to buy too many dresses at once because the next year they would be completely outmoded. Only actresses such as the spendthrift Sarah Bernhardt could break the rules.[10] The Duchess of Marlborough, by comparison, seemed to have an innately honed fashion sense that later served her well in the spartan era of World War I and beyond.

Her husband's love of spectacle, however, was unchecked. Marlborough took Consuelo to Russia for the New Year's festivities in 1902 after buying her additional jewels, furs, and assembling a suitable entourage.[11] In Russia, Consuelo danced with Grand Duke Michael, one of the tsar's brothers, at a New Year's ball and dined with Nicholas II at the even more exclusive Bal des Palmiers, noting the tsar's resemblance to his cousin, Edward's son, the new Prince of Wales (later King George V).

Although the notoriously unsocial tsarina failed to grant the young duchess a private audience, Consuelo visited Dowager Empress Maria Feodorovna at the Anichkov Palace. Consuelo neglects to mention in her memoir, *The Glitter and the Gold*, exactly what she saw there, but it seems likely that she was shown the *Imperial Blue Serpent Egg* given to Maria Feodorovna by Alexander III on Easter day in 1887. During her Russian trip, Consuelo commissioned St. Petersburg's House of Fabergé to create another clock based on this *pendule*, but in pink.[12]

Fabergé's display of imperial Easter eggs at the 1900 Paris Exposition Universelle, which the duchess visited, may have been her first interaction with these exclusive works. The *Blue Serpent Egg* was also on rare public view in March 1902 in a charity exhibition at the Von Dervis mansion on the English Embankment, one of the most fashionable of St. Petersburg's streets.

The appeal of Fabergé for British royals was pervasive, and the royal family's personal collections of enamel frames, miniature eggs, hardstone animals, and jeweled flowers grew with

each gifting season.[13] To order a full-size Fabergé egg, however, was to make a profound statement because these extraordinary bibelots carried with them a royal cachet. It was even more impressive when commissioned by an American.

While Fabergé was driven to outdo himself with imperial eggs each year, he never repeated himself stylistically. His nonimperial commissions, however, often took an existing imperial egg as its direct inspiration, perhaps revealing the owner's aspirations. The clock commissioned for Consuelo is a near copy of the *Imperial Blue Serpent Egg*. Most notable differences between the two include the Marlborough egg's larger size, rosy pink enamel, and the duchess's coat of arms. Rather than containing surprises, both were made to be working clocks, with a serpent's tongue perpetually marking time. Each also winds with a chased gold knob rather than a key, as other Fabergé clocks do.[14] They are exquisitely feminine objects, with the diamond serpent appearing not only as a neoclassical motif, but also evoking Cleopatra's venomous death toll.

After Consuelo's return from Russia, all London was consumed with preparations for the coronation, as Queen Victoria had died in

Fig. 29. Barbara Kelch's impressive silver tea set was included in *Artistic Objects and Miniatures by Fabergé*, the Von Dervis exhibition of 1902, along with the *Imperial Blue Serpent Egg*, the work that prompted the Duchess of Marlborough to order her own version.

Fig. 30. The young tsarina Maria Feodorovna painted by Ivan Nikolaevic Kramskoj just three years before she received her first Fabergé Easter egg and instituted a historical tradition.

Fig. 31. The *Duchess of Marlborough Egg* (near right) is the only large Fabergé egg known to have been commissioned by an American.

The *Imperial Blue Serpent Egg* inspired Consuelo Vanderbilt's commission in 1902 (cat. 56).

Below: Fig. 32. The Duchess of Marlborough in her robes at the coronation of Edward VII just months after her trip to Russia.

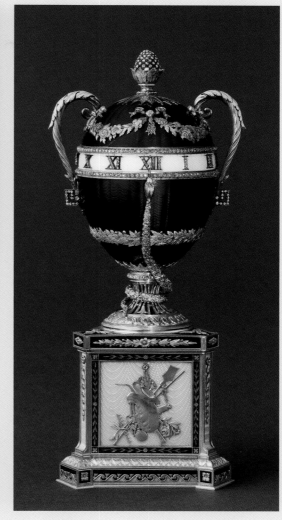

January 1901. At the coronation Consuelo sat among the other peeresses, a mass of scarlet and sparkling diamonds, gracefully doffed a coronet at the appropriate moment, and raised the canopy over the new queen as she knelt before the archbishop.[15] The *New York Times* commented on her "tall and graceful" presence, focusing almost entirely on her jewelry: "Her new diamond coronet gave her a regal appearance ... she did not wear her long ropes of pearls but around her neck was a high collar of pearls with rubies and diamonds [and] around her slim waist was a belt made entirely of brilliants."[16]

It seems that as Consuelo's marriage soured, her philanthropic spirit gained strength. In 1906, her Edwardian marriage of convenience came to an end, and her equally Edwardian legal separation was facilitated by a young Winston Churchill, cousin to the duke but more enamored with the duchess. Now independent but still a titled duchess, she parlayed her name into a force behind women's issues and charitable causes for the rest of her life.

The American duchess grand enough to commission a Fabergé egg sold it in 1926 a few years after her divorce became final and just after she and her husband had the union annulled. When a group of social workers approached her with the idea of founding a French hospital for the middle class, she auctioned off much of her personal collection in order to raise funds.[17] Among these treasures was her pink-enameled Fabergé clock, still unique in being the only egg commissioned by an American. Polish soprano Ganna Walska purchased it, and when her collections were later auctioned, Malcolm Forbes acquired it as the first Fabergé egg to enter his collection. Today, the egg has returned to Russia, purchased in 2005 by industrialist Viktor Vekselberg for the Link of Times Foundation with the goal of repatriating important Russian art that was lost as a result of the Communist revolution.

Yet the *Blue Serpent Egg* has not gone back to Russia. After being kept in the Anichkov Palace from 1887 until 1917, it was taken along with other treasures to the Moscow Kremlin Armory under Prime Minister Alexander Kerensky's provisional government. It was sold in 1927, probably by an official of the Antikvariat, to Michael Norman of the Australian Pearl Company in Paris. After changing hands twice more, on 7 May 1974 it was given to Prince Rainier III of Monaco to celebrate the twenty-fifth anniversary of his reign. The egg has remained in Monaco, where it is known to have been much loved by Rainier's wife, Princess Grace, the former Grace Kelly of Philadelphia, another American married to European royalty a half century later than Consuelo Vanderbilt. The egg now belongs to H.S.H. Prince Albert II, their son, and in many ways embodies the long history of Russian relations with the Principality of Monaco, which was at the turn of the century one of the most exclusive playgrounds for Russian aristocracy.

Varvara Kelkh (often anglicized to Barbara Kelch), another heiress, had much in common with her contemporary, the Duchess of Marlborough. Born and raised in Moscow, Varvara Petrovna Bazanova also came from

a merchant family. In the 1860s her grandfather had cofounded companies in Siberia that mirrored the American industrial scene, such as gold mines, railways, and shipping concerns. On her grandfather's death, Barbara and her mother inherited his wealth and became businesswomen in their own right.

Just as Consuelo Vanderbilt was about to do, Barbara married a short-on-cash hereditary nobleman, Nikolai Ferdinandovich Kelkh, in 1892. Widowed two years later, she married her husband's younger brother Alexander in a marriage of convenience and went on to have two children. Much like Consuelo, Barbara enriched her husband's coffers but maintained her own financial independence. While said to be gifts of Alexander Kelch, Barbara actually purchased her own Easter eggs from the House of Fabergé each year for seven years.

Barbara Kelch gave herself Fabergé eggs each year for seven years, including the *Rocaille Egg* at left (cat. 65).

Although inspired by the Easter eggs made for the imperial family, all the Kelch eggs, including the *Bonbonnière Egg*, are larger in scale (above, cat. 64).

The Kelch eggs were meant to compete with the imperial eggs by Fabergé in quality and extravagance. The *Kelch Bonbonnière Egg* (1903) is beautifully worked in neoclassical design, evoking an eighteenth-century paneled wall wrapped around its fragile surface. In this way, it strongly resembles the *Imperial Gatchina Palace Egg* from just two years earlier, and both are thought to have been fabricated by Fabergé workmaster Mikhail Perkhin, who was known for working in the Louis XV style.

The House of Fabergé created the last Kelch egg in 1904, the *Chanticleer Egg,* which has a mounted clock in the neoclassical style of the *Blue Serpent Egg.* That same year, the Russo-Japanese War sent shockwaves through Russia, and a first attempt at revolution occurred in 1905. Barbara and Alexander Kelch legally separated and went their own ways. Barbara moved to Paris, most likely taking her eggs and other precious objects with her. Alexander remarried and

purportedly was reduced to selling cigarettes on the street. Ultimately, the Communists arrested him in 1930 and sent him to a gulag where he eventually perished.[18]

These two extraordinary women—Consuelo Vanderbilt and Barbara Kelch—led parallel lives, and though it remains undocumented, they may well have crossed paths. Like the American-born duchess, Barbara Kelch was involved with charities, including Russia's own Red Cross and the Imperial Musical Society, and she even lent her massive, Gothic-style silver *surtout de table* by Fabergé to the Von Dervis exhibition in 1902. The event raised money for the Imperial Women's Patriotic Society Schools, of which Barbara was benefactress.[19] Her offering stood out among the imperial loans as unique, just as these two women stood out in their own time as exceptional.

Had the House of Fabergé not been shut down by the Soviets, more of these commissions may have come about. Certainly, as the world's governments moved from monarchies to fledgling democracies and America's consumer strength grew exponentially, there might have been more pressure to balance imperial commissions with other orders. In the end, however, the firm was destined to close during World War I, and Peter Carl Fabergé escaped to Switzerland where he died in 1920. Unfortunately, one can only speculate as to how Fabergé would have fared in the 1920s against his competitor Cartier, who supplied the era's celebratory mood with Art Deco jewels and luxury goods for a new kind of royalty—the movie star. By contrast, the House of Fabergé encapsulates imperial Russia, Edwardian England, and its European extended family.

Catherine Walworth

1. Elsie Bee, "The Love for Jewelry," *Jewelers' Circular* (6 February 1901): 13.

2. "Not at the Rehearsal: Duke of Marlborough Staid [*sic*] Away from St. Thomas's, Spent the Time in Shopping," *New York Times*, 5 November 1895, 1.

3. "Such weddings as the Marlborough-Vanderbilt and Paget-Whitney have a stimulating effect upon all the higher branches of the jeweler. It is true that perhaps but a half dozen dealers at most benefit directly through them, but the whole trade profits by the examples set by the participants of these high social affairs." *Jewelers' Circular* (1 November 1895): 23.

4. "She is Now a Duchess," *New York Times*, 7 November 1895, 1.

5. The London Gentlewoman, "The Coming Ducal Marriage," *New York Times*, 20 October 1895, 23.

6. Amanda Mackenzie Stuart, *Consuelo and Alva Vanderbilt: The Story of a Daughter and a Mother in the Gilded Age* (London: HarperCollins, 2005), 184–85.

7. "The low-cut neck is responsible for one of the latest fads. The Duchess of Marlborough is credited with introducing the fashion of wearing a separate high stock-collar of lace and ribbon with the décolleté bodice. . . . Here, by the way, it may be timely to remark that the forehead jewel, of which one occasionally hears, has also been affected by the fashionable personage already mentioned." Amy Varnum, "Dress and Ornament," *Jewelers' Circular* (31 July 1901): 12.

8. Ibid., 12, 14.

9. One international incident on this score pitted American quick wit Mark Twain against French novelist Paul Bourget. Bourget's *Outre-Mer* (1895), a novel based on his observations of America, scoffed at the egregious excess of Newport's wealthy. Although Twain was an unlikely defender since it was he who coined the sharp-edged term "Gilded Age," he penned an attack, "What Paul Bourget Thinks of America," published that year in the *North American Review*.

10. *Illustrated American* 18, no. 306 (28 December 1895): 836.

11. Consuelo Vanderbilt Balsan, *The Glitter and the Gold* (New York: Harper, 1973), 122.

12. Ibid., 127. According to Jessie McNab Dennis, Julia Grant, granddaughter of President Grant, lived in St. Petersburg and also visited the dowager empress's rooms at the Anichkov Palace where she saw hardstone animals by Fabergé; see Jessie McNab Dennis, "Fabergé's Objects of Fantasy," *Metropolitan Museum of Art Bulletin*, n.s., 23, no. 7 (March 1965): 229.

13. Reinforcing their status as a gift boutique, the Fabergé ledgers record large leaps in sales at Christmastime; see Elspeth Moncrieff, "Grandest Gift Shop in the World: Fabergé in London and Wartski's," *Apollo* 136, no. 370 (December 1992): 330–32.

14. Marina Lopato, "A Few Remarks Regarding Imperial Easter Eggs," in Géza von Habsburg and Marina Lopato, *Fabergé: Imperial Jeweler*, exh. cat., State Hermitage Museum and tour (Alexandria, Va.: Art Services International, 1993), 83.

15. For a description of Consuelo's part in the coronation festivities, see her autobiography, Balsan, *Glitter and Gold*.

16. "Brilliant Show at Westminster," *New York Times*, 10 August 1902.

17. Balsan, *Glitter and Gold*, 199. The land purchased for the new hospital came with a distinct pedigree. It had been owned by Jean Worth of the premier nineteenth-century Parisian fashion firm House of Worth.

18. For a full discussion of the Kelch family history and their various commissioned Easter eggs, see Tatiana Fabergé et al., *The Fabergé Imperial Easter Eggs* (London: Christie's, 1997).

19. See the Link of Times Foundation's online publication of imperial eggs (2005), http://www.treasuresofimperialrussia.com.

A New Order

Using glass cabochons and a sleek profile, Lalique's later headbands represented a radical departure from his flamboyant hair ornaments of around 1900 (cat. 168).

Below: Lalique developed a distinctive opaque patination that he used to enhance the subtle decoration of his glass, the precise recipes for which have yet to be deciphered (cat. 149).

At the turn of the nineteenth century, the concept of artistic luxury was grounded in the desire to apply art to the creation of a useful object, as well as the need to market and sell it. There was no divorcing the two; "artistic luxury" was in use a long time before the maxim "art for art's sake" became known. As a term of description, it satisfied a need for qualification and discrimination—the evidence of, or at least the development of, connoisseurship in the eyes of the beholder. Subsequent generations of scholars and museum curators have tended to apply the term "artistic" only to the work of reform—work that looks sculptural, painterly, or avant-garde in concept or execution; yet, to do so is to rob the past of its complexity and nuance. Without the delicate balance between what is traditional and what is progressive, a certain disruption to the pace of change occurs, resulting in either retrenchment and boredom or chaos and self-indulgence.

Such was the case in 1900, when a seemingly endless century finally came to a close. Consumers and those who designed for them suddenly looked to a new century with no end in sight, even though the prevailing spirit of the nineteenth century would not end, arguably, until World War I. Everyone's world changed in some way with the "Great War," though in 1900 there was still more than a decade before revolutions and political convulsions would throw off the old order and beckon a new one. If the theme of the 1900 Exposition Universelle was indeed the "Summation of a Century," then it's no wonder that the big idea of the fair turned out to be Art Nouveau, as if simply by saying one's art is new makes it new. The Art Nouveau, in reality, belonged as much to the nineteenth century as it did the twentieth since its premise was not really enough of a rejection of the old aesthetics to be able to put anything truly new on the table. This theory may explain why Art Nouveau was passé by 1904 in St. Louis, the next big comprehensive international gathering after Paris. Subsequent explorations of new forms, geometry, abstract decoration, and new color palettes, not to mention a new political and social landscape, would eventually effect the change necessary to proclaim a new century.

In the first two decades of the twentieth century Tiffany & Co. was faced with a crisis when Charles Lewis Tiffany died in 1902. His son, Louis Comfort Tiffany, took the helm as design director and immediately clashed with Paulding Farnham, the talented designer of his father's generation.

Once Louis had consolidated his power within the firm, he probably faced the biggest challenge of his career: should he change everything his father had achieved and move Tiffany & Co. toward more progressive design? Or should he maintain Tiffany & Co.'s conservative identity? In the end, Louis kept his studio as a separate company and began to integrate aspects of his modern design into Tiffany & Co.'s production. Tiffany then began making modern jewelry settings with collaborators at Tiffany Studios to be sold at Tiffany & Co., thus linking the two concerns while keeping the concept of "modern" as a novelty. By 1912, this practice was in full swing as Tiffany & Co. would routinely advertise that they could "reset and reconstruct jewelry in modern styles."[53]

René Lalique faced nearly the same challenge as Tiffany since so much of his world was intertwined in the promotion of Art Nouveau as an art movement. However, because of his experience in marketing himself as an artist and his works as art to a buying public, Lalique was able to take the leap to a new level of his career—a complete reinvention of his work. Between 1909 and 1912, he experimented increasingly with making glass on a mass-production scale. He explored how to turn one design into many while keeping the quality high. In doing so he first turned to surfaces and techniques that had distinguished his jewelry for several years prior, including colored patination and mirrored backs. These techniques preserved Lalique's signature aesthetic of soft, luminous surfaces. While no documentation has come to light to link any substantive influence of Louis Tiffany in Lalique's decision to abandon his jewelry career and remake himself as a glass designer, Lalique must have realized that there was much more money to be made making objects on a grand scale than singular works of jewelry. That decision ultimately led him to a vastly successful new career and another triumph in 1925 with his truly forward-looking Art Deco designs.

For Peter Carl Fabergé, of course, life literally careened out of control once World War I began and life as he knew it in Russia effectively ended. He fell prey to the Russian Revolution, and although not physically harmed, he limped along in St. Petersburg evaluating pieces for the new government and resetting stones in old settings. Finally, he fled to Switzerland in 1918 and lived out his few remaining days in miserable exile like so many other White Russians after the war. He died in 1920, a broken man. While his destiny was seemingly controlled by others, his works remain as a legacy to bear witness to his talent as both an artisan and a major player in the sad drama that ended in the overthrow of the last tsarist regime. The imperial family was the sun around which everyone he sought as clients revolved, and he may well have kept alive the myth of absolute monarchy in the eyes of the court by plying them over and over again with the baubles that ultimately became the symbols of excess and a source of their demise. Had there not been a Fabergé or a Rasputin, how history might have been changed.

One force would not have been different, however: world war and unfathomed destruction of the old order. It was enough to change the world forever, and when the last gun had sounded and the ink was dry on the fragile peace, the nineteenth century and its world of artistic luxury were over.

The application of mirroring to the backs of opaque glass produced a murky luminosity that became a distinctive characteristic of Lalique's work in glass, enabling him to achieve depth and definition in his forms (above, cat. 188; right, cat. 125).

Among Lalique's many experiments in the manipulation of glass for decorative effect was the blowing of molten glass directly into a bronze framework such the sugar bowl seen on page 73 (cat. 182).

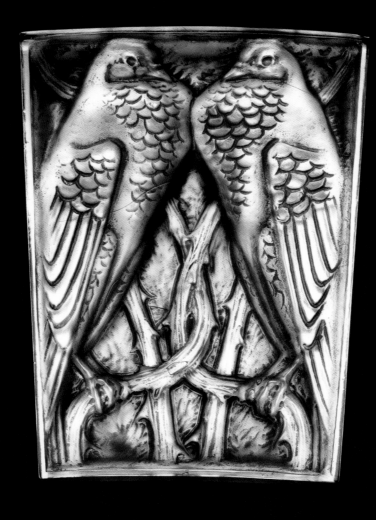
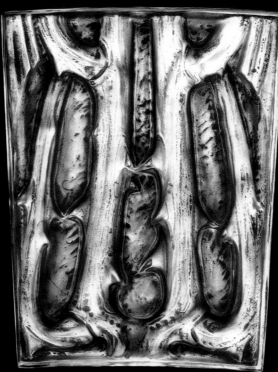

Epigraph. Irene Sargent, "A Recent Arts and Crafts Exhibition," *Craftsman* 4, no. 2 (May 1903): 71. Sargent's article reviews the Arts and Crafts exhibition held in Syracuse, New York, in 1903.

1. For recent comprehensive considerations of international design reform in this period, see Wendy Kaplan, *The Arts and Crafts in Europe and America: Design for the Modern World*, exh. cat. (Los Angeles/New York: Los Angeles County Museum of Art/Thames and Hudson, 2004); and Karen Livingstone and Linda Parry, *International Arts and Crafts*, exh. cat. (London: Victoria and Albert Museum, 2005).

2. Frederick S. Lamb, "Lessons from the Expositions," *Craftsman* 3, no. 1 (October 1902): 49.

3. John Russell Taylor, "The Belle Epoque," *Art & Artists* (July 1982): 8.

4. Ibid.

5. Ibid., 10.

6. For a more recent and thorough exploration of the significance of portraiture in society, see Gabriel Badea-Päun, *The Society Portrait: From David to Warhol* (New York: Vendome, 2007).

7. Taylor, "Belle Epoque," 11–12.

8. Nancy Troy, "Towards a Redefinition of Tradition in French Design, 1895 to 1914," *Design Issues* 1, no. 2 (Autumn 1984): 54.

9. Ibid.

10. Gabriel Mourey, "Decorative Art in Paris: The Exhibition of 'The Six'," *International Studio* 4, no. 13 (March 1898): 83.

11. F. Hamilton Jackson, "Electric Light Fittings of To-day, Part 1, Foreign Fanciful Designs," *Magazine of Art* 1 (1903): 540.

12. Ibid.

13. Dr. H. Pudor, "Dokumente des Modernen Kunstgewerbe," *Craftsman* 5, no. 6 (March 1904): 620 (as quoted in English translation from the original German).

14. As referenced in Jacqueline Viruega, *La Bijouterie Parisienne, 1860–1914: Du Second Empire à la Première Guerre mondiale* (Paris: L'Harmattan, 2004), 328.

15. Ibid.

16. Ibid., 329.

17. The most comprehensive scholarship on the subject of Bing and his endeavors remains the pioneering work of Gabriel P. Weisberg. For a complete bibliography of his published works on Siegfried Bing, see especially Weisberg's work with Edwin Becker and Evelyne Possémé, *The Origins of L'Art Nouveau: The Bing Empire*, exh. cat. (Amsterdam/Paris/Antwerp: Van Gogh Museum/Musée des Arts Décoratifs/Mercatorfonds, 2004). For a thorough and insightful discussion of both Bing's L'Art Nouveau and Meier-Graefe's La Maison Moderne, see Nancy J. Troy, *Modernism and the Decorative Arts in France: Art Nouveau to Le Corbusier* (New Haven/London: Yale University Press, 1991).

18. As listed by Jane Shadel Spillman, *Glass from World's Fairs 1851–1904* (Corning, New York: Corning Museum of Glass, 1986), 57–58.

19. The secondary literature on Louis Comfort Tiffany and Tiffany & Co. is extensive. For a recent discussion of Louis Comfort Tiffany's participation in world's fairs, see Marilynn A. Johnson, *Louis Comfort Tiffany, Artist for the Ages* (London: Scala, 2005). Tiffany & Co.'s exhibitions at world's fairs are recounted in Clare Phillips, ed., *Bejewelled by Tiffany 1837–1987*, exh. cat., Gilbert Collection (New Haven/London: Yale University Press/Gilbert Collection Trust/Tiffany & Co., 2006).

20. The work of Yvonne Brunhammer is seminal to the modern understanding of Lalique's career. For a recent interpretation, see Yvonne Brunhammer, ed., *René Lalique, Exceptional Jewellery, 1890–1912*, exh. cat., Musée du Luxembourg (Milan: Skira, 2007).

21. As quoted in ibid., 281.

22. For more recent work on the cultural ties between France and Russia at the end of the nineteenth century, see Wilfried Zeisler, "Fabergé et l'Alliance Franco-Russe," *La Revue des Musées de France, Revue du Louvre* 3 (June 2005): 69–75.

23. Géza von Habsburg, "Fabergé and the Paris 1900 Exposition Universelle," in Géza von Habsburg and Marina Lopato, *Fabergé: Imperial Jeweler*, exh. cat., State Hermitage Museum and tour (Alexandria, Va.: Art Services International, 1993), 116. For a more thorough discussion of traditional Russian folk traditions and renewed interest in them during this era, see Wendy Salmond, "A Matter of Give and Take: Peasant Crafts and Their Revival in Late Imperial Russia," *Design Issues* 13, no. 1 (Spring 1997): 5–14.

24. From the *Russian Jewellers' Directory*, as translated and quoted in Tatiana Fabergé et al., *The Fabergé Imperial Easter Eggs* (London: Christie's, 1997), 225.

25. For an excellent perspective on American art at the 1900 Paris Exposition Universelle, see Dianne P. Fischer, ed., *Paris 1900, The "American School" at the Universal Exposition*, exh. cat., Montclair Art Museum and tour (New Brunswick, N.J./London: Rutgers University Press, 1999).

26. Habsburg, "Fabergé and the Paris 1900 Exposition Universelle," 116.

27. Ibid., 121.

28. Lalique repeated an exotic motif at the 1901 Salon, where he exhibited early experiments with glass in a large box-shaped case seemingly held at the corners by four raised serpents with open mouths.

29. "Modern Jewellery at the Paris Exhibition," *Artist* (January 1901): 193.

30. Ibid.

31. At this point, Louis Comfort Tiffany had not yet begun to make jewelry for public sale. For a contemporary illustrated discussion of the distinction between *bijouterie* and *joaillerie*, see O. Massin, "Un Ornament de Corsage en Joaillerie," *Revue des Arts Décoratifs* 19 (1899): 173–78; and Charles Saunier, "La Bijouterie et la Joaillerie a l'Exposition Universelle," *Revue des Arts Décoratifs* 20 (1900): 73–81.

32. "The Imperial Russian Jewelry," *Jewelers' Circular* 41, no. 13 (24 October 1900): 1.

33. Ibid. The Azova, Pansy, and Coronation eggs are discussed in a brief article from a few months earlier; see "The Easter Eggs of the Czarina," *Jewelers' Circular* 41, no. 5 (22 August 1900): 62. The Fabergé clock, which is mentioned in the longer October article, is now at Hillwood Museum in Washington, while the eighteenth-century version from which he based his design is in the collection of the Walters Art Museum in Baltimore.

34. René Chanteclair (1900) as quoted in Habsburg, "Fabergé and the Paris 1900 Exposition Universelle," 124.

35. Ibid.

36. For example, see Jean Bilibine, "L'Art Populaire du Nord de la Russie," *Mir Iskusstva* 11 (1904); Z. de Wassilieff, "Les Industries d'Art en Russie," *Revue des Art Décoratifs* (1898), 85–92; Irene Sargent, "The Racial Art of the Russians," *Craftsman* 4 (October 1903), 42–51; Gabriel Mourey, "L'Art Populaire Russe," *Art et Décoration* 14 (July–December 1903), 237–46; Denis Roche, "Un Milieu d'Art Russe: Talachkino," *La Revue de l'Art, Ancien et Moderne* 22 (July–December 1907), 223–27; Netta Peacock, "The New Movement in Russian Decorative Art," *Studio* 13, no. 49 (March 1901): 268–76.

37. Janet Zapata, "The Rediscovery of Paulding Farnham, Tiffany's Designer Extraordinaire: Part 2, Silver," *Antiques* 139, no. 4 (April 1991): 728.

38. Heinrichs remains an elusive figure from this period as quite a lot of his metalwork survives with the backstamp of "Jos. Heinrichs/Paris New York" although no record of his ever having actually established a retail arrangement or a shop in Paris has been found. I am grateful to Wilfried Zeisler for sharing his research in the *Bottin du Commerce* (city directories) of Paris for Heinrichs.

39. Fischer, *Paris 1900*, 139–41.

40. *The Paris Exposition of 1900: Special Number of the Watchmaker, Jeweler, Silversmith & Optician* (London: Heywood & Co., [1900]), 102–3, 105. Now marked with spurious Paul Storr hallmarks along with an engraved mark, "Goldsmiths & Silversmiths Company Ltd.," this service has been in the collection of the Cleveland Museum of Art since 1943 and even published as Paul Storr (N. M. Penzer, *Paul Storr: The Last of the Goldsmiths* [London: B. T. Batsford Ltd, n.d.]). However, analytical testing revealed a late-nineteenth-century alloy content, which suggested a much later date than indicated by the 1812 hallmarks. The discovery of this publication from 1900, which illustrates the centerpiece and describes it at the fair, has rehabilitated this monumental work of historicism. The service is also discussed in the column "Ladies' Pages," *Illustrated London News* 116 (12 April 1900): 552. Here the centerpiece is described as depicting "the King of the Seas with his chariot and steeds, and attendant nymphs and ocean creatures."

41. *Report of the Commissioner-General for the United States to the International Universal Exposition Paris, 1900* (Washington, D.C.: Government Printing Office, 1901), 5:615.

42. For more on the symbolism of design at the fair and the contrast between traditionalism and modernism, see Gabriel P. Weisberg, "Italy and France: The Cosmopolitanism of the New Art," *Journal of Decorative and Propaganda Arts* 13 (Summer 1989), 110–27.

43. For a comparative discussion of Gallé's work with that of Tiffany, see W. Fred, "Glass and Ceramic Industry at the Paris Exhibition: I. Glass," *Artist* 29 (October 1900–January 1901), 66–74.

44. "M. Lalique's Exhibition," *London Times*, 12 June 1903, 4; "Silver and Jewels at South Kensington," *London Times*, 16 November 1903, 7; for a closer look at the exhibition at the Agnew gallery, see Diana Scarisbrick, "René Lalique in London: Agnew's 1905," *Apollo* 126 (July 1987): 16–19.

45. Much of Jeptha Wade II's collection of geological specimens, including polished and unpolished stones as well as jewels in settings, was given to the Cleveland Museum of Natural History, where they form the major display of gems in its mineralogical galleries. Wade's archival records (Jeptha Homer Wade Family Papers) were donated to the Western Reserve Historical Society.

46. *Collector* (1 May 1892): 208.

47. Ibid.

48. *Catalogue of the Tiffany & Company Collection of Jade and Rock Crystal* (New York: Tiffany & Co., 1899).

49. "The Genius of American Jewelers and Silversmiths, Exhibits at the Paris Exposition, Gorham Mfg. Co.'s Exhibit," *Jewelers' Circular* 41, no. 1 (1 August 1900): 7.

50. Caroline de Guitaut, *Fabergé in the Royal Collection* (London: Royal Collection, 2003), 15.

51. Alexander von Solodkoff, "Fabergé's London Branch," *Connoisseur* 209, no. 840 (February 1982): 102. For a more recent discussion of the London operations including images of the shop interiors, see Kieran McCarthy, "Fabergé in London," *Apollo* 169 (July 2006): 34–39.

52. *Town & Country* 59, no. 8 (30 April 1904): 40.

53. Advertisement, "Tiffany & Co.," *Craftsman* 23, no. 2 (December 1912), n.p.

France: The Ascendancy of Lalique

Emmanuel Ducamp

While the nineteenth century is often defined as the century of revivals, it can also be described as the century of revolutions: political, industrial, technical, and artistic. These upheavals—challenges to the traditional institution of monarchy, with little lasting success except in France; the rise of industrial mass production; the meteoric growth of railways; and the breach of the edifice of classical academicism by reform movements in the arts—were to shake established hierarchies to their very foundations.

In 1900 a revolution in art circles that had been gathering strength in the latter half of the nineteenth century reached its zenith at the Exposition Universelle in Paris. This rebellion embraced all the arts and was indissolubly linked with Art Nouveau. A fundamental examination of the traditional hierarchy within the arts, it was a quest, both spiritual and material, that sought their unity. The primacy of the fine arts—architecture, painting, sculpture, and engraving—was called into question by both critics and practitioners of art. The decorative arts, too long considered of minor importance, then rose up in dazzling style.

Left: *Sheaves of Wheat Chalice* (detail, cat. 184). René Lalique.

At the 1900 Exposition Universelle in Paris, Maison Cardeilhac exhibited a silver service in the pattern of the chocolate pot above that reflects a blend of the naturalistic motifs of the prevailing French Art Nouveau with the abstracted rhythm of early Austro-German modernism (cat. 12).

Liberty & Co. became synonymous with design reform movements at the turn of the century. This diadem in the form of barley corn demonstrates the English brand of early modernism favoring a subtle color palette, here enhanced by luminous moonstones (cat. 198).

The seeds of this revolution were sown in England. In *The Stones of Venice* (1853), John Ruskin set out his view of historic cultures, especially the medieval world, as the ideal cradle for artistic creation. By arguing that all good art should imitate nature, whether by accident or design, Ruskin linked art and nature to man and morals. He was a pioneering advocate of purity and simplicity in design, which in his view were central to the dignity of man.[1]

William Morris, the designer, artist, poet, political activist, cultural critic, and leading member of the Arts and Crafts movement, embodied this universal vision as well. Morris believed that art was a primary necessity of life and belonged to everyone. It was therefore essential to rid art of its hierarchies. Morris aimed to produce household objects that were both beautiful and reasonably priced so as to be accessible to all levels of society. This democratization of the arts became the guiding principle behind the founding of his design firm Morris, Marshall & Faulkner in 1861 (to become Morris & Co. in 1874).

Likewise, an idealized notion of the medieval craft guilds inspired the creation of the Art Workers' Guild (1884), the Century Guild (1882) founded by A. H. Mackmurdo, and the Guild of Handicraft (1888) founded by C. R. Ashbee. These organizations fought against the distinction between the fine and applied arts, and favored the use of authentic materials and the rejection of illusion and imitation.

While these British-born ideas found considerable resonance in continental Europe, they also had direct equivalents in the social art movement in France. Proponents of social art seemed to be a world away from the pessimism of Ruskin and the revolutionary socialism of Morris, both nourished by a profound skepticism regarding the capability of modern technology to create beauty and well-being for all.[2] However, there were many voices in France who disputed the pre-eminence accorded British critics in the modern art revolution, more the result of national pride than any real disagreement with the essential reform ideas espoused in Britain. In 1899, the French critic Roger Marx rejected "this doctrine that subjects our genius to the British yoke . . . before William Morris, Victor Hugo and his disciples, followed by Viollet-le-Duc, had already declared the benefits of beauty in everything and for everyone."[3]

Paris saw the birth of the Société du Progrès de l'Art Industriel in 1845, which fought for recognition of the status of creative artists and stressed the fundamental importance of education in artistic industries. A generation later, under the name the Union Centrale des Arts Décoratifs, the organization campaigned for reform of the draftsmanship training given to industrial artists and called for a revision of the status of the "minor" arts. When the Union Centrale

Fig. 33. Aubrey Beardsley's illustrations for Oscar Wilde's controversial play *Salomé* (1891–94) epitomized the decadent and overtly sexual undertones associated with Art Nouveau design.

Left: A great affinity developed between ceramists, glass artists, and jewelers around 1900, resulting in many collaborative projects. This vase by Auguste Delaherche demonstrates the lyrical quality possible with such a blend of talents (cat. 23).

Fig. 34. The complex patterns of William Morris's textile and book art used nature in such a rhythmic way that the overall effect became abstracted, a device that appealed greatly to the early modernists.

championed plans for a public collection of ancient and modern objets d'art, prompted by a growing interest from collectors and scholars in the "bric-à-brac of history," it placed decorative artists on a level with fine artists, sculptors, and architects.

At this point museums, the so-called temples to the arts, began to accession furniture and wall hangings, ceramics and glassware, as well as gold and silverware on an equal footing with painting and sculpture. The decorative arts finally began to acquire "the aesthetic value that the traditional hierarchy of academicism had denied them since the intellectualization of art in the early Renaissance."[4]

Prior to the elevation of decorative arts to the level of recognition enjoyed by the fine arts, the major event in the Paris art world had been the Salon, an exhibition of artists organized annually under the tutelage of the Académie des Beaux-Arts in the Palais des Champs-Elysées. Following the traditional hierarchy of the genres, the only works accepted by the Salon outside the fields of painting and sculpture were drawings, sketches for ceiling paintings, and maquettes for sculpture that could be placed in the category of monumental decorative schemes.

In 1882 the fledgling Société des Artistes Français took over the running of the Salon from the Beaux-Arts but kept these restrictions in place. Determined to challenge the status quo, the Union Centrale then entered the fray, organizing a breakaway independent exhibition that lasted only two years. However, its impact was far-reaching as it led to a new sense of entitlement of decorative arts craftsmen to show their efforts publicly.

Numerous artists, including René Lalique and Émile Gallé, had for some time demanded broader recognition for their art than that offered by the universal exhibitions held every five or so years around Europe since the Great Exhibition in London in 1851. Faced with the intransigence of the Société des Artistes Français, which persisted in refusing them admission to the Salon, a group of artists founded the Société Nationale des Beaux-Arts. Initially they organized their own salon, and in February 1891 they inaugurated a new section dedicated to "original objets d'art," in other words, objects that had been made by hand without the aid of mechanical processes. In 1893 the Société Nationale des Beaux-Arts itself broadened its definition of decorative art to embrace furnishings and interior decoration, and two years later the Société des Artistes Français finally admitted such works to its Salon, confounding all expectations with its liberal interpretation of the new rules. The struggle for legitimacy for the applied arts was won at last.

The New Total Work of Art

At the same time as these developments, a new style of design and decoration was emerging in both England and Belgium, so closely parallel that it is difficult to attribute its origins to either country exclusively. One of its earliest manifestations is generally held to be an illustration by Aubrey Beardsley for Oscar Wilde's *Salomé*, published in the first edition of the progressive *Studio Magazine* in March 1893. An androgynous figure with locks of hair like tentacles—a vision of a diabolical, corrupt, and enigmatic beauty—is shown gazing with depraved lust at the severed head of St. John the Baptist, eyes closed in death and lifeblood flowing in a sinuous, whiplash line. That same year saw another development with the building of a villa for the industrialist Émile Tassel by Belgian architect Victor Horta in the Saint-Gilles quarter of Brussels. Its sinuous form featured flowing uninterrupted lines. Already viewed by some as a major innovation, this style was dubbed Art Nouveau or simply *moderne*, a term that emerged in about 1880 to describe the work of a group of artists who in 1884 were to style

themselves La Société des Vingt. Their aim, pursued in the pages of the magazine *L'Art Moderne*, founded in Brussels in 1881 by the writer Octave Maus, advocated wholesale reform of both art and society. The artists and theorists of this new style posed social questions that were inextricably bound with its formal manifestations, which in turn were associated with technical, economic, and political changes that would inevitably bring about a radical transformation of the established order in the world of design.

In 1894 the Belgian architect and designer Henry Van de Velde published his *Déblaiement d'Art*, proclaiming, like the prophet of a new era: "The time has come . . . art will return to the light in a new form. The earth has been worked from which the new flower will rise; but we will not see the rise before the complete obliteration of the present."[5] The function of art had changed; the new world required a new art. In the words of the German intellectual Julius Meier-Graefe, "If the uses of art change, art itself must change."[6] A new stylistic phase had begun to coincide with the call for reform in art itself, indeed a "completely new art."[7]

Quite apart from its novelty, this Art Nouveau was also a total art: merging and melding with life itself, it found expression in every aspect of life and in all its everyday objects. The term *Gesamtkunstwerk* (total work of art) could therefore be applied to life itself and to all the material objects that make it possible.

If life itself is a total work of art, it follows that there should no longer be any hierarchy among the different forms of art, no more major or minor, aristocratic or vernacular arts. In the words of Gallé,

Belgian architect and designer Henry Van de Velde emphasized the importance of strong linear elements often completely devoid of naturalistic or figural motifs, as in this gold, sapphire, and green amethyst necklace (cat. 317).

In this pendant brooch for Liberty & Co., British designer Archibald Knox used opal mosaic to depict a painterly scene of a boat outlined by a fiery sunset on London's Thames River (cat. 199).

"There are no castes among the artisans of art … there are no mean and plebeian arts."[8] A tract published in 1898 to accompany the Paris exhibition of the Groupe des Six (also known as l'Art dans Tout) expressed this point of view clearly: "It is necessary to make art part of contemporary life, to make the ordinary objects that surround us into works of art."[9]

This new art, so liberated and ostensibly so revolutionary, found expression in formal and stylistic terms where its identifiable influences interweave an eclectic variety of elements inherited from the European artistic tradition; from historical styles; from the cultures with which Europe had come into contact through trade and colonial expansion, especially that of Japan; and from the intellectual and aesthetic researches and their visual manifestations, specific to influential artistic circles.

The British Lineage

Once again, Britain's role in these new artistic developments appears to have been decisive.[10] Espousing the same philosophy as Ruskin, Morris added his own essential contribution to this reform through his organic view of the natural world. This approach led to his use of naturalistic and often stylized motifs, together with simple forms that rejected all allusions to the historical styles that had dominated artistic tastes since the early nineteenth century. Likewise, the Pre-Raphaelite Brotherhood, founded in 1848, helped to diffuse a new image of womanhood—languid, mysterious, and abstract—rooted in a mixture of archaism inherited from the Renaissance and contemporary Symbolism.

To complicate matters further, the 1880s saw the emergence of the Aesthetic movement, consisting this time of dandies and intellectuals who championed "art for art's sake" and exalted the individual experience, though without the social, moral, and artistic vision that was so central to the Arts and Crafts philosophy. The artists who made up the Aesthetic movement, which was never in fact a unified movement with common aims or ideals, were often lumped together with their fellow artists in the Arts and Crafts. In fact, the aspirations of the two groups had little in common apart from the quest for an aesthetic based on stylized, simplified forms undertaken by a number of aesthetes, whether architects and designers, such as Christopher Dresser, C. F. A. Voysey, and E. W. Godwin; illustrators in the tradition of Walter Crane; or painters, such as J. A. M. Whistler.

A figure who was indisputably a major driving force of the Aesthetic movement was Arthur Lasenby Liberty. At the great London emporium Liberty & Co., which he founded in 1875, customers of taste and fashion could buy not only treasures from exotic lands (Persia, China, India, or Japan) but also a whole range of objects designed by contemporary artists in every field of interior decoration and luxury articles: furniture, fabrics, clothing, glassware, metalwork, and jewelry. Thanks to Liberty's, especially after the opening of a Paris branch in 1889, the modern movement came to be viewed as a remarkably cosmopolitan affair. It was always

Fig. 35. Liberty & Co.'s linear patterned textiles followed from the Japanese-inspired designs of William Morris and expressed a more lyrical quality typical of Art Nouveau trends elsewhere in Europe.

Fig. 36. As seen in this interior view from 1895, Siegfried Bing's design emporium L'Art Nouveau was laid out to resemble both a museum and a department store.

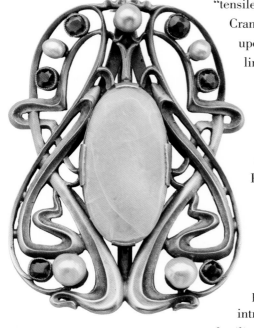

Edward Colonna worked in America, at times in collaboration with Louis Comfort Tiffany, before joining Bing's stable of designers in Paris. This opal and gemstone buckle in gold was likely shown at the 1900 Paris Exposition Universelle (cat. 20).

invariably associated with its overriding and defining feature, perfectly encapsulated by Beardsley: "tensile lines [that] describe a rigorous, asymmetrical composition."[11] Or in the words of Walter Crane: "Line is all important. Let the designer, therefore, in the adaptation of this art, lean upon the staff of life of line—line determinative, line emphatic, line delicate, line expressive, line controlling and uniting."[12]

The "Moderne" in Paris: Siegfried Bing

In Paris, one of the earliest commercial ventures that attempted to capitalize on the fervor for these new theories of art was L'Art Nouveau, the gallery and exhibition space opened in the rue de Provence in 1895 by the Hamburg-born art dealer Siegfried Bing. Passionately interested in Japanese art, Bing had opened a gallery selling oriental art in Paris a decade earlier, and above all had fostered the popular taste for Japanese decoration (Japonisme) with his periodical *Le Japon Artistique*. Thirty-six editions of the journal, in French, German, and English, were published between 1888 and 1891.

Through his gallery and the objects on sale there, Bing set out to "modernize the interior of the contemporary home in order to make it both practical and aesthetically pleasing."[13] The influence on Bing of Meier-Graefe (friend of Van de Velde, to whom he introduced Bing in Brussels in 1893) was clear. The program laid out for Bing's gallery has a familiar ring to modern ears: "L'Art Nouveau will strive to eliminate what is ugly and pretentious in all things that presently surround us, in order to bring perfect taste, charm, and natural beauty to the least important utilitarian objects."[14]

Amid interiors commissioned from Van de Velde, Bing exhibited objects and artworks that he had selected from all over Europe and America, where he was one of the earliest and most fervent admirers of Louis Comfort Tiffany, retaining exclusive distribution rights over his work until the Exposition Universelle of 1900. While their collaboration is well documented, it was not just the innovative nature of Tiffany's glass that won Bing over but the spirit that guided the Tiffany workshop:

> a vast central establishment grouping together under one roof an army of craftsmen in all media: glass makers, jewel setters, embroiderers and weavers, casemakers and carvers, gilders, jewelers, cabinetmakers—all working to give form to the carefully considered concepts of a group of directing artists . . . united by a common current of ideas.[15]

The organization of such a workshop, in which no distinction in quality or superiority was drawn according to activity or materials, reinforced the essential refrain of these pivotal years: that there was no correlation between artistic luxury and the intrinsic value of the materials used. This was a luxury derived, paradoxically, from "the simplicity, harmony, and perfection" that Bing, for one, had discovered in Japanese objets d'art. In an article published in 1903 in the *Craftsman*, Bing cautioned artists "to avoid, as one would flee from leprosy, the falsehoods of a fictitious luxury consisting in falsifying every material and in carrying ornament to extremes."[16] Gradually Bing moved away from his role as a dealer to become an artistic director with his own workshops, creating coherent, unified ensembles consonant with his personal vision and with the philosophy of the total artwork.

Although it was aimed at a younger, less wealthy clientele than that of Bing, Meier-Graefe's Maison Moderne, which opened in Paris in September 1899, was also symbolic of this process of reorientation and unification. Meier-Graefe commissioned a poster from Manuel Orazi in 1900 that was indicative of the ideal client. It featured the celebrated figure of Cléo de Mérode adorned with jewels

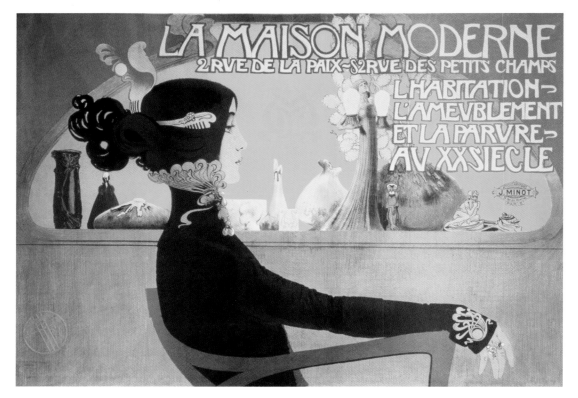

made in the Maison Moderne studios and seated in profile in front of a shop window filled with the goods she might buy there.

The intelligence and flair of Bing and Meier-Graefe lay in their grasp of the fact that the best way to spread the principles of design reform was through commercial ventures. Bing had seen similar enterprises in the United States in 1895, most notably Tiffany & Co., when Henri Roujon, director of the Société Nationale des Beaux-Arts and a japoniste like Bing, sent him to lead an enquiry into the decorative and industrial arts in America. The results were published in 1896 under the title *La Culture Artistique en Amérique*.

Their battle lay with a market that was saturated with mass-produced, overdecorated, historicist products. Bing's choice of name, *Salon de l'Art Nouveau,* for his exhibition was also symptomatic of this weighty past, nodding as it did in the direction of the great fine art salons of the Champs-Elysées. So, too, were the collaborations he set up between the fine and decorative arts, with artists Pierre Bonnard, Ker Xavier Roussel, Félix Vallotton, Édouard Vuillard, and Henri de Toulouse-Lautrec creating cartoons for stained-glass windows made by Louis Comfort Tiffany; Vuillard also made designs for a set of porcelain plates. This association of artists and decorators was not unusual.

Bing and the Critics

The critics were by no means unanimous in their support of Bing's initiative. In the eyes of Louis de Fourcaud, academician and professor of aesthetics at the École des Beaux-Arts, Tiffany's panels represented some kind of "bizarre manifesto,"[17] while Edmond de Goncourt castigated Van de Velde's furniture designs as "hard and angular . . . [conceived] for a rude cave or lake dweller."[18] Arthur Maillet, editor of the influential magazine *L'Art Décoratif Moderne,* was even more scathing in his verdict on Bing's shop and the works on sale there, opining that "their originality lies solely in their

Fig. 37. Parisian courtesan Cleo de Mérode, rendered here in a poster by Manuel Orazi for Julius Meier-Graefe's design showroom La Maison Moderne around 1900, was famous for her signature hairstyle and an ideal model for the shop's avant-garde combs and jewels.

After first seeing Louis Comfort Tiffany's work at the 1893 Columbian Exposition, Julius Lessing, director of Kunstgewerbemuseum in Berlin, purchased the vase at right and other Tiffany Favrile glass at the 1900 Paris world's fair (cat. 304).

ignorance of the most fundamental rules of art. This type of art is not a form of progress; rather it is a return to barbarism."[19]

Only the critic Roger Marx, an ardent admirer of reform, discerned an "absolute beauty" in Tiffany's stained glass, which, "far from insignificant quality in our eyes, glowed like jewels."[20] If the battle to gain recognition for the decorative arts on a level equal to the fine arts was almost won, the struggle for this Art Nouveau, this totality of art with its emphasis on furniture alongside objects, continued to attract barbs and diatribes that today form an illuminating study, encapsulating as they do the criticisms flung at both the artists and their tentative first steps in this new direction.

The august curator of the Louvre, Émile Molinier, regretted the excessive number of *bibelots* (objects for display placed around a room or in showcases) and the fact that the artists tended to "lose sight of the ultimate goal of their efforts, which is to endow everyday objects with the qualities of art."[21] He continued:

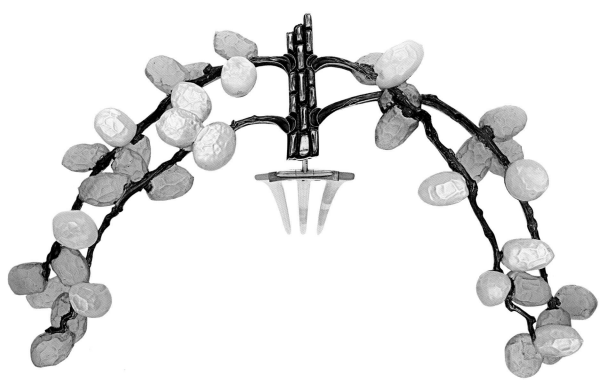

They must be careful not to create objects that are dead from their conception, that will soon take their place in museum displays without ever having been used. If this is always to be the case, I would consider that all the efforts of the past forty years or so would have been wasted. If the decorative arts do not have the embellishment of everyday life as their goal, if they are to be limited to creating museum pieces, then let us give up the whole thing now and make do with what we have.[22]

Departing from both the form and composition of traditional tiaras, Lalique's design for this hair ornament implies the naturally occurring shape formed of the twigs of an arbutus tree (cat. 155).

Fig. 38. Henry Nocq's jewelry was held in high esteem by art periodicals, here illustrated in *Art et Décoration* (1898), whose critics compared him to Lalique.

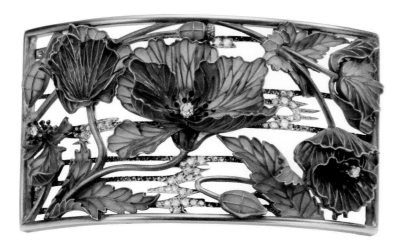

In a few pithy phrases, Molinier sums up one of the most immediate dangers of luxury in art: a danger in which museums played a significant part, making it a point of honor at each Salon or exposition to purchase contemporary and modern works, inevitably tempting artists to create exclusively with this end in view.

Molinier's highest praise was reserved for the jewelry of Henry Nocq and René Lalique, saluting their "most welcome reaction against the banality of modern jewelry" and their attempts to "breathe new life into this branch of the decorative arts, turning to best advantage a happy combination of gold, silver, enamel, and precious stones."[23] Nocq was one of the Groupe des Cinq (later the Groupe des Six), who exhibited at the Galerie des Artistes Modernes in rue Caumartin beginning in December 1896. The preface to the catalogue of their exhibition, which they specifically denied was a manifesto, explained their position unambiguously:

> We are wholly committed to the successful renewal of the domestic arts . . . the works that we exhibit are intended first and foremost to be used. . . . Artistic integrity, respect for materials, the necessary use of objects intended to become part of the fabric of our daily life: these are the values we seek to uphold.[24]

It was not the materials used that defined luxury but the spirit in which the work was conceived. An article on Lalique's jewelry design in the popular and influential magazine *Art et Décoration* was quite specific: "We cannot congratulate M. Lalique too warmly on his . . . new look for jewelry, and especially on the combination of luxury with simplicity."[25] Gallé went further in the *Gazette des Beaux-Arts,* where he emphasized the fact that Lalique had brought to jewelry "unexpected new developments and . . . laid the ground for definitively modern jewelry."[26]

Parisian jeweler Louis Aucoc designed the dog collar plaque above in the same naturalistic motif as Lalique (cat. 1).

Inspired by the asymmetry of Japanese design, Lalique's depictions of flora, as in this dog collar plaque of poppies, are nonetheless carefully composed to look undisturbed from their natural state (cat. 175).

In his review of the salons of 1898, Molinier noted the influence Lalique had begun to have on the work of his pupils and imitators and the link between design and commercial appeal:

> highly artistic in a word, yet . . . not fabulous in price . . . I imagine that jewelers' stocks of tinware will eventually be exhausted, to be replaced, thanks to an evolution that it is now easy to predict, by pieces distinguished in both form and taste, which . . . thanks to machine production, can be produced at extremely reasonable prices.[27]

In 1899, Marx also raised the stakes: "Henceforth we must break away from old-fashioned decoration, escape from the narrow confines of pure jewelry; thus, by a supreme effort, René Lalique has succeeded in casting off these chains and, climbing up from one freedom to the next, has risen to the rank of liberator and master of modern French jewelry."[28]

Modernism Faces Its Critics

The reception given to the modernists, and to Lalique in particular, was on the whole a warm one, especially in the specific context of jewelry within the decorative arts in general. But some critics with a particular interest in jewelry were dissenting voices, recognizing not only the merits of the rising generation but also its faults. In an article published in *La Revue des Arts Décoratifs* in 1896, Lucien Falize, for example, decries the fickle whims of the fair sex, the vanity of their husbands, the voracity of dealers, and the power of couturiers as arbiters of fashion, using all as an opportunity to draw attention to his own creations, with illustrations, for the House of Boucheron and House of Vever. Feeling obliged to mention Lalique, the new arrival to the salons of the previous year, Falize made a remarkably astute connection, linking these creations to the world of theater. In his view, the theater lobby was the new "testing ground," replacing the primacy of the old royal court as a playing field for ladies of fashion to conduct their elegant rivalries.[29]

Lalique's designs for the theater had to be large and prominent so as to be seen by the audience. He made this diadem for stage personality Julia Bartet easier to wear by using lightweight aluminum as the frame (cat. 142).

Striking serpents guard the contents of the purse at right by Lalique presented at the 1903 Paris salon of the Société des Artistes Français, and later illustrated in the American Arts and Crafts magazine the *Craftsman*, published by Gustav Stickley (cat. 177).

Both on stage, where Sarah Bernhardt and Julia Bartet, two of the most celebrated actresses of the day, were clients of Lalique, and in the audience, *élégantes* continued this noble tradition to show off their finery. In his definitive book on nineteenth-century jewelry, Henri Vever described the response to "a very large tiara in the form of Isis" that Lalique created in 1899 for Bartet in the role of Bérénice:

Although the craftsmanship was very delicate and the weight of the jewel very light for its size (it was made of aluminum), the diadem was generally thought to be too large, even though that was what the actress had wanted. . . . However, Lalique was only moderately attracted to theatrical jewelry, which he said, stood midway between the trinket and the true jewel.[30]

In his essay on jewelry at the salons of 1898, Vever had already made remarks of a similar nature. He termed the display of Lalique's work "an enchantment for the eyes," the artist himself a virtuoso, his industriousness unflagging, his colors "gentle and harmonious," his efforts "of an originality unique to himself, in unerringly elegant taste." However, after such a litany of compliments the ax was bound to fall. Lalique's jewels, he lamented, were destined for collections and museums; they were bibelots, wearable only by actresses. Even Molinier, though a great champion of Lalique, expressed his regret that Lalique should create jewels that were not "objects of practical value; but *objets de vitrine* [objects of display] rather than jewels that can be worn."[31] This is one of the fundamental criticisms of Lalique. To these critics, any creation in the field of the applied arts must suit its function; hence, a jewel should be wearable.

In 1901, Molinier extended his criticism to include one of Lalique's favored techniques, enamelwork. In his view only two types of jewels were suitable for wearing in the evening—gold pieces and works in pearls and diamonds: "Enamel jewelry has no fire and loses much of its brilliance and delicacy in artificial light."[32] Therefore, to Molinier and others, Lalique's brilliant pendants, hair combs, brooches, and corsage ornaments that featured translucent plique-à-jour enamel were disappointingly useless, being that their beauty was silenced as soon as they were put on the wearer.

The critic Charles Plumet was also later to criticize Lalique's creations for "their overdone appearance, too showy, too theatrical, too anxious to be noticed . . . made to adorn remote or even inaccessible idols." While he recognized their "strange . . . disturbing, spellbinding, even diabolical charm," he regretted that it was only rarely that they recalled "the discreet charms of the feminine sex" or their "discreet and intimate sensibility."[33]

Nadar

Artistic Jewelry and the Theater

Actress Virginia Earle's heavy-lidded stare confronted readers from the front page of the *Jewelers' Circular* in September 1896. The beauty wore a million dollars' worth of diamond jewels. A diamond lizard slithers up the crook of her arm, and bejeweled butterflies, "mercury" wings, birds, and flowers envelope her hair and dangle on her forehead. The photographer struggled to capture the image with his nineteenth-century explosive flash because the "diamonds seemed a chain of fire and sent upward rays of light that acted as footlights to the necklaces above." Mrs. T. Lynch's jewelry store in New York's Union Square hired Miss Earle to pose for this image sparked by diamonds.[1]

Inside the *Circular*, however, was a less thrilling story. Statistics revealed a lull in American jewelry production. Luxury sales were undermined by everything from the bicycle fad to a decreased tariff on foreign jewelry.[2] European firms, particularly German and Austrian, were allegedly using inside knowledge of American buyers and marketing tactics, perhaps gleaned from participating in Chicago's Columbian Exposition of 1893, to infringe on the American market.[3]

Yet celebrity endorsement could be powerful marketing. Much has been written on the French actress Sarah Bernhardt's patronage of René Lalique, a relationship that helped secure his early fame in Europe.[4] With the undeniable impact of celebrity endorsement on fashion, Bernhardt's tours seem also to have had a substantive impact on the American jewelry market and the increasing penchant for "Lalique jewelry," as the genre became known.[5]

James B. Metcalfe wrote in the popular magazine *Cosmopolitan*, "Let an actress who is successfully posing as a beauty adopt some peculiar detail of style . . . [and] its popular adoption by other women, particularly those of the cheaper type of would-be fashionables is pronounced and rapid."[6] Actresses, then as now, were tastemakers, and nineteenth-century theater was synonymous with jewelry and fashion. Theatergoing wives competed with mistresses for extravagance. In the absence of a manager willing to spend thousands on costuming, admirers showered actresses with diamonds and modish dresses.[7] Max Freeman, another correspondent for *Cosmopolitan*, wrote of the elevation of stage costume at the turn of the century:

> The stage princess no longer wears a fustian gown and sham diadem; nowadays her robes are modeled after those worn by titled ladies in European courts, and are made by the best modistes and of the costliest material. Her laces are real, her silks and satins are real, her velvets are real, and so too are her jewels.[8]

Imperial ballerina Mathilda Kschessinskaia, a former paramour of Tsar Nicholas II, wore Fabergé jewels on stage, even when portraying penniless characters such as Esmeralda the street dancer.[9] When performing with Sergei Diaghilev's Ballets Russes in London in 1911 and 1912, Kschessinskaia sent her jewels to Fabergé's London branch for cataloguing. An official from the firm brought the proper jewels to her for each performance and took them away again for safekeeping.[10]

As a result of such opulence, the literary,

Fig. 39. Lalique created an oversized lotus brooch for actress Sarah Bernhardt in her role as the Hindu princess in the play *Izéyl*, written for her by Armand Sylvestre and Eugène Morand.

artistic, and moneyed coveted invitations to dress rehearsals and first nights at their favorite theaters. In Paris, decadents in their 1830s bohemian dress flocked to the Théâtre de l'Oeuvre, while the well-heeled intelligentsia frequented the French state theater, the Comédie-Française, which had been a beloved institution since the days of Molière.[11] Until the last quarter of the nineteenth century, audiences shared their reactions, and fashions, quite out in the open. Lights glowed over the audience during the performance and dimmed during intermission. It was only in the 1880s that electric houselights began replacing gaslights, leading to the darkened voyeuristic theatergoing experience we know today.[12]

International stage stars such as America's Lillian ("Diamond Lil") Russell, England's Lillie Langtry, Russia's Mathilda Kschessinskaia, and France's Sarah Bernhardt promoted luxury consumption by their very example. In Russia, the imperial family showered dancers with Fabergé gifts, either for their performances on stage or as "favorites" of the grand dukes. Elizabeta Baletta of the Imperial Mikhailovsky Theater had an important collection of Fabergé, including the *Baletta Vase*, a gift from Grand Duke Alexei Alexandrovich, one of Nicholas II's uncles. Celebrity association contributed to Fabergé's reputation at home and, most likely, abroad in the wake of Diaghilev's tour to such centers as London, Vienna, and Monte Carlo.[13]

After two decades of acting, Sarah Bernhardt resigned from the Comédie-Française a second time, forming her own company, the Théâtre Sarah Bernhardt, in 1879. Now independent, the "divine Sarah" capitalized on her strong commercial wits. Her association with Alphonse Mucha, a Czech designer living in Paris in the 1890s, kept her image before the public. In December 1894, Mucha designed a poster for her lead role in *Gismonda* that was so powerfully different from anything before that she put him under contract to style her promotional image, stage costumes, and jewelry.[14] Mucha's sinuous graphic style became

so popular that Art Nouveau was often dubbed "Le Style Mucha." With this kind of mass appeal, advertisers lined up to use both Mucha and Bernhardt in their marketing schemes.

Bernhardt was the promotional face of turn-of-the-century luxury goods such as perfumes, cigarettes, candies, and jewelry. The *Jewelers' Circular* from 1901 featured a half-page advertisement for Providence Stock Co.'s "Sarah Bernhardt Chain Bracelet." Bernhardt's endorsement read "It's simply perfect." Made of rolled plate and sterling silver wire, the bracelet was a very simple and unadorned band except for a heart-shaped locket. Although far from luxurious, it came with glamorous name recognition. Similarly, the American jewelry firm Whiting & Davis assured profit from "Alice Nielsen" jewelry to retailers in 1901.[15] Named for the pixiesh operetta star, these snake-themed bracelets came in various gold and enamel finishes. Affordable jewelry based on historical revival styles, as well as artistic jewelry by Lalique and Mucha, could make a middle-class housewife feel like Cleopatra with a clip at the wrist. Popular culture provided the modern woman with creative options to redefine herself, proving that all the world was indeed a stage. Even as late as 1911, the *New York Times* described the adventurous everyday woman "who has the style of a French marquise or a Jane Austen heroine, or a medallion by Lalique."[16]

While fashion magazines reported on Bernhardt's "at home" style, affluent audiences in jewelry centers such as Cleveland, Chicago, and New York would have seen Bernhardt in Lalique jewelry. Lalique fashioned an immense lotus corsage ornament with a pale, iridescent sheen for Bernhardt's title role in *Izéyl* (1894), which premiered in Paris but appears prominently in Bernhardt's studio photographs taken later in New York and London. She must have had it with her on her 1896 American tour, and the jewel's image continued to circulate in print.[17] Bernhardt even appears in an 1897 advertisement for "Coombe

Russian Grand Duke Alexei Alexandrovich gave this carved topaz vase from the House of Fabergé to Elizabeta Baletta, prima ballerina at the Imperial Mikhailovsky Theater in St. Petersburg around 1900 (cat. 96).

and Son, Aerated Water Manufacturers" as Izéyl wearing Lalique's lotus.

For Bernhardt's portrayal of Mélisande in *La Princesse Lointaine (The Faraway Princess)*, which premiered in April 1895, Lalique is thought to have executed Mucha's design for a tiara that set giant pearl-paved lilies on either side of the actress's head.[18] Lalique also created a haunting pendant miniaturizing Bernhardt's character in a scene from *La Princesse Lointaine*, in which she walks in a darkened forest beside her sleek hound, surrounded by the moonlit glow of diamonds and a large amethyst drop.

In Cleveland, one of the wealthiest cities of the day, Bernhardt performed *Izéyl* and Sardou's *Fédora* in 1896, but local advertisements featured her in the lily diadem for *La Princesse Lointaine*.[19] Whether worn on stage or in the press, the extraordinary diadem would have been seen by Americans throughout the tour and afterward. Mucha featured Bernhardt from *La Princesse Lointaine* on his 1904 *Lefèvre Utile* cookie tins, postcards, and posters. Intriguingly, the famous Lillian Russell, who appeared on many of the same stages as Bernhardt, posed for photographs in 1897 wearing a near copy of Mucha and Lalique's headdress. As Bernhardt influenced other stage personalities' jewels, so too did she multiply the impact of artistic jewelry's influence on American audiences.

The exaggerated scale of Lalique's jewelry, seen as fit for stage projection rather than daily wear, received persistent criticism.[20] The players of one 1901 French revue actually dressed as Lalique jewels in an elaborate spoof. This play on scale may have been a parody of Lalique's large dimensions or his popularity driven by stage personalities and their friends.[21] One French reviewer attributed Lalique's bizarreness to his relationship with Bernhardt.[22] She was not, however, the only diva to wear Lalique.

After Bernhardt left the Comédie-Française in anger in 1879, Julia Bartet succeeded her. Jeanne Julia Bartet was just in her mid twenties when she took over Bernhardt's role as the Queen in Victor Hugo's *Ruy Blas*. Reportedly, the older actress said she would never forgive Hugo for letting Bartet play the part, to which he retorted that Mlle Bartet played the part so well, "that her name deserved to be indissolubly connected with it in future."[23]

Bartet acted in productions by the nation's leading playwrights, including Jean Racine and Alexandre Dumas. She played the title role in *Antigone* in an ancient Roman open-air theater at Orange, France, in 1888, a production that proved

Below: Fig. 40. The elaborate lily diadem covered in pearls that Sarah Bernhardt wore in *La Princesse Lointaine* (*The Faraway Princess*) was designed by Alphonse Mucha and likely made by Lalique in 1895.

Right: Fig. 41. Actress Lillian Russell's diadem in this photograph is a near copy of the one Sarah Bernhardt wore on her American tour just the year before and seen in the photograph below.

SARAH BERNHARDT

F.C&Cⁱᵉ
272   BARTET
                dans "Le Réveil"

influential to the revitalization of Greek tragedy and open-air theater.[24] One witness described Bartet's spellbinding portrayal of Antigone on the ancient stage as well as the poetry of her exit through a grove of trees.[25] In 1899, Lalique created a large, but lightweight, aluminum diadem for another of her Greek characters, the title role in *Bérénice*. Bartet made history in 1905 as the first woman awarded the Legion d'Honneur, but nearly a decade earlier the Paris correspondent for *Harper's Weekly* gave her another accolade, calling Julia Bartet one of the two most influential women in the world for fashion.[26]

Rival jewelry designer Henri Vever criticized Lalique's extravagance in a Salon review in 1898:

> Not everyone is Sarah Bernhardt or Cléo de Mérode, and a number of these lovely admirers are a little frightened by the originality, even she who personifies it and, at times, touches on eccentricity. In effect, who is the woman, so elegant in herself, who can easily hold back her hair with one of these combs, including this one in the full display cabinet?[27]

While the self-assured and eccentric woman may have worn Lalique jewels as an expression of her allegiance to decadent art and poetry, such was not often the case with women of high society. Elsie Bee, fashion correspondent for the *Jewelers' Circular,* said it was not until the summer of 1901 that Art Nouveau jewelry became fashionable for the general public. In Bee's opinion, artistic jewelry demanded too much focused attention to read its often allegorical or narrative compositions. Yet Bee could not deny that Art Nouveau's influence was pervasive and that the new art and the old "seem likely to run their course together."[28] Stage stars and avant-garde celebrity socialites stimulated the popularity of Lalique and his imitators among fashion-craved audiences. They wore artistic jewels on stage and in studio portraits that circulated in print, trickling down to product advertising, and from art into life.

Catherine Walworth

Fig. 42. French stage actress Julia Bartet set the fashions for Paris and for readers of magazines such as *Harper's Bazaar*, who reported on her style.

1. "How $1,000,000 Worth of Jewelry May be Worn," *Jewelers' Circular* 33 (2 September 1896): 1, 4.

2. The 1890s bicycle fad cut into the business of other luxury trades by becoming the ultimate gift. "The jeweler avers that where the paterfamilias celebrated the birthdays and anniversaries of the 'home circle' with gifts of jewels, jewels are now at a discount, and the 'home circle' clamors for the fascinating bike. Even the newly-engaged girl turns her back on more sentimental gifts and eagerly proclaims her preference for the 'silent steed'

above all other possessions." J.H.N., "As Seen Through a Woman's Eyes," *Illustrated American* 28, no. 288 (24 August 1895): 250. Tiffany & Co. followed suit by selling bicycles bedecked in ivory, precious and semiprecious stones, silver, and gold. "Diamond" Jim Brady gave one to singing star Lillian Russell, who rode it everywhere to much fanfare. David V. Herlihy, *Bicycle: The History* (New Haven: Yale University Press, 2004), 273.

3. "The Wilson Act and the Jewelry Industry," *Jewelers' Circular* 33 (2 September 1896): 21.

4. Jane Abdy's critically important examination of the details of their association and what evidence remains can be found in "Sarah Bernhardt and Lalique: A Confusion of Evidence," *Apollo* 125 (May 1987): 325–30.

5. For a discussion of Lalique's fame in the United States, see Gabriel P. Weisberg, "The Reception of René Lalique in America: 1901–1920," in *The Jewels of Lalique*, exh. cat., Cooper-Hewitt, National Design Museum, Smithsonian Institution, and tour (Flammarion: New York, 1998), 80–97. The author credits Lalique's early fame in America to his success at the 1900 Paris Exposition Universelle, as well as articles by Irene Sargent and Tristan Destève in the *Craftsman* between 1902 and 1904.

6. James B. Metcalfe, "The Stage and the Beauty Problem," *Cosmopolitan* 22, no. 1 (November 1896): 19.

7. Lenard R. Berlanstein, *Daughters of Eve: A Cultural History of French Theater Women from the Old Regime to the Fin de Siècle* (Cambridge: Harvard University Press, 2001), 111–12.

8. Max Freeman, "Fin de Siècle Stage Costumes," *Cosmopolitan* 22, no. 3 (January 1897): 290.

9. Mindy Aloff, *Dance Anecdotes: Stories from the Worlds of Ballet, Broadway, the Ballroom, and Modern Dance* (London: Oxford University Press, 2006), 206.

10. Mathilde Kschessinska, *Dancing in Petersburg: The Memoirs of Mathilde Kschessinska*, trans. Arnold Haskell (New York: Doubleday, 1961), 133.

11. In the midst of this luxurious display of the latest styles at theaters, theatrical architecture also reappeared in nineteenth-century department store design, with colonnade-style open tiers overlooking a central exhibition space, which can be seen in period photographs of the Bon Marché department store, Siegfried Bing's gallery L'Art Nouveau, and the Comédie-Française. In the age that gave birth to the department store, designers prioritized visual spectacle over practical floor space.

12. For a detailed description of nineteenth-century theater practices, see F. W. J. Hemmings, *The Theatre Industry in Nineteenth-Century France* (New York: Cambridge University Press, 1993).

13. Marvin C. Ross, *The Art of Karl Fabergé and His Contemporaries: Russian Imperial Portraits and Mementoes* (Norman: University of Oklahoma Press, 1965), 9.

14. Mucha designed elaborate jewelry and headdresses for his images of women in paint and print. His imaginings came to fruition in signature pieces created for Parisian jeweler Georges Fouquet, and he designed an equally artistic interior for Fouquet's boutique on the rue Royale with elaborate peacocks and floral lighting fixtures.

15. *Jewelers' Circular* (27 March 1901): 8, 10.

16. Anne Rittenhouse, "Now is the Time to Take Stock of Clothes and See Where One Has Made Mistakes," *New York Times*, 2 July 1911, X6.

17. Photographic studios in New York specialized in promotional photography. Hundreds of images were taken to be displayed around town during the production's run and then sent on to towns on the rest of the tour. For a detailed description of photography's development alongside theater promotion, see Daniel Frohman, "Actress Aided by Camera," *Cosmopolitan* 22, no. 4 (February 1897): 413–20.

18. Bernhardt coproduced this play with Mucha, as the author Edmond Rostand was still an untested playwright. Jane Abdy suggests that, because Lalique and Mucha had a friendly working relationship and because Robert de Montesquiou seems to have described seeing this very piece ("les lys emperlés de la Princesse Lointaine") in Lalique's workshop in *Roseaux Pensants* (1897), it can be attributed with some assurance to Lalique. Abdy, "Sarah Bernhardt and Lalique," 327–28.

19. This similarity to Gismonda's poster and the closeness in creation date has led some to attribute the diadem to Gismonda by mistake, including the Cleveland *Plain Dealer*, 19 May 1896.

20. "J'ai conscience d'avoir fait autrefois à Lalique—je ne crois pas que ce soit dans *Art et Décoration*, le reproche de créer parfois des bijoux impossibles à porter, incommodes ou en dehors de l'échelle humaine, par conséquent des oeuvres qui dès leur naissance étaient condamnées à devenir des objets de vitrine, des objets morts par conséquent aux trois quarts." Émile Molinier, "Les Objets d'Art aux Salons," *Art et Décoration* 9 (January–June 1901): 189.

21. Katharine De Forest, "Recent Happenings in Paris," *Harper's Weekly* (30 March 1901): 13, 34.

22. "On sait, en particulier, que M. Lalique a beaucoup travaillé pour Mme Sarah Bernhardt; et peut-être est-il permis de découvrir là la raison de ces aspects un peu étranges que révèle parfois son art, et qui constituent le seul reproche qu'on puisse lui addresser." G.S., "Les Bijoux de M. Lalique," *Art et Décoration* 1 (January–June 1897): 160.

23. Jules Huret, *Sarah Bernhardt* (Chapman & Hall: London, 1899), 85.

24. Frank Jones, "Scenes from the Life of Antigone," *Yale French Studies* 6 (France and World Literature) (1950): 97.

25. Thomas A. Janvier, "The Comédie Française at Orange," *Century Magazine* 1, no. 2 (June 1895): 180.

26. Katharine de Forest, "Our Paris Letter," *Harper's Weekly* (7 March 1896): 183.

27. Henri Vever, "Les Bijoux aux Salons de 1898," *Art et Décoration* 3 (January–June 1898).

28. Elsie Bee, "The Love for Jewelry," *Jewelers' Circular* 42, no. 1 (6 February 1901): 13.

Contemporaries of Lalique

Lalique's works came onto an already crowded scene of serious jewelers working to please their equally serious critical peers. Henri Vever's comprehensive history of French jewelry helped establish him as the dean of Parisian jewelers, with many other rivals clawing for recognition. Encompassing more than 1,000 pages, Vever's tome reads like a who's who of French jewelry at the time, especially since many contemporary firms had formed in the early years of Napoleonic France. The objects Vever described and illustrated throughout most of the book were largely formal arrangements of diamonds and pearls, which then stood in marked contrast to the emerging jewelry of Lalique and others working at the end of the century. Vever's work is remarkable in visually setting up this contrast as he continued to illustrate traditional designs alongside those of a more avant-garde nature, principally those of Lalique and his contemporaries. In this way, Vever joined the ranks of his fellow critics and jewelers who, while they frequently recognized the benefits of modernism in their writings, also offered a much more faithful image of the jeweler's art in general during this period, giving equal attention to the masters of classic jewelry who represented a large proportion of contemporary production.

There is a tendency to view this world in terms of a dichotomy between revolutionary jewelry in the modern style, as personified by Lalique, and the classic, traditional work embodied by jewelers such as Chaumet and Cartier. In fact there would seem to be a case for broadening that view and rediscovering a much wider aesthetic spectrum embracing an eclectic mix, in which a good many jewelers, including Vever, Boucheron, Coulon, Roger Sandoz, René Foy, Écaille, Téterger, and Aucoc, oscillated between the two styles, classic and modernist.

Charles Saunier, writing about the jewelry at the 1900 Exposition Universelle, pointed out the modernist tendencies adopted by the great classic jewelers who paid "the supreme tribute . . . to René Lalique by following in his footsteps." Thus he noted that Vever, as a jeweler, mingled gold, silver,

Maison Boucheron in Paris created elegant formal jewelry in historicist styles such as the long necklace of blue steel, diamonds, zircons, and pearls at left in the French Régence taste of the early 1700s (cat. 6).

Ornamented with floral motifs and specimen agate facings, Henri Téterger's design for a jewelry box derives from the form of eighteenth-century French chests of drawers (cat. 220).

Left: Around 1900, Parisian jewelers such as Henri Vever might depict a traditional motif—in this case a young French Breton woman—in the new style with an unconventional pose, rendered in enamel and delicate swirling lines (cat. 319).

Right: Composed of Mississippi River pearls for flower petals and plique-à-jour leaves, this extraordinary bodice ornament by Vever was shown at the 1900 Exposition Universelle in Paris, illustrating the dominant theme of nature in its wildest forms (cat. 318).

Below: Georges Fouquet's interpretation of an orchid in this brooch is a somewhat stylized and controlled version of the exotic flower, as if to tame its complex features (cat. 104).

precious stones, and enamel but "also reserves an important role for diamonds. The proof may be seen in his figure of a Breton woman, with her ruff, bonnet, and bonnet strings picked out in brilliants." Vever's joint creations with Eugène Grasset were thought to possess "a robustness reminiscent of the handsome jewelry of old Hungary."[34] Léonce Bénédite, a curator at the Musée du Luxembourg, also accorded a special place to Vever, who sought "reform and evolution within the context of tradition,"[35] while Marx acknowleged his "bias toward precious stones."[36] Maison Boucheron, "although belonging to the old school of jewelry," was singled out by Saunier for its "respect for diamonds," but also for its "modernist vision."[37]

One jeweler, Georges Fouquet, was known for his collaborations with artist Alphonse Mucha. However, the complex Symbolist works that resulted were not always received with praise. One critic declared that he preferred pieces in which Fouquet had invested "his personal taste alone" to those designed in collaboration with Mucha, with their "dazzling, ostentatious opulence . . . which may well produce a dramatic effect at the theater . . . but which cannot usefully complement the charms of the ladies of Paris."[38] Another drew attention to their "rather exotic emphasis, not without piquancy or charm," as well as their "savage opulence."[39]

Although in most of these articles the work of Alexis Falize and Falize Frères was illustrated by pieces that were unambiguously historicist and japoniste in inspiration, Saunier saw an unexpected connection between Falize and modernism in his "return to nature, from 1889 and earlier."[40] Bénédite, by contrast, regretted that his work was not more "enlivened by artistic inspiration."[41]

Other jewelry houses such as Chaumet operated almost exclusively within the traditional canon of formal jewelry, producing grand ornaments paved in diamonds. The "imposing parures of Marret frères" and "graceful ornaments" of M. Desprez are today all but long forgotten.[42] Yet, it is worth noting that jewelers who continued to work in the conventional style around 1900 did not necessarily incur the modernists' wrath. Even Marx, a champion of Lalique and the new styles, could be generous in his praise for traditional work:

Historicist designs, such as this necklace and bracelet in the Renaissance style, remained popular alongside the era's more avant-garde jewels (cat. 101).

Diamonds reigned supreme in formal evening jewelry at the turn of the century, as in this perfectly symmetrical butterfly bodice brooch by an unknown French maker composed of matching pairs of stones (cat. 309).

Fig. 43. For some ladies of society it was not enough for diamonds to glitter on their own. In the design below for an elaborate stomacher intended for Princess Yusupov, 1910, Parisian jewelers Chaumet added rubies to enhance the bowknot and tassel cascading effect.

In an unexpected twist on a traditional accessory, Lalique's enameled lorgnette at right takes the form of a gently trailing wisteria vine (cat. 196).

Among all these jewels, take the piece that is the largest in scale, the most sumptuous, the most magical: the *devant de corsage* [large brooch] by M. Chaumet. You will observe that it undoubtedly owes its splendor less to the number and size of diamonds used than to the art with which they are arranged, which creates the effect of a shimmering cascade or a glittering burst of fireworks.[43]

The classicists, meanwhile, could prove susceptible in their turn to the charms of Lalique. Henry Havard described him as "the most justly celebrated of the protagonists of a neo-style," capable of daring touches that were "completely unexpected, such as depicting the rising sun or setting the moon on plaques for a bracelet; ripening diamond hazelnuts on sapphire foliage; and allowing glimpses, through trailing fronds of honeysuckle, of female profiles with long, flowing tresses and lips hungry for kisses, melting away as though in a dream."[44]

Lluís Masriera, between Catalan Modernisme and International Art Nouveau

In 1888, the first universal exposition in Spain was held in Barcelona. This Catalan city, an industrial center that had been rapidly expanding since the mid nineteenth century, took advantage of the occasion to adapt its urban planning to new needs, following the path of cultural modernity then prevalent in Europe. The Catalan middle class was growing ever larger, and much of Spain was immersed in a serious political and economic crisis, still trapped in the ways of the past. Barcelona, on the periphery, took a stand against the center, Madrid, and looked to Paris as a social and artistic model. Then the cultural capital of Europe, Paris was just entering the era of Symbolism and Art Nouveau.

Catalan artists, who up until then had been trained in Rome, now swapped Rome for Paris and chose bohemia and creative freedom over the academy. It was not just painters and sculptors who chose this model but also applied and decorative artists, who were then beginning to take on a very important role in the art of their time. Such was also the case in Barcelona, and objects of art, including jewelry and gold items, began to take on a leading role.

The Masriera lineage was founded by Josep Masriera Vidal (1812–1875). He came from a town near Barcelona, the city where he did his apprenticeship as a master jeweler in 1838. The Masriera family became one of the leaders in jewelry arts,

Fig. 44. As a young artist in Barcelona, Lluís Masriera kept abreast of European art movements.

Masriera's designs echoed those of other fashionable jewelers across Europe and in America who depicted flowers in gemstones and enamel, as in this carnation brooch (cat. 207), with its design (cat. 209b) from around 1900.

especially in Art Nouveau and Art Deco, from the end of the nineteenth to the beginning of the twentieth century.

At the Barcelona world's fair in 1888, the Masriera firm—then run by Josep Masriera Vidal's sons Josep Masriera Manovens and Francesc Masriera Manovens—was awarded a gold medal for its creations and the prize awarded by the Jewelry and Silverware Artifacts Association of Barcelona for the best presentation of such pieces. Not just jewelers, the brothers were also painters much admired by Barcelona's middle class. Their paintings brought them great recognition, even in Paris at the 1889 Exposition Universelle. The aesthetic side of their work was typical of the time, but at the end of the century the scenario began to change when Josep Masriera Manovens's two sons, Josep Masriera Rosés and especially Lluís Masriera Rosés, joined the firm.

Lluís Masriera began in the family workshop quite young. In 1886, he enrolled at the School of Fine Arts in Barcelona, leaving for Geneva in 1889 to study different enameling techniques. Enameling was one of the specialties of the Masriera firm, and Geneva was the place to complete one's knowledge. Training under Frank-Édouard Lossier, Lluís excelled in enamel painting and grisaille. After returning to Barcelona, he visited Geneva occasionally. Nonetheless, he remained well aware of artistic developments in Europe because of his travels, subscriptions to the main decorative art magazines, commercial relationships, and friends. One notable friendship was with the Bing family, gallery owners and art dealers whose Parisian establishment, L'Art Nouveau, lent its name to the end-of-the-century style. Lluís Masriera's designs gradually evolved toward the characteristic forms of Art Nouveau.

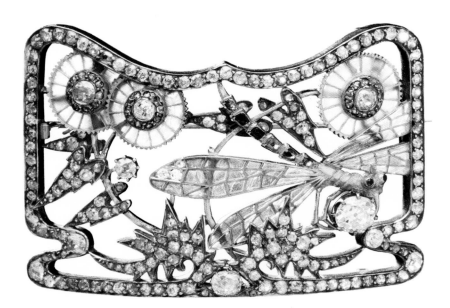

After 1900, Masriera became increasingly associated with the international Art Nouveau movement. The composition of this dragonfly dog collar plaque, now converted to a pendant brooch (cat. 208), reflects these sensibilities even if the liberal use of diamonds speaks to a more traditional taste. The original design drawing below (cat. 209a) suggests the plaque was intended for use as a dog collar necklace.

Fig. 45. The figural brooch at bottom left of around 1900–1910 displays Masriera's particular style of enamelwork, in which he delicately shaded colors to give depth and tonality to his pieces.

By 1901, floral decoration, sinuous lines, and stylized female figures began to appear in his works. These were the features of Modernisme (modernism), the name given to Art Nouveau in Catalonia. Originally Modernisme was only a way of defining the cultural aspirations of a set of intellectuals and artists who wanted to build a modern country and create a new art form.

In the years just before the full upsurge of Modernisme, from the universal exposition in 1888 until the late 1890s, Catalonia was culturally immersed in Romanticism. In artistic and architectural terms this fascination mainly involved

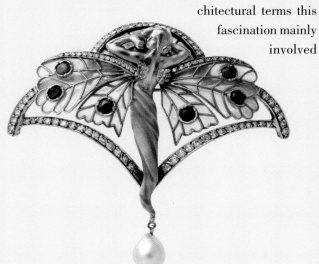

an extensive review of the region's history during the Middle Ages to find the roots of a national identity.

Many of Masriera's pieces made during the closing years of the nineteenth century contained dragon motifs, an element from the medieval past typical of a premodernist style that has sometimes been called the Renaixença (Renaissance). The word actually refers to a broad romantic and cultural movement focused on regaining Catalan

Fig. 46. Because Masriera almost always drew his designs on the same kind of paper, they could be assembled into books. The original molds prepared from the drawings were an important step in creating the form before decoration could be applied.

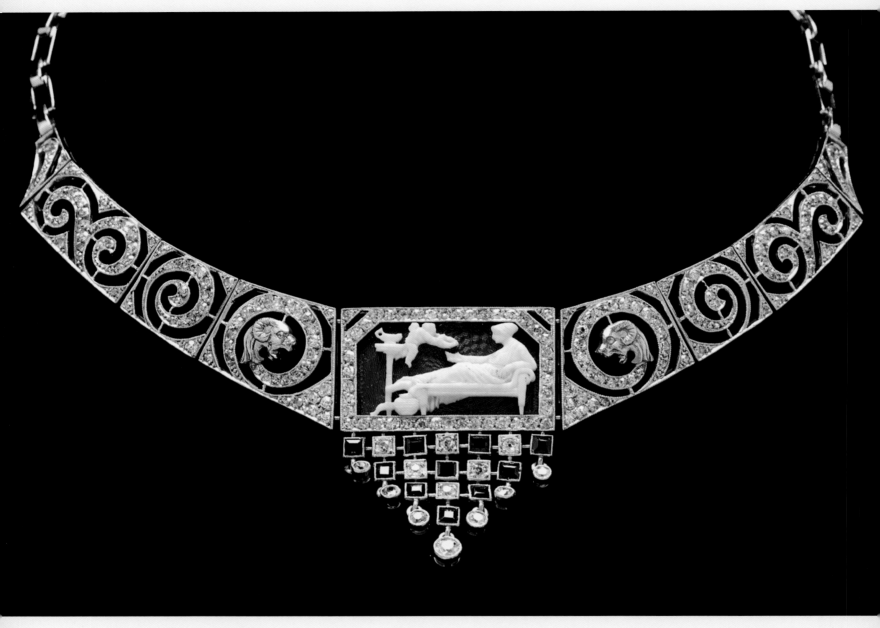

language and culture. Following a visit to the 1900 Exposition Universelle in Paris, which was an international triumph for Art Nouveau, the legendary Lluís Masriera became obsessed with achieving the most refined enamels possible. Shutting himself away in his Barcelona workshop to concentrate on the task, he became completely wrapped up in Art Nouveau aesthetics. He achieved his goal, developing a plique-à-jour (translucent enamel) and the extremely fragile "cameo" enamel or "Barcelona enamel," as it is now known. On 21 December 1901 during

the Christmas fair, he presented his modernist pieces in the display cases of his shop in Carrer de Ferran, in Barcelona's most important shopping center at the time. Masriera's jewelry was so successful he came to be recognized as a great Catalan modernist jeweler and enameler.

Lluís Masriera's fame coincided with the direction the family firm was taking: to produce new works in the Art Nouveau style. Lluís designed the jewelry and, using pencil and watercolor, drew the various pieces with great care; he was a very talented draftsman. These drawings are now

In marked contrast to the fluid lines of the Art Nouveau, the early modern movement's influence on Masriera can be seen in the sleek neoclassical decoration completely contained within the form of this necklace (cat. 210).

kept in just over a hundred small albums, making a fine index of his refined creations. Dragonflies, butterflies, frogs, insect-women, fairies, flowers of all kinds, forest trees, radiant suns, and winter landscapes are the most characteristic motifs of his pieces, with gold, plique-à-jour, *basse-taille* (low-cut) and cameo enamel, diamonds, pearls, wild pearls, sapphires, rubies, ivory, tortoiseshell, and coral, the most common materials.

Another feature typical of Masriera's designs was that each could be produced in a series. He used highly precise molds and cutting tools, enameled the resulting objects in different colors, and added stones designed for each individual piece. Thus many works had the same central motif—insects, nymphs, fairies, flowers—but no two were exactly the same. Art, industry, and commercial sense all played a role in Masriera's designs, which can still be produced today thanks to the molds and models preserved in workshops now owned by the Bagués-Masriera firm.

Lluís Masriera was commissioned to create unique high-quality jewelry and gold pieces—royal gifts, commemorative pieces, and the like. The workshop books, which have fortunately been preserved, allow us to see which models were most highly valued by his customers. Between 1901 and 1915 he added new, more classical themes to his Art Nouveau repertoire. By the 1920s his designs could be described as Art Deco.

The Bagués-Masriera firm is one of the oldest in Europe. While the company has gone through various name changes, it has operated continually and does so today, 170 years after the firm was founded by Josep Masriera Vidal and more than two centuries after the Carreras family, Masriera's partners, also goldsmiths, began working in Barcelona. The two firms merged to create Masriera y Carreras in 1915. For several decades, Masriera's workshops were the most important in Catalonia because they could carry out the entire process of making jewelry: there a project could be started, worked on, finished, and brought to market. There were divisions for melting down metal bought in bulk, for chiseling, embossing, and polishing metal, for setting stones, and for various kinds of enameling.

Lluís Masriera was also a painter, dramatist, and set designer, a member of the Academy of Fine Art, and a respected figure in Barcelona's cultural life. Above all, however, he was the prototypical global artist who sought to create complete works of art and play a leading role in integrating the arts characteristic of the end of the nineteenth and beginning of the twentieth century and Art Nouveau.

Dr. Pilar Vélez

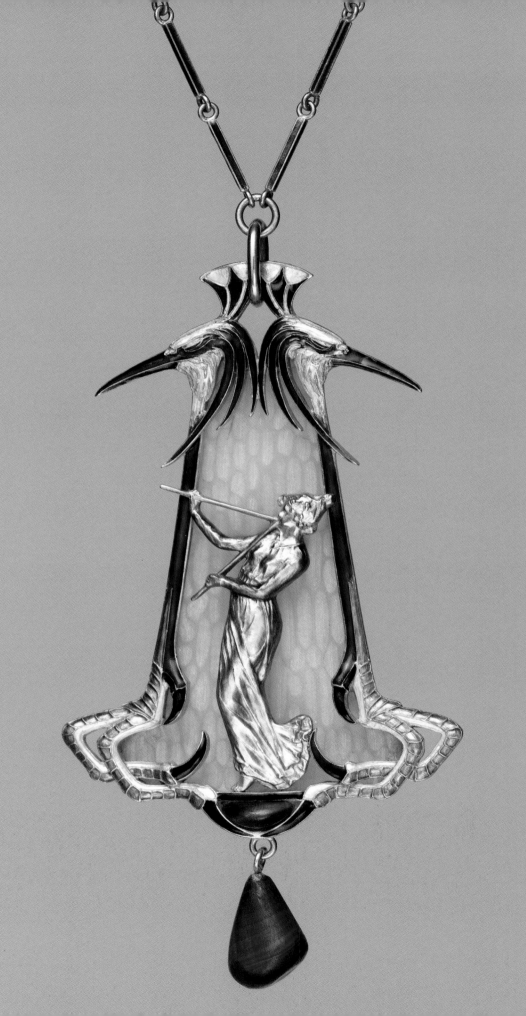

Lalique: Poet of Artistic Luxury

Inspired by the Symbolist literary movement around 1900, with whose members he was well acquainted, Lalique created allegorical works such as this enamel pendant in which a pied piper mockingly dances amid the claws of a bird of prey in a metaphor of life itself (cat. 190).

One of the most noticeable features to emerge from a study of contemporary texts is the striking frequency with which critics drew parallels between the art of Lalique and the realms of dreams and poetry:

> Who does not treasure childhood memories of unforgettable images of Aladdin's garden? The very name conjures up—as though by the rubbing of the genie's lamp—vistas of enchanted orchards with opalescent paths of mother-of-pearl, of white peacocks with tail feathers encrusted with pearls, of mysterious trees laden with wonderful fruit, all sparkling in the magical light of a thousand supernatural flames.... Recently a figure made his appearance who suddenly reawakened in us the enchanted delights and splendors of the *Thousand and One Nights*. It was Lalique.[45]

This was not the first time links had been drawn between modern decorative art and literature. Gallé had already made liberal use of such comparisons, to the point of prompting acerbic remarks from the critics. In his review of the salons of 1897, Molinier wearily observed the plethora of texts from St. Francis of Assisi, Victor Hugo, Verlaine, Baudelaire, Maeterlinck, and Robert de Montesquiou that accompanied the catalogue descriptions of Gallé's work: "If only M. Gallé could do away with all this literature, which is quite irrelevant to his work; literature often makes a poor guide to art."[46]

Ironically, Gallé was also commissioned to review the same salons of 1897 for the *Gazette des Beaux-Arts*. A poet himself, he wrote of Lalique: "In his prisms we seek reflections of our souls, in his constellations the hidden light of a familiar thought, from the heights of which we may better view the stars."[47] In Gallé's view, the artist was invested with an almost mystic and spiritual duty:

> Let Lalique therefore realize our hopes: for we yearn for ingenuity to govern the confection of our *lacs d'amour*, for jewelry to be a sublimely childish creation to serve our needs, to adorn lovers and fiancées, and to limn a halo of memory around life's happiest and harshest hours.[48]

Fig. 47. Paul Helleu's portrait of Parisian writer and friend of Lalique, Robert de Montesquiou, known by his moniker "the bat," who praised Lalique's work in his 1897 work *Roseaux Pensants*.

In typical Symbolist fashion, Lalique included images of both day (blooming flowers) and night (sleeping figure) in his designs for pocket watches (cat. 174, front and back).

The objet d'art or jewel not only had its own identity, but also represented something else, more intangible, but almost more important to contemporary eyes: the link between art and life. This link was not merely valuable but imperative in their view. It was a joining of art in the philosophical sense of the term; artistic creation, in the material sense of the term; and life, encompassing everything from dreams and sublime passion to more prosaic everyday events.

The common denominator between Lalique and Gallé was the creation of a physical object. It didn't matter whether it was a jewel or a glass vase, the distillation in metal, enamel, and precious stones of "this power to evoke . . . this quest for meaning . . . this invitation to meditation" was paramount.[49] One observer wrote that in Lalique's work the "bats flutter among diamond stars . . . swans glide silently on opal waters . . . fish undulate through enamel waves . . . [and] writhing snakes disgorge strings of precious stones from their gaping jaws."[50] Bénédite pointed out that Lalique's crowning achievement was the creation of "an art of the imagination, amusing and charming, through the close conjunction of imagination and technique, of feeling and intellect."[51] Lalique's contemporaries attributed his imaginative prowess to, above all, his close observation of nature.

Nature

Above: Reminiscent of Claude Monet's early water lily paintings, Lionel-Aristide Le Couteux's ornamental comb uses tortoiseshell for a murky watery effect (cat. 21).

Émile Gallé's glass was as synonymous with the Art Nouveau movement as was Lalique's jewelry around 1900. Gallé created veritable sculptures in glass, enhanced in some cases by the collaborative work of other makers, as in the vase at left with mounts of undulating seaweed and marine life by Bapst and Falize (cat. 109).

The natural world was perhaps Lalique's deepest source of inspiration in the two decades surrounding 1900. One of his contemporaries imagined Lalique "strolling through the fields, head down in order to contemplate the works of nature," noting that it was:

> an equally profound understanding of rural life, acquired in woods and gardens, in his studio, and even in the museum, that enabled [Lalique] to lend his works inspired by nature the only interpretation that befits decorative art: neither slavish imitation nor literary translation studded with pretentious symbolism.[52]

Lalique employed more than the usual hierarchy of favorite blooms, which also set his efforts apart. He found nobility in the lowest orders of nature: "the wild flowers of the woods, meadows, and paths—violets, cowslips, nasturtiums, dandelions, and those humble flowers that have earned popularity and the status of enduring classics in French jewelry, such as mistletoe, thistles, honesty, and wood anemones."[53]

Speaking reverently of the objects Lalique displayed at the 1900 Paris Exposition, curator Bénédite remarked that the artist "observes intently as the buds open, and the flowers unfurl their

petals to the dawn."[54] He had become the celebrant of the vital principle underlying each flower, each insect, and each flutter of a butterfly's wing, offering an interpretation that quivered with life and melody, transforming them into lyrical "commandments." In Bénédite's view, the direct source of inspiration for this new style lay in the same nature to which Lalique gave such close study, "tracing this profusion of sinuous lines, these curves—vanishing or broken, gentle or bold—avoiding scrolls and whorls, and executed with such elegance and nonchalance that they appear to have been borrowed from the swelling of a bloom or curve of a stem, from stamens or pistils."[55] For Lalique, the form and execution, not just the subject, derived from nature.

Contemporaries attributed much of the visual and spiritual inspiration for Lalique's passion for nature to the influence of japonisme and to his study of Japanese art. In Europe a fascination with exoticism has existed since the seventeenth century, and after Japan opened its ports in 1853, European eyes were opened to its culture and its art, regularly shown at the great universal exhibitions. In addition, the Meiji government encouraged

Previous pages: Two distinctively different renditions of the popular thistle motif show the evolution from the Art Nouveau as rendered by Lucien Gaillard (left, cat. 108) to a more rhythmical, modernist look in the work of René Lalique (right, cat. 187) after 1900.

The influence of Japan continued to be an important force in design at the turn of the century. Each panel of this match holder and cigar cutter by Falize at right is a varicolored japonesque scene (cat. 100).

Lalique's treatment of natural subjects was at times both literal and lyrical, as with the orchid hair ornament at left infused with both an obsessive attention to detail and a soft expressive tonality seen in nature only at the moment of budding (cat. 167).

Gaillard rendered the coloration of a moth's wings with such precision and symmetry in this pendant that the whole work begins to take on an abstraction typical of early modern design (cat. 107).

Instead of using gemstones to simulate the design of a moth's wings as others might have done, Lalique precisely rendered the night butterfly clip at right in enamelwork of such absolute perfection it rivals only Nature itself (cat. 166).

the production and export of Japanese objets d'art, the influence of which was clear to see on the work of artists such as Félix Bracquemond and Eugène Rousseau in France, and Christopher Dresser, E. W. Godwin and J. A. M. Whistler in England. The critic Louis de Fourcaud acknowledged the depth of this influence: "The Japanese have invited us, through examples of their work, to reopen the book of nature, that profound, many-faceted, fascinating, harrowing, consoling volume in which all is recorded, and all is to be discovered."[56] To those observing the decorative arts in Paris, Lalique was the one most profoundly influenced by Japanese art because he used the philosophy of Japanese form and arrangement in his works, not just the obvious decorative motifs.[57]

In his depictions of the natural world, Lalique alternated between two different approaches. Paul Greenhalgh observes that sometimes the "poetic imagination [was] to be expressed through natural form without strictly following the natural world," while in other works he "used the bestial to create a sense of mystery. Animals, reptiles and insects [were] often depicted realistically, without the taming element of conventionalization."[58]

Other artists of the period, for example Falize Frères, were drawn to subject matter derived from the natural world, adopting the stylized forms and flat patterning found in the work of their Japanese counterparts. Bing played a significant role in this area as well, mounting exhibitions of Japanese prints in Paris that furnished numerous modernist artists not only with inspiration for subject matter but also with a whole new aesthetic direction.[59] In 1900, Hermann Baur declared that Japanese art had "set us free and made us bold."[60] Furthermore, the European interpretation of this remote and exotic land corresponded to the ideal that modernist artists, champions of art that was total and all-encompassing, had set as their ultimate goal. The Japanese appeared to make no distinction between arts and crafts, and the interiors depicted in their prints had all the appearance of the European concept of Gesamtkunstwerk.[61]

Some of Lalique's contemporaries continued to depict natural motifs after 1900 in increasingly literal ways as in these ornamental combs of dragonflies by Gaillard (above, cat. 105) and cicadas by Gaston Chopard (below right, cat. 19). Lalique, however, began to embrace the tenets of early modernism typified by this headband (bandeau) also depicting dragonflies but in a much more abstract way than his counterparts (cat. 145).

Overleaf: Lalique's mother-of-pearl fan with butterflies recalls Japanese hand-cut stencil art known as *katagami*, popular in the Meiji period (1868–1912) in Japan (cat. 147).

René Lalique and the Presentation of Perfume

He [René Lalique] breathed new life into the jeweler's art, and, I dare say, prepared the way for the final stages of modern jewelry."[1] With these words Émile Gallé conveyed his admiration for Lalique, whose latest jewelry creations had just been exhibited at the Salon du Palais de l'Industrie. Unfortunately, Gallé died in 1904. Had he lived at least ten years longer, he would also have been able to state that René Lalique breathed new life into the art of presenting perfume and prepared the way for the final stages of modern flacons.

Through the mid nineteenth century perfume had been an artisanal product sold in small shops. Although a luxury in Europe, perfume had been sold in utilitarian glass bottles and after purchase decanted into decorative flacons with imaginative shapes, occasionally made of fancy glass or crystal but more generally of porcelain, semiprecious stones, rock crystal, and precious metals. The advent of the Industrial Revolution, world's fairs, department stores, and modern advertising led to the beginning of the perfume industry. Perfumers faced direct competition and quickly understood the importance of more original and elegant packaging to express the style of the house and the identity of each perfume. However, very little attention was paid to the design of the bottles, which were all of similar shapes and almost hidden under large paper labels printed with colorful, often exuberant flower motifs matching the graphics of the paper boxes.

Before the end of the nineteenth century René Lalique had created a few decorative flacons, which, as the works of an artist inspired by nature, resembled his high style Art Nouveau jewelry designs. The *Serpent* flacon (about 1898–99) was made of a beautiful chunk of jasper, the pattern of its internal inclusions similar to that of snakeskin. The stone was polished and drilled to create a hollow area, a realistic gilt-silver snake coiled around the flacon, with its menacing head serving as the stopper. Another flacon, *Chardon (Thistle)*, created especially for the 1900 Exposition Universelle in Paris, was made of carved animal horn, with a stopper of mold-pressed glass—a juxtaposition Lalique had already used in earlier jewelry creations. These two flacons were not intended to be functional but rather to be displayed as objets d'art.

Two other artists exhibited their flacon creations at that exhibition. The first was the painter, illustrator, and sculptor Louis Chalon, who

Created for the 1900 Exposition Universelle in Paris, the *Chardon* flacon combines animal horn and glass, a union that appeared first in Lalique's jewelry designs (cat. 134).

Left: Lalique sometimes evoked Symbolist associations in his designs for early decorative flacons that incorporated both fragrant flowers and venomous snakes, obvious allusions to temptation in the Garden of Eden (cat. 181).

Hector Guimard's design for the *Kantirix* flacon, shown at the 1900 Paris Exposition Universelle, was an intricate Art Nouveau creation. However, the Art Nouveau style was not fully accepted by the public and the perfumers (cat. 112).

Illustrator and sculptor Louis Chalon designed this suite of flacons to be shown at the 1900 Paris world's fair (cat. 18). This restrained design was much more successful than high-style Art Nouveau.

also trained as a jeweler and costume designer. *Bouquet Nouveau (New Bouquet),* created for a Roger & Gallet perfume, featured a gilded-brass surface ornamentation that was a mixture of Art Nouveau plant motifs carefully controlled by repetition and symmetry. The overall classic shape created the illusion that the flacon had been molded into this metal ornamentation, thus emphasizing the contrast between the fluid lines of the glass surface and the rigidity of the metal constraints. The second artist was Hector Guimard, the great architect of the Paris Métro entrances. For the perfumer Félix Millot, Guimard designed a perfume pavilion at the exhibition and the singular and extravagant flacon *Kantirix,* crafting a quintessential Art Nouveau shape. However, the perfume industry totally rejected this style because of its complexity and production difficulties.

Lalique opened his first shop in Paris at 24 place Vendôme in 1905. Then, in 1908, François Coty opened a luxurious establishment at 23 place Vendôme. The two men met, became friends, and Coty commissioned Lalique to design Art Nouveau lettering for perfume labels. Initially they were applied to standard tester

François Coty contracted Lalique to design the lettering for the tester flacons at left, which were then assembled in wooden cases for Coty boutique displays (cat. 183).

flacons, produced by the Dépinoix glassworks and presented in a splendid wood case embellished with a gilded-bronze plaque, also created by Lalique. The case with twelve tester flacons in this exhibition was used in the Coty place Vendôme boutique.

When he was later interviewed, Lalique recalled that in 1909 he created his first perfume flacon, *Cyclamen*, for a Coty perfume.[2] This flacon was a complete departure from the classic shape used at the time and displayed a truly modern shape, contrasting with its surface decoration, an Art Nouveau style woman-dragonfly—a motif Lalique had often used in his jewelry. Instead of a

paper label, "Coty Cyclamen Paris" was molded on the top of the stopper, and "Lalique" appeared as a visible signature, molded on the lower part of the flacon. These surface elements were all highlighted with light-green cold patination—one of the great innovations in the production of glass. The flacon was displayed and packaged in a luxurious but understated leather box, similar to a jewelry case, and "Coty Paris France" appeared in very small gilded letters stamped at the bottom of the satin lining on the inside lid of the case.

Only one year later in 1910, Lalique fashioned several completely coordinated presentations for the Roger & Gallet line of products marketed under the name *Cigalia*. One of Lalique's preferred design concepts for Art Nouveau style jewelry and objets d'art had been the use of confronting insects. Lalique successfully used this design concept for the *Cigalia* products as well, with four cicadas molded on the vertical edges of the perfume flacons, and two cicadas stamped on the boxes for perfume and soap. Even the soap itself was molded with this motif. The paper label on the flacons featured the *Cigalia* name in Art Nouveau style lettering. Rather than using jewelry style cases, all the boxes for the *Cigalia* products were made of cardboard covered with

Left: *Cyclamen*, for Coty, was Lalique's first commercially produced flacon (cat. 141). It represented a complete stylistic departure from traditional perfume bottles, which had been dominated by large colorful paper labels.

paper, simulating wood, on which the insects appeared with an iridescent finish.

In 1909, Lalique rented a glassworks at Combs-la-Ville, which he purchased in 1913. While working for Coty and other perfumers, such as L. T. Piver, Roger & Gallet, and d'Orsay, Lalique continued to design and produce decorative flacons and other glass objects for René Lalique et Cie. His research and acquired knowledge of glassmaking became one of his greatest strengths, enabling him to develop new industrial techniques to meet his artistic needs.

Pavot (Poppy), a decorative flacon of 1910, was a creative landmark and presented several innovations. The flacon was molded in three parts: body, neck, and base, which were joined together while the glass was still in fusion. Such a

technical innovation had to be invented because the opening of the neck was very small in relation to the body, and glassmaking techniques of the period would not permit molding in one piece. The *Pavot* flacon presented several design innovations as well: a very small stopper and a very short neck; a prominent and very complex collar around the top of the neck; a black glass stopper with a clear glass flacon; and incursions of opaque red glass below the surface of the clear glass flacon, highlighted with black patina. Above all, however, this flacon is a piece of sculpture. Seen from above, it represents a flower—the stopper and collar are the center, with the body

simulating wilted petals. This dramatic model expresses the death of a flower, an Art Nouveau theme, and represents one of Lalique's most important achievements.

Another decorative flacon, *Fougères (Ferns)*, created in 1912, presented other technical innovations. It was molded with identical concave oval receptacles, front and back. The two receptacles met inside the flacon in the center, surrounded by a hollow portion into which perfume could be poured. An oval glass medallion was inserted into each receptacle, which had been lined with metallic foil. Each medallion portrayed the upper part of a different female figure. The same two female figure designs had been used as medallions in Lalique jewelry pieces around 1900–1903. The example of *Fougères* shown in this exhibition is a prototype made of electric blue glass with pale gray patina, the receptacles having been lined with platinum leaf. Lalique would often explore technical and design innovations in the creation of decorative flacons, which he would later incorporate into flacon models for perfumers.

In 1913, Lalique created the complete presentation (flacon, label, and box) for *Misti*, a perfume of L. T. Piver. This circular flacon, whose diameter is greater than its height, was decorated

Left: Produced for Roger & Gallet, these boxed sets designed by Lalique contained *Cigalia* perfumes and soaps based on the form of the cicada, the symbol of Provence (cat. 136).

Top right: The female figures on the flacon called *Fougères (Ferns)* also appeared in Lalique's jewelry from about 1900 to 1903 (cat. 148).

One of the most technically complex of all his early flacon designs, *Pavot (Poppy)* is cast in three parts, reflecting Lalique's innovative experimentation in the production of artistic glass. Later he would apply these principles to the creation of various glass objects (cat. 170).

with a butterfly motif and presented a rare element—a convex base that allows for a curious vibrating movement of the flacon and its perfume, perhaps to simulate the flapping of the butterfly wings. The box was covered with paper printed with a matching butterfly motif, rendered to resemble a lithographic stone. The inside of the box was slightly raised in the back, so that the flacon is displayed at an angle. The label was attached to the neck of the flacon by a silk cord so it appeared to be a hanging medallion, and the flacon was attached to the box with the same silk cord. In order to remove the flacon from its box, this silk cord had to be cut, which explains why the label was usually lost.

The impact of the early Lalique innovations for the perfume industry inspired many others. Baccarat, the venerable crystal works founded in 1764, had produced many high-quality crystal flacons of classic shapes with highly polished surfaces and recut stoppers. However, Baccarat immediately met the challenge posed by Lalique's entry into the world of perfume by introducing a wide range of imaginative flacon designs created by a new group of artists. The sculptor, goldsmith, and jeweler Pierre-Georges Deraisme was greatly influenced by Lalique, for whom he had worked during the latter part of the nineteenth century.[3] Deraisme created flacons as an independent artist, and in 1913 he designed the flacon *Nelly* for a perfume by d'Orsay that Baccarat produced. The perfume paid homage to soprano Nellie Melba, then at the height of her career. The flacon was a contrast between polished crystal and frosted crystal highlighted with gray patina, with the lower part molded into a frieze of eight faces representing the singer, separated by eight polished oval "windows."

Another talented glass artist, the sculptor Julien Viard, was also inspired by Lalique's creations and designed the flacon *D'ara* for a Tokalon perfume of 1914. The ancient city of Dar'â, in contemporary Syria, was believed to have been the birthplace of perfume, especially

the traditional Arabic rose water. Viard's stopper presented a veiled female nude resembling a statue from antiquity, reclining on a marble tombstone. The flacon was molded with four identical reclining and veiled female nudes, placed at the edges opposite one another. All the figures were patinated black. The label featured a female figure enjoying the scent of a branch of roses.

In 1919, Lalique created several magnificent decorative flacons with oversized stoppers referred to as "tiara" models. Of these designs, *Bouchon Eucalyptus* (*Eucalyptus Stopper*) had the most exaggerated proportions. The stopper was molded with eucalyptus flowers and elongated leaves that almost completely framed the very tall, thin, unstable flacon. Lalique remained active in the perfume industry until his death, and his creative contributions changed forever the ways in which perfume would be presented, clearly establishing this domain as a true art form. René Lalique went through several artistic periods; he seemed to have

The complete ensemble for *Misti*, a perfume by L. T. Piver, was designed by Lalique, including the label and box (cat. 163). When filled with perfume, the flacon vibrates because its base is convex, and the butterflies on the upper surface appear to flutter.

One of Lalique's early collaborators, sculptor and jeweler Pierre-Georges Deraisme, designed the flacon for *Nelly*, a d'Orsay perfume, which features eight portraits of soprano Nellie Melba (cat. 24). Baccarat, the venerable French crystalworks, realized this perfume bottle.

Above: The fragrance *D'ara*, for Tokalon, pays homage to Dar'â, an ancient city still in existence in present-day Syria, thought to be where perfume orignated (cat. 321). The bottle, with its reclining female figures, was designed by Julien Viard, another of Lalique's contemporaries.

With its exaggerated form reminiscent of a tiara, *Bouchon Eucalyptus (Eucalyptus Stopper)* was part of a series of flacons by Lalique that featured extravagant stoppers surmounting relatively simple flacons (cat. 126).

possessed an instinct to anticipate trends and then modify or even transform his style without losing the uniqueness of his artistic vision.

Christie Mayer Lefkowith

1. Émile Gallé, "The 1897 Salons. Objets d'Art," *Gazette des Beaux-Arts* 18 (September 1897): 247–49.

2. Félix Marcilhac, *René Lalique 1860–1945, maître-verrier, analyse de l'oeuvre et catalogue raisonné*, 3rd ed. (Paris: Les Éditions de l'Amateur, 2004), 68.

3. Henry Vever, *La Bijouterie au XIXe siècle* (Paris: H. Floury, 1908), 3:730.

The Many Faces of Woman

Lalique's repertoire of subject matter was not confined to the flora and fauna of the wild but equally derived from the most noble of natural creations—the human form. He embraced the female form as the most perfect expression of nature, capable of transformation and of dramatic contradictions: "Lalique introduced the human figure, the female form, in numerous and expected guises, genuinely expressive, tragic and untamed, a combination of femme fatale, sphinx, and siren."[62] Like an omnipotent demigod, Lalique, master of the re-creation of his world, performed metamorphoses between the three kingdoms of nature. In one after another of his creations, "memory wanders at will through images of this world of imaginative vision and reality, in which faces have haloes of undulating tresses studded with flowers, in which the female form veils and reveals its fluid nudity at whim, in which the

Fig. 48. View of René Lalique's stand at the 1900 Paris Exposition Universelle featuring a bestiary of bats, snakes, and butterfly women.

Lalique's design for the bronze grille that served as the backdrop for his jeweled creations at the 1900 Paris world's fair captured a woman spreading her metaphorical wings as if she were a butterfly emerging from its chrysalis (cat. 178).

Delicate ivory plaques with the soft, contemplative image of a woman often adorned Lalique's accessories for men such as the cigar case at right (cat. 137).

human body is transformed into an insect or fronds of greenery."[63]

In so doing, Lalique metaphorically reveals the mutual interdependence of the three kingdoms of creation: woman transforms into dragonfly, into snake, into flower, while flowers become women, "involv[ing] the fusion of human, animal, and plant in a mystical recognition of the ascent of nature."[64] Woman sprang from nature, from its trailing fronds of caressing leaves and buds promising eternal youth; but in Lalique's world, these buds could then open to reveal thistle flowers armed with treacherous spines.

Just as the modernist aesthetic of nature could be linked directly to the Japanese influence, so could the contemporary aesthetic of the female form be clearly related to European literary movements of the late nineteenth century, most notably the Symbolists. Scientific and technological progress had plunged intellectuals into many debates between, on the one hand, rationalists who espoused scientific advances and, on the other, romantics who were fascinated by spirituality and might even venture into the realms of mysticism or occultism. Esoteric themes were therefore common currency in the late nineteenth and early twentieth centuries, finding expression in "haunted inspirations that exasperated the more subtle of their contemporaries."[65]

The most appropriate vehicle for these "inspirations" seemed to be the female form, in every manifestation from the airily

ethereal to the frankly sensual. Woman was to be the inspiration for images ranging from purity and serenity to temptation and the fall, from chaste virgins to seductive sirens, via maidenly nymphs. And presiding over the virtuous extreme was the figure of woman as angel, woman as salvation.[66]

At the other extreme of the repertoire lay the fallen woman, a combination of youthful grace, sexual allure, and stony-hearted love. Lalique's dragonfly woman (Calouste Gulbenkian Foundation, Lisbon), her bosom swelling with desire, wears an expression interpreted by some as enigmatic and by others as frankly ecstatic. Is she in the process of being devoured by this grotesque clawed creature from whose jaws she emerges? Is she drowsy with postcoital pleasure? Is she meant to evoke a vampire, reputed to feed off the blood of other creatures? Or is she the monster itself, with its azure wings and its forked sting, "symbol of the feminine spirit, deceptive and delightful, lyrical and chimerical, making promises it will not keep?"[67] Plumet went so far as to recognize in Lalique's jewelry "a bizarre charm ... disturbing, spellbinding, even satanic."[68]

It is significant that the repertoire of Sarah Bernhardt, ahead of her time in responding to Lalique's talent and supporting it, encompassed Edmond Rostand's *Samaritaine* (1897), Jules Barbier's *Jeanne d'Arc* (1898), Catulle Mendès's *Sainte Thérèse d'Avila* (1906) and *Médée* (1898), Dumas fils' *Dame aux Camélias* (1898), and Victorien Sardou's *Cléopâtre* (1890). These roles ranged from holy ecstasy to murderous motherhood, via the repentant sinner and the courtesan-as-victim. In the role of "Théodora" (1884), empress of Byzantium, by Sardou, the woman responsible for reintroducing the worship of images, she wore a crown dripping with precious stones but appeared on stage behind a veil. In a drawing for the same role a decade later, Lalique imagined crowning her with menacing snakes, perhaps reincarnating the Medusa whose stare turned men to stone.

Salomé, epitome of the castrating femme fatale, is another central figure in the literature of the late nineteenth century. She loomed large in the works of decadent and aesthetic authors such as J.-K. Huysmans (1884), Jules Laforgue (1886), Oscar Wilde (1893), Jean Lorrain (1897), and Catulle Mendès (1900). Bénédite also made reference to her in his review of works by Lalique at the 1900 Exposition Universelle, impressed by "the silhouettes of strange and troubling creatures, Salomés and Salammbôs."[69]

It was only a short step from the cause of decadence to that of feminism. A new woman rose up from decades of male domination at the turn of the century, casting off her corsets and the straitjacket of tradition to the loud disapproval of many of her contemporaries. Writing in *La Plume*, Victor Jozé earnestly wished that women "would remain as nature has made them, an ideal of womanhood, man's helpmeet and lover, and mistress of the home."[70] In 1892 the exhibition *Les Arts de la femme* (The Womanly Arts),

Fig. 49. Sarah Bernhardt (above) as "Théodora," empress of Byzantium, by Victorien Sardou, wearing an elaborate, though conventional, bejeweled headdress. By contrast, Lalique's crown design (left, fig. 50) for Bernhardt in the same role a decade later featured a mass of writhing snakes, recalling the mythical Medusa. Though never executed, the design inspired a large snake bodice ornament exhibited at the 1900 Paris Exposition Universelle.

Fig. 51. Lalique's display at the Turin world's fair in 1902 showed the great bodice ornament in the shape of a woman as dragonfly along with the snake stomacher; both had been shown at the 1900 Paris world's fair.

described as "a prophetic manifesto of the relationship between Art Nouveau and women as both clients and subject matter," provoked an outburst from those who would castigate this model of a "new woman."[71]

Lalique's creations were intended for this new woman. However, his notion of womanhood had little to do with needlework and interior decoration, taking its inspiration instead from the all-embracing power of woman as temptress and as earth mother, as sorceress and daughter of the moon, as the "ivory nymph" suspended "in gold and enamel from some of his pendants," showering mere mortals with diamonds.[72]

Lalique's Techniques

More than forms and subjects classified Lalique's luxurious works as art. In fact, to contemporary critics objects by Lalique were artistic as much for their execution and impeccable technique as for their composition. Molinier noted in his review of the 1898 salons that Lalique had become "a master of his art, handling gold and enamels, pearls and precious stones with charming flights of the imagination."[73] In a few words he seems to sum up the broad outlines of this revolution, led by Lalique and other reformists, to blur the established lines between conventional and artistic.

As Saunier stressed, "There is henceforth no place for the distinction between the work of the *joaillier* and that of the *bijoutier*" as a result of the "revolution in the hierarchies of precious stones and metals," and more particularly of "a more discreet use of stones and the rehabilitation of gemstones that had virtually fallen out of use."[74] Lalique had put an end to "the despotic rule of diamonds

A mocking jester confronts the user of this hand mirror by Lalique, while stag beetles proclaim the true beauty of the beholder on the reverse (cat. 158, front and back).

Left: The identity of the maker of this Symbolist masterpiece is unknown, though the ivory figure of a woman is thought to have been carved by sculptor Edmond-Henri Becker (cat. 3). His heroine rises into the night as the apotheosis of beauty lifted by bat wings to the moon and stars.

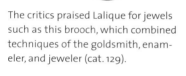

in the art of jewelry" as he had "no regard whatever for the commercial value of his stones, turning the established hierarchy on its head and using them simply according to his requirements."[75]

A radical upheaval was turning upside down the age-old hierarchy that placed the art of joaillerie above that of bijouterie. According to the critic Gustave Kahn:

> Before René Lalique, what was a *bijou?* A parure, naturally, but, more than that, a crass show of luxury, an ostentatious display of wealth. The masterpieces of his predecessors, all founded upon the brilliance of diamonds, were like portable châteaux of light.... The old idea of jewelry is founded upon the notion of wealth; the new one on the principle of art.[76]

Bénédite concurred:

> The great revolution that Lalique has achieved will be shown to be in his creation of jewelry for the sake of art, not for the opulence of the materials. . . . He brings together and mingles all the delicate arts of the jeweler, the goldsmith, the enameller, the medalist, the engraver of precious stones [and] just as he mingles techniques, so he mingles materials: gems, pearls, ivory, enamel (whether translucent, openwork or painted), and metals of all types, with a variety of discreet patinas.[77]

Lalique's work was therefore innovative in all aspects: the composition and form of his designs; the materials he chose to give them shape and texture; and the technique and colors he employed to enliven them.

The critics praised Lalique for jewels such as this brooch, which combined techniques of the goldsmith, enameler, and jeweler (cat. 129).

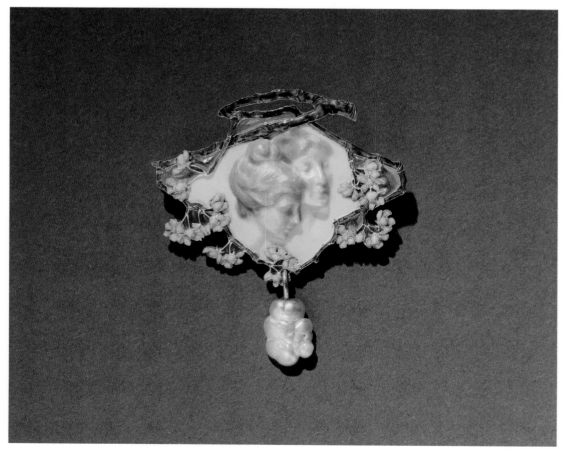

Composition and Form

After 1900 Lalique's sculptural prowess began to emerge in his jewelry, bronzework, and first uses of glass. But until his move into exclusive glass production in 1912, his jewelry remained the central medium of his expression. Writing in 1905 Kahn declared, "The outstanding feature of René Lalique's achievement is the way in which he has harnessed all the plastic arts and channeled them into the creation of jewelry."[78] Lalique's perennial champion Roger Marx also extolled his work in a continued attempt to classify Lalique as an artist of the highest rank:

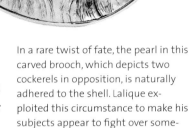

> Sculpting tool in hand, this "sculptor of jewelry" lends his work with precious stones the grandeur
> of high sculpture: Like some charming figurine, medallion, silhouette, or bas-relief, these minuscule
> works of art offer a fluidity of form of the utmost freedom, vitality, and delicacy.[79]

Once again, Lalique's interest in sculpture is linked with that of his contemporaries and his work had to be defended against the potential criticism that he was just like those who sold their work for reproduction.

The invention of the system of mechanical reduction perfected by Frédéric Sauvage in 1836 gave fine art sculptors a means to supplement their income by selling the right to reproduce miniature versions of their works. This debasement of sculpture into mundane ornaments blurred the boundary between work by artists such as Lalique and the creations of applied artists, then known as industrial artists. Sculptors had invaded "areas of artistic production with which earlier generations had had only occasional and distant contacts."[80]

This situation encouraged industrialists in their growing refusal to recognize the creative role of the artist in the production process. As soon as sculptors started to supply models, however occasionally, for table centerpieces, clocks, or jewelry, their status was called into question and the guilds of jewelers and goldsmiths had to put up a vigorous fight to gain recognition for their contribution.

The presence of the artist's signature, acknowledged as a matter of fundamental importance by the Union Centrale des Arts Décoratifs, was debated at the Congrès des Arts Décoratifs in 1894 but not finally settled until 1902 by the introduction of the law giving to model makers and industrial artists the status of sole creators. Luxury objects, meanwhile, often posed an additional difficulty—that of collaboration. Very elaborate pieces frequently called for the skills of different artists at different stages of production. The richly worked hand mirror designed by Félix Bracquemond, first illustrated in 1906,[81] was actually a collaborative venture, created by a sculptor, chaser, and enameler working together. Auguste Rodin carved the model for the central plaque; Alexis Falize constructed the goldwork frame, and Alexandre Riquet did the cloisonné enamelwork.

Lalique shared with fellow artist Jean Dampt, a follower of Ruskin who was close to the Symbolists, a taste for the fantastic, the mysterious, and the unusual as well as a penchant for refined materials. Like another of his contemporaries, the jeweler Alexandre Charpentier, Lalique included carvings in many of his compositions and refused to depict modern dress, preferring instead figures that were unclothed, veiled, or garbed in historic costumes. But Lalique went beyond the purely decorative

In a rare twist of fate, the pearl in this carved brooch, which depicts two cockerels in opposition, is naturally adhered to the shell. Lalique exploited this circumstance to make his subjects appear to fight over something neither can have (cat. 138).

The silver and glass inkwell below by Lalique is so richly adorned with sculpted elements that its intended use is almost completely obscured (cat. 122).

Elaborate collaborative ventures were relatively common at the turn of the century among artists and artisans in Paris, as in the mirror at right for Baron Joseph Vitta, which encompasses the work of four great masters of their art: Bracquemond, Rodin, Falize, and Riquet (cat. 8).

character of Charpentier's reliefs, making his own reliefs a central element in his compositions. A plaque on an ornamental hair comb with medieval figures in the Calouste Gulbenkian Museum depicts a scene of courtly love and recalls a medieval reliquary. The plaque stands out against a field of pale horn with sides of angular design redolent of the Gothic, echoing the frieze of enameled gold with cabochon sapphires that forms a framing device to top and bottom.

In the realm of sculpture, Lalique deployed an inventive flair rarely seen by any sculptor before him, playing with the obverse and reverse of carved features and lending them movement either by projecting figures forward as though they were about to step out of the carving or, when using translucent or transparent materials such as glass or rock crystal, by carving both sides—in intaglio on the reverse and in cameo on the obverse. In his hand, figures appear to be seeking each other but are prevented by an insurmountable barrier such as in *Le Baiser (The Kiss)*, the simple, yet complex brooch now at the Musée des Arts Décoratifs in Paris.

Left: Lalique used carved ivory plaques to advance allegorical themes such as the medieval scene of courtly love in this ornamental comb (cat. 139).

Fig. 52. The often painful barrier between lovers is powerfully rendered by Lalique in the brooch above, called *Le Baiser (The Kiss)*, in which the man is carved on the front face and the woman on the reverse. Although their lips look as if they are about to meet, the glass forever prevents them from touching.

After 1900, the plethora of imitators frustrated Lalique. Here his lyrical drawing of two swans on a lake (fig. 53) stands in stark contrast to the ambitious composition of a pendant by Parisian jewelers Plisson & Hartz (cat. 213).

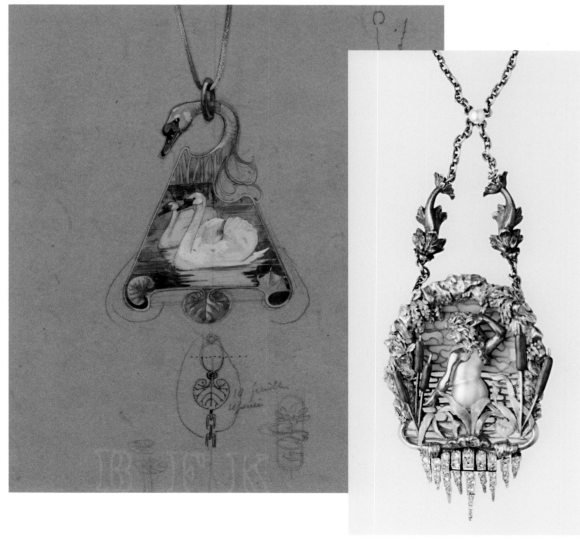

Materials and Color

Form and composition were the framework of Lalique's designs, but his innovative use of materials gave richness and depth as well as a measure of symbolism to his works that served to entice the eye, not blind it as some did with diamonds. When he used precious stones, he did so as with semiprecious, drawing no distinctions, employing them only to enhance his designs and bring visual definition. This inventive technique naturally drew the notice and sometimes the shock of curators and critics. In 1900, Bénédite drew up an inventory of the novel materials Lalique used:

> Corundums, onyx and sard [chalcedony], jade, agate and carnelian, opals, which he values particularly for their opaque, pearly mistiness or their creamy, iridescent transparency, as well as simple hardstones, jasper and coral, and other materials that are obscure or even beyond the pale, such as horn, and worse still—vulgar glass cabochons.[82]

While Bénédite may have been repelled by Lalique's use of common horn, it was a medium he returned to time and again for his most sculptural creations. For Lalique, horn was a malleable material that combined the virtues of plasticity and translucency:

> Diaphanous, intangible butterflies flutter on a haircomb of translucent horn, hardly less substantial than the comb itself, which by a technical tour de force [the horn being carved on both sides] reveals the transparency of the gossamer-light wings.[83]

Lalique used precious stones in sparing ways, often in a secondary role merely to enhance or define edges within the composition, as in this pendant brooch in the form of a pansy (cat. 169).

Not content with exploiting the transparent qualities of horn, Lalique also turned to both its natural color and the ease with which it could be dyed. In the magnificent *Hair Ornament* in the Rijksmuseum in Amsterdam, the foliage takes on the naturalistic gold shades of autumn, while the two prongs are carved in the form of viburnum branches. Just as in nature, the flowers droop in autumn, so in Lalique's graceful depiction they bow their heads in a shower of diamonds.

The translucent quality of horn provided the perfect canvas for Lalique's subtle arrangement of butterflies on this ornamental comb (cat. 131).

Even with the use of thousands of tiny diamond chips to enliven the hair comb at right in the form of a viburnum branch, Lalique forces the eye to consider them as part of the whole composition, not just as stones themselves (cat. 156).

In this extraordinary ornamental comb, Lalique exploits the natural variegation of the horn to create the illusion of two swallows flying toward each other, preparing to make a nest in a lady's hair (cat. 165). The drawing for this design shows the pencil grid for working out the proportions (fig. 54).

In the *Nesting Swallows Hair Comb* noted at the 1908 Salon by M. P. Verneuil, to suggest movement Lalique played with lighter and darker shades on the breast of one of the birds and the back of the other.[84] With great creativity, he extended the tips of their wings to form the prongs, and one of the birds appears to be bringing the other, possibly as a token of love, a blade of wheat made of gold with little diamonds forming the grains. Lalique conjures up as well a great irony in the pairing of the most humble material with the most precious.

The glass cabochons mentioned by Bénédite, meanwhile, were an allusion to Lalique's unusual use of common glass, whether clear or colored, for the sake of its intrinsic qualities alone and not paste or colored glass in imitation of precious stones as might be imagined. The advantages of glass were numerous: it could be molded on virtually any scale and with much less work than carved pieces of similar dimensions; it could be colored, creating at least a similar effect, if not an imitation, of precious stones, and at minimal cost; the color could be added in such a way as to create

Lalique found glass to be a suitable material for creating depth and translucency within his jewelry. Whether carved in relief, as in this dog collar plaque (left, cat. 192), or cast to form the petals of flowers, as in this pendant in the form of chrysanthemums (below, cat. 135) and poppies (right, cat. 176), glass provided a quiet counterpoint to the enamel and diamonds within each composition.

nuances and shadings impossible to find in natural stones; and finally colored glass could be patinated, enameled, or layered with another color in order to produce precisely the desired effect.

Lalique made virtuoso use of these processes to create jewels of the greatest refinement and elegance. This was especially the case when he combined the use of glass with other techniques, for instance creating the stalks of poppies in enamel picked out with diamonds, with the matte surface of the glass capturing the filmy texture of the natural petals with striking fidelity. He even used glass for figures, such as the angel on a hair comb of horn in the Cincinnati Art Museum. Just as in the *Nesting Swallows Hair Comb*, the prongs here are fashioned from an inherent feature of the design, the angel's elongated wings. The figure of an angel appears in relief, ethereally rendered in sky blue glass against the golden horn. Her form is subtly enlivened by gradations of color, from pale at her feet to deep at her head, as though symbolizing an intensity of spirit converging in the upper part of her body. This effect is emphasized by one further detail: she holds a sapphire heart with both hands against her breast, proffering it solemnly as though for the adulation of the faithful.

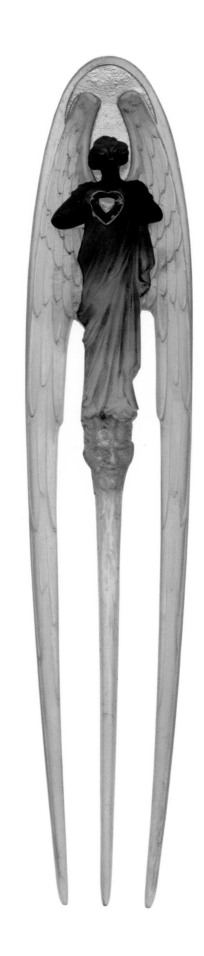

Cast figural forms increasingly found their way into Lalique's work after 1900, both because molds could easily reflect the carver's intent and because infinite translucent effects were possible. Here cast glass forms the knob of a chalice (cat. 133) as well as the central figure in a haunting ornamental comb in the form of a winged angel (cat. 124).

In addition to nonprecious stones, horn, and molded glass, Lalique was a virtuoso exponent of work in ivory, a material prized by other nineteenth-century artists such as Dampt and Falize. In 1897, Molinier had drawn attention to praiseworthy developments in ivory carving.[85] As Émile Dacier pointed out in an article entitled "L'Art de l'Ivoire," many artists, more or less traditional in their approach, were working in ivory by this time, including Falize, Vever, Boucheron, Gaillard, Cardeilhac, and René Boivin.[86] Among modern artists, Lalique and his contemporary Nocq were major practitioners.

With its smooth and richly colored surface, ivory was especially suited to depictions of the human form. Lalique not only exploited this quality but harnessed it in his most dramatic sculptural elements. In the great *Abduction Pendant* acquired by Calouste Gulbenkian in 1902, the male figure leaps toward the viewer, every muscle tensed, as he endeavors in vain to wrest the female figure from the ivory to which she obstinately clings. It is almost possible to hear the cries of this commanding figure, his flesh browned by the sun, and the protests of the pale, terrified woman. In a brooch depicting the scene in which the orator Hyperides defended the celebrated Greek courtesan Phryne, mistress of Praxiteles, by disrobing her before the jury, Lalique used the ivory to suggest the whiteness of her skin and the diaphanous transparency of her veils. And in the *Breton Women Hair Comb*, another of Gulbenkian's acquisitions of 1902, Lalique combined carved ivory with horn, using the contrasting tones and textures to animate the women in their traditional Breton coiffes as they appear at a house window, gossiping and squabbling.

Ivory was also the medium chosen to carve a series of magnificent hair combs in the form of orchids around 1900 that are so realistic they almost deceive the eye. The largest, now in a private collection, perfectly represents in carved ivory the enticing and seductive qualities of a cattleya orchid, only subtly enhanced by pale green cloisonné leaves punctuated with small diamonds.[87]

In Saunier's view, it was from developments in the other arts and their "initiation into color"[88] that Lalique took his inspiration for his highly innovative palette, "with its thousands of nuances, enabling him to create evanescent harmonies as gentle as a languorous caress,"[89] using, as has been mentioned above, an equally novel range of stones.

Above: To enliven his compositions, Lalique often carved figures in motion, appearing to leap from the work as in this pendant called *The Abduction* (cat. 123).

Facing page: Ivory was especially well suited for depictions of the human form because of its fleshlike color and smooth surface. Its soft tones also work in harmony with translucent glass in this brooch showing the Greek courtesan Phryne, the mistress of Praxiteles (cat. 172).

Lalique often intended that his carved ivory panels interact visually with their metal framework, as in the pilgrim flask above (cat. 173) where the river god appears to release the ivory as if it were water from its mouth, or this comb below (cat. 140) where the figures seem to lean from the windows of the frame itself.

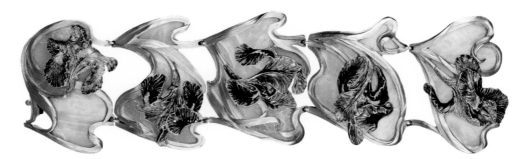

Undoubtedly Lalique's use of opals, with their ever-changing cerulean hues, attracted the most attention from his contemporaries. The large opal cabochons set amid tendrils of gold seaweed in the handsome necklace in the Metropolitan Museum of Art might be miniature versions of the foaming pools in which the female figures are poised to refresh their spirits, naked figures with impassive features and frondlike arms who seem to be rounding up the haughty black swans drinking from an amethyst stream. Opals also form the petals of water lilies above pads paved with diamonds, and the surface of the water seems to tremble in the waves of pearls that hold the central plaque of a choker.

But if Lalique was expert at exploiting the possibilities of colored stones and glass, he achieved his most elegant and sophisticated results with enamel, especially when combined with other materials. In 1901, Molinier recognized that there was no one who could exceed Lalique in "setting off the translucent pale green and violet shades of enamel, in combination with opals, pearls, and the full gamut of precious stones and glass in the most exquisite shades."[90]

As the *Studio* noted when reviewing his 1905 exhibition at Thos. Agnew's gallery in London, Lalique "reintroduced enamels, which were the glory of the jewellery work of the Middle Ages and the Renaissance"[91] carrying this technique of the past to the most poetic extremes. Indeed, the *Studio* article acknowledged that, "thanks to [Lalique], the jeweller's art has been absolutely transformed," having succeeded "in giving to an art in which, until he came, had been cold and stationary, that variety which is movement, and that movement which is life." As the critic stated, "There is no doubt the whole teaching of his art is that all

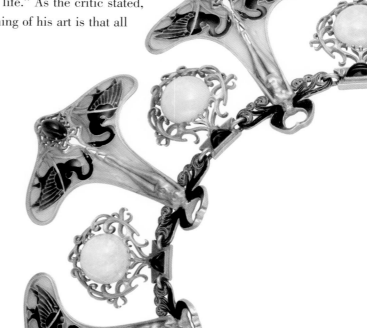

Facing page: Lalique's choice of ivory for this magnificent hair ornament in the form of a cattleya orchid demonstrates his ability to match humble materials with rare and noble subjects to perfection (cat. 132). The ivory instantly relates the seductive qualities of the orchid itself.

In his typical way of relegating rare stones to the shadows, Lalique exploited the iridescent sea-blue colors of the opal as the perfect backdrop for the delicately enameled blue iris of the bracelet above, shown at the 1900 Exposition Universelle in Paris (cat. 161).

Philippe Wolfers used opals to form the iridescent spots on the butterfly brooch above (cat. 322).

Large cabochon opals alternate with plique-à-jour enamel in the same color to give a unified palette to this celebrated black swan and insect woman necklace featured in Lalique's booth at the 1900 Paris world's fair (cat. 164).

expressive art must move forward, it can never stand still," but that movement should definitely not be understood as a voluntary distanciation from the past.

For his contemporaries, the art of Lalique is deeply rooted both in the styles of the past and in French tradition. Yet "He sought to find some expression for his own time and for all the knowledge which from the past as a legacy remained to him," for "the designer must be going forward, not toward novelty, but towards a close and more genuine knowledge of what is really of himself and of his time."[92]

Opals are used as enhancements to the composition of this dog collar necklace by Lalique (cat. 143).

Lalique's enamel technique was trumpeted by the critics who noted the different ways enamel was used to create decorative effects. In this inkwell (cat. 159), Lalique's technique rivals that of his contemporary Eugène Feuillâtre, retailed by Tiffany & Co.

While straightforward as a monotone palette, the opalescent white enamel on this decorative cup and saucer by Lalique is far from a simple application, given the intricate nature of the composition (cat. 194).

As if bubbling up from the surface, the glass in Lalique's chalice of wheat motifs is harnessed by the metal surface in a pairing of materials that he used to great effect (cat. 184).

1. John Ruskin, "The Deteriorative Power of Conventional Art," lecture delivered at the South Kensington Museum in 1858, text reprinted in Ruskin, *Sesame and Lilies: The Two Paths & The King of the Golden River* (London, 1859).

2. Rossella Froissart Pezone, *L'Art dans Tout* (Paris: CNRS Editions, 2004), 16.

3. Roger Marx, "René Lalique," *Art et Décoration* 5 (January–June 1899): 13–14.

4. Pezone, *L'Art dans Tout*, 23.

5. Henry Van de Velde, *Déblaiement d'Art* (Brussels, 1894).

6. Julius Meier-Graefe, *Modern Art: Being a Contribution to the New System of Aesthetics* (London: Heinemann, 1908), 1.

7. Tim Benton and Charlotte Benton, eds., *Form and Function: A Source Book for the 'History of Architecture and Design,' 1890–1939* (London: Crosby Lockwood Staples, in association with the Open University Press, 1975), 21.

8. Émile Gallé, "Les Salons de 1897: Objets d'Art," *Gazette des Beaux-Arts* 39, no. 18 (September 1897), as cited in Maria Teresa Gomes Ferreira, *Lalique— Bijoux* (Lisbon: Calouste Gulbenkian Museum, 1999), 311.

9. *Les 6. Deuxième exposition*, exh. pamphlet (Paris: Galerie des Artistes Modernes, 1898), unpaginated.

10. For the best recent survey of Art Nouveau, see Paul Greenhalgh, *Art Nouveau 1890–1914*, exh. cat. (London: Victoria and Albert Museum, 2000).

11. Ibid., 143.

12. Ibid., 227.

13. Gabriel P. Weisberg, "Lost and Found: S. Bing's Merchandising of Japonisme and Art Nouveau," *Nineteenth-Century Art Worldwide* 4, no. 2 (Summer 2005), http://www.19thc-artworldwide.org/summer_05/articles/weis.shtml.

14. Gabriel P. Weisberg et al., eds., *The Origins of Art Nouveau, the Bing Empire*, exh. cat. (Amsterdam/Antwerp: Van Gogh Museum/Mercatorfonds, 2004), 15.

15. Siegfried Bing, *La Culture Artistique en Amérique* (Paris, 1896), 91.

16. Siegried Bing, "L'Art Nouveau," *Craftsman* 5, no. 1 (1903): 4.

17. Louis de Fourcaud, "Les Arts Décoratifs aux Salons," *La Revue des Arts Décoratifs* 15 (1894–95): 42–103.

18. Edmond and Jules de Goncourt, *Journal: Mémoires de la vie littéraire*, trans. Christina Contandriopoulos and Harry Francis Mallgrave (Monaco: Fasquelle & Flammarion, 1956), 4: 156–57 (30 December 1895).

19. *L'Art Décoratif Moderne* (February 1896): 81.

20. Roger Marx, "Le Salon du Champ-de-Mars," *Revue Encyclopédique* 5 (1 May 1895): 170.

21. Émile Molinier, "Les Arts décoratifs," *La Revue de L'Art Ancien et Moderne* 22 (1897): 169.

22. Ibid.

23. Ibid.

24. *Première exposition*, exh. cat. (Paris: Galerie des Artistes Modernes, 1896), 1.

25. G.S., "Les Bijoux de M. Lalique," *Art et Décoration* 1 (January–June 1897).

26. Gallé, "Les Salons de 1897: Objets d'art."

27. Émile Molinier, "Les Arts Appliqués à l'Industrie," *La Revue de L'Art Ancien et Moderne* 3 (January–June 1898): 542.

28. Roger Marx, "Les Maîtres Décorateurs Français: René Lalique," *Art et Décoration* 6 (1899), 15.

29. L[ucien] Falize, "Le Goût Personnel des Femmes dans l'Invention des Bijoux," *La Revue des Arts Décoratifs* 16 (1896): 111–19.

30. Henri Vever, *French Jewelry of the Nineteenth Century*, trans. Katherine Purcell (London/New York: Thames and Hudson, 2001), 1227. Originally published as *La Bijouterie Française au XIXe Siècle* (Paris: H. Vever, 1908), 718–19.

31. All material quoted in this paragraph is from Molinier, "Les Arts décoratifs" (1897), 169.

32. Émile Molinier, "Les Arts décoratifs," *La Revue de L'Art Ancien et Moderne* 10 (July–December 1901): 46–47.

33. Charles Plumet, "L'Art Decorative au Salon," *L'Art et les Artistes* 4 (April–September 1907): 173–74.

34. Charles Saunier, "La Bijouterie et la Joaillerie à l'Exposition Universelle," *La Revue des Arts Décoratifs* 20 (1900): 23.

35. Léonce Bénédite, "Le Bijou à l'Exposition Universelle," *Art et Décoration* 8 (July–December 1900): 65–82.

36. Roger Marx, "La Décoration et les Industries d'art," *Gazette des Beaux Arts* (1902): 81.

37. Saunier, "La Bijouterie et la Joaillerie à l'Exposition Universelle," 23.

38. Ibid., 23.

39. Marx, "La Décoration et les Industries d'Art" (1902), 80.

40. Saunier, "La Bijouterie et la Joaillerie à l'Exposition Universelle," 23.

41. Bénédite, "Le Bijou à l'Exposition Universelle," 65–82.

42. Henry Havard, "Le Métal: l'Or," *La Revue de L'Art Ancien et Moderne* 7 (January–June 1900): 448. Havard also wrote the celebrated *Dictionnaire de l'Ameublement et de l'Histoire de l'Orfèvrerie Française*.

43. Marx, "La Décoration et les Industries d'Art," 81.

44. Havard, "Le Métal: l'Or," 448.

45. Léonce Bénédite, "La Bijouterie et la Joaillerie à l'Exposition Universelle de 1900," *La Revue des Arts Décoratifs* 20 (1900): 201.

46. Molinier, "Les Arts Décoratifs" (1897), 178.

47. Gallé, "Les Salons de 1897: Objets d'Art."

48. Ibid.

49. Marx, "Les Maîtres Décorateurs Français: René Lalique," 17.

50. Marx, "La Décoration et les Industries d'Art," 82.

51. Bénédite, "La Bijouterie et la Joaillerie à l'Exposition Universelle de 1900," 206.

52. Pol Neveux, "René Lalique," *Art et Décoration* 8 (July–December 1900): 130.

53. Bénédite, "Le Bijou à l'Exposition Universelle," 66.

54. Bénédite, "La Bijouterie et la Joaillerie à l'Exposition Universelle de 1900," 208.

55. Bénédite, "Le Bijou à l'Exposition Universelle," 66.

56. Louis de Fourcaud, "Artistes Contemporains, Émile Gallé," *La Revue de L'Art Ancien et Moderne* 9 (January–June 1902): 37.

57. Bénédite, "Le Bijou à l'Exposition Universelle," 66.

58. Greenhalgh, *Art Nouveau 1890–1914*, 61–62.

59. *Les Maîtres de l'Estampe Japonais*, an exhibition at the École des Beaux-Arts (1890), and *Blanc et Noir* (1892) at L'Art Nouveau.

60. Hermann Baur, review of the Japanese exhibition of the Secession (1900), quoted by Anna Jackson in "Orient and Occident," in Greenhalgh, *Art Nouveau 1890–1914*, 107.

61. The Japanese influence was not the only factor in the omnipresent emphasis on the natural world at this time. Since the late eighteenth century, scientific interest had prompted the publication of illustrated volumes on botanical (frequently exotic) and biological themes, such as the *Flore Ornementale* (1865) by Victor-Marie Ruprich Robert, *Plants and their Application to Ornament* (1897) by Eugène Grasset, and the *Étude de la Plante, son Application aux Industries d'art* (1900) by M. P. Verneuil.

62. Bénédite, "Le Bijou à l'Exposition Universelle," 67.

63. Marx, "La Décoration et les Industries d'Art," 82.

64. Greenhalgh, *Art Nouveau 1890–1914*, 67.

65. Saunier, "La Bijouterie et la Joaillerie à l'Exposition Universelle," 18.

66. A significant development in this regard was the revival of Rosicrucianism, with exhibitions at the Durand-Ruel gallery from 1892 to 1897. Symbolist artists, many of them rejected by the official Salon, took advantage of these occasions to show works that took as their subject matter "legend, myth, allegory, dreams, scenes from high poetry, and lyricism in all its forms." Championed by the mystical writer Joséphin Péladan, self-proclaimed Grand Master of the order, Rosicrucianism traced its roots back to Christian Rosenkreuz, a celebrated fifteenth-century visionary who used the rose and cross as symbols of Christ's resurrection and redemption.

67. Félix Albinet, "Lalique," *L'Art Décoratif pour Tous* (July 1902): 10.

68. Plumet, "L'Art Décoratif au Salon," 173–74.

69. Bénédite, "La Bijouterie et la Joaillerie à l'Exposition Universelle de 1900," 202.

70. Stephen Escritt, *L'Art Nouveau* (Paris: Phaidon, 2002), 88. English ed. *Art Nouveau* (London: Phaidon, 2000).

71. Ibid.

72. Gustave Kahn, "L'Art de René Lalique," *L'Art et les Artistes* 1 (April–September 1905): 148.

73. Molinier, "Les Arts Appliqués à l'Industrie," 542.

74. Saunier, "La Bijouterie et la Joaillerie à l'Exposition Universelle," 23.

75. Bénédite, "La Bijouterie et la Joaillerie à l'Exposition Universelle de 1900," 206.

76. Kahn, "L'Art de René Lalique," 147–48.

77. Bénédite, "La Bijouterie et la Joaillerie à l'Exposition Universelle de 1900," 242.

78. Kahn, "L'Art de René Lalique," 148.

79. Marx, "Les Maîtres Décorateurs Français," 19.

80. Pezone, *L'Art dans Tout*, 35.

81. Maurice Guillemont, "Félix Bracquemond: Décorateur et Ornamiste," *L'Art et les Artistes* 3 (April–September 1906): 14–23.

82. Bénédite, "La Bijouterie et la Joaillerie à l'Exposition Universelle de 1900," 242–43.

83. Prince Bojidar Karageorgevitch, "Les Objets d'Art au Salon des Artistes Français," *L'Art Décoratif* (January–June 1906): 12.

84. M. P. Verneuil, "L'Art Décorative aux Salons," *Art et Décoration* 23 (January–June 1908): 195.

85. Molinier, "Les Arts Décoratifs" (1897), 169.

86. Émile Dacier, *La Revue de L'Art Ancien et Moderne* 14 (July–December 1903): 72.

87. Four versions of this orchid, in varying sizes and depictions, are known to exist. They currently reside in the Gulbenkian Museum in Lisbon, the Walters Art Gallery in Baltimore, the Anderson Collection at the University of East Anglia in England, and a private collection.

88. Saunier, "La Bijouterie et la Joaillerie à l'Exposition Universelle," 18.

89. Marx, "Les Maîtres Décorateurs Français: René Lalique," 19.

90. Molinier, "Les Arts Décoratifs" (1901), 48.

91. "The exhibition of Jewellery by René Lalique," *Studio* (London) (1905), as cited in Ferreira, *Lalique—Bijoux*, 337.

92. Ibid.

Box (Monnaie du Pape) (cat. 127). René Lalique.

Russia: Fabergé and His Competitors

Emmanuel Ducamp and Wilfried Zeisler

Far from being cut off from the rest of the world, Russia attracted, assimilated, and was inspired by Western innovations in art. As the French art historian Louis Réau noted bombastically in 1909:

> Russia is one of the countries that is most propitious for the study of the expansion of French art during the eighteenth and nineteenth centuries. Thanks to the patronage of the great Moscow merchants, the influence of French art continued to spread throughout this period. This influence on Russian art has never been stronger than it is today, with Paris—having absorbed the traditional clientele of Rome, Munich and Düsseldorf—now the undisputed capital of European art.[1]

Réau, who published numerous works on Russian art in French, displays a degree of national bias that turns a blind eye to the place occupied in turn-of-the-century Russia by German, English, and American art, and above all by Russian art itself. Since the eighteenth century, France had been known in Russia for its luxury objects reserved for an aristocratic clientele. Yet in 1892, a French report noted a decline in the position of French goods in the Russian market: "Today the generally admitted superiority of French products no longer enjoys its former influence."[2]

Russia had maintained close links with France since the 1880s. The exoticism of Russian art had caused a sensation at the world expositions in Paris up to this point, and economic exchanges had intensified, with France receiving its first financial loans from Russia in 1888. The finest, and often prize-winning, creations displayed by French enterprises at the Exposition Universelle of 1889 were moreover purchased by the Russian imperial family at subsequent Franco-Russian exhibitions in Russia. At the exhibition in Moscow of 1891, the tsar and tsarina chose lamps by the bronzesmith Gagneau, and the tsarina added jewels by Louis Aucoc and Coulon & Cie to her vast collection.[3] Some of the grand dukes also followed suit, acquiring objets d'art and furniture from the goldsmiths Boin-Taburet and Christofle and from the furnituremaker Sormani.

Exhibitions were an important vehicle in forging a strong link between France and Russia in the late nineteenth century. The most notable was the Russian Red Cross Exhibition, another Franco-Russian effort, staged at the Stieglitz Museum of Decorative and Applied Arts in St. Petersburg in 1899. The brainchild of Princess Lobanov-Rostovsky, head of the Red Cross and a regular visitor to Paris and its jewelers,[4] this show was a fundraising venture[5] for a hospital to be built in memory of the late tsar Alexander III.[6] The princess received the support of major industrialists and manufacturers such as Marcerou and Shreter, agents in Paris who paid for transportation; the court architect R. F. Meltzer, a committee member; and the goldsmith Khlebnikov. The French exhibitors consisted principally of firms that already had close links with Russia and the imperial family, such as the gunsmith Fauré-Lepage and the bronzesmith Soleau.

Supervised in France by the Ministry of Commerce, the Red Cross Exhibition was divided into the following sections: metalwork, furniture, glass, ceramics, jewelry, accessories, and graphic arts.[7] Opened with great ceremony by Grand Duke Konstantin Konstantinovich, this lavish display brought together thirty-five exhibitors from France, plus ten more French concerns established in Russia, all

Kremlin Tower Clock (detail, cat. 68). House of Fabergé.

of whom made numerous sales.[8] Spread over a floor space of 2,500 square meters, the exhibition encompassed the great entrance hall, central hall, and three other galleries of the museum established by Baron Alexander von Stieglitz.

Baron Stieglitz's Museum and School of Applied Arts

Baron Stieglitz founded his museum and school in the spirit of the great European museums of the decorative arts that were established in the wake of the founding of the South Kensington Museum in London, which became the Victoria and Albert in 1899.[9] Following the model laid down in Europe, where a strong emphasis was placed on the education and training of artists and artisans, Stieglitz also set up a school of applied art. In Moscow, the Stroganov Academy of Fine and Industrial Arts had been founded in 1860 to amalgamate the city's various schools of applied art, including the first Stroganov school, founded in 1825.

Following the example of the Stroganov Museum, which was attached to the academy opened in 1864, Stieglitz, a privy councilor and banker to the court, financed the establishment of his new institution, authorized by Tsar Alexander II in 1876 and opened in 1881. On his death in 1884, the baron endowed the school and museum with the colossal sum of 9,690,642 rubles (approximately $6.3 million in the 1880s), enabling his daughter Nadejda Polovtsova and son-in-law Alexander A. Polovtsov, state councilor, politician, industrialist, and collector, as trustees to enrich the school and the museum's collections and library.[10]

The collections of the Stieglitz Museum were founded on antique works acquired from great Russian collectors,[11] as well as from the European dealers and antiquaries frequented by the very cosmopolitan Polovtsov.[12] In order to complete the universality of its vision, the museum also commissioned copies of celebrated works, notably furniture.[13] Many of these were made by Henry Dasson, while the goldsmiths Elkington & Co. and Christofle created copies of known masterpieces of the goldsmith's art. Examples of oriental art, including Japanese vases, bronzes, and lacquerwork, were purchased from Siegfried Bing in Paris.

Meanwhile, Alexander Polovtsov took advantage of his visits to France to select objets d'art reflecting the latest artistic innovations of the late nineteenth century. For example, in 1889 he bought several glass pieces from Léveillé[14] and a small vase from Émile Gallé, the celebrated "magician in glass," in Nancy.[15] Between 1878 and 1900, the museum purchased at least seven works by Gallé; Polovtsov also bought enamelwork from Bapst & Falize in 1890 and 1892.[16]

The revolutionary Parisian jeweler René Jules Lalique was naturally one of the master artists chosen by Polovtsov for representation in the museum's collections. He acquired at least seven pieces by Lalique, including two ornamental combs in horn embellished with gold and silver[17] and a pendant in enameled gold consisting of six entwined serpents, two of them holding baroque pearls in their jaws.[18] Lalique revisited the serpent theme, a popular fin-de-siècle motif, on several occasions, most notably in an opulent *devant de corsage* (stomach brooch) preserved in the Calouste Gulbenkian Museum in Lisbon[19] and in a design that was possibly the model for the jewel now in the State Hermitage Museum in St. Petersburg.[20] Creations by Louis Comfort Tiffany were also well represented among Polovtsov's selections, supplied by L'Art Nouveau, Siegfried Bing's Paris shop. In 1897 Polovtsov bought 1,200 francs' worth of Tiffany's Favrile glass[21] from Bing, probably the two vases now in the Hermitage,[22] and in 1901 a stained-glass panel with magnolias, which was a fine example of Tiffany's "American glass" of international repute and exhibited in Paris at the Exposition Universelle the year before.

Five works were purchased from René Lalique's studio in 1902 for the museum of the Stieglitz School of Applied Arts in St. Petersburg, including this pendant based on the artist's recurring theme of intertwined serpents clasping pearls with their fangs (cat. 171).

The important collections of the Stieglitz Museum, officially opened in the presence of the imperial family in 1896,[23] formed a remarkable center for study and experimentation among the creative, avant-garde, and eclectic spirits of Russia's native artists and artisans. The Art Nouveau character of the objects available for the Stieglitz art students to study provided an important cosmopolitan inspiration for the output of the imperial workshops.

International Exhibitions in Russia

The Imperial Society for the Encouragement of the Arts, erected in 1870, fulfilled a similar role as the Stieglitz Museum and School in St. Petersburg. After the 1900 Exposition Universelle in Paris, where the Russian section made a great impression with its creations in the Art Nouveau style, known as the "Style Moderne" in Russia, the Red Cross decided to mount a new international exhibition of the arts. The venue was to be the headquarters of the Society, and the patron was to be Princess Eugenia of Oldenburg, a member of the imperial family well versed in Parisian luxury.[24]

The work of Russian artists was represented at the exhibition, as was that of their German, Austrian, Belgian, Italian, and Japanese counterparts, but the French section was the largest. Everything about it was calculated to attract St. Petersburg's wealthy elite: the district in which it was held also housed the premises of the city's most celebrated jewelers, such as Bolin and Fabergé; the time of year chosen (December 1901–January 1902) coincided with the period when wealthy Russians had returned to the capital from their foreign travels; and finally, the objects on display, consisting essentially of jewelry and gold- and silverwork with a few bronzes and amusing playthings, would make ideal gifts for Christmas and New Year's: "It was therefore to be hoped, in the interests of both this fine charitable organization [the Red Cross][25] and the exhibitors, that visitors would be seduced by the taste and perfection they would encounter in French products, and make many large purchases."[26] On the day the exhibition opened, the French section and its jewelry aroused the admiration and enthusiasm of the Russians, with august visitors, led by the tsar, yielding to the temptation to make purchases.

The following year, Grand Duchess Xenia Alexandrovna, sister of Tsar Nicholas II, became a patron of another new exhibition, this time more historical in character: the International Exhibition of Historical and Modern Costumes and Accessories, held at the Tauride Palace in St. Petersburg in 1902–3. This sketchily documented event, in which the Parisian goldsmith and jeweler Boin-Taburet, greatly appreciated in Russia, played a particularly important part, brought together not only historic items but also a range of creations that were put at the disposal of clients.

Although none of these exhibitions was an outstanding commercial success, they helped draw attention within Russia to European artistic luxury as well as technical and stylistic innovations that readers could also discover in the pages of numerous periodicals devoted to the arts, both in Russia and abroad. Information and illustrations printed in *Studio* (London), *Art et Décoration*, or *La Revue des Arts Décoratifs* were often incorporated in articles in Russian published in *Stroitel*, *Zodchy*,[27] and above all, *Mir Iskusstva*.

Originally a society of contemporary artists, among them Alexandre Benois, Léon Bakst, Evgeni Lanceray, and Kostantin Somov, who considered themselves progressive, Mir Iskusstva (World of Art) organized exhibitions of work by Russian and foreign artists on a regular basis after 1898 in St. Petersburg and Moscow, as well as Paris, Berlin, and Venice. Its magazine *Mir Iskusstva*, edited by designer Sergei Diaghilev and supported in its early days by the great collector and patron Savva

Fig. 55. This cover of the Russian art journal *Mir Iskusstva* (World of Art) from 1899 announces the group's admiration for the international Art Nouveau, which came to be known as the Style Moderne in Russia where it often incorporated native folk traditions.

Mamontov and subsequently by Princess Maria Tenisheva, was clear in its objectives. Its sole aim, it declared, was "the encouragement of the development of Russian Art Moderne, both in its purely aesthetic manifestations and in its applications to Industry."[28]

Available in Berlin, Munich, Paris, and St. Petersburg, *Mir Iskusstva* documented in words and images the developments in European art from which Russian artists were meant to draw inspiration, while at the same time reflecting the activities of the association's numerous members.[29] These artists were comparable to their European counterparts, in that they worked in the same spirit of Art Nouveau or the *Gesamtkunstwerk* (total work of art). They were active not only in the field of painting but also in decorative arts, performing arts, and book design. The association's first exhibition, entitled *International Exhibition of the Fine Arts Organized by Mir Iskusstva,* opened in January 1899. Significantly, the exhibition was held in the buildings of the Stieglitz Museum and School, demonstrating convincingly that these painters were not afraid to be associated with an institution devoted to the decorative arts.

Lalique and Russia

The inclusiveness and generosity of spirit characteristic of the artists of Mir Iskusstva, or World of Art, is apparent in the catalogue of their 1899 exhibition. At the back, following the list of works by the artists Giovanni Boldini, Claude Monet, Gustave Moreau, and J. A. M. Whistler among many others,[1] comes a surprising mention of a display case of jewels by Lalique, whose part in the exhibition seems hitherto unheralded; of another case devoted to glass by Tiffany; and of a third containing works by Tiffany, Jacquin, and Gallé alongside pieces from the Abramtsevo workshops and embroideries by Elena Polenova.[2] These Russian artists represented the avant-garde of the Russian Art Nouveau that would be displayed in Paris the following year at the 1900 Exposition Universelle. Although it is not known which pieces Lalique selected for display at the 1899 exhibition, the fact that he, Gallé, and Tiffany were invited to take part reveals how clearly the members of World of Art had perceived the innovative nature of their work and the necessity of including them in their first exhibition.

While the membership of World of Art consisted largely of painters, another Russian art society founded on the same principles, L'Art Contemporain (Contemporary Art), focused on the application of modernism in the decorative arts. Financed by two Muscovite art patrons, Prince Sergei Scherbatov and the industrialist Vladimir von Meck, this society had its offices in the heart of St. Petersburg and luxury sales premises at 33 Bolshaia Morskaia. Its artistic director was the distinguished Igor Grabar, who in 1903 organized a show of Style Moderne interior design and furniture. The exhibition also included a number of design schemes by World of Art members, including a teremok (small hall) by A. Golovin, a tea room by K. Korovin, and a bedroom by Léon Bakst. Once again, Lalique was invited to exhibit his work alongside that of members of Contemporary Art, and he related his adventures in St. Petersburg in a series of letters to his wife.[3] The tale of his troubles with customs officials gives a tantalizing glimpse into both the type of work Lalique was displaying as well as the difficulties of getting it in and out of Russia in the period.

Apparently in the commotion of departure Lalique had forgotten his passport, and could only present the Russian customs officers with letters of recommendation from Grabar and "a telegram from Prince Scherbatov urging him to leave [France quickly] in order to be at the exhibition for the Tsar's visit." Unimpressed, the customs officers became even more suspicious when they discovered what he was carrying in his bags. During their search they managed to damage a "bracelet by Jacharin" and a comb. Most of the pieces were of little interest to them, however, as they were of horn. Lalique had moreover taken the precaution of carrying two combs and a lorgnette on his person. Detained at the border, he lost no time in dispatching a telegram to Prince Scherbatov but was obliged to spend the night there.

Lalique was eventually allowed into Russia when the colonel of police received detailed instructions to that effect: Prince Scherbatov sent messages directly to the colonel, as well as to the minister and to the French ambassador.[4] When

This pendant of a winter scene by Lalique was purchased by the Hamburg Kunstgewerbemuseum from the 1900 Exposition Universelle in Paris (cat. 195). The Stieglitz Museum of Decorative and Applied Arts in St. Petersburg acquired another from the same series directly from Lalique's studio in 1902.

Lalique at last arrived at the Hôtel Bellevue in St. Petersburg, "it was the same performance all over again" as far as his papers were concerned. After meeting Grabar in the exhibition rooms he lunched with Prince Scherbatov,[5] who broke the news to him that the opening of the exhibition had had to be delayed by a week, as the tsar was indisposed and not all the exhibits had yet arrived from Paris. Lalique noted the disappearance of a "small comb with dancers," which had possibly been left behind at the border, but as "the display cases look[ed] very good and the exhibition look[ed] promising," he seemed quite happy, particularly since the ambassador had intervened. In a short telegram to his wife, he announced that he was to be received by Nicholas II, who would perhaps buy some jewels from him.[6]

As photographs published in the magazine *Mir Iskusstva* in 1903 confirm,[7] the items exhibited by Lalique included a large tiara in gold and enamel, in the shape of a cockerel holding a large jonquil diamond in its beak,[8] described by Vever at the Paris Exposition Universelle of 1900 as "this cockerel proudly holding in its beak an enormous yellow diamond."[9] The amethyst that now adorns the work was a replacement for the original yellow diamond. The tiara was bought from Lalique by Portuguese collector Calouste Gulbenkian in 1904.[10] Also reproduced in *Mir Iskusstva* were a choker in the shape of dragon-flies, two large anemone pendants, a very wide collaret, the brooch mentioned above with pearls cascading from the jaws of intertwined serpents, a large dagger, a vermeil brooch, and a chalice.

By this time Lalique had already worked for the Russian tsar and his entourage, supplying them with cane knobs, one of which is preserved in the Hermitage.[11] A design for a knob dating from 1893–95 bears the letter "K" beneath an imperial crown, suggesting that it was intended for Grand Duke Kyril Vladimirovich, first cousin to the tsar, or for another of his cousins, Grand Duke Konstantin Konstantinovich.[12] Another design from the years 1895–97, depicting the head of a warrior with his helmet elongated to form

the curve of the cane, bears the inscription "Her Majesty Alexandra Feodorovna."[13]

Among the most remarkable of Lalique's designs for the imperial family is a design for a fan exhibited at the Musée du Luxembourg in 2007.[14] Dominated by the imperial eagle, double-headed and crowned, the armature, probably embellished with brilliants, is further adorned with flowers and, in their upper part, a young cupid chasing a colorful butterfly. Two female figures separate this section from the handle, also decorated with flowers and a pair of tassels, each decorated with an imperial crown. The fan itself was described in 1926 as belonging to the crown jewels transferred from St. Petersburg to Moscow in 1914, on the outbreak of war.[15] It was then described as "a superb example of the jeweler's art" as practiced in Paris during the reign of Nicholas II (1900).[16]

The future tsar Nicholas II possibly commissioned the fan from Lalique in 1894, the year in which he became engaged and was married. When he was staying in London at the time, numerous jewelers presented their jewelry to him, and his name appears in the accounts of Boucheron, while Vever is mentioned in the

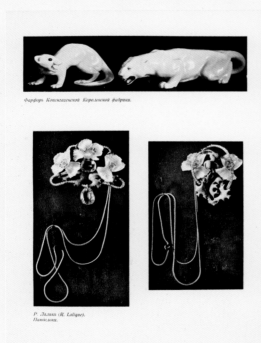

Фарфоръ Копенгагенской Королевской фабрики.

Р. Лаликъ (R. Lalique).
Павоглазки.

241

Р. Лаликъ (R. Lalique).
Колье и головное украшеніе.

242

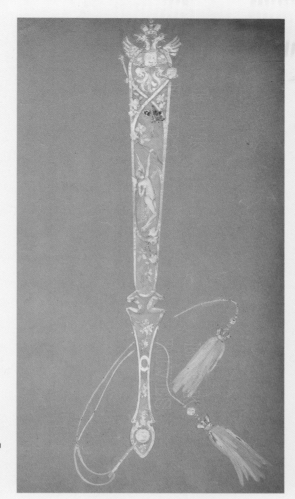

Fig. 56. While Nicholas II shopped Paris jewelers on a visit in 1894, he may have commissioned a relatively unknown Lalique to create a fan with a double-headed eagle. Photographs of Alexandra Feodorovna frequently show the tsarina holding the fan.

Figs. 57a–b. In 1903 Lalique was invited to participate in the contemporary art exhibition organized by Prince Scherbatov and Vladimir von Meck, and the World of Art group published his works in its journal, *Mir Iskusstva*. Among the works presented were the poppy pendant series and the cockerel tiara (both facing page), both now in the Calouste Gulbenkian Museum in Lisbon, as well as a sword hilt, chalice, and the great serpent stomach brooch, one of the masterpieces of his 1900 Paris exposition display (right).

accounts of the imperial cabinet. The fan is subsequently seen in several photographic portraits of Tsarina Alexandra Feodorovna, notably one taken by Pasetti at St. Petersburg in 1894.[17] The fan is also recognizable in several photographs taken in 1923 showing the Russian crown jewels as the inventory of them was being taken, but its current whereabouts are unknown.[18]

Lalique's work had obviously caught the attention of the young Nicholas. A bill from Lalique entered by the tsar's cabinet in December 1900 attests to further expenditures for "1 chain, 12 pearls, 2 ladies' pendants gold and translucent enamel, pairs baroque pearls" for a price of 5,200 francs in November 1898, and "1 pendant, 2 cockerels enameled gold, 3 natural pearls" for 13,000 francs in June 1900. The sum was paid to Lalique through the Russian embassy in Paris in January 1901.[19]

Other members of the imperial family also manifested an interest in Lalique's work. In December 1899, Grand Duke Vladimir Alexandrovich, uncle of Nicholas II, received bills from the jeweler for a total of 1,550 francs: 750 francs for "1 cat pendant enameled silver

Р. Лаликъ (R. Lalique).
Брошь и кинжалъ.

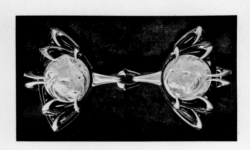

Р. Лаликъ
(R. Lalique).
Брошь.
Кубокъ.

1 baroque pearl," and 800 francs for "1 enameled ladies' brooch and butterfly wings."[20] This
last item recalls the *Elf* brooches and *Naiad* and
Elf pendants with butterfly wings recorded by
Sigrid Barten,[21] all clearly invoking the enigmatic insect-woman, a motif greatly identified with
Lalique.

A stylized female figure was also the dominant ornamental motif on the jewel bought at
the 1900 Exposition Universelle for 900 francs
by Grand Duchess Vladimir, in all likelihood a
pendant described in Lalique's account ledgers
for that year as "engraved stone head and bust,
red-enameled gold mount."[22]

Wilfried Zeisler

1. Other artists mentioned include L. Bakst, A. Boeklin,
J. [Frank] Brangwyn, A. Vasnetsov, Ch. [sic] Degas, F.
Lehnbach, I. Levitan, M. Liebermann, P. Maliavin, R.
Ménard, P. Puvis de Chavannes, I. Raffaelli, H. Rivière,
V. Serov, and F. Thaulow.

2. "Exposition Internationale des Beaux-Arts Organisée
par la Revue 'Le Monde Artiste,'" exh. brochure (six
pages listing 322 works, 3 display cases, and 2 collections
of works and fabrics) (n.d.).

3. Documentation from the Musée des Arts Décoratifs,
Paris, copies of telegrams and letters, of which one, dated
19 February 1903, is reproduced in Philippe Thiébaut,
*René Lalique: Correspondance d'un Bijoutier Art Nouveau,
1890–1908* (Paris: La Bibliothèque des Arts, 2007),
134–39.

4. Ibid.

5. Lalique also dined with the prince that night and
considered him as "truly a great aristocrat."

6. Dated 10 February 1903. *The Fabulous Epoch of
Fabergé—St. Petersburg, Paris, Moscow*, exh. cat.,
Catherine Palace, Tsarskoe Selo (St. Petersburg, 1992),
235.

7. *Mir Iskusstva*, nos. 5–6 (1903): 237, 241–44 (nine
reproductions).

8. Ibid., 242.

9. Henri Vever, *La Bijouterie française au XIXe siècle*
(Paris: H. Floury, 1908), 3:738.

10. Sigrid Barten, *René Lalique Schmuck und Objets d'Art
1890–1910* (Munich: Prestel, 1989), 170, no. 11.

11. Ibid., 54. The inventory number given to the piece in
the Hermitage is Э–17258.

12. Ibid., no. 1601.

13. Ibid., 54–55, no. 1608, ill. 95, p. 129.

14. Exh. cat. (Paris, 2007), 66, no. 43, ill. p. 45; Maison
Lalique, Paris, inv. 6.1.001.

15. A. E. Fersman, *Les Joyaux du trésor de Russie*
(Moscow: Commissariat National des Finances, 1924–26),
Livraison 4, no. 295, p. 38.

16. The 1926 description specifies that the tortoiseshell
leaves bore a painted scene signed "Mingart," depicting
the castle of Fredensborg in Denmark, which probably
links it with Tsarina Maria Feodorovna, a Danish princess
by birth.

17. Gossudartsvenny Arkhiv Rossiskoï Federatsii (ГАРФ)
(State Archive of the Russian Federation), Moscow,
reproduced in Olga Barkowez et al., *Peterhof ist ein Traum*
(Berlin: edition Q, 2001), 228. Another print, signed
"Alexandra 1899," is in a private collection. See also I.
Schélaïev et al., *Nikolaï II, Stranitsi Jizni* (St. Petersburg:
Likii Rossii, 1998), 136, ill. 143. Alexandra Feodorovna in
court dress by the photographer K. Bulla.

18. Nikolai Ilin et al., *Prodannie Sokrovischa Rossii*
(Moscow: Trilistnik, 2000), 27, 33.

19. Rossisky Gossudartsvenny Istoritchesky Arkhiv
(РГИА) (State Russian Historial Archive), St. Petersburg,
fund 468, file 14, act 364, pp. 2, 3, 6–8. Several different
medallions with two cockerels reproduced in Barten, *René
Lalique*, nos. 636–37, are probably very similar to the item
supplied for Nicholas II.

20. РГИА, fund 528, file 1, act 1684, p. 181.

21. Barten, *René Lalique*, nos. 963–64 and nos. 567–68.

22. Yvonne Brunhammer, ed., *René Lalique: Bijoux
d'Exception 1890–1912*, exh. cat. (Paris: Musée du
Luxembourg, 2007), no. 279.

Foreign Jewelers

René Lalique had clients in Russia, but he was not the only jeweler to enjoy a high reputation there. Members of the imperial family were equally appreciative, if not more so, of the often more traditional creations of the great western European jewelers who were eager to embark on their own conquest of the Russian market. Before opening its Moscow premises in 1898–99, the firm of Boucheron had already wooed the future tsar Nicholas II during his stay in London with his young fiancée, Alix of Hesse. In his diaries the tsarevich made several references to contacts with jewelers. On Monday, 27 June 1894, he and Alix admired the wares of one of the four jewelers who had sent him their cards;[30] on 5 July, he bought a piece of jewelry from each of the two jewelers who had displayed their creations in his room,[31] one of whom must have been Boucheron or one of his sales representatives. Indeed, the archives of the Paris firm record that on 17 July 1894, the future tsar bought a "couronnette fleurettes brilliants and pearls" for the sum of 27,500 francs.[32] Boucheron exhibited several different models of these pearl and diamond coronets at the great exhibitions of 1889 and 1900, probably influenced by the work of Gabriel Lemonnier, who made Empress Eugénie's tiara and coronet in 1853.[33] The diamond coronet by Boucheron was a very personal gift from Nicholas to his future bride, who wore it regularly after their marriage.[34] In 1898 it appears in a portrait on ivory by I. Zehngraf;[35] in 1906 on a set of official photographs taken at Tsarskoe Selo;[36] and in 1914 in a family photograph.[37]

Nicholas II's name made another appearance in the Boucheron account books on 20 May 1898, when he purchased a *sautoir* of diamonds and rubies most probably intended as a gift for the tsarina, whose birthday was 25 May.[38] These two purchases of unique items cost Nicholas 41,000 francs,[39] a considerably greater expenditure than that of his cousin Grand Duchess Anastasia Mikhailovna, even though, like many other Romanovs, she was a faithful client of Boucheron from 1891 to 1916.[40]

Following in the footsteps of Boucheron, a veritable French pioneer in Russia with his Moscow showroom, Cartier organized shows in St. Petersburg and Moscow. The most celebrated was in 1908, when the imperial family paid a visit and Nicholas II bought three brooches: one in the form of a crown with pearls and diamonds; the second in rubies and diamonds; and the third in emeralds and

Maison Boucheron vied for clients among Russia's imperial family, perhaps inspiring a stylized motif that references the imperial double-headed eagle seen above in this brooch designed by Lucien Hirtz for Boucheron (cat. 4).

Fig. 58. The imperial family sits for an intimate portrait, with the tsarina wearing the Boucheron coronet given to her as an engagement gift by a young Nicholas II.

This Easter egg presented to Tsar Nicholas II on behalf of the city of Paris in 1912 was Maison Cartier's most overt interpretation of the Fabergé style (cat. 14).

Cartier sold hardstone animals in the Fabergé style in its Paris showroom in the rue de la Paix, including the whimsical family of kangaroos above, complete with a joey (baby kangaroo) in its mother's pouch (cat. 16).

The cigarette case below by Cartier demonstrates how well the firm's craftsmen duplicated the forms and palette of Russian enameled luxury goods (cat. 13).

diamonds. Tsarina Alexandra Feodorovna, meanwhile, is mentioned in the Cartier account books of 1908 for her purchase of a necklace with two pearls, and again in 1910 for a watch.[41]

Influenced by the Russian market, in 1906 Cartier even created an imperial egg as a gift to Nicholas II from the city of Paris in 1912. The entire composition—a jeweled egg topped by a crown and surmounted on a cushion—was undoubtedly influenced by the miniature models of the Russian imperial crowns exhibited by Fabergé at the 1900 Exposition Universelle, now preserved at the State Hermitage Museum.[42] Like Fabergé, Cartier concealed a surprise inside his imperial egg: a portrait of the tsarevich, Grand Duke Alexis Nikolaievich, framed in diamonds and set on an onyx support in the modern style. Similarly, Cartier also produced enamel cigarette cases very close in style to Fabergé's, as well as hardstone animals and naturalistic flowers and trees.

Long before Boucheron or Cartier, Chaumet had enjoyed great popularity with Russian clientele, beginning in the 1830s.[43] Later, one of his more celebrated patrons in Russia was Grand Duchess Maria Pavlovna, whose husband, Grand Duke Vladimir Alexandrovich, was an uncle of Nicholas II. Chaumet also achieved renown for having altered the jewelry of Grand Duchess Irina Alexandrovna, granddaughter of Alexander III, after her marriage to Prince Felix Yusupov, in order to suit contemporary tastes.[44] In addition to these private displays of interest, the presence of modern French objets d'art in late nineteenth-century Russia was encouraged by developments in political relations between the two countries.

The Franco-Russian Alliance and Its Artistic Manifestations

Following the warmly received visit of the French fleet to the Russian naval port of Kronstadt in 1891, visits between the two countries—outward signs of the alliance then under negotiation—multiplied and were accompanied by the exchange of diplomatic gifts. These gifts reflected each country's traditional areas of artistic prowess: Gobelins tapestries and Sèvres porcelain from France were matched by Russia with gold creations made by the finest goldsmiths working for the imperial court or large decorative vases carved at the imperial factories of hardstones from the Ural or the Altai mountains.[45] Other French gifts, however, were in the Art Nouveau style, and they served to encourage, or to strengthen, the imperial family's taste for artistic novelty.

One of the earliest masterpieces sent by France was the Gallé table *Flore de Lorraine*, presented to Alexander III by a delegation of the citizens of the region of Lorraine during the visit of the French fleet in 1893.[46] The delegation, which was closely involved in this venture, also presented their Russian hosts with other official gifts that were equally representative of the Art Nouveau style. Most of these gifts were reproduced in the *Livre d'Or de la Lorraine*,[47] which illustrates a punch bowl made by the goldsmith André Kauffer to the design of Camille Martin[48] and a Franco-Russian Alliance champagne goblet created by Auguste Daum in 1893 and presented to the Russian officers.[49] A pair of Gallé vases by Émile Hinzlen and mounted by Lucien Falize[50] was presented to the imperial couple by the city of Paris during their state visit, known as the "Russian week," in 1896. The vases were followed in 1897 by a set of Lalique presentation boxes and brooches, the gift of President Félix Faure, decorated with two female heads, representing France and Russia.[51]

On his state visit to St. Petersburg in 1902 President Émile Loubet, ever eager to promote France's foremost contemporary artists, presented the metropolitan bishop of St. Petersburg with an Orthodox cross by Lalique.[52] With his customary brilliance, Lalique set a molded crystal cross in a mount and chain made to imitate the spines of Christ's crown of thorns, thus evoking the Passion with twofold intensity. And because the Crucifixion also prefigures the Resurrection and redemption, Lalique placed the features of Christ in agony at the center of the crystal cross but silhouetted against a luminous sunburst evoking eternal light.

The French president also presented the tsar and tsarina with Sèvres porcelain and an impressive set of twelve Gallé vases, some with bronze mounts.[53] Among these vases and other objets d'art reproduced in *L'Illustration* in 1902, Philippe Deschamps described a number as "triumphs of symbolism." Notable among them was "an electric lamp or *Instant de Lumière* . . . of crystal and light bronze . . . with blooms enclosed within the crystal."[54] He also mentioned the "*Cattleya Empress of Russia* vase, diamond-patterned in snowy crystal striated with amethyst" and a "low jardinière in the shape of a nautilus shell, crystal engraved with two fleets and a décor of seaweed and shells."[55] These works were all embellished with inscriptions emphasizing the importance of moments of meeting and union, thus highly appropriate to the diplomatic exchanges that they accompanied.[56]

On 28 July 1908, at a dinner given in his honor aboard the imperial yacht *Standart* during his state visit to Tallinn (Revel) on the Baltic Sea, President Armand Fallières presented the imperial couple with a pair of silver vases by Falize as a gift from the French Republic.[57] The fact that most of these diplomatic gifts were subsequently

To celebrate the Franco-Russian alliance and the visit of France's president to St. Petersburg in 1897, Lalique created the portrait brooch above featuring Mother Russia and Mother France under twin stars (cat. 150).

Fig. 59. Gallé vases with naturalistic mounts by Fabergé were among the imperial family's collection.

Fig. 60. The view at right of Tsarina Alexandra's drawing room in the Winter Palace from about 1917 shows Gallé glass vases that were enhanced by the addition of silver-gilt mounts and retailed by the House of Fabergé.

placed in their private apartments is evidence of the favor they found with the imperial couple. As an example, the Gallé vases with mounts by Falize given to them in 1896 were put on display in Tsarina Alexandra Feodorovna's Louis XVI salon at the Winter Palace.[58]

The Tastes of Nicholas II and Alexandra Feodorovna

Although the imperial couple was open-minded toward artistic creations from abroad and attracted by their novelty, it should not be assumed that their residences were largely furnished in this style. Their private apartments in the Winter Palace were laid out in 1894–95 by the architect Alexander F. Krasovsky, assisted by Kramskoi and Danini, and furnished to designs by the architect N. V. Nabokov, who had previously worked on the imperial yacht *Polar Star*. Most of the furniture was created by the celebrated Russian furnituremakers Feodor Meltzer and Svirsky in late nineteenth-century eclectic taste, mingling Empire and Louis XVI drawing rooms with a Louis XV study, dining room, and Gothic Revival library. This eclecticism was not confined to architectural interiors, but rather was highly typical of the variety of styles ubiquitous in luxury items produced at this time.

Advised by Grand Duchess Elizabeth, sister of the tsarina, the imperial couple applied themselves conscientiously to the decoration of their apartments, clearly shown in Nicholas II's journal.[59] As early as July 1894, when the future tsar was staying in London to see his young fiancée, he had taken advantage of the opportunity to make some purchases from an antique dealer: "I went into a shop selling antique furniture, where I bought a handsome bed, a dressing table, a small table and an Empire mirror that I liked very much."[60] It was a habit that stayed with him after he became tsar. In 1896, he paid visits to shops selling furniture and antiques during a visit to the grand duke of Hesse, brother of the tsarina.[61] Inventories taken in 1909[62] and again when some of their contents were sold in the 1920s show that the private apartments of both Nicholas and Alexandra in the Winter Palace contained many examples of international luxury items, especially Gallé vases.

The imperial family's taste for Gallé glass was not a new one. Of the 350 vases and other objects in glass and crystal listed in 1925 in the palace of Gatchina, the favorite residence of Alexander III

and Maria Feodorovna, 16 were by Gallé: bottles, vases, and goblets, often in several layers of colored glass, and generally decorated with motifs inspired by flowers or plants. Similar pieces were to be found in the private apartments of Nicholas II and Alexandra Feodorovna. The tsarina kept a tall vase of lilac-colored orchids on a small table in her drawing room,[63] and on her work table a small vase in shades of orange.[64] Gallé vases were also on display in the tsar's apartments, notably on a shelf in his study, where the 1909 inventory described a small vase decorated with leaves and deep pink flowers,[65] and a glowing red pot engraved with flowers and leaves mingled with dragonflies and may bugs.[66]

The authenticity of these pieces was of little real concern to the tsar and tsarina, who were more interested in their modern style. Alexandra Feodorovna displayed, for example, a small vase in "Gallé style," in the form of a lilac-colored tulip on a base of silver foliage,[67] while Nicholas II showed a small vase in the "Gallé taste," in shades of green and yellow mounted with silver vine leaves by the Russian goldsmith Bolin.[68] Moreover Gallé was not the only foreign artist whose work found favor with the imperial couple. The imperial inventories list glass by Tiffany and Daum, bronzes by Siot-Decauville, furniture by Millet and l'Escalier de Cristal, and lamps and small ornaments by the goldsmith Boin-Taburet and, once again, Lalique.

The palace of Pavlovsk still has, for example, a perfume burner that stood in the tsar's study at the Winter Palace, mentioned in the 1909 imperial residence inventory and described as a small vase in patinated bronze with chased and applied decoration, embellished with twenty agates of various sizes. The decoration extended to the burner's three feet and long straight handle topped with the head of a wildcat. The handle is signed "R. Lalique" and dated 1896.[69] The same room also contained an ashtray by Lalique[70] and a small zoomorphic jug of patinated bronze in the form of a frog whose mouth forms the spout.[71]

The tsar and tsarina's proclivities toward the latest fashions from Paris also led them to explore the work of Parisian goldsmith Gustave Keller.[72] Numerous sources in France and Russia testify to the important relationship between the Russian court and the House of Keller, further confirmed by

Fig. 61. These lamp bases and the silver hunting knife, buckle, and modernist pitcher (facing page) owned by Tsar Nicholas II and his uncles were exhibited by Parisian silversmiths Keller Frères at the 1900 Paris Exposition Universelle to promote its close association with Russia's imperial family.

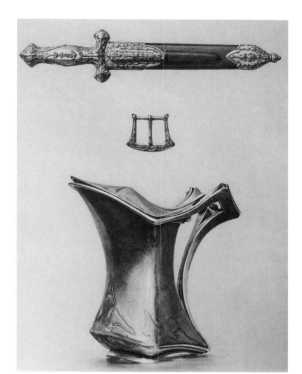

the Keller pieces belonging to members of the imperial family displayed at the Exposition Universelle of 1900. The creation of these works was probably linked to the Imperial Warrant granted to Keller Frères in 1900 as supplier to the Russian court.[73] At the 1900 exhibition Keller Frères illustrated the firm's chief characteristic techniques and style, including its celebrated technique for creating mounts for porcelain. This method was used on the bases of two lamps made for the tsar, which were not only mentioned in the numerous press reports devoted to the exhibition but also described and reproduced in an album published by Keller for the occasion.[74] The bases of both lamps were produced in fired stoneware with cast and chased bronze mounts. Where these lamps are now is unfortunately not known, but one was still in the imperial apartments at the Winter Palace when their contents were inventoried during the 1920s. The second lamp is recognizable in a period view of Alexandra Feodorovna's Louis XVI drawing room, also known as the Silver Salon[75]—in all likelihood, the same lamp described in the 1909 inventory as standing on a round table.

The modern "Keller style" was also to be found in other items exhibited at the 1900 Exposition Universelle, including traveling cutlery in chased gold and a silver hunting knife and buckle made for Grand Duke Alexei Alexandrovich (an uncle of Nicholas II),[76] who is known to have been interested in French art.[77]

The hunting knife, the silver parts of which were hammered throughout, was described as a "tour de force."[78] Grand Duke Paul Alexandrovich, Alexei Alexandrovich's brother and Tsar Alexander II's third son, was also a regular visitor to Paris, and eventually made his home there. In 1900, Keller exhibited a silver ewer belonging to Grand Duke Paul Alexandrovich,[79] one of a set of ewers of an originality that startled commentators on the exhibition.[80] The normally reticent critic André Bouilhet described their "strange, rough forms," which bore witness to a "bold ingenuity and rare dread of the commonplace" while acknowledging the excellence of the workmanship and its virtuoso use of the goldsmith's traditional techniques.[81] Victor Champier, meanwhile, recognized the "goldsmith's work of great excellence, recalling a form of primitive art, at once healthy, naïve, and strong."[82] With its angular forms, the ewer belonging to Paul Alexandrovich is relatively close to the lidded example in the collections of the Musée d'Orsay, except that on its base and lid it has a chased and repoussé decoration in a design similar to many of the modern creations of the House of Keller. The ewers exhibited by Keller in 1900 were unusually innovative in their spare, simple lines, far removed from the naturalistic decorations then in vogue.

Alongside these modern French objects and Russian furniture, the Russian imperial apartments also contained objects of Russian workmanship in considerable quantities. A study of the archives yields a strong impression of eclecticism, in both the style and the origins of the pieces concerned. Old photographs of the Alexander Palace at Tsarskoe Selo (the more or less permanent residence of Nicholas and Alexandra after 1905)[83] reveal an eclectic mix of Russian and Western antique furniture,[84] large Russian court portraits of the eighteenth and nineteenth centuries, and modern porcelain vases of Danish or Russian manufacture.[85] In the private apartments of the imperial couple, which had been refurbished in contemporary taste, the decorations by Meltzer were modern throughout, as was most of the furniture. The paintings, meanwhile, were nearly all contemporary and the objets d'art were modern in style, both from abroad and from within Russia, and notably from the Russian imperial porcelain and glass factories.

The Imperial Porcelain Factory and Glassworks

When the Imperial Porcelain Factory sent its creations to Paris for the 1889 Exposition Universelle, the critics castigated them for their lack of originality. Despite the technical innovations of the 1880s on the model of Sèvres and the construction of new kilns inspired by Sèvres, Meissen, and Berlin, director of the procelain factory Count Dmitri Guriev remained a stalwart champion of tradition.[86] Many of the factory's products, such as the Raphael service manufactured beginning in 1884, were considered nothing more than copies of existing works or at the very least were heavily inspired by them. One of the few innovations introduced to the factory workshops at this time was porcelain with underglaze decoration of the type exhibited by the Royal Copenhagen Factory in 1888 and greatly favored by Alexander III and Maria Feodorovna, who was, coincidentally, born a Danish princess.

In 1890, the former Imperial Glassworks was merged with the Imperial Porcelain Factory for economic reasons, thus creating a single factory on the same premises and under the same management. In 1894, Count Guriev was replaced by Baron Nicholas von Wolf, who had worked for Alexandra Feodorovna and enjoyed a close relationship with her. His main concern was to rejuvenate the factory's output and restore its prestige. From that point forward, the baron decided to make a rule of

The House of Fabergé provided silver mounts for a range of materials, including ceramics and elaborate rich-cut glass, such as these ruby-colored examples in the British Royal Collection (cat. 80).

employing graduates of the Stieglitz school. Not surprisingly, the glass produced in the factory's workshops soon bore the unmistakable stamp of the eclectic, innovative spirit that reigned at the school.

The first category of new work from the glass workshops was more classic in style. The architect N. V. Nabokov, for instance, who had participated in the refurbishment of the imperial apartments at the Winter Palace, produced designs in the Empire Revival style, combining highly elaborate faceted cut glass with gilt-bronze mounts.[87] Interestingly, cut glass of this type is often found in work by Fabergé, mounted in a style that is at once classic and Russian.[88] A remarkable pair of Fabergé decanters in the collection of Queen Elizabeth II incorporates mounts in the form of Baroque-style dolphins that are fine examples of Fabergé's work in a style resembling Art Nouveau, but the identity of the supplier of the more Baroque cut glass remains unknown. These vessels display compelling similarities, however, with earlier work by the Imperial Glassworks, which from the 1830s and especially under the reign of Nicholas I had been known for its remarkable cased cut-crystal creations in two layers of different colors.[89]

Another group of pieces created after 1890 at the Imperial Glassworks, notably under the direction of Ivan Murinov, who was responsible for cut, engraved, and painted glass from 1894 to 1901, consists of items, especially vases, in translucent crystal, cut in highly intricate fashion and a variety of styles. An example may be seen in the tall, double-headed eagle vase in the collection of Grand Duke Vladimir.[90] There is also another made in 1899 for the palace of Gatchina, engraved in Japanese style, with a carp motif.[91] Other notable work in this style includes the group of small zoomorphic glass vases in imitation of hardstones, made in 1905–6 by A. Zutov after models by Avgust Thymus. These animal forms recall not only Japanese netsuke but also the celebrated hardstone figures created by Fabergé.[92]

A third category of works by the Imperial Glassworks consists of creations that set out to break with the past, frequently similar in spirit and technique to the work of the great modernist glassmakers such as Gallé. The factory craftsmen were able to draw inspiration and ideas from the factory museum, which contained 280 contemporary pieces, alongside 2,000 older works.[93] Under Murinov's direction, the workshops produced primarily crystal vases—translucent or colored in a great variety of shades as well as engraved, painted, or shaped with motifs generally derived from the plant world.

There were also works in multi-layered glass of such impeccable technical quality they could be mistaken for work of French manufacture, with engraved patterns generally etched by hand rather than by acid, as was the case in the Gallé workshops. The *Iris* vase (1900),[94] for example, which before the Revolution stood in Alexandra Feodorovna's dressing room, was specially made in the tsarina's favorite shade of lavender, with gold and cobalt added to the glass.[95] Today the State Hermitage Museum still preserves other pieces of multi-layered glass from the imperial apartments, such as the *Azaleas* vase (1901),[96] while the palace of Pavlovsk retains a vase called *Lily* (1902), formerly in Nicholas II's study.[97]

As in the glass section, the output of the porcelain section of the St. Petersburg imperial factory in the 1890s and 1900s oscillated between classic pieces and much more modern work. Traditional wares still occupied a relatively important place, if only to replenish the numerous services the factory had produced since its inception—especially throughout the nineteenth century—that were still in regular use at the numerous formal court receptions. But as in the glass section, Baron von Wolf was determined to carry out a fundamental reorganization of the porcelain workshops; of the laboratory responsible for the chemical formulation of the pastes, where graduates of the University of St.

Overleaf left: As the imperial family favored the French Art Nouveau, nearly every Russian firm created objects in this style, such as this pair of vases with poppies by the Imperial Glassworks (cat. 116).

Overleaf right: With branches in Moscow and later St. Petersburg, the Parisian firm of Boucheron competed with Russia's greatest firms for the patronage of the tsar with works similar to this vase (cat. 5), also rendered in the prevailing style of Art Nouveau.

Petersburg and the Institute of Technology were now employed; of the painting studio, run from 1906 by Rudolf Wilde; and of the modeling studio, where Avgust Thymus took over the management from August Spiess. New kilns, a casting unit for large vases, and the capability of firing soft pastes at lower temperatures all enabled the factory to produce larger pieces with underglaze decoration. In 1906, the factory produced no fewer than 200 such pieces, including vases, large cache-pots, and platters decorated by artists such as Grigory Zimin, generally in the Art Nouveau style influenced by the work of the Royal Copenhagen Factory.[98] No imperial interior was complete without examples of such pieces: at Gatchina and at the Anichkov Palace; in the apartments of the dowager empress, who nurtured a veritable passion for this type of porcelain whether Russian or Danish;[99] in the apartments of Nicholas II and Alexandra Feodorovna at Tsarskoe Selo; and at the Vladimir Palace, residence of Grand Duke Vladimir Alexandrovich, uncle to the tsar and president of the Academy of Arts.[100] The coexistence of both antique and contemporary objets d'art, from abroad or of national make, is finally illustrated by the masterpieces by Fabergé that found their way into every single imperial household.

Fabergé and the Imperial Court

The House of Fabergé was founded by Gustav Fabergé in 1842 in St. Petersburg and later taken over by his sons Carl and Agathon.[101] Carl's tastes had been formed in contact with collections both within Russia and in Europe, where he visited the museums of Dresden, Frankfurt, Florence, and Paris during the 1860s. From 1866 the Fabergé workshops had from time to time supplied the imperial court with precious objects, but during the reign of Alexander III these items began to assume a place of

great importance in deliveries to the court. By 1903 Fabergé was a business of international standing, with showrooms not only elsewhere in Russia (Moscow, Odessa, and Kiev) but also in London.

In 1885 the House of Fabergé obtained its imperial warrant as supplier to the court with the delivery of its first imperial Easter egg to Alexander III. The most symbolically charged of all the imperial eggs, this first creation took the form of a chicken egg in white-enameled gold that opened to reveal a golden hen. The hen in turn concealed a second surprise, a miniature replica in diamonds of the imperial crown, which contained a final surprise: an egg pendant in rubies, which accounted for 2,700 rubles of the total price of 4,151 rubles. The egg symbolized the promise of new life—for Christians the eternal life promised when Christ rose from the dead. This rebirth is central to the Orthodox tradition of exchanging gift eggs after the evening service on Easter Saturday, which marks victory over death and the passage from darkness to light. In this tradition, every Easter Sunday from 1885 on Alexander III gave Maria Feodorovna an egg, each a unique creation by Fabergé, that opened to reveal a surprise, sometimes linked with contemporary events or with members of the imperial family and their residences.

The superb *Lapis Lazuli Egg* containing a crown and a ruby

Above left: Likely made in Dresden, where hardstone carving was an honored tradition, the eighteenth-century agate snuffbox at left illustrates the type of imaginative objects that inspired Fabergé during his youthful days volunteering at the Hermitage Museum (cat. 316).

Fig. 62. Large windows dominate the first floor of Fabergé's original studio and shop in this view from about 1900 of his building at 24 Bolshaia Morskaia Street in St. Petersburg. Courtesy Wartski, London.

The House of Fabergé's emphasis on the use of native Russian materials can be seen in the lapis lazuli exterior of the Easter egg above, which opens to reveal a replica of the imperial crown in diamonds, springing up on a spiral mechanism. Inside the crown is a pink sapphire pendant (cat. 51).

egg pendant now in the Cleveland Museum of Art is very similar to the first imperial egg. Fabergé also used a crown surprise in the *Imperial Rosebud Egg* (Link of Times Foundation Collection, Moscow) that Nicholas II gave to Alexandra Feodorovna in 1895 (priced at 3,250 rubles) and repeated the egg theme again in red enamel for Barbara Kelch in 1898 (Link of Times Foundation Collection, Moscow). Eighteenth-century eggs on the same model are to be found in the Danish royal collection and the Kunsthistorisches Museum in Vienna. One of the illustrations to the article "The New Gallery of Treasures at the Imperial Hermitage," published in the magazine *Starye Gody* (Old Years) in 1911, shows some other eighteenth-century eggs from which Fabergé probably drew inspiration.

An illustration to another article[102] shows a clock by André Lepaute, preserved in Russia, that is very similar to the *Imperial Blue Serpent Egg* presented to Maria Feodorovna in 1887 at a cost of 2,160 rubles. Fabergé had undoubtedly been inspired by the pieces on display in the gallery of precious objects in the Hermitage, to which he enjoyed privileged access over many years in his capacity as appraiser to the Imperial Cabinet, a post to which he was appointed in 1890. Moreover, the first of his creations to attract the attention of the imperial family, in 1882, were reproductions of works from the Hermitage's collection of Greek antiquities.

Fabergé created most of the imperial eggs using gold, precious and semiprecious stones, hardstones, rock crystal, and usually enamel on *guilloché* (machine-worked metal), in a style that was on the whole fairly classic and more rarely Art Nouveau. During the reign of Nicholas II, Fabergé's

commission doubled as the new tsar wished to give an egg every year to his mother and another to his wife. In 1899, for example, he gave Maria Feodorovna a magnificent egg in the Art Nouveau style, the *Imperial Pansy Egg* (priced at 5,600 rubles), in which delicate branches in twisted gold support a nephrite egg with appliqué pansies in enamel and diamonds. The surprise is composed of a large white enamel heart bordered with diamonds and sitting on an easel; eleven red enamel medallions like holly berries open at a click to reveal miniature portraits of eleven members of the imperial family. This egg was among those the imperial family allowed to be shown in Fabergé's display at the 1900 Exposition Universelle in Paris.

Other eggs are more topical in their allusions, such as the *Imperial Red Cross Egg* with triptych, given to Alexandra Feodorovna in 1915, when the First World War was at its height.[103] In commemoration of the Red Cross work undertaken by the tsarina and grand duchesses, this white egg features a simple red cross on each side; set in the center of each cross is a portrait of one of the two oldest grand duchesses, Olga and Tatiana. The egg opens to reveal a triptych formed by a miniature depiction of the Resurrection and the Harrowing of Hell, flanked by portraits of saints Olga and Tatiana.

As well as being masterpieces of elegance and refinement, the imperial eggs were tours de force of technical virtuosity. In order not to damage the yellow background enamel of the *Imperial Coronation Egg* (Link of Times Foundation Collection, Moscow) given by the tsar to Alexandra Feodorovna in 1897 (at a price of 5,500 rubles) during the application of the trelliswork design with the double-headed eagle motifs, the enamel had to be pierced while the egg was entirely submerged in water so as not to raise the temperature of the enamel and risk cracking the surface.[104] The same process may well have been repeated for the *Imperial Rose Trellis Egg* that Nicholas II gave to his wife, in which the guilloché enamel egg is covered with a diamond trellis in the form of lozenges with enamel roses and leaves of gold (8,300 rubles including the

Fabergé often drew inspiration from motifs of the eighteenth century, the great age of the goldsmith, when creating works for the imperial family in historical styles. The *Imperial Blue Serpent Egg* in the form of a clock (left, cat. 56) reflects the lines of a French desk clock (above, fig. 63) by Jean André Lepaute from about 1785, later published in the popular Russian magazine *Starye Gody* (Old Years).

The House of Fabergé made two imperial Easter eggs in 1915 that honored the contributions of the tsarina and her two eldest daughters, Olga and Tatiana, to the war effort as Red Cross Sisters of Mercy. One of the two, the *Imperial Red Cross Egg*, now in the Cleveland Museum of Art, becomes an icon when opened, revealing the patron saints of the tsarina's daughters (cat. 62).

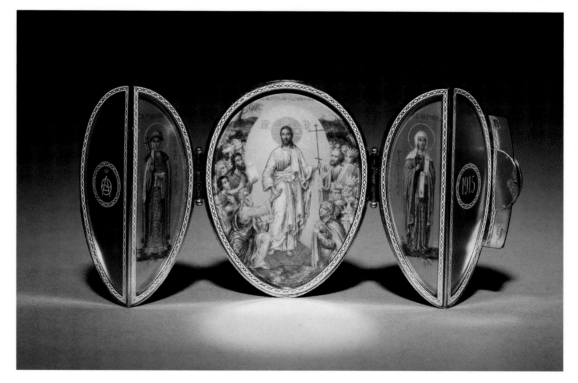

surprise, a miniature portrait of the tsarevich on a diamond necklace).

These highly precious objects also had great sentimental value to the imperial family. The imperial eggs were displayed in the heart of the family's apartments, where as historian Richard S. Wortman suggests, they also assumed a symbolic power: "Their splendor and importance indicate the shift in the locus of representation from the arena of the court to the private setting, where the symbols and events of the Imperial house could become the object of the members' own fascination and adulation."[105] Thus, public events such as the coronation (*Imperial Coronation Egg*, 1897), the construction of the Trans-Siberian railway (*Imperial Trans-Siberian Railway Egg*, 1900, Armory Palace, Kremlin Museum, Moscow), and the tercentenary of the Romanov dynasty (*Imperial Romanov Tercentenary Egg*, 1913, Armory Palace, Kremlin Museum) became not only symbols of their gift of themselves to the Russian nation but also the occasion of their private pleasure.

By 1909, Alexandra Feodorovna's apartments at the Winter Palace contained ten imperial eggs.[106] The majority were displayed in *Artistic Objects and Miniatures by Fabergé*, the 1902 exhibition devoted to Fabergé at the Von Dervis mansion in St. Petersburg.[107] In addition to being a public, and on this occasion imperial, tribute to the talent of Fabergé (the tsarina and dowager empress having loaned numerous pieces from their personal collections), this exhibition marked an intriguing evolution in the image that the imperial family sought to project. As Preben Ulstrup noted, "A prominent place was given over to objects of sentimental importance, tokens of affection intended for the privacy of the Imperial circle, as though the emotional bonds between members of the Imperial Family were being set forward as an example."[108] At a time when the autocratic regime was subject to a barrage of criticism, this was one of the weapons it used to counter and disarm its detractors; the customary official portraits were supplanted henceforth by numerous photographs showing Nicholas II with his wife and children, living the life of a model family, perhaps one of the few real assets then left to the tsar.

The exhibition at the Von Dervis mansion also featured the jeweled flowers that were another Fabergé specialty,[109] including a rose in a rock crystal vase, probably the same one mentioned with the eggs in the inventory of 1909,[110] and the *Imperial Lilies of the Valley Basket* presented to

The miniature frames at left with images of Tsar Nicholas II and Princess Olga were among the intimate family collections lent to the exhibition of Fabergé's works organized by the tsarina at the St. Petersburg mansion of the Von Dervis family in 1902 (left, cat. 59; right, fig. 64).

Fig. 65. The view of the Von Dervis exhibition below shows the two vitrines filled with Fabergé's imperial Easter eggs, most of them likely shown two years earlier at the 1900 Paris world's fair.

The *Imperial Rose Trellis Egg* (right) was presented in 1907 to Tsarina Alexandra Feodorovna by Nicholas II (cat. 63).

Overleaf: A group of Fabergé's bejeweled flower studies along with a little ladybug pill box promised an imperial spring, especially during the long Russian winter (left to right, cats. 73, 43, 314, 69, 97, 81, 52, 44, 72, 98).

Fabergé's workshop often accented its hardstones and precious metals with other innovative materials; here asbestos fibers recreate a delicate network of dandelion seeds (cat. 46).

The crowning achievement of Fabergé's jeweled flower creations is the basket of lilies of the valley nesting in moss of spun gold (cat. 60). Presented to Tsarina Alexandra Feodorovna by the merchants of Nizhnii Novgorod as a coronation gift, Fabergé borrowed it for the 1900 Exposition Universelle in Paris.

Fig. 66. As a resource for many of his creations for the imperial family, Peter Carl Fabergé turned to the collections of the Hermitage, particularly those of Catherine the Great and Elizabeth I, including the eighteenth-century bejeweled flower bouquet at right by Jérémie Pauzié, from c. 1740.

Tsarina Alexandra Feodorovna by the merchants of Nizhny Novgorod on the occasion of her husband's coronation and loaned by the tsarina for display at the Exposition Universelle of 1900.[111]

The hardstone and colored enamel flowers were probably interpreted by Fabergé from the jeweled bouquets created in the eighteenth century for tsarinas Elizabeth I and Catherine II. Originally intended as brooches or hair ornaments, mounted *en tremblant* on sprung stems that enabled them to move like natural flowers in a breeze, they were later displayed at the Hermitage as though they were real flowers, in rock crystal vases simulating water. In order to recreate these greatly admired compositions, Fabergé made full use of the palette offered by the colors of hardstones and enamel in order to render his blooms as close to nature as possible. Between 1897 and 1915 the tsar, tsarina, and dowager empress purchased several examples,[112] but the member of the imperial family who developed a veritable passion for these flowers was Grand Duchess Maria Pavlovna, sister-in-law of Alexander III. Among her thirty-three examples were cornflowers, forget-me-nots, cactus flowers, and dandelions.[113]

Among other precious objects, Fabergé also supplied the imperial family with animals modeled in silver and animals and small figurines carved from hardstones from the Ural and Altai Mountains. From the second half of the eighteenth century Russian mineral deposits (jasper in many varieties, lapis lazuli, and malachite) had played an important role in the decoration of the imperial residences, used lavishly to create both entire decorative schemes, as in the Agate Rooms at Tsarskoe Selo, and decorative items such as vases, tazza, and candelabra. Such objects were placed in the imperial palaces in St. Petersburg, or presented as diplomatic gifts—as quintessential expressions of Russian materials or techniques, such as mosaic especially in malachite and lapis lazuli. The three imperial hardstone factories, at Ekaterinburg[114] in the Urals (founded in 1765), Peterhof on the outskirts of St. Petersburg (founded in 1775), and Kolyvan near Novosibirsk in western Siberia (founded in 1787), specialized chiefly in the production of large-scale objects. Private workshops, meanwhile, including artisans who worked for jewelers, created smaller pieces.

In 1893, at the World's Columbian Exhibition in Chicago, exhibits from the three imperial factories included cabinets with mosaic panels[115] and vases in nephrite, rock crystal, white quartz, and jasper, while

the firm of Korchakov-Sivitsky from Radomiesl (province of Kiev) displayed items carved exclusively from labradorite, highly prized for its blue-gray tones that vary according to the light. The Woerffel workshops of St. Petersburg submitted "articles of stone"[116] including small figurines, which so impressed Tiffany that he later ordered some.[117]

This type of small figurine was also sold by Fabergé, for whom Woerffel worked exclusively from 1907 until his death in 1912, perhaps inspired by the work of another master craftsman, A. K. Denisov-Urlasky.[118] These works offered the court jeweler opportunities to make his own extraordinarily subtle use of the great variety of Russian hardstones. He adapted the colors of the different stones to the various elements of the traditional Russian costumes of his figures, in the tradition of the porcelain figurines created by the imperial porcelain factory from the eighteenth century, or to the plumage or fur of small animals, probably inspired by eighteenth-century zoomorphic snuffboxes.

By endowing these figures with individual or characteristic expressions, or even with recognizable identities, such as the gypsy singer Vara Panina, Fabergé created unique pieces of rare charm. After Grand Duchess Olga received one of them as a gift from her brother on her feast day in 1912, she wrote to her sister Xenia: "Nicky has sent me such a beautiful Fabergé babushka with a bundle and broom: too appetizing."[119] The well-known menagerie of animals from the royal estate at Sandringham in England, commissioned by Edward VII for Queen Alexandra, hints at a possible rivalry between the two sisters in this regard.

Animals were an especially popular subject for Fabergé's creative wit, either as paperweights such as a little seated bulldog (above, cat. 33) and playfully balanced elephants on a bellpush (below, cat. 27), or as whimsical desk ornaments (facing page, top, cats. 82, 85).

Left: Fabergé created, in hardstones, a series of figures of traditional folk heroes and heroines, such as gypsy singer Vara Panina, who reputedly drank poison after an unrequited romance with a member of the Imperial Guard (cat. 54).

Agate was a popular material for men's accessories such as the cigar case at right from the House of Fabergé, as it represented the collecting of specimen minerals (cat. 35).

Like other works of Fabergé imitated by Cartier, the study of a Japanese apple blossom at the far right is obsessive in its attention to detail (cat. 15).

The inventory drawn up in 1917 by Major-General Yerekhovich, director of Anichkov Palace, the dowager empress's residence in St. Petersburg, lists more than one hundred such figures.[120]

As the German army closed in on Petrograd during the First World War, the provisional government under Alexander Kerensky decided to evacuate works of art from the Hermitage Russian Museum and some of the imperial palaces. On the night of 15 September 1917, a train was sent to the Kremlin Armory Palace in Moscow, its forty wagons carrying notably eighty-four cases of treasures from the Anichkov Palace.[121]

The inventory offers extremely detailed, almost photographic images of the interiors of the palaces and the treasures they contained on the eve of the Revolution. Maria Feodorovna's "mineral zoo" apparently contained

fish, insects, and wild and domestic animals in Kalkan or Orsk jasper, Bieloretsk quartz, Altai porphyry, carnelian, citrine, and rock crystal.[122]

The dowager empress bought these figures not only for herself but also to offer as gifts. In 1892 on a visit to her parents in Copenhagen, for example, she took with her no fewer than four elephants, an animal particularly highly regarded in Denmark as it recalled the most distinguished order of the Danish crown, the Order of the Elephant, reputed to have been created in the twelfth century by Knut IV.[123] Two of the elephants were in nephrite (at 75 rubles), one in smoky topaz with howdah (at 175 rubles), and the last a larger model in nephrite (at 550 rubles). In presenting them to her family, Maria Feodorovna was well aware that she was offering gifts that were not only charming and sophisticated but also uniquely Russian, and impossible to obtain elsewhere, as indicated by her lament in a letter to her sister Alexandra in 1906: "Now that silly Fabergé has his shop in London, you have everything, and I can't send anything new, so I'm furious. You must be understanding and accept my little things with love."[124]

Most of Fabergé's other creations in materials as characteristically Russian as hardstones were *objets de vertu* such as snuffboxes, small boxes and bottles, as well as whimsical items; or everyday items such as clocks, electric lamp bases, photograph frames, candlesticks, bellpushes, pen and pencil trays, stamp boxes, seals, tumblers, cigarette jars, and small pots for glue or matches.

Here, once again, clear similarities exist between the jeweler's creations and "historic" precious objects in the same materials, as demonstrated by an interesting series of articles published in *Starye Gody* before the Revolution by Baron von Foelkersam, in which the author examined hardstones and their uses in the arts since the Renaissance.[125] Fabergé evinced a public pride in choosing to work in characteristically Russian materials such as Siberian nephrite and made it a point of honor to use these materials to create categories of objects that were no less distinctively Russian, such as the kovsh form, or works that sported authentically Russian designs.[126]

The combination of rare minerals, such as bloodstone, diamonds, and gold, creates a seductive pairing in a little box by Fabergé designed only to amuse (cat. 70).

Historical styles dominated the designs of the House of Fabergé. Both of the frames at left draw on eighteenth-century precedent for their inspiration (cats. 45, 86).

The use of Siberian nephrite reflects the Russian character of this traditional kovsh, given as a diplomatic gift on behalf of Tsar Nicholas II, whose monogram adorns the handle (cat. 66).

Grand Duchess Maria Pavlovna and Grand Duke Vladimir: Enthusiasts of Artistic Luxury

Tsar Alexander III's brothers—the grand dukes Vladimir, Alexei, Sergei, and Paul—enjoyed many privileges under his reign and that of Nicholas II. They traveled abroad, especially to France, more frequently than the tsar and had access to considerable means, allowing them to patronize the greatest suppliers of artistic luxury. In his *Memoirs,* Grand Duke Alexander Mikhailovich, a cousin of Nicholas II, details the fortunes that a grand duke to the last tsars had at his fingertips. At age twenty, every grand duke was financially emancipated. Grand Duke Alexander received an annual allowance from his parents of 210,000 rubles (approximately 800,000 francs or $325,000 in the 1880s), plus the money he had been entrusted as a minor. In addition, the tsar offered another 150,000 rubles.[1] A few years earlier, in 1867, Grand Duke Vladimir Alexandrovich had, for his twentieth birthday, received an annual allowance of 140,000 silver rubles as well as 600,000 rubles allocated to build his palace.[2]

Archival documents in Germany, France, and Russia reveal certain aspects of the life of Grand Duke Vladimir and his wife, Grand Duchess Maria Pavlovna of Mecklenburg-Schwerin, one of the oldest ruling dynasties in Europe. Maria Pavlovna married Grand Duke Vladimir, president of the Academy of Fine Arts, on 16 August 1874. The Mecklenburg-Schwerin dynasty was traditionally drawn to Western art, an interest he shared. Passionate about painting, Vladimir also collected ancient icons and loved the ballet, becoming one of the first to support the legendary impresario Sergei Diaghilev.[3] As the third lady of the empire—after the dowager empress

Maria Feodorovna and the tsarina Alexandra Feodorovna—Maria Pavlovna played a noteworthy role in Russian high society and was often described as having a strong personality.[4]

The Vladimirs' collections were housed in the so-called Vladimir Palace, close to the Winter Palace along the banks of the Neva. Built between 1867 and 1874 in the style of an Italian Renaissance palazzo by the architect Alexander I. Rezanov, commissioner of education of the Academy of Fine Arts, the palace included apartments decorated in the eclectic spirit of the nineteenth century: Gothic, Renaissance, Louis XV, Louis XVI, Moorish, and Russian. The grand-ducal couple lived in the palace until the 1917 revolution and commissioned several renovation projects, one to the architect M. E. Mesmacher

Fig. 67. Grand Duchess Maria Pavlovna married Grand Duke Vladimir Alexandrovich, one of Nicholas II's powerful uncles, and ranked as third lady of Russia, establishing a dazzling court circle that rivaled that of the tsar and tsarina as well as the dowager empress.

Fig. 68. Grand Duke Vladimir chose a Boucheron scarf necklace for his wife on one of their many shopping trips to Paris.

of all the great European houses. Proof of her numerous acquisitions appears both in Russian accounts and in the archives of the great Paris houses. According to Grand Duke Alexander,[6] the Vladimirs traveled to France twice a year on average and were fixtures in Belle Époque high society. The archives reveal that in 1882, when the grand duchess left St. Petersburg for a long visit to Europe, she brought along twenty-four jewels, several of which were by Tiffany & Co., notably a sapphire and brilliant bracelet and a pearl brooch.[7] During this same year the Paris boutique of the famous New York company became the official supplier to the imperial court of Russia. It should come as no surprise, then, that Tiffany & Co. objects were among Maria Pavlovna's private belongings.

Once she arrived in Paris, the grand duchess headed straight to the eminent jewelers and, in January 1883, spent a total of 2,700 francs at Tiffany & Co.[8] She is also mentioned in the accounting records of the Maison Boucheron (founded by Frédéric Boucheron in 1858). The Vladimirs made their first purchases there around 1880. On 14 October 1882, the grand-ducal couple is mentioned as having acquired a "vine branch with three leaves" for 3,450 francs and a "spiral necklace with a matte gold vine branch motif and roses" for 2,500 francs.[9] One can imagine the prized realism and particularly modern shape by taking into account contemporaneous models designed by Paul Legrand and introduced by Boucheron at the 1878 world's fair.[10] A loyal Boucheron client, Grand Duke Vladimir in 1883 then chose a precious scarf necklace, one of the specialties of the house, for which he paid 8,800

executed between 1880 and 1893. At the turn of the century, they hired A. I. von Goguen and A. S. Pronine, architects who specialized in modern interiors, and the famous Meltser firm, which had designed most of the Art Nouveau interiors for Nicholas and Alexandra.

The greatest Russian artisans were commissioned to decorate the palace—furniture and statue manufacturers, imperial porcelain and glass factories, and other suppliers to the court, including the silversmiths Nicholls & Plincke and Khlebnikov. Yet many of the objets d'art came from abroad: fine silver from Christofle in Paris,[5] silk from Tassinari and Chatel in Lyon, and glassware from Salviati in Venice.

With regard to jewelry, Grand Duchess Maria Pavlovna was the classic important Russian client francs.[11] Boucheron retains an antique photograph of the model. With its gold mesh, fringe, and pearls, the necklace is reminiscent of the model shown at the 1889 world's fair: "a knotted, flowing scarf, made from gold that is as fine and soft as silk; its warm color embellishes the two white and black pearl fringes at its ends."[12] Between 1883 and 1893, the grand duchess is mentioned by Boucheron only once, in 1891, for a modest purchase of 400 francs.[13] In 1893, however, two days before New Year's Eve, Grand Duke Vladimir spent the considerable sum of 65,000 francs on "two button earrings" composed of two very large white pearls, one 95 grains, the other 108 grains.[14] While in Paris in 1895, the grand duchess purchased a diamond necklace for 1,900 francs.[15] She is once again mentioned in the accounting records in 1897.[16]

The grand duchess had mostly patronized jewelers such as Boucheron and Tiffany until then, but around 1900 her taste evolved. Maria Pavlovna was entranced by Lalique, just as were her brothers-in-law.[17] In December 1899, her husband received an invoice from Lalique totaling 1,500 francs: "one silver cat pendant studded

French designer Gaston Lafitte designed the pendant at left for the House of Fabergé and exhibited a similar piece at an exhibition of Lalique and his followers in 1903 (cat. 84).

Figs. 69, 70. Maria Pavlovna (far left) wore her waterfall-style tiara by Parisian jewelers Chaumet, similar to the one at left, fitted into her elaborate headdress at the famous 1903 costume ball with a seventeenth-century theme that was staged at the Winter Palace.

Fig. 71. The House of Chaumet adapted to the taste of its Russian clientele by creating traditional jewels such as the miniature Easter egg pendants above, shown in a period archival photograph.

with a baroque pearl" for 750 francs and "one brooch of a woman with studded butterfly wings" for 800 francs.[18] The latter is reminiscent of the *Elf* brooches and the *Water Nymph* and *Elf* pendants with butterfly wings that Sigrid Barten lists.[19] The jewel Grand Duchess Vladimir purchased in 1900 for 900 francs was also a female figure and in all likelihood a pendant. In Lalique's accounting records that year, it is described as an "engraved stone head and bust with gold setting enameled red."[20]

Also in 1899, on 28 July, Maria Pavlovna appeared for the first time in the records of the House of Chaumet. For 60,000 francs, she ordered a "waterfall" tiara with three floral bouquets and dangling diamond briolettes (75 carats in all), which, with movement, resembled dewdrops.[21] The grand duchess wore it to the

famous costume ball at the Winter Palace in 1903. Dressed in a seventeenth-century Russian style, she donned an impressive *kokoshnik* (tiara in a traditional Russian shape) studded with precious stones; three openings allowed views of the three diamond drops on the Chaumet tiara. Maria Pavlovna also ordered a tiara with an interlace motif in 1904[22] and then another in 1910 made in the Louis XVI style. Chaumet has retained the design in its collection.[23] In 1911, the grand duchess chose a new form, a band made of diamonds and pearls, and in 1914, in St. Petersburg, she acquired a second one, in an undulating shape made of diamonds, for which she paid 1,800 rubles.[24] She also purchased a bell made of petrified wood inspired by the *Tsar Bell* at the Kremlin.[25] It was sold to her by Marcel Chaumet on the occasion of her visit to St. Petersburg in 1911, as two invoices in the Moscow archives indicate. One, dated 5 April 1911, concerns twelve eggs, some of which include the inscription "XB," the Russian initials for "Christ Is Risen," a phrase repeated during Eastern Orthodox ceremonies at Easter.[26] This purchase confirms that Chaumet was able to adapt to the customs of the Russian market. Relations with Russia were still very much alive and well on the eve of World War I. In 1914, for example, Chaumet sold a new tiara to Grand Duchess Vladimir, demonstrating her continued interest in French jewelers and securing for him a place at her charity event the following year.[27]

The House of Cartier (founded in 1847) was concerned about its rival's success in the Russian market,[28] and attempted to capture that market in the first years of the twentieth century. Maria Pavlovna, who liked to visit Cartier during his outings and exhibitions in St. Petersburg, placed her first order with him at the beginning of the new century: a pearl choker decorated with two diamond Russian eagles, which she provided.[29] The grand duchess in fact often brought stones or jewels to Cartier to be modernized. She did so in 1902[30] and again in 1908, when she once again had a ruby tiara designed around her "Beauharnais ruby."[32] During the winter of 1908–9, Maria Pavlovna rented part of one of her palace outbuildings to Cartier and then placed an order for a tiara that again incorporated older pieces. It was shaped like a kokoshnik with round sapphires and diamonds set around an enormous center cushion-cut sapphire of 137 carats and six cabochon sapphires totaling 102 carats.[33] Louis Cartier himself brought the tiara to Russia in March, receiving the grand duchess's compliments in person when he arrived.[34]

For Christmas 1909, Grand Duchess Vladimir wanted a devant de corsage that, in the jeweler's own words, would be "entirely worthy of the large sapphire tiara."[35] Cartier therefore provided another very large 162-carat sapphire for the center.[36] The order for 175,000 francs included adjustments to a dog collar necklace studded with

diamonds valued at 75,000 francs, also supplied by the grand duchess.[38] A document housed in the national archives in Moscow[39] details the work Cartier completed for the grand duchess between 1909 and 1911, including a "tiara with a row of brilliants between two rows of pearls set in platinum" purchased on 7 January 1910. In April, there is mention of a "neck chain in beaded fabric" reminiscent of the scarf necklace Pavlovna had chosen at Boucheron years before.

The range of purchases made by the grand duchess extends beyond jewels: in May 1911, for example, Cartier provided her with a "rock crystal candy bowl with miniature diamonds encrusted in the lid" and later "a platinum square bracelet-watch with diamonds, moiré ribbon, 'W' initialed clasp, diamonds." To this impressive list must be added a diamond drop and a series of evening platinum-mesh clutches in 1913 and finally, the following year, on the eve of World War I, an enormous 39-carat pear diamond, for the colossal sum of 121,000 francs, payable over three years.[40]

The grand duke and grand duchess also amassed an impressive array of fine silver. In 1892 they commissioned Lucien Falize and the

Fig. 72. The grand duchess's first commission to Cartier was a pearl choker with two Russian eagles not unlike this design for a stomacher exhibited by the firm's competitor Chaumet at a St. Petersburg exposition in 1902.

Grand Duke Vladimir commissioned Parisian silversmith Lucien Falize to create this centerpiece featuring Peter the Great and honoring the Russian navy (cat. 102). It was designed by the Russian sculptor Mark Antokolsky and sent to the 1900 Paris world's fair.

Russian sculptor Mark Antokolsky to create an extraordinary silver centerpiece, the *Vessel of Russia*. Peter the Great, wearing the uniform of the Preobrajensky regiment, takes the helm of this ship, "which bears the destinies of Russia."[41] The bow is decorated with the Russian two-headed eagle, the sides with cannons coming out of lion muzzles. On the bridge, the navy flag rests beneath the imperial crown. The vessel tears through a rocaille-style sea, embellished with shells, acanthus and oak leaves, and a dolphin. Since medieval times, large stately ships had decorated the tables of rulers, and in this tradition, the *Vessel of Russia* commemorates the 1696 foundation of the navy by Peter the Great, "the father of the Russian fleet."

The composition of the *Vessel of Russia* was in all likelihood inspired by the navy's symbolic founding of St. Petersburg in transferring Alexander Nevsky's relics there from the Nativity Monastery in the city of Vladimir. After several months of transport, on 30 August 1724 the tsar himself led a galley carrying relics to the new Alexander Nevsky Monastery in St. Petersburg. The figure of Peter the Great clearly evokes Antokolsky's 1872 full-length portrait of the tsar (State Tretyako Gallery, Moscow), using the same proud posture, the embodiment of power. At the turn of the nineteenth century, Peter the Great was the subject of a wealth of national commemorations and became one of the favorite symbols of the Russian Empire. The government used his likeness in much the same way the French used the image of Henri IV during the July Monarchy.[42] As Falize did for many pieces, he appointed an assistant, the silversmith Joindy. Introduced in the Franco-Russian exhibition organized at the Stieglitz Museum in 1899, the *Vessel of Russia* was also displayed at the 1900 Paris Exposition Universelle.[43]

These new revelations about the purchases and patronage of foreign jewelers and luxury goods merchants highlight the important links that existed between Russia and the Western world around 1900. Russian aristocrats, blessed with the means and ability to travel, visited every fashionable capital of the world. Grand Duke Vladimir and Grand Duchess Maria Pavlovna were among the world's most celebrated society figures, on a par with American industrialists, whose lives, like their own, were led in stark contrast to those of their countrymen.

Wilfreid Zeisler

1. Alexander of Russia, *Einst war ich ein Grossfürst* (Leipzig: Paul List Verlag, 1932), 94.

2. Iekaterina S. Khmelnitskaïa, "The Palace of Grand Duke Vladimir Alexandrovich: History of the construction and problems of the stylistic evolution in the state rooms. Second half of the nineteenth century–beginning of the twentieth century" (master's thesis, St. Petersburg University, 2007) (in Russian), 40.

3. Alexander of Russia, *Einst war ich ein Grossfürst*, 141.

4. *Von Mecklenburg nach Russland—Maria Pawlowna—ein Leben am Ende einer Epoche*, exh. cat. (Schwerin: Schwerin Schloss, 2001), 19.

5. Rossisky Gosudarstvenny Istoritchesky Arkhiv (РГИА), St. Petersburg (State Russian Historical Archive), fund 528, file 1, act 939 (1869–82), p. 133. Account provided by Iekaterina S. Khmelnitskaïa; see also Khmelnitskaïa, "The Palace of Grand Duke Vladimir Alexandrovich," 22.

6. Alexander of Russia, *Einst war ich ein Grossfürst*, 140.

7. РГИА, fund 528, file 1, act 341.

8. Ibid., act 342–43.

9. Archives Boucheron (AB), Paris, MC 11, folio 165. My thanks to Emannuelli and Sablier Paquet for their kind assistance during the research conducted at the archives of the Department of Heritage at the House of Boucheron, Paris.

10. *Rapport de l'Exposition Universelle de 1878, groupe IV, classe 39* (Paris, 1878), 26: "In the window, one first sees a thistle branch composed of two leaves and a flower, worked with astonishing care, an imitation of nature."

11. AB, MC 13, fol. 8. The grand duke stayed at the Continental hotel at the time.

12. *Rapport de l'Exposition Universelle de 1889, groupe III, classe 24* (Paris, 1889), 780.

13. AB, MC 20, fol. 414.

14. AB, MC 23, fol. 29.

15. AB, MC 25, fol. 149.

16. AB, MC 27, fols. 359, 371, 389.

17. Henri Vever, *La Bijouterie française au XIXe siècle* (Paris, H. Floury, 1908), 3:746.

18. РГИА, fund 528, file 1, act 1684, p. 181.

19. Sigrid Barten, *René Lalique: Schmuck und Objets d'art 1890–1910* (Munich: Prestel, 1989), nos. 963–64 and nos. 567–68.

20. Yvonne Brunhammer, ed., *René Lalique: Bijoux d'exception 1890–1912*, exh. cat. (Paris: Musée du Luxembourg, 2007), no. 279.

21. Diana Scarisbrick, *Chaumet, joaillier depuis 1780* (Paris: Alain de Gourcuff, 1995), 195, 197, illus. 56 (photograph of a similar model, collection Chaumet); Géza von Habsburg, ed., *Fabergé–Cartier. Rivalen am Zarenhof*, exh. cat., Kunsthalle der Hypo-Kulturstiftung Munich (Munich: Hirmer, 2003), 119; Alexander von Solodkoff, "Grossfürstin Wladimir und ihre Passion für Schmuck und Pretiosen," in Habsburg, ed., *Fabergé–Cartier. Rivalen am Zarenhof*, 112 and 111, illus. 4. See also Hans Nadelhoffer, *Cartier* (Paris: Edition du Regard, 1984), 70, pls. 59 and 79; Geoffrey C. Munn attributes this object to Cartier; see Geoffrey C. Munn, *Tiaras: A History of Splendour* (Paris: Antique Collectors' Club, 2001), 319, illus. 289.

22. Diana Scarisbrick, "Russland und Chaumet 1900 bis 1917," in Habsburg, ed., *Fabergé–Cartier. Rivalen am Zarenhof*, 119.

23. Ibid., 124.

24. Scarisbrick, *Chaumet, joaillier depuis 1780*, 341; Scarisbrick, "Russland und Chaumet 1900 bis 1917," 120.

25. Scarisbrick, *Chaumet, joaillier depuis 1780*, 168; Scarisbrick, "Russland und Chaumet 1900 bis 1917," 125.

26. The two documents were given to me by Iekaterina S. Khmelnitskaïa.

27. Scarisbrick, *Chaumet, joaillier depuis 1780*, 341.

28. Habsburg, ed., *Fabergé–Cartier. Rivalen am Zarenhof*, 439, correspondence between St. Petersburg and Paris, 24 March 1910 and 14 April 1910: "The House of Ch[aumet] bothered him to the point that he became angry and made it known that C[haumet] should not bother him any further in the future."

29. Nadelhoffer, *Cartier*, 50; Solodkoff, "Grossfürstin Wladimir und ihre Passion für Schmuck und Pretiosen," 114.

30. РГИА, fund 528, file 1, act 952, p. 9.

32. РГИА, fund 528, file 1, act 952, pp. 1–3; Nadelhoffer, *Cartier*, 117.

33. Munn, *Tiaras: A History of Splendour*, 318, illus. 288; François Chaille, *La Collection Cartier—Joaillerie* (Paris: Flammarion, 2004), 58, illus. Bestowed to Queen Marie of Romania, it can now be found in a private collection in the United States; see Munn, *Tiaras: A History of Splendour*, 308.

34. Nadelhoffer, *Cartier*, 117, pl. 63, and Solodkoff, "Grossfürstin Wladimir und ihre Passion für Schmuck und Pretiosen," 114.

35. РГИА, fund 528, file 1, act 952, p. 7: letter from Louis J. Cartier to the Grand Duchess Vladimir, 25 March 1910.

36. The list of jewels provided by the grand duchess as well as the design of the devant de corsage are in the Russian archives РГИА, fund 528, file 1, act 952, pp. 4, 5, 7.

38. Payment was made over three years. Cartier's letter accompanying the "sapphire and diamond devant de corsage" delivered by Léon Farinés to the grand duchess is dated 25 March 1910; Géza von Habsburg, "Cartier in Russland," in Habsburg, ed., *Fabergé–Cartier. Rivalen am Zarenhof*, 84.

39. Document provided by Iekaterina S. Khmelnitskaïa.

40. For the candy bowl, bracelet-watch, and diamond drop, see Nadelhoffer, *Cartier*, 120; for the clutches, see Habsburg, "Cartier in Russland," 87; for the pear diamond, see Nadelhoffer, *Cartier*, 120.

41. Gustave Geoffroy, *Les industries artistiques françaises et étrangères à l'Exposition Universelle de 1900* (Paris: Librairie Centrale des Beaux-Arts, 1900), 33–34.

42. A statue of Peter I, in all likelihood drawn from the Antokolsky model, decorated an ink stand on the table in Nicholas II's audience hall in his apartments in the Alexander Palace in Tsarskoe Selo. It can be seen in a photograph in the palace guide written by A. V. Saditsky in 1939 (p. 47).

43. Geoffroy, *Les industries artistiques françaises et étrangères à l'Exposition Universelle de 1900*, 33–34.

Russian Enamels

The technique of enameling metal was certainly by no means new in fin-de-siècle Russia. The art of brilliantly colored cloisonné enamel, perfected in the Kremlin workshops in the seventeenth century, had given way in the eighteenth to surface enameling (*en plein*) characteristically found on snuffboxes of this period before becoming a subject of study once more in the mid-nineteenth-century context of artistic historicism that emerged during the reign of Nicholas I (r. 1825–55).[127] Spurred on by institutions such as the Stroganov and Stieglitz schools, numerous goldsmiths such as Pavel Ovchinnikov and Ivan Khlebnikov became tireless champions and practitioners of enamelwork once more.

These artisans promoted the old style and technique of enamelwork to such an extent that it came to appear as quintessentially Russian at all the great exhibitions and world fairs of the second half of the nineteenth century, so much so that from the 1880s onward, many diplomatic gifts consisted of cloisonné enamelwork in the "traditional Russian" style.[128] Fabergé was also an ardent practitioner, especially in his Moscow workshops, where this type of work enjoyed particular favor with his clientele living in the Russian capital city. Sometimes these objects in bright enamels also featured enamel

paintings—cartouches, medallions, the cover of a box—occasionally in sepia tones, commissioned from one of the finest artists of the period, Fedor Rückert, whose mark was often carefully replaced by that of Fabergé. But the field in which Fabergé left all his contemporaries behind was that of enameling on metal, most often gold, with a guilloché pattern.

Many factors contributed to Fabergé's undisputed position as leader in this field. Even more crucial than his artistic flair, arguably, was his ability to set up and run a large-scale business that appeared unified and singular from the outside, when in reality it consisted of a number of more or less autonomous workshops under the stewardship of master craftsmen who were themselves highly experienced. These artisans included, among others, Mikhail Perkhin, August and Albert Holmström, August Hollming, and Henrik Wigström, all working under the same roof but with very different tasks.[129]

Moscow silversmith Fedor Rückert specialized in neo-Russian enameled decoration and traditional forms such as this bejeweled kovsh (drinking cup) (cat. 217).

Fig. 73. The view at left of the design studio on the upper floor of Fabergé's St. Petersburg studio, around 1910, shows animal studies, enamel charts, and a series of unfinished kovshi in the foreground. Courtesy Wartski, London.

The silver presentation box below with early modern motifs by Fabergé and sepia-painted scenes of the Kremlin and St. Petersburg financial buildings (cat. 28) was a commemorative gift to a member of the Russian insurance firm Lloyd from its regional offices.

This gold cigarette case of intertwining serpents at right (inset, cat. 40), given by Princess Cécile Murat to Charles Luzarche d'Azay on 1 January 1912, compares closely to its preparatory drawing from Fabergé workmaster Henrik Wigström's workshop of the previous year (fig. 74).

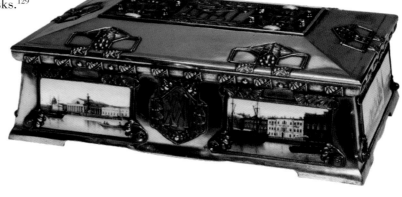

12756, 25/

1/XII 1911.

12753 19/XII 1911

12646, 1/XII 1911

A volume of workshop drawings, the only one known to have survived the Russian Revolution, is striking in the way it reveals the inventiveness of the designers who worked in House of Fabergé workshops, in this case that of Henrik Wigström. Their designs show an eclectic array of styles, ranging from Renaissance, Louis XVI, Russian, and Empire to Art Nouveau and moderne.[130] This variety was offered in response to the wishes of the Fabergé clientele, who were considerably more open-minded in their tastes than is often imagined and who were not looking for a particular style in preference to all others, but rather for an item that combined luxury with artistry. Contemporary magazines were faithful mirrors of tastes and vogues, and it therefore comes as no surprise to find *Mir Iskusstva* publishing articles and various series of illustrations on topics as diverse as Aubrey Beardsley, French modern art, Charles Rennie Mackintosh, the estate of the Yusupov princes, Arkhangelskoe Palace (just outside Moscow), classical architecture in Moscow, and northern Russian folk art.[131]

In addition to the gamut of styles to be found in guilloché enamels by the House of Fabergé, the variety of patterns carried out by the workshops was far wider than in the eighteenth century, sometimes with several different types incorporated on a single item. Moreover, the range of enamel tones from the lightest to the darkest was vast, encompassing some 140 different shades.[132] Fabergé sometimes incorporated antique pieces within an enamel setting, thus reenacting an antique process, es-

A small gold box from Henrik Wigström's workshop at the House of Fabergé features a classical cameo scene of suppliants coming before Alexander the Great (cat. 34).

pecially as to antique cameos, richly mounted in precious settings from the Middle Ages onward.

The inexhaustible range of shapes and colors, which both stimulated and satisfied his clients' desires, included quite a few whimsical objects. The Cleveland Museum's miniature chair in the Louis XVI style, for example, takes on the shape of a tiny bidet, making a luxury object into a seemingly useful one, in this case a miniature box, just as a writing set from Catherine the Great preserved in the Hermitage treasury assumes the shape of a sofa, to hide in its cushions all the necessary writing implements.

Enameled frames were also particularly sought after by Fabergé's clients because frames could transform the portraits of a new, modern form of art (photography) into the miniatures of the past that had until then often been framed in elaborate or precious settings to convey the degree of attachment to a particular person. Fabergé's masters went to delightful imaginative extremes to evoke the particular occasion for which each

Henrik Wigström was one of the House of Fabergé's most talented workmasters. He achieved a level of enameling seldom reached by others, as the range of unfinished parts and colorful guilloché enamel from his shop attest (left, cat. 89).

Fabergé became known for his intricate and completely useless objects of fancy such as miniature furniture in the Louis XVI style, which might have encompassed moving parts but were hardly functional as anything but amusing decorations (left to right, cats. 75, 77, 74).

Fabergé's personalized frames were a favorite gift for his clients and the royal families of Europe. Here the Roman numeral X is used to commemorate the tenth wedding anniversary of Grand Duke Mikhail Mikhailovich and Countess Sophie von Meremberg (cat. 53).

Monogrammed cigarette cases by the House of Fabergé (right, cat. 38) became a staple in fashionable Russian courtly society at the turn of the century, much like the bejeweled snuffboxes at the French court of the eighteenth century.

Queen Alexandra, in an act of sentimental kindness, reputedly returned the blue enamel and diamond cigarette case below by Fabergé to King Edward VII's mistress Alice (Mrs. George) Keppel upon his death in 1910 (cat. 37). It still contains the stub of the king's last cigar.

frame was created. One frame, presented by Grand Duke Mikhail Mikhailovich (Alexander II's grandson) to his wife, Countess Sophie von Meremberg, on the occasion of their tenth wedding anniversary, contains portraits of him and their three children, with birthdates, framed in enameled hearts and shown with views of four of their residences, all symmetrically displayed around a large enameled X, to represent the anniversary in a Roman numeral.

Snuffboxes had been the ultimate expression of luxury in the eighteenth century, exploring any possible technique and material; cigarette cases replaced them during the late nineteenth century, displaying a similar variety and imagination in materials and designs through the skills of Fabergé's masters. If some were indeed close to eighteenth-century designs in style, such as the white enamel and diamond cigarette case with a cipher in the center, others were strikingly contemporary. The case presented by Alice (Mrs. George) Keppel to Edward VII in 1908 is a masterpiece, uniting with utter refinement a particular technique with a related motif. While the background is worked in deep blue guilloché enamel, a diamond motif in the shape of a whirling snake creeps over and around the case in a typically Art Nouveau mood; here the undulating pattern of guilloché work gives the impression of wavy waters in which the snake is slithering, itself an unending creature as it holds its tail in its mouth.

Charles Luzarche d'Azay, a French officer, received as gifts from Princess Murat numerous cigarette cases by Fabergé, including these two showing the creative range of Fabergé's designs (left, cat. 36; right, cat. 39).

Desk accessories such as the barometer below in rich wood and gilt bronze were an important mainstay of the House of Fabergé's stock-in-trade of luxurious goods (cat. 25).

Workmaster Viktor Aarne designed this mount for a miniature Tiffany Favrile glass vase (right, cat. 307) for the House of Fabergé, adapting the swirling pattern of the glass through the device of intertwined snakes. A preparatory study shows how closely Aarne's design was followed to completion (cat. 47).

Other Fabergé cigarette cases display remarkable sculptural qualities in metalwork. One of the many cases presented by Princess Murat (née Cécile Ney d'Elchingen) to her friend Charles Luzarche d'Azay shows two similar snakes, this time composed in relief and intertwined. The snakes' bodies are modeled in platinum, engraved with scales, and highlighted with gold spots echoing the polished gold used for the body of the case. Once again, the serpents appear to have just crawled out of a liquid golden pond. Another case from the Luzarche d'Azay-Murat collection is chased in gold, showing the front view of an imposing elephant, seemingly plodding toward the viewer. On its forehead glitters a rose diamond crescent moon, an exotic motif found on other cigarette cases of Luzarche d'Azay, who had spent some time in the Middle East—as a French spy, so the legend says. But while this crescent might seem nothing more than an innocent decorative detail to friends and acquaintances, the crescent actually opens to reveal a miniature portrait of Princess Murat, the French gentleman's friend or *amie de coeur* for many years. Their liaison, though the talk of the town, had to remain impeccably proper, so much so that on their regular visits to the spa town at Evian they always dined at separate tables for the sake of convention.[133] Still another of the Luzarche d'Azay cigarette cases is neither Art Nouveau nor sculptural but totally modernist in spirit, with three types of colored gold modeled into a geometrical pattern nearly heralding later designs. Some other pieces by Fabergé also illustrate the use of less precious materials and could just as well have been made in Paris by Boucheron, Chaumet, or Cartier, boasting simply an international style and impeccable craftsmanship.

In addition to decorative and everyday items, the House of Fabergé, like other European luxury firms, supplied the imperial family with mounted crystal or ceramic vases. Viewing his firm as a business of international dimensions, with a sophisticated clientele who could expect to find examples of the latest fashions from abroad—as at Tiffany & Co. in the United States—Fabergé created mounts, generally in silver or silver gilt, not only for Russian ceramics

but also for French, English (Royal Doulton), and Danish (Röstrand) porcelain, as well as for glass from France (Gallé) and America (Tiffany). The 1909 inventory of Tsarina Alexandra Feodorovna's Winter Palace rooms records a small Tiffany crystal vase mounted in silver gilt in her Louis XVI drawing room[134] and a Tiffany green vase and small perfume bottle (flacon) mounted in silver gilt with a silver stopper in her cabinet.[135]

Like many of the great jewelers of the age, Fabergé was also a celebrated goldsmith. Accounts of the Imperial Cabinet show that numerous gold and silver pieces were purchased from the House of Fabergé for use at court. Generally this silverware went to complete the large services of the imperial residences, created in the eighteenth century by foreign or Russian goldsmiths, notably during the reigns of Catherine the Great and Nicholas I. For example, in 1895–96 Fabergé supplied the court with 260 silver-gilt teaspoons, 10 teapots, and 100 sugar bowls, as well as designs for two large centerpieces (surtouts de table).[136] One of these centerpieces, in the Louis XV Rococo style so popular in late-nineteenth-century Russia, is of international workmanship and could have been designed by French goldsmiths such as Louis Aucoc or Boin-Taburet, firms that were well known in Russia and had exhibited, alongside Fabergé, works in this style at the 1900 Exposition Universelle.[137] The other drawing is of a more restrained design in neoclassical style, also popular with European craftsmen and their clients at this period.[138]

A tea service with its own matching Karelian birch table, now in the Fine Arts Museums of San Francisco, is another example of these exclusive commissions. Formerly the property of Grand

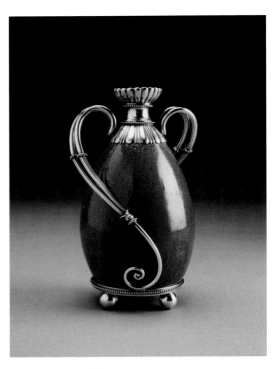

Above: The House of Fabergé was well known for its silverwork, supplying silver and gold accessories from full table services to mounts for ceramics, including this green stoneware vase (cat. 95).

Left: The French goldsmiths Louis Aucoc Fils, well known in Russia, were one of Fabergé's greatest competitors for aristocratic clients there. The firm created grand table services such as this tea kettle and stand, the model for which was shown at the 1900 Paris world's fair (cat. 2).

Right: Despite the vigorous competition from both Russian and European silversmiths, Fabergé remained number one in the minds of courtly aristocrats, producing rich, grand services in historical styles such as this sumptuous tea and coffee ensemble (cat. 92).

Duchess Victoria Melita, wife of Grand Duke Kyril Vladimirovich, this service is a rare instance of the few pieces of furniture either made by or retailed by the House of Fabergé. As was the case with many of his other creations, Fabergé's silver tableware is often in an overtly historicist style and reflects the eclecticism of its time, including the interest in Russian art and architecture of the late eighteenth and early nineteenth centuries discussed in artistic circles such as the World of Art group.

Not only did the journal *Mir Iskusstva* illustrate contemporary Russian art, it also drew attention to the wealth of Russia's national heritage in painting, architecture, and the decorative arts. Both Moscow and St. Petersburg hosted "historical" exhibitions that bore witness to this revival of interest in the relatively recent past, featuring objets d'art in Moscow in 1901 and at the Stieglitz Museum,

These Louis XVI-style silver candelabra demonstrate Fabergé's command of historical design, which fueled the Russian aristocracy's passion for conservative good taste (cat. 79).

St. Petersburg, in 1904; Russian portraits at the Tauride Palace, St. Petersburg, in 1905, organized by Sergei Diaghilev under the patronage of Nicholas II; and architecture and the decorative arts, organized at the Academy of Arts by the Museum of Old Petersburg in 1911. Such events were not only a melting pot of inspiration for artists such as Fabergé but also an endorsement for an art that was viewed as intrinsically Russian, of which they were ensuring the continuance in dazzling style.

Competitors of Fabergé

While Fabergé received a large number of commissions from the imperial court, he was nevertheless far from being the only supplier of such stature in Moscow or St. Petersburg, sharing the limelight with other distinguished goldsmiths to the court. One of them, the Muscovite firm founded in 1851 by Pavel Ovchinnikov (a former serf of Prince Wolkonsky), rapidly gained a glittering reputation for the excellence of its work, particularly in the Russian style. In this aspect, the Ovchinnikov firm was carrying on the work of the goldsmith Ignati Sazikov, whose creations in the "national" style never failed to attract attention at Russian exhibitions and world fairs in the second half of the nineteenth century.[139] What the Sazikov firm produced stood in marked contrast to the slavish imitation of foreign models that dominated the work of so many other Russian goldsmiths of this period.[140] Sazikov worked in association with the sculptors Ivan Vitali and Baron Klodt, a favorite of Nicholas I, as well as with the academician Feodor Solntsev, commissioned by Nicholas to carry out a study of Russian antiquities of the sixteenth and seventeenth centuries, which he published in *Antiquities of the Russian State*. Sazikov also appears to have been the first Russian goldsmith to use an engine turning machine for guilloché work.[141]

Fabergé provided every luxurious object needed to accessorize the rich life at court. The St. Petersburg nobility commissioned this Russian triptych icon in the form of the royal doors to commemorate the birth of Grand Duchess Olga, personalized with the patron saints of her parents, Tsar Nicholas II and his wife, Alexandra Feodorovna, and presented to them on 3 November 1895 (cat. 94).

Conceived in the same spirit as that of Sazikov, Ovchinnikov's work was primarily sculptural and historical in the use of typically Russian subject matter such as Cossacks, boyars, or other figures in native costume, as well as technique—the cloisonné enamel of sixteenth- and seventeenth-century Russia. Ovchinnikov either copied from new academic sources describing religious objects or reinterpreted and adapted his designs from secular ones. Sometimes he also combined cloisonné enamelwork with other techniques, such as gold filigree. In 1882, Ovchinnikov broadened his research to include colored en-plein enamelwork with embossed gold motifs, inspired by Japanese work and later applied to pieces in the Art Nouveau style, and to exceptionally challenging translucent plique-à-jour work similar in level of quality to that being achieved elsewhere in Europe.[142] Since the complexity of these techniques demanded highly experienced craftsmen, firms such as Ovchinnikov began progressively to establish apprenticeship schools within their workshops in order to control and accelerate the training of their employees. These communities of workers were similar to Arts and Crafts cooperatives sprouting up in Europe and America where an emphasis on creating a total educational environment meant ultimately a better skilled and productive worker.[143] The subjects taught in these schools included drawing, calligraphy, modeling in clay and wax, and even gymnastics and singing.[144] Ovchinnikov's school was awarded a silver medal at the All Russian Industrial Exhibition held in Moscow in 1882. Another firm of great repute was that of P. I. Olovianishnikov and Sons, specialists in liturgical objects and particularly inventive in their combination of several techniques, such as cloisonné enamel, engraving, and filigree.

The brightly contrasting colors of Russian enamelwork compared favorably with that of similar traditions in Europe around 1900, as seen in these two exquisite examples of plique-à-jour enamel: a vase by the Norwegian Marius Hammer (left, cat. 113) and a bowl by André Thesmar of Paris (right, cat. 221).

Fabergé's greatest rival in ecclesiastical wares was the firm of Olovianishnikov & Sons in Moscow. The chalice at right demonstrates an early modern adaptation of a classic form with carved ivory, semiprecious cabochon jewels, and medieval-style enameling (cat. 212).

The company founded by Ivan P. Khlebnikov was a regular exhibitor and prizewinner at the great exhibitions held in Vienna, Chicago, and Paris. They supplied pieces not only to Grand Dukes Konstantin Nikolaievich and Vladimir Alexandrovich but also to numerous foreign courts, including Austria, Denmark, the Netherlands, and Serbia. In his two establishments in St. Petersburg and (from 1871) Moscow, Khlebnikov attracted attention not only for his enamelwork but also for his use of the ancient and characteristically Russian technique of niello, in which a black metal mixture is fused onto silver or sometimes silver gilt (vermeil).[145]

In 1881 Khlebnikov was succeeded by his sons, Mikhail, Alexei, and Nikolai, who in 1887 took over the firm, and who received commissions from the imperial court to supply, with the goldsmith Vladimir I. Morozov, sets of coffee pots, teapots, cream jugs, and sugar bowls, as well as hundreds of teaspoons for the services in use at the Winter Palace.[146] Like Fabergé, the firm of Khlebnikov was also commissioned to supply surtouts de table and various services in gold or silver plate for weddings such as that of Grand Duchess Olga Alexandrovna, sister of Nicholas II, to Duke Peter of Oldenburg in 1901. In 1896, Khlebnikov also made the immense iconostasis in chased and enameled gilt bronze for the Cathedral of the Annunciation in the Kremlin, one of the most important churches in Russia and the private chapel of the tsars. The Khlebnikov brothers employed nearly 300 artisans and had their own school of apprentices with a roll of thirty-five, while the Ovchinnikov school counted 130 apprentices.

It is significant that in Russia, as in France, commercial businesses began to subscribe to the principle of improving the education of craftsmen in the decorative arts, as already championed by professional institutions such as the Stieglitz Museum and School in St. Petersburg and the Imperial Stroganov Central Industrial School in Moscow. The role of the Stroganov School in the comprehensive restructuring of the educational system was one of crucial importance, relying not only on the teaching of theory and an obligatory apprenticeship in drawing but also on mandatory practical

A bejeweled fan revealing a painted bridal scene by Fabergé was just one of the many gifts from Russian firms commemorating the marriage of Grand Duchess Olga Alexandrovich to Duke Peter of Oldenburg in 1901 (cat. 57).

Fig. 75. View of a room in Princess Maria Tenisheva's artist colony Talashkino around 1900, which was inspired by folk art and celebrated native Russian craftsmanship and traditions.

training courses in a range of different techniques.[147] These advances were advocated at levels as illustrious as learned societies such as the Imperial Society for the Encouragement of the Arts, which founded a school of technical drawing, the Russian Industrial Art Society or Society for the Rebirth of Artistic Russia. By 1917, more than 100 of these technical and craft schools had been set up with 140 other institutions offering courses in this field.[148]

The role of private patrons and collectors in this movement, such as Savva Mamontov, Princess Tenisheva, and Peter Shchukin, should not be overlooked.[149] Mamontov maintained an artists' colony on his estate at Abramtsevo, near Moscow. Meanwhile, at Talashkino, near Smolensk, Princess Tenisheva assembled an important collection of folk art that was to inspire Elena Polenova in the creation of her distinctively Russian objects and furniture for the Russian display at the 1900 Exposition Universelle. And in Moscow Peter Shchukin, brother of Sergei, the visionary collector of Matisse and Picasso, created an encyclopedic decorative arts collection for teaching purposes, including an important Russian section that set out to emphasize the special contribution of Russian artists in this area. Against the backdrop of the nationalistic political climate of the time, manifested in the artistic sphere by prizes and exhibitions designed to stimulate creativity and competition, it is no coincidence that institutions, commercial businesses, and private individuals such as these should have chosen to favor a style that was specifically Russian.

Moscow and St. Petersburg

A distinction in stylistic terms has long been made between Moscow and St. Petersburg. The capital of the empire, St. Petersburg, largely open to Western influences since its foundation, is often viewed as the more European in spirit and style of the two cities, while Moscow, more deeply attached to its Russian roots, encouraged the Russian style virtually to the exclusion of all others. The Byzantine revival in architectural design that emerged in Moscow during the reign of Nicholas I reinforced this

Fig. 76. View of the great towers at
the Kremlin gate in Moscow, c. 1890.

Made of rare, large pieces of rhodonite from the Ural mountains, this
clock, which was likely from Fabergé's
Moscow shop, depicts the great tower clock at the gate of the Kremlin
surmounted by the imperial double-
headed eagle (cat. 68).

idea. Architect Konstantin Ton's Grand Kremlin Palace (1838–49), Cathedral of Christ the Redeemer (1839–89), and Armory Palace (1838–49) all look back to the Byzantine roots of Moscow. Their colorful exteriors and elaborate traditional interiors encouraged the first decorative art objects in this style.

Traditional Russian architecture then became a subject of study culminating in the grand public buildings built during the last years of the nineteenth century: the Historical Museum by Vladimir Sherwood (1883); the Moscow City Duma by Dmitri Chichagov (1892); and the Upper Trading Row, known today as the GUM department store, by Alexander Pomerantsev (1893). From 1900 there also appeared a style known as "neo-Russian," which was, in fact, a specifically Russian interpretation of Art Nouveau steeped in historical references and folk art traditions.

In the realm of decorative arts, the differing sensibilities of Moscow and St. Petersburg are apparent in the work of goldsmiths such as Ovchinnikov and Khlebnikov. Their works resonated with the characteristics of each particular locale. Similarly, the Fabergé workshops in Moscow produced objects principally in the Russian style, while those in St. Petersburg devoted themselves equally single-mindedly to "European" items in styles such as Louis XVI and Renaissance. This distinction did not just reflect taste and fashion. It was the result of the methodical division of labor between the various workshops, creating groups of specialized workers led by specific talented workmasters from each region. The Moscow workshops also benefited from new levels of technical specialization that had emerged in the wake of the transformation of the educational system promulgated by the Stroganov School among others. This trend was especially true at a time when taste was so inextricably linked with politics.

Tsar Alexander III's role as a patron of Russian art was key to the flowering of this national pride in Russian art and decoration. While still heir to the throne, Alexander had displayed a manifest attraction to Russian art, acquiring Russian works from the collection of Vassili Kokorev[150] along with paintings by European artists.[151] Significantly, at his coronation he chose to wear short and voluminous "Russian-style" trousers. He subsequently embarked on a massive campaign of art acquisition and patronage. This development of the imperial collection was carried out through the intermediary of the Ministry of the Imperial Court and the Academy of Arts under the directorship of the tsar's younger brother Grand Duke Vladimir Alexandrovich, whose funds were tripled. This imperial patronage was later to culminate posthumously in the creation of the Russian Museum in St. Petersburg, which opened its doors in 1895, after Alexander's death. Even Grand Duke Vladimir had his St. Petersburg palace redecorated in the Russian style by the architects Ippolit Monighetti and Alexander Rezanov.[152]

The design chosen by the tsar for the St. Petersburg sanctuary built over the spot where his father, Alexander II, was assassinated, the Cathedral of the Savior on Spilt Blood, could hardly have

Tsar Nicholas II presented this silver kovsh by Fabergé, decorated with bogatyrs (the medieval Russian folk heroes who protected their native land from foreign invaders), to the officers of the French battleship *Vérité*, where he had dined during a visit to Russia by the French president in 1908 (cat. 67).

Fig. 77. Throughout his reign, Nicholas II promoted native Russian culture, design, and decoration. Here the tsar is seen with his tsarina at the great costume ball held at the Winter Palace in 1903, to which the guests wore traditional seventeenth-century Russian costume.

Fabergé answered the call for Russian-styled objects by emphasizing native materials in the products he made, such as in this sleek letter opener incorporating a Russian black bear claw (cat. 71).

been more Russian, inspired as it was by St. Basil's Cathedral on Moscow's Red Square.[153] The Russification of the empire was a political necessity, pursued on many fronts in an attempt to convince the people of the empire that they shared a common culture, although in reality this was far from the case.

Under the reign of Nicholas II, the Russian state and to a degree the imperial family were to pursue this nationalistic tendency. Consequently, many of the diplomatic gifts commissioned by the Imperial Cabinet were chosen in order to show off either Russian materials or the Russian style. After having been shown in the Russian jewelry section of the Paris 1900 Exposition Universelle, a large map of France executed in hardstone mosaic from the imperial factory at Ekaterinburg was presented by Nicholas II to the French president Émile Loubet.[154] Each French regional department is represented in a different stone, and the seas, rivers, and lakes are depicted in platinum with major cities picked out in precious stones. Paris was marked by a ruby-colored "siberite."[155]

When the French president Armand Fallières went to visit the tsar at Revel, now Tallinn (capital of Estonia), Nicholas II presented the officers of the battleship *Vérité*, on which he was invited to dine, a monumental kovsh created in the Moscow workshops of Fabergé.[156] The decoration depicts *bogatyrs*, heroes of traditional Russian epic poems, sailing in a small vessel, recalling the legendary Russian heroes painted by Viktor Vasnetsov, the champion of a highly national style of painting.

The two most glittering manifestations of Russia's return to its roots during the reign of Nicholas II were undoubtedly the great Russian costume ball held at the Winter Palace in 1903, to which all the guests wore costumes inspired by seventeenth-century Muscovite dress, and the tercentenary celebrations of the Romanov dynasty ten years later, with its remarkable neo-Russian Kremlin in miniature, built across the park from the Alexander Palace at Tsarskoe Selo. Photographs of the ball of 1903 are revealing.[157] The ladies' costumes in particular are embroidered with thousands of freshwater pearls, characteristic of Russian women's jewelry, or with precious stones of striking proportions. Most of the members of the imperial family are there, posing with pride and clearly more concerned about their appearance than the alarming realities of the empire.

Russian Jewelry

The lavishness with which Russian society, led by the imperial family, patronized the great jewelry houses of Europe is well known, but Russian jewelers were also competitive. Fabergé was the first to apply the same care to his jewelry creations that he applied to his objets d'art, insisting on designs of the highest quality and encouraging his master craftsmen to employ talented artists such as Alma Pihl, niece of the head of the Fabergé jewelry workshop, and Albert Holmström, whose designs were of unparalleled charm.

The quality and size of the stones were often equally remarkable, doubtless because clients tended to be susceptible to these features. Fabergé, like counterparts in Europe and America, seemed to derive a particular pleasure from setting stones of native origin, such as Siberian aquamarines and amethysts, creating jewels that combined an elegant design with the finest Russian stones. The jewels created by Fabergé remained relatively classic in style, featuring many contemporary reinterpretations of traditional ornaments and forms such as the *kokoshnik* (tiara in a traditional Russian shape), no doubt because Russian society remained fairly conventional, and court life was still highly formal. The same is true of the creations of Fabergé's competitors in the Russian market.

The House of Fabergé was not the only supplier of jewelry to the imperial family and the court; indeed, his rivals were numerous. In 1889 the number of jewelers and goldsmiths established in St. Petersburg was estimated at fifty-two firms and workshops, with a workforce of nearly 2,500 making jewelry to the colossal value of 2.8 million rubles annually.[158] Within just four years, in 1893, the production of gold and silver objects had more than doubled, to reach a value of 7 million rubles, with foreign exports amounting by comparison to a mere 809,000 rubles.[159] At the Pan-Russian exhibition in Moscow in 1882, the jeweler Bolin had attracted attention with a pearl and diadem tiara valued at 120,000 rubles, which was bought by Alexander III's brother Grand Duke Vladimir Alexandrovich.

The firm of Bolin, Swedish in origin like many of the other goldsmiths in St. Petersburg, was one of Fabergé's most serious competitors in the field of jewelry. Supplier to the court since 1839 and successor to the court jeweler Roempler, who had himself succeeded Gottlieb Jahn, Bolin maintained premises at 10 Bolshaia Morskaia. Critics at the Great Exhibition of 1851 held at the Crystal Palace in London were greatly impressed by Bolin's creations, finding them superior even to the work of the great French jeweler Lemonnier, supplier to Empress Eugénie.[160]

In 1852, Henrik Conrad Bolin opened a shop

in Moscow, where he concentrated on gold and silver wares and luxury accessories. At the time Moscow was a rapidly expanding market as a result of the early effects of the Industrial Revolution. The site he chose was not far from the spot where Fabergé was to open a Moscow branch in 1888. In St. Petersburg, Henrik Bolin's brother, Carl Edward, presided over the family business with such success that he was sometimes able to buy the wares of other jewelers, particularly Finnish-born Alexander Tillander, and sell them under his own name.[161] Bolin's specialty was ceremonial jewelry with large stones mounted in unusually light settings, which explains why Tsar Alexander II turned to Bolin for the ruby and diamond parure that he gave to Grand Duchess Maria Alexandrovna on her marriage in 1874 to Alfred, Duke of Edinburgh, Queen Victoria's second son.[162] After this date the name Bolin appears regularly in the accounts of the Imperial Cabinet beside commissions for parures and tiaras for the imperial family or the treasury. In 1888 a turquoise and diamond parure was commissioned from Bolin for the imperial crown jewels, consisting of a tiara and a brooch valued at 27,315 and 15,229 rubles, respectively.[163]

One way to combat the long, cold Russian winters was to attend the many court balls and state dinners. Fabergé provided exquisite diamond winter scenes and snowflakes to brighten the frigid nights (above left, cat. 90).

Fabergé's reputation for using extraordinary Siberian gemstones, such as these amethyst (far left, cat. 32), star sapphire (far bottom left, cat. 31), aquamarine (bottom left, cat. 29), and pink mecca brooches (far right, cat. 30), was not unlike that of Tiffany & Co., which used Montana sapphires and other American stones to achieve the same effect.

Alma Pihl, daughter of one of Fabergé's workmasters, allegedly designed a series of winter pieces, including the rock crystal pendant at top right, when she noticed frost on her workshop window (cat. 55).

While some commissions from jewelers such as Bolin were intended as additions to the crown jewels, others were destined to form or enrich the private collections of members of the imperial family. A document of particular interest in this regard is the inventory of jewels belonging to Grand Duchess Xenia, sister of Nicholas II, which lists the 426 items of jewelry she received between 1894 and 1912, accompanied in most cases by a watercolor illustration and the name of the donor.[164] On her marriage to her cousin Grand Duke Alexander Mikhailovich at Peterhof in 1894 (less than three months before the death of Alexander III), Xenia's parents gave her an impressive collection of jewels comprising the four parures deemed imperative by the highest expectations of society at this period—in diamonds, rubies, emeralds, and sapphires—not to mention endless ropes of indispensable pearls. Bolin supplied the diamond parure, consisting of two tiaras, one a traditional kokoshnik shape, a two-row necklace (*rivière*), and a brooch with pendants. Bolin also made the ruby and diamond parure, including a tiara with flowerets, a matching necklace, and a large brooch.

The invoices preserved in the Russian archives mention not only the prices of certain pieces but also the separate costs of the stones and the labor.

Fig. 78. Grand Duchess Xenia wore her wedding jewels to the 1903 costume ball at the Winter Palace in St. Petersburg.

The long necklace, or sautoir, at left by Fabergé features cabochon gemstones in a more modern version of the ropes of pearls popularized in the Edwardian era (cat. 88).

Right: A Russian enameled and bejeweled butterfly brooch for day wear (left, cat. 311) closely compares to one by a French maker of the same period (right, cat. 310).

The ruby tiara, for example, was priced at 42,100 rubles (2,570 for the labor and the box), and the necklace at 42,000 rubles (2,511 were for the labor and box). Another piece supplied by Bolin was the sumptuous five-row pearl necklace at a price of no less than 126,400 rubles (the diamond catch with a single large pearl accounted for 4,000), a reminder that at that time pearls were at least as highly prized, and as expensive, as diamonds.

Although Grand Duke Alexander Mikhailovich, Grand Duchess Xenia's husband, asserted in his memoirs that "all the jewels were by Bolin, the finest goldsmith in St. Petersburg,"[165] the archives reveal an interesting detail. Ever anxious to avoid favoring one jeweler at the expense of all others, the tsar gave the commission for Xenia's emerald parure to another St. Petersburg jeweler, Nicholls & Ewing, probably to avoid concentrating all the imperial commissions in the hands of Bolin.[166] This parure consisted of a large tiara with pear-shaped cabochon emeralds, a necklace of extremely large cabochon emeralds, and a large brooch with pendant.[167] The identity of the creator of the parure of cabochon sapphires in a style similar to Bolin's, delivered to the grand duchess in April of the following year, is unknown. The inventory also mentions a very large bodice ornament in diamonds and rubies with pearl pendants, a gift from the grand duchess's future husband, as well as other more modest jewels given by her future brothers-in-law, by "Nicky and Alix" (a diamond star), and by "Uncle Bertie and Aunt Alix," the Prince and Princess of Wales (a tortoiseshell comb with diamond wings). Even if Bolin adopted the Art Nouveau for part of his production in the years after 1900, these imperial commissions retained a conventionally classic style reminiscent of the work of French jewelers such as Boucheron, Chaumet, and Cartier.

The scale of the wedding commissions for Grand Duchess Xenia is an indication of the economic impact of these events. Since the reign of Nicholas I the custom had been for the tsar to give each grand duchess (his daughters and granddaughters) a dowry of a million rubles on her marriage. No ruler was more aware than Alexander III of the potential effects of these commissions on the health of the Russian economy and employment and therefore of the obligation to award them to Russian

suppliers rather than to foreign firms. Nicholas II was to follow his father's example. But the biggest client in the empire was not strictly speaking the imperial family, but rather the Imperial Cabinet, which was in charge of all official and personal expenditure and above all the gifts and honors dispensed by the tsar and tsarina.

Aquamarines and white enamel were especially suited for use in the winter, as in this elegant fur clasp by the House of Fabergé from around 1900 (cat. 41).

The Imperial Cabinet

Introduced during the reign of Peter the Great and reorganized initially under Nicholas I in 1827 then again under Alexander III in 1884 and 1893, the Imperial Cabinet was the most important body of the Ministry of the Imperial Court and an essential mechanism in the functioning of the court. Within its purview fell the responsibility for and administration of the crown jewels and insignia, the payment of purchases made by the tsar and tsarina, the appointment of purveyors to the court, and the bestowing of court ranks and titles. The Imperial Cabinet therefore controlled the presentation of gifts and awards by the Russian sovereigns both at home and abroad.[168]

At the court of Louis XIV in France, the distribution of offices was designed to bind a hitherto rebellious aristocracy to the service of the king not only by requiring their constant presence at Versailles but also by making the distribution of pensions conditional upon this service and a direct reward for it. Similarly, the distribution of awards by the Russian tsars was intended to "create bonds of loyalty between the ruler and those who served in his name as well as to promote efficiency and zeal in carrying out official duties. Gifts and honors were compensation for service, both political and administrative, rendered to the State and thus indirectly to the emperor." The process of rewarding thus became in itself "an important instrument of ruling."[169]

The distribution of awards was linked to the existence of the Table of Ranks established by Peter the Great in 1722, which formed the fundamental code underlying a system that was both extremely

Fig. 79. One of the first tasks of the new revolutionary government was to inventory all the jewels and regalia of the former tsarist regime illustrated in this photograph from 1922.

complex and highly organized. The table laid down fourteen ranks or grades that established a pre-ordained path for promotion within state service, whether in the military, the navy, the civil service, or the court, with explicit rules governing advancement from one rank to the next, generally seniority of service in addition to personal qualities meriting promotion. Although no female offices appeared in the Table of Ranks, ladies who held positions at court—grand mistress and mistress of the court, ladies of honor, maids of honor of the bedchamber, and maids of honor—observed a strict order of precedence and were rewarded with jewels, official insignia, and gifts.

For the sovereign, court offices also offered the opportunity to single out individuals by conferring on them a post that did not require any active service. This explains the large number of appointees sometimes filling the same office: in 1914, for example, there were 135 masters of the court, with a mere 33 in active service; 45 masters of ceremonies of whom 17 were active; and no fewer than 386 chamberlains.[170] To further complicate the system, the bestowing of titles and decorations functioned in parallel with the Table of Ranks. Thus, advancement up the Table of Ranks sometimes brought automatic ennoblement, as might the bestowing of a particular decoration; the bestowing of a decoration, meanwhile, could also trigger promotion through the ranks, each order being further subdivided into fourth, third, second, and first class, with diamonds.

The Table of Ranks was originally intended to turn the Russian regime into a meritocracy in which every subject would have the opportunity of entering the service of the state and forging a career without the advantage of noble birth (Peter the Great being as wary of the boyars [Russian nobility] of Moscow as Louis XIV was of the aristocrats of Paris). But after two centuries the system had become institutionalized; while it still functioned according to the same principles, it sometimes also revealed its shortcomings. Promotion was generally accompanied by the bestowal of pensions, decorations, and in particular, gifts. Valuable tokens frequently served as a significant supplement to the recipient's income, since they could discreetly be returned to the cabinet in exchange for their value in cash.

Every year, accordingly, the Imperial Cabinet was required to commission gifts from Russian jewelers and goldsmiths in impressive quantities and considerable variety, according to the ranks of the individuals for whom they were intended, including portrait medallions (miniature portraits of the sovereign or sovereigns bordered with diamonds, one of the most distinguished gifts of all), insignia, cigarette cases, watches, jewels, rings, cufflinks, objets d'art, and more. This system contributed greatly to the employment and development of court purveyors.[171] The gifts were stored by the Imperial Cabinet before being distributed to members of the imperial family, court, clergy, diplomatic corps, and anyone else designated for an award. Under Alexander III, the value of this stock of gifts was estimated at 10 million rubles, excluding the regular purchases required to top up stocks.[172]

One of the lists preserved in the archives mentions among other gifts 15 portrait medallions,[173] 22 insignia of the Order of St. Andrew with diamonds, 188 insignia for maids of honor, 133 pectoral crosses, 228 snuffboxes, 538 cigarette cases, and 3,477 watches embellished with the imperial coat of arms (for a value of 277,472 rubles).[174] The register of rewards distributed during the reign of Nicholas II reveals that over eighteen years these gifts amounted to a value of 8,325,746 rubles, with spending peaking at 867,758 rubles in the coronation year of 1896, and 774,687 rubles in 1913, the year of the Romanov Tercentenary.[175] Although it is difficult to give precise equivalents of the value of these imperial awards and purchases, a rough approximation is nonetheless instructive. The price of one of the tiaras given to Grand Duchess Xenia as a wedding gift, for instance, was equivalent to two years of a ministerial salary (18,000–20,000 rubles); a nephrite snuffbox bearing a portrait of the tsar or diamond monogram was equal approximately to the annual rent on a seven-room apartment on Bolshaia Morskaia in the heart of St. Petersburg (2,000 rubles); and a gold watch embellished with the imperial eagle was roughly the same as the annual salary of an unskilled worker in the Winter Palace workshops (180 rubles).[176]

The Firm of Pavel Buhre, which specialized in jeweled watches, such as this one bearing the imperial double-headed eagle, was one of the many Russian firms providing diplomatic gifts and chivalric decorations for the Imperial Cabinet (cat. 11).

The firms who supplied these goods to the Imperial Cabinet were numerous, and each had its own specialty.[177] Their activities were sometimes influenced by government legislation. In 1881, for example, in order to protect Russian production, Alexander III imposed a supplementary tax on watches imported from abroad, while the regulations brought into effect in May 1890 regarding the wearing of orders, medals, and other decorations among the ranks of the bourgeoisie prompted an increase in the commissions jewelers received. Another significant figure was the taxes raised annually on the gold and silver worked throughout the empire and assayed by the state, which rose almost tenfold between 1880 and 1894. Furthermore, it should be noted that the introduction of the gold standard in 1885, which established paper money as a stable form of saving, also had repercussions on the artistic quality of jewelers' work, as modest savers ceased viewing small items of jewelry as a form of safe investment.[178]

Many of the items furnished by the Imperial Cabinet belonged to the eclectic style of the late nineteenth century, such as the presentation boxes bearing the imperial cipher or portrait in gold, enamel, and precious stones. These gifts also included pieces in characteristically Russian materials such as nephrite or in the Russian style, as discussed above, most notably as applied to traditional Russian items such as the kovsh and the bratina. The kovsh, which formed part of the Russian goldsmith's repertoire from the fourteenth century, was a boat-shaped drinking vessel derived from the traditional Russian wooden vessel with a long or short handle. Always a prized gift or award, the kovsh became a specific symbol of traditional Russian culture and pre–St. Petersburg art. It was in the same spirit of nationalism that the bratina, a word derived from брат (brother), came into vogue in the nineteenth century. A gold or silver loving cup passed from guest to guest when toasts were drunk and, like the kovsh, a symbol of fraternity, the bratina also rose to prominence as a diplomatic gift. Many examples were thus exchanged in diplomatic circles around 1900. A list dated 23 May 1908 and preserved in the State Russian Historical Archive in St. Petersburg details the gifts commissioned for this visit.[179] The bratina *ladia* (boat) for the officers' wardroom on board the *Vérité* appeared on an invoice for a total of 12,725 rubles, dated 6 November 1908 and addressed to the Imperial Cabinet by Fabergé.[180] The organization of Fabergé's Moscow workshops, opened in 1887, does not identify the makers of particular pieces, unlike in St. Petersburg. In Moscow, as Franz Birbaum has observed, Fabergé concentrated on the creation of objects that derived inspiration for their form and decoration from traditional Russian art, such as the bratina in the Musée de la Marine: "In most cases these were bratini, carafes, kovshi, caskets, decorative vases, etc., heroic figures, tales and poems from folklore and historic events or characters inspired their decoration, in the form of groups of figurines or bas reliefs. These pieces were made working from wax models and were unique."[181] The *Vérité* bratina, with a gilded interior, is decorated with stylized scrolls that, although borrowed from the vernacular ornamental vocabulary, evoke above all the spirals of the modern style, the Russian Art Nouveau.

As these commissions by the Imperial Cabinet demonstrate, Russian artistic luxury at this period belonged to the international eclectic style, often historicist and open to Western influences, while at the same time remaining imbued to some extent with the strong Russian national tradition. The work of Mikhail A. Vrubel, who was close to the Abramtsevo circle of artists interested in reviving Russian tradition, offers a fine example of this Russian-inspired work. In addition to painting, sculpting in majolica, and designing costumes for the operas of Rimsky-Korsakov, Vrubel also designed stained glass and jewelry, as shown by two designs for hair combs published in *Mir Iskusstva* in 1899.[182] One of these, conceived with the naturalistic verve to be found in Lalique's

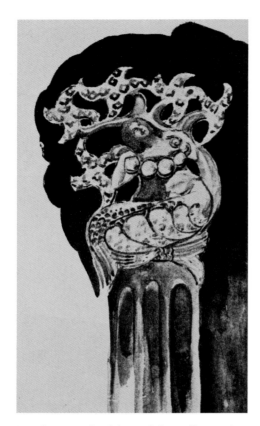
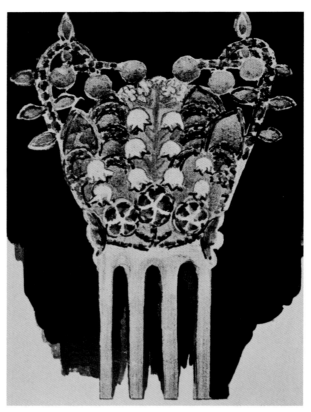

jewelry, mingles lilies of the valley with more stylized flowers in the Russian tradition, as found in the most innovative creations of the late nineteenth century. The other hair comb, a similar reflection of the Russian modern style, is decorated with a female figure, a Symbolist resurgence of the birds of paradise Sirine and Alkonost adapted from folk art and from a current of Russian Art Nouveau. Both expressions of a specifically Russian aesthetic, these two pieces are fine examples of the quality that constitutes the interest, the charm, and the beauty of Russian art at the turn of the century: a "melange of Art Nouveau, Slav renaissance, and symbolism."[183]

Fig. 80. Russian designer Mikhail Vrubel published these studies for jeweled and enameled combs in an issue of the art journal *Mir Iskusstva* of 1899.

Even the Symbolist imagery in the Art Nouveau work of Fedor Lorié took on a Russian tone in this depiction of a Russian chimera, or bird of paradise (cat. 200).

1. Louis Réau, "L'Art Français en Russie," *La Grande Revue* (10 November 1909): 170.

2. As quoted in Anne Kratz, *Le Commerce Franco-Russe: Concurrence & Contrefaçons* (Paris: Les Belles Lettres, 2006), 337.

3. The whereabouts of these jewels are unknown. Léon Plarr, *La France à Moscou: Exposition de 1891* (Paris: De Soye et Fils, 1891), 221–22; *Journal de l'Exposition Française à Moscou en 1891*, no. 5 (26 May 1891): 4.

4. Notably as a client of Boucheron and Cartier.

5. Ten percent of the proceeds was passed to the Red Cross by the Crédit Lyonnais in St. Petersburg; see Madame Pégard (chief representative of the exhibition), *Comité Français des Expositions à l'Étranger, Exposition Franco-Russe de Saint-Pétersbourg, sous le Haut Patronage de S. A. I. le Grand-Duc Constantin, Section Française, Rapport* (Paris, 1900), 31.

6. Ibid., 6.

7. Ibid., 28.

8. Ibid., 40.

9. See G. Prokhorenko and G. Vlasova, *Baron Stieglitz Museum, The Past and the Present* (St. Petersburg: Sezar, 1994).

10. These collections were housed in an imposing building started by R. A. Hedike and A. I. Krakau in partnership with the architect M. Messmacher, who subsequently took sole charge of the project. Led by Polovtsov's son Alexander, his daughter, Princess A. A. Obolenskaia, and son-in-law Count A. A. Bobrinsky, these acquisitions continued until the Revolution.

11. Such as Prince Gagarin, Prince Trubetskoy, Prince Lobanov-Rostovsky, Count Bobrinsky, and the art critics Stasov and Botkin.

12. Such as Davis, Seligmann, and A. Beurdeley fils.

13. Including, for example, the Swedish cabinetmaker Haupt's replica of the great mineralogy cabinet of the Prince de Condé at Chantilly.

14. Purchased for 640 francs. Arkhiv Gosudartvennog Ermitaja (АГЭ), St. Petersburg (State Hermitage Archive), fund I, file 9, act 1, p. 22.

15. Purchased for 1,550 francs. Ibid.

16. The Bapst & Falize works included an enameled gold plaque to the value of 12,000 francs (1890) (ibid.) and an unidentified piece at 6,000 francs (1892) (ibid., 28).

17. Inv. PH 378 and Э 17578.

18. Purchased with five other objects in 1902 for the sum of 4,500 francs; State Hermitage Museum, inv. Э 15364.

19. Sigrid Barten, *René Lalique Schmuck und Objets d'Art 1890–1910* (Munich: Prestel, 1989), 392, no. 947.1.

20. Yvonne Brunhammer, ed., *René Lalique: Bijoux d'Exception 1890–1912*, exh. cat. (Paris: Musée du Luxembourg, 2007), 92, no. 105.

21. АГЭ, fund I, file 9, act 1, p. 35.

22. Inv. K 1372 and K 3357.

23. The collections of the Stieglitz Museum were sent to the Hermitage beginning in 1923.

24. The Oldenburgs were regular clients of the jeweler Boucheron.

25. As in 1899, ten percent of the proceeds was donated to the Red Cross.

26. Martial Bernard, *Exposition Internationale Artistique de Saint-Pétersbourg 1901–1902, Section Française, Rapport* (Paris: Georges Petit, 1902), 34.

27. Philippe Thiébaut, "Le Style Moderne Russe et l'Art Nouveau Européen," in *L'Art Russe dans la Seconde Moitié du XIXe Siècle: en Quête d'Identité* (Paris: Musée d'Orsay, 2005), 332.

28. *Mir Iskusstva* 1, nos. 1–12 (1899).

29. The artists most discussed included Bakst, Benois, I. Bilibin, Dobuzhinsky, Lanceray, Maliavin, Repin, and Somov, among others.

30. Nicholas II, *Journal intime* (Paris: Payot, 1925), 69 (27 June 1894): "After lunch Alix came to my apartments and together we looked at the jewels of one of the four jewelers who had sent me their cards."

31. Ibid., 76: "Two jewelers showed me all their jewelry in my room. I bought one item from each of them."

32. If the difference between the Julian and Gregorian calendars is taken into account, this date corresponds within a day to the date Nicholas II mentioned.

33. Bernard Morel, *Les joyaux de la couronne de France* (Paris: Albin Michel, 1988), 344, 348 (ill.).

34. The fate of this piece after the Revolution is problematic. It was not included in the jewels transferred to Moscow at the outbreak of war and recorded by Fersman (A. E. Fersman, *Les Joyaux du trésor de Russie* [Moscow: Commissariat National des Finances, 1924–26]), nor did it appear at the sale of many of the Russian crown jewels organized by the Soviet authorities at Christie's London on 16 March 1927. As an item of personal jewelry, it was possibly among the jewels and precious objects the imperial family took with them into exile in Siberia. See William Clarke, *The Lost Fortune of the Tsars* (New York: St. Martin's Press, 1994), 72, 153.

35. Collection of the Kremlin Museums, reproduced in Tatiana N. Muntian and Irina A. Rodimtseva, *Fabergé Velikie Iuveliry Rossi/The World of Fabergé* (Moscow: Red Square, 2000), 15.

36. Gossudartsvenny Arkhiv Rossiskoï Federatsii (ГАРФ), Moscow (State Archive of the Russian Federation); see reproduction in ibid., 22.

37. Ibid.; see reproduction in *Nicholas & Alexandra, the Last Imperial Family of Tsarist Russia* (New York: Broughton International, 1998), no. 518.

38. Archives Boucheron, Paris, MC 28, fol. 260. The fate of this sautoir remains unknown.

39. A sum approximately equivalent to 131,330 euros, or about $200,000 (March 2008).

40. Her total expenditure amounted to 37,027 francs.

41. Hans Nadelhoffer, *Cartier* (Paris: Edition de Regard, 1984), 116.

42. Inv. ЭРО 4745.

43. Diana Scarisbrick, *Chaumet* (Paris: Alain de Gourcuff Editeur, 1995), 60–62.

44. Ibid., 62–68, illus. pp. 173, 175, 201.

45. The Altai is a mountain range in central Asia between western Siberia and northwestern Mongolia.

46. Tamara Rappe, "Pamiatniki russko-frantsuskikh sviazeï poslednogo desiatiletnya XIX veka," *State Hermitage Journal* (St. Petersburg) (1991), 21–24; State Hermitage Museum, inv. Э–3867.

47. Ibid., 20–21; State Hermitage Museum, inv. Э–13529–13612. All the drawings in this book are reproduced in *Orchidées lorraines* (St. Petersburg: State Hermitage Museum, 1999).

48. State Hermitage Museum, inv. Э–13577, illustrated in ibid., 150. No examples of this bowl have been found.

49. State Hermitage Museum, inv. Э–13548, ibid., 134. Examples of this goblet are preserved in various collections: Musée d'Orsay, Paris, inv. OAO 964; Musée des Beaux-Arts, Nancy, inv. 95. 1. 27; Musée Historique de Moscou; Palace-Museum of Tsarskoe Selo.

50. State Hermitage Museum, inv. Э–23413–23414.

51. See *Fabergé–Cartier, Rivalen am Zarenhof* (Munich: Hirmer, 2003), 436, no. 957.

52. The cross is reproduced in *L'Illustration* 1 (24 May 1902): 376; the drawing in Barten, *René Lalique*, no. 839.

53. The vases were reproduced in *L'Illustration* 1 (24 May 1902): 376.

54. Philippe Deschamps, *Le Président de la République française en Russie, 15–27 May 1902* (Paris: A. Lemerre, 1902), 67.

55. *L'Illustration* 1 (24 May 1902).

56. One of these vases, *Passiflora*, is now in the State Hermitage Museum (inv. ФБ-1633). The whereabouts of the others are unknown.

57. *Le Figaro*, 29 July 1908; *L'Illustration*, no. 3415 (8 August 1908): 87–88. The whereabouts of the Falize vases are currently unknown.

58. See the period photograph reproduced in V. Nesin, *The Imperial Winter Palace during the Reign of the Last Emperor (1894–1917)* (St. Petersburg: Neva, 1999), 144; E. A. Anissimova, "Vazy raboty Emilia Gallé is litchnikh pokoev Nikolaïa I Alexandry Feodorovny v Zminem Dvortse Sudby muzeïnikh kollektsiy," *Materialy* 7, Tsarskoselskoï naoutchnoï konferentsii—Gosudartsvenni muzeï zapovednik Tsarskoïe Selo (St. Petersburg, 2001), 202–8.

59. Nicholas II, *Dnievnik* (Moscow: Orbita, 1991), 49.

60. Nicholas II, *Journal intime* (Paris: Payot, 1925), 75 (5 July 1894).

61. Nicholas II, *Dnievnik*, 173.

62. АГЭ, fund I, file 8 (Г), act 7 (1909).

63. АГЭ, fund I, file 8 (Г), act 7, p. 40, no. 147: vase signed "Emile Gallé Nancy Paris 38957." АГЭ, fund I, file 8 (Г), act 30, p. 6, no. 40: sent to Gosfond.

64. State Hermitage Museum, inv. 23409.

65. АГЭ, fund I, file 8 (Г), act 7, p. 114, no. 570. АГЭ, fund I, file 8 (Г), act 27, p. 9, no. 90 [570]; whereabouts unknown.

66. АГЭ, fund I, file 8 (Г), act 7, p. 7, p. 120, no. 603; vase signed "Cristallerie de Gallé à Nancy," fund I, file 8 (Г), act 27, p. 13, no. 116 [603]; sent to Gosfond, signed "Modelle e decore et deposé" [*sic*]. This piece must have been very similar to the vase from the Stieglitz Museum now preserved in the State Hermitage Museum (inv. K 1434).

67. АГЭ, fund I, file 8 (Г), act 7, p. 61, no. 251. АГЭ, fund I, file 8 (Г), act 30, p. 15, no. 103; sent to Gosfond.

68. АГЭ, fund I, file 8 (Г), act 7, p. 116, no. 581; АГЭ, fund I, file 8 (Г), act 27, p. 11, no. 99 [581]; sent to Gosfond.

69. АГЭ, fund I, file 8 (Г), act 7, p. 123, no. 618; АГЭ, fund I, file 8 (Г), act 27, p. 14, no. 128 [618].

70. Ibid.

71. The original provenance of this piece remains unknown.

72. Wilfried Zeisler, "Frantsuskii Art Nouveau v Rossii i imperatorskie pokupki izdielii firmy Keller," in *Na rubeje vekov … Iskusstvo epokhi moderna* (St. Petersburg: State Hermitage Museum, 2006), 137–43.

73. V. V. Skurlov and A. N. Ivanov, *Postavchiki visotchaïtchevo dvora* (St. Petersburg, 2002), 20. Gustave Keller received this honor in 1900, when he was described as a porcelain manufacturer, probably as the result of a confusion with the celebrated firm of Keller et Guérin.

74. Gustave Keller, *Keller Frères, 1900, Exposition Universelle, classes 94 et 98* (Paris: Keller, 1900), pls. I, II.

75. Vadim Nésin, *The Imperial Winter Palace during the Reign of the Last Emperor 1894–1917* (St. Petersburg: Lenizdat, 1999), 144–45. The photograph also shows the two Gallé vases that were a gift from the city of Paris in 1896 (State Hermitage Museum, inv. Э–23413 a–b and 23414 a–b).

76. Keller, *Keller Frères, 1900*, pls. III, IV. Each item bears the grand duke's monogram and a crowned anchor, symbol of his position in the imperial navy.

77. The whereabouts of these pieces are currently unknown. The grand duke's taste for work by Keller is evident from the inventory of the contents of his palace, drawn up in 1909 before the sale of his collections by his heirs. The inventory mentions a number of items of gold and silverware bearing the mark "Keller Paris."

78. Victor Champier, "Les Industries d'Art à l'Exposition Universelle de 1889 et de 1900," *Revue des Arts Décoratifs* (1902): 193. The same knife is described on page 194, attributing its ownership to the tsar.

79. Keller, *Keller Frères, 1900*, pl. IV. The example belonging to the grand duke seems to have disappeared. There is no mention of it in the guide to Princess Paley's palace-museum published around 1918, either in the list of objects transferred to the Hermitage when this museum's collections were sold off the following year or in the sale of her collections held at Christie's in London in 1929.

80. Four ewers from this set have recently been acquired by French public collections in Paris: two by the Musée d'Orsay (inv. OAO 1284, h. 31.7; and OAO 1283, h. 29), one by the Musée des Arts Décoratifs (inv. 997.119.1), and the last by the Petit Palais (inv. ODUT01796). To this list should also be added an engraved crystal ewer mount in silver by Keller Frères, acquired by the Musée d'Orsay in 2005 (inv. OAO 1444, h. 33 cm).

81. *Rapport de l'Exposition Universelle de 1900, groupe XV, classe 94*, 257–58.

82. Champier, "Les Industries d'Art à l'Exposition Universelle de 1889 et de 1900," 193.

83. G. K. Loukomsky, *Les Demeures des Tsars* (Paris: Editions Nilsson, 1929); Marilyn Pfeifer Swezey, ed., *Nicholas and Alexandra/At Home with the Last Tsar and His Family/Treasures from the Alexander Palace*, exhibition organized by the American-Russian Cultural Cooperation Foundation (Washington, D.C., 2004); Larissa Bardovskaia, *Tsarskoe Selo, Residence d'été des Empereurs de Russie* (St. Petersburg: Alfa-Colour, 2005).

84. Such as the large set of gilded wood chairs in Louis XVI style, commissioned from Georges Jacob by Catherine the Great.

85. On this subject see the exhibition catalogue by V. Znamenov and N.V. Vernova, *Datsky Farfor v'Rossii* (Danish Porcelain in Russia) *1880s–1917* (St. Petersburg: Abris, 2006).

86. Galina Agarkova and Natalya Petrova, *250 Years of Lomonosov Porcelain Manufacture St. Petersburg 1774–1994* (Switzerland: Desertina, 1994), 59–61.

87. T. Malinina et al., *Imperial Glass Factory: 225th Foundation Day Anniversary, 1777–1917* (St. Petersburg: Slavia, 2004), 101–3.

88. The archives of the firm of Baccarat contain records of supplies of cut glass to Fabergé, Grachev, Kirliukov, Morozov, and Ovchinnikov.

89. Malinina, *Imperial Glass Factory*, 54–56, 92–93, 97.

90. Ibid., 107, no. 509.

91. State Hermitage Museum, inv. ЭРС 1976.

92. Malinina, *Imperial Glass Factory*, 109, 114, nos. 518–24.

93. Agarkova and Petrova, *250 Years of Lomonosov Porcelain Manufacture*, 86.

94. State Hermitage Museum, inv. ЭРС 2432; Malinina, *Imperial Glass Factory*, 106, 111, no. 503.

95. Malinina, *Imperial Glass Factory*, 106.

96. State Hermitage Museum, inv. ЭРС 2427; Malinina, *Imperial Glass Factory*, 112, no. 505.

97. Pavlovsk Palace, inv. ЦХ 9941. 1; Malinina, *Imperial Glass Factory*, 113, no. 510.

98. Agarkova and Petrova, *250 Years of Lomonosov Porcelain Manufacture*, 86–87.

99. W. A. Fedorov et al., *Imperator Alexandr III Imperatritsa Maria Feodorovna* (Moscow: Manege 2006), 188–91, nos. 444–48.

100. I. I. Khmelnitskaïa and E. S. Khmelnitskaïa, *Dom Outchenikh Im. M. Gorkovo: Dvorets Velikogo Kniazia Vladimira Alexandrovitcha* (St. Peterburg: Rossiiskaïa Akademia Nauk–Russkaïa Klassika, 2003), 72, illus. pp. 22, 25, 66.

101. Gustav Petrovich Fabergé (1814–1893), Carl Gustavovich Fabergé (1846–1920), and Agathon Gustavovich Fabergé (1862–1895).

102. G. Lukomsky, "The Historical Display of Architecture and Decorative Art," *Starye Gody* (April 1911): 46–47.

103. There is no known surviving invoice for this work.

104. A. Kenneth Snowman, *The Art of Carl Fabergé* (London: Faber & Faber, 1953).

105. Richard S. Wortman, *Scenarios of Power: Myth and Ceremony in Russian Monarchy* (Princeton, 2000), 2:280.

106. АГЭ, fund I, file 8 (Г), act 7 (1909), pp. 48–53. Transported to Moscow in May 1917, some of them were later sold abroad by the Soviet authorities. From the court inventories, one display case apparently contained the following imperial eggs: *Rosebud Egg* (1895) (Link of Times Foundation Collection, Moscow); *Coronation Egg* (1897), with its surprise of a miniature version of the imperial carriage (Link of Times Foundation Collection, Moscow); *Lilies of the Valley Egg* (1898), which cost 6,700 rubles (Link of Times Foundation Collection, Moscow); *Bouquet of Lilies Egg* (1899), 6,750 rubles (Armory Palace, Kremlin Museum, Moscow), *Trans-Siberian Railway Egg* (1900), 7,000 rubles (Armory Palace, Kremlin Museum, Moscow); *Basket of Wild Flowers Egg* (1901), 6,850 rubles (Royal Collection, England); *Clover Egg* (1902), 8,750 rubles (Armory Palace, Kremlin Museum, Moscow); *Peter the Great Egg* (1903), 9,760 rubles (Lillian Pratt Collection, Virginia Museum of Art, Richmond); and *Rose Trellis Egg* (1907) (Walters Art Museum, Baltimore). There was also an egg in rock crystal, perhaps the *Revolving Miniatures Egg*, 6,750 rubles, now in the Lillian Pratt Collection at the Virginia Museum of Art.

107. See the illustrations in *Fabergé Joaillier des Romanov* (Brussels: Espace culturel ING, 2005), 22–23.

108. Preben Ulstrup, "The House of Romanov and the House of Fabergé," in *Ruslands skate: Kejserlige gaver/Treasures of Russia: Imperial Gifts/Sokrovishcha Rossii i Imperatorskie Dary* (Copenhagen: Det Kongelige Sølvkammer, 2002), 180.

109. Marilyn Pfeifer Swezey et al., *Fabergé Flowers* (New York: Abrams, 2004).

110. Doubtless the "yellow enameled rose in a rock-crystal vase" that appears on a Fabergé bill of 1895, mentioned by Tatiana Muntian in "Kejserinde Maria Fjiodorovnas ejendele i samlingerne i Moskvas Kreml (The Kremlin Collection of the Empress's Personal Belongings)" in *Kejserinde Dagmar Maria Feodorovna: en udstilling om den danske prinsesse som blev kejserinde af Rusland* (Maria Feodorovna, Empress of Russia) (Copenhagen: Det Kongelige Sølvkammer, 1997), 328.

111. So highly regarded was this piece that is was reproduced opposite the bust of Fabergé in the famous "interview" with Fabergé published in the magazine *Stolitsa i Usadba*, in which he questioned the artistic spirit governing the creations of Tiffany, Boucheron, and Cartier; *Stolitsa i Usadba*, no. 2 (15 January 1914): 14.

112. Swezey, *Fabergé Flowers*, 108–13.

113. Muntian, "Kejserinde Maria Fjiodorovnas," 328.

114. Also known as Yekaterinburg and Sverdlovsk in the Soviet era.

115. Almost certainly the Louis XVI-style cabinets in mahogany (by A.V. Shutov), gilt bronze (by A.Y. Sokolov), and mosaic panels from the Peterhof factory, commissioned for Alexander III and Maria Feodorovna for the Anichkov Palace in St. Petersburg. Today the first two are preserved in the State Hermitage Museum and the third in the Fersman Mineralogical Museum in Moscow.

116. *World's Columbian Exhibition, 1893, Chicago: Catalog of the Russian Section* (St. Petersburg, 1893), 187, 189, 191.

117. Information kindly supplied by Valentin Skurlov.

118. Marina Lopato, "Court Jewelers," in *The Fabulous Epoch of Fabergé: St. Petersburg–Paris–Moscow* (Moscow: Nord, 1992), 41.

119. Tsarina Maria Feodorovna to Queen Alexandra, 18 December 1906, Hoover Institution, Stanford, quoted in Ulstrup, "House of Romanov and House of Fabergé," 187.

120. State Moscow Kremlin Museums, Department of Manuscripts, Graphics, Prints, and Photographs, f.20, list from 1917, arch 5.

121. Muntian, "Kejserinde Maria Fjiodorovnas," 318.

122. Only a few of these figurines are still in the Armory Palace (a rock crystal dog, piglet, and hare, a carnelian fish and fly, a citrine bulldog, and an agate monkey); Muntian and Rodimtseva, *Fabergé Velikie Iuveliry Rossii/The World of Fabergé*, 67–68.

123. Fabergé was also well known for his gold and silver items featuring elephants, notably the monumental vermeil kovsh given by Alexander III and Maria Feodorovna to the latter's parents, Christian IX and Queen Louise of Denmark, for their golden wedding anniversary on 26 May 1892, and a pair of wine coolers given by the tsar and tsarina and members of the European royal houses related by marriage to Christian IX and his wife. The three items were invoiced together by Fabergé on 15 October 1892 for a total of 10,000 rubles. Muntian, *Kejserinde Dagmar Maria Feodorovna*, 445–47.

124. Tsarina Maria Feodorovna to Queen Alexandra, 18 December 1906, Hoover Institution, Stanford, quoted in Ulstrup, "House of Romanov and House of Fabergé," 186.

125. Baron A. von Foelkersam, "Rock Crystal and Its Artistic Applications," *Starye Gody* (December 1915): 3–14; "Chalcedony and Its Artistic Applications" and "Aventurine and Its Artistic Applications," *Starye Gody* (March 1916): 3–18 and 19–23.

126. *Stolitsa i Usadba*, no. 2 (15 January 1914): 13–14.

127. Publications that gave prominence to the techniques of enamelwork included notably *Dvernosti rossiiskogo gosudartsva* (Antiquities of the Russian State), commissioned by Nicholas I from the academician Feodor Solntsev (1849–53); and a study by the historian Ivan E. Zabelin, *A Historical Review of Enamel and Precious Work in Russia* (1853).

128. Alexander von Solodkoff, *Russian Gold and Silver* (London: Trefoil Books, 1981), 62.

129. Ula Tillander-Godenhielm et al., *Golden Years of Fabergé* (New York/Paris: A La Vieille Russie/Alain de Gourcuff Editeur, 2000), 21–36.

130. See ibid., 56, 77, 83, 123, 125, 130.

131. O. McCall, "Aubrey Beardsley," *Mir Iskusstva*, no. 7–8 (1900): 74–84; J. Meyer-Graefe, "L'Art moderne français," *Mir Iskusstva*, no. 7–8 (1900): 87–100; *Mir Iskusstva*, no. 12 (1903): 255–58; A. Benois, "Arkhangelskoïe," *Mir Iskusstva*, no. 2 (1904): 31, 87–100; I. Fomine, "L'Architecture classique à Moscou à l'époque de Catherine II at Alexandre Ier," *Mir Iskusstva*, no. 7 (1904); J. Bilibine, "L'Art populaire du nord de la Russie," *Mir Iskusstva*, no. 11 (1900).

132. Anne Odom, *Russian Enamels: Kievan Rus to Fabergé* (Baltimore/ Washington, D.C./London: Walters Art Gallery/Hillwood Museum/Philip Wilson Publishers, 1996), 174.

133. Tillander-Godenhielm, *Golden Years of Fabergé*, 84.

134. АГЭ, fund I, file 8 (Г), act 7, p. 33, no. 100, "le vase représentant des poissons nageant. Les yeux des poissons en pierre taillée."

135. АГЭ, fund I, file 8 (Г), act 7, p. 43, no. 164. АГЭ, fund I, file 8 (Г), act 7, p. 59, no. 240; and "un petit vase sans couvercle genre Tiffany sur un support en argent à huit pieds" (АГЭ, fund I, file 8 (Г), act 7, p. 59, no. 238).

136. Baron A. von Foelkersam, *Inventory of the Silverware Preserved in the Furniture Storage of the Imperial Palaces, Winter Palace, Anichkov Palace, Palace of Gatchina* (St. Petersburg: Golick and A. Wilborg, 1907), 2:432, ct (page) 129, 486–89. The silver designs are now preserved in the archives of the State Hermitage Museum (АГЭ).

137. *Fabergé: Orfèvre des Tsars* (Paris: Musée des Arts Décoratifs, 1993), 410–11, illus. 329–32.

138. Ibid., 412, illus. 333–34.

139. Viatcheslav Mukhin, "The St. Petersburg Branch of the Sazikov Firm and Russian Silverware of the 19th and Early 20th Centuries," in *Fabulous Epoch of Fabergé*, 44.

140. *Report on the Moscow 1882 All-Russia Industrial Art Exhibition* (St. Petersburg, 1883), 5–6:305.

141. Mukhin, "The St. Petersburg Branch of the Sazikov Firm," 48.

142. Galina Smorodinova, "Pavel Ovchinnikov and Russian Gold- and Silversmithery," in *Fabulous Epoch of Fabergé*, 59.

143. For the best description of these communities and their philosophies, see Wendy Kaplan, *The Arts and Crafts Movement in Europe and America: Design for the Modern World, 1880–1920*, exh. cat. (Los Angeles/New York: Los Angeles County Museum of Art/Thames and Hudson, 2004).

144. Galina Smorodinova, "Gold and Silverwork in Moscow at the Turn of the Century," *Journal of Decorative and Propaganda Arts*, no. 11 (Winter 1989): 30.

145. Evgenia I. Kirichenko and Mikhail Anikst, *Russian Design and the Fine Arts, 1750–1917* (New York: Abrams, 1991), 131.

146. Foelkersam, *Inventory of Silverware*, 438ff.

147. From 1902, students wishing to obtain the diploma of applied art at the Stroganov School had to reach the required standard not only in general theory but also in practical courses in no fewer than eighteen different workshops such as engraving, enameling, and mounting. In the wake of this reform, only 4 of 1,500 students were awarded the diploma, while 53 qualified as draftsmen. Smorodinova, "Pavel Ovchinnikov and Russian Gold- and Silversmithery," 33.

148. Sergei M. Gontar, "Alexander III's Reforms in the Decorative Arts," in *Kejserinde Dagmar Maria Feodorovna*, 286.

149. See Oleg Neverov and Emmanuel Ducamp, *Great Private Collections of Imperial Russia* (London: Thames and Hudson, 2004).

150. See the remarkable study by John O. Norman, "Alexander III as a Patron of Russian Art," in *New Papers on Russian Soviet Artistic Culture*, 4th World Congress of Soviet and East European Studies, Harrogate, 1990 (New York: St. Martin's Press, 1994), 26.

151. Notably through the intermediary of the Russian painter Alexei Bogoliubov (1824–1896), drawing master to Maria Feodorovna.

152. Kirichenko and Anikst, *Russian Design and the Fine Arts*, 122–23; also Khmelnitskaïa and Khmelnitskaïa, *Dom Outchenikh Im. M. Gorkovo*, 54–57.

153. Designed by Alfred Parland, 1883–1907.

154. This map was much discussed in the popular press. Weighing nearly 350 kilograms, and measuring 1.25 by 1.25 meters, it no doubt made for an impressive, if curious, sight.

155. G. de Wailly, *A travers l'exposition de 1900* (Paris: Fayard, 1900), 5–35; *Un tsar à Compiègne Nicolas II, 1901* (Château de Compiègne, 2001), 124, no. 1.

156. Wilfried Zeisler, "Fabergé et l'Alliance franco-russe," *Revue des musées de France-Revue du Louvre*, no. 3 (2005): 39–45.

157. Rifat Gafifullin et al., *Costume Ball in the Winter Palace*, 2 vols. (Moscow: Russky Antiquariat, 2003).

158. Magdalena Ribbing et al., *Jewelry & Silver for Tsars, Queens and Others: W. A. Bolin 200 Years* (Stockholm: W. A. Bolin, 1996), 64.

159. Ibid.

160. Quoted in ibid., 42.

161. For a brief history of this firm, see Herbert Tillander, "A. Tillander Jewelers from St. Petersburg to Helsinki," in *Fabulous Epoch of Fabergé*, 28–32.

162. Ribbing, *Jewelry & Silver for Tsars, Queens and Others*, 26, 27, 41.

163. Rossisky Gosudarstvenny Istoritchesky Arkhiv (РГИА), St. Petersburg (State Russian Historical Archive), fund 468, file 7, act 248.

164. *Ruslands skate: Kejserlige gaver/Treasures of Russia: Imperial Gifts/ Sokrovishcha Rossii Imperatorskie Dary* (Copenhagen: Det Kongelige Sølvkammer, 2002), 252–64.

165. "Aller Schmuck war von Bolin, dem besten Goldarbeiter in St. Petersburg angefertigt," in Alexander of Russia, *Einst war ich ein Grossfürst* (Leipzig: Paul List Verlag, 1932), 135.

166. *Ruslands Skate*, 256–58.

167. Costing 41,417 rubles (tiara); 38,944 rubles (necklace); and 18,944 rubles (brooch with pendant), respectively.

168. Ulla Tillander-Godenhielm, *The Russian Imperial Award System During the Reign of Nicholas II 1894–1917* (Helsinki: Vammalan Kirjapaino, 2005), 145–47.

169. Ibid., 397.

170. Ibid., 17.

171. D. Iuferov, "Historique de la gérance du trésor de Russie," *Les joyaux du trésor de Russie*, Livraison no. 3 (1926): 9–25.

172. Tillander-Godenhielm, *Russian Imperial Award System*, 145–47.

173. The value of each portrait estimated at nearly 10,000 rubles.

174. Gontar, "Alexander III's Reforms in the Decorative Arts," 276.

175. We are indebted to Valentin Skurlov for his groundbreaking research into the records of the Imperial Cabinet. Cited in Tillander-Godenhielm, *Russian Imperial Award System*, 145–46.

176. Ibid., 489–90.

177. In her study, Tillander-Godenhielm lists the jewelers Carl Fabergé, C. E. Bolin, Carl Blank, Carl Hahn, Köchly, Butz, and A. Tillander; the goldsmiths I. E. Morozov, Ovtchinnikov, and Gratchev Brothers; and the clockmaker Buhre/Bouret. Ibid., 379–87.

178. Gontar, "Alexander III's Reforms in the Decorative Arts," 278.

179. РГИА, fund 468, file 43, act 963, p. 40.

180. Ibid., p. 76.

181. "Birbaum Memoirs," trans. Felicity Cave, in Géza von Habsburg, *Fabergé: Imperial Jeweler* (St. Petersburg/Washington, D.C./London: State Hermitage Museum/Fabergé Arts Foundation/in association with Thames and Hudson, 1993), 448.

182. *Mir Iskusstva*, nos. 13–24 (1899): 85.

183. *Fabergé, orfèvre à la cour des tsars* (Paris: Musée Jacquemart-André, 1987), 23.

America: A Tale of Two Tiffanys

Jeannine Falino

Visitors to the 1900 Exposition Universelle in Paris could not have missed the remarkable displays of Charles Lewis Tiffany's firm, Tiffany & Co., and beside it, the Tiffany Glass & Decorating Co. owned by his son, Louis Comfort Tiffany. For those who could not attend the fair, the many awards won by both Tiffanys, father and son, were widely reported in newspapers and magazines.[1]

Tiffany & Co. presented a blend of historical and exotic designs translated into a panoply of luxurious goods by craftsmen skilled in metalsmithing and the lapidary arts. Necklaces, tiaras, stomachers, brooches, corsage ornaments, and just about anything else that could be adorned with precious jewels beckoned the curious to look and the seriously wealthy to buy. While their display caused one zealous potentate, the shah of Persia, to appoint Tiffany & Co. Gold and Silversmiths to His Imperial Majesty,[2] thereby receiving the shah's royal warrant, one critic decried the firm's display for its emphasis on valuable and expensive stones:

> The show-cases unite the most valuable jewels, the largest diamonds, the
> rarest rubies and sapphires. The mounted pieces show the aiming at the
> most showy combinations of gold and jewels: bouquets of glittering emer-
> alds and diamonds in floral shapes, with brilliants as dewdrops. It would be
> difficult to imagine anything more brutal in the way of jewelry. Every piece has
> only one meaning: to appear as concentrated money.[3]

Tiffany & Co. became known for its stock of rare yellow diamonds, often procured by the firm's gemologist, George Frederick Kunz. This example at left is paired with emeralds in a gold filigree setting designed by Louis Comfort Tiffany and for sale by Tiffany & Co. (cat. 268).

Fig. 81. The large iris brooch at right, composed of Montana sapphires, demantoid garnets, topaz, diamonds, and gold, was sold to the American collector Henry Walters at the 1900 Paris Exposition Universelle for $3,500.

Fig. 82. This close-up view of Tiffany & Co.'s jewelry display at the 1900 Paris exposition shows the iris brooch at slightly left of center.

This same reviewer went on to liken Tiffany's customers to savages from faraway islands who wear coins strung around their necks, a sure sign that the mood of the critics was sharp and unwavering in their support for new trends in artistic jewelry prevalent elsewhere in the fair.

Louis Comfort Tiffany's firm, the Tiffany Glass & Decorating Co., strategically placed next to the booth of his father's Tiffany & Co., exhibited works of a more experimental and avant-garde nature, grounded in the close study of nature and embracing unorthodox materials and techniques. Louis Tiffany's experiments in the aesthetic possibilities of glass had already led to an international renewal of interest in the artistic possibilities of this medium. Besides the blown glass he named Favrile, which was used in stained glass, lamps, and vessels of all shapes and sizes, his company offered ceramic vessels, bronze work, textiles, silverware, hollowware, furniture, and design services for every type of interior, from churches and civic structures to high-end residences. Tiffany's designs were realized by many talented artists and craftsmen working under his direction, including Arthur J. Nash, the Englishman who helped develop Favrile glass in 1892.[4]

At once reminiscent of Japanese gourds and Roman vessels, Favrile glass objects were appealing as singular works of art, with a remarkable iridescence that could be likened to a peacock's feather, a beetle's back, or a fragment of oxidized ancient glass. Both associations were relevant to the artistic world at the end of the century and assured that Tiffany's creations would be taken seriously by the critics.[5]

High exposure and critical notice, in Europe especially, was crucial to establishing Tiffany's reputation in America as a source of "artistic" objects of museum quality that could sell for large sums. Although Tiffany was able to establish an identity for himself and his firm independent of his

Fig. 83. This view of Louis Comfort Tiffany's booth at the 1900 Exposition Universelle in Paris shows his work in stained glass, Favrile glass, ceramics, and enamel as well as signs indicating the many awards he received at that fair.

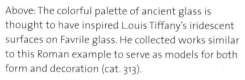

Above: The colorful palette of ancient glass is thought to have inspired Louis Tiffany's iridescent surfaces on Favrile glass. He collected works similar to this Roman example to serve as models for both form and decoration (cat. 313).

Above, right: Early shapes of Louis Tiffany's Favrile glass often took the form of Japanese gourds in opaque colors with abstract patterning (cat. 302).

Right: Tiffany was not the only American artist to admire ancient glass. F. Walter Lawrence set an actual fragment of Roman glass in the hair ornament (cat. 197) seen here next to a perfume bottle by Tiffany (cat. 296).

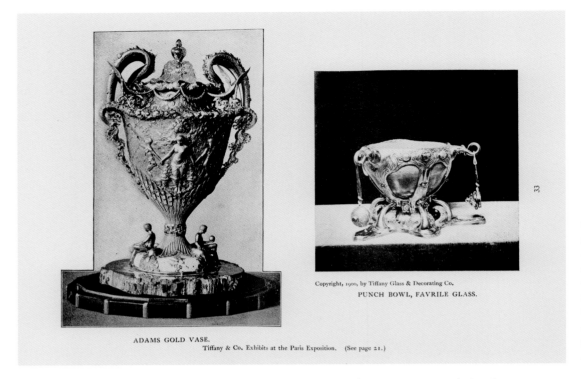

Copyright, 1900, by Tiffany Glass & Decorating Co.
PUNCH BOWL, FAVRILE GLASS.

ADAMS GOLD VASE.
Tiffany & Co. Exhibits at the Paris Exposition.   (See page 21.)

Fig. 84. Because their booths stood next to each other at the 1900 world's fair in Paris, critical comparisons highlighting differing aesthetics were inevitable between the work of Louis Tiffany and that of his father's firm, Tiffany & Co. The *Adams Vase* and the *Lava Punch Bowl* appear side by side on this page from the *American Art Annual* (1900–1901).

Fig. 85. Charles Lewis Tiffany (in hat) and Tiffany & Co.'s vice president Charles T. Cook in the ground-floor showroom of the firm's Union Square store around 1887.

father's renowned firm, association with the Tiffany name and reputation was obviously opportune. The location of his booth next to his father's at the 1900 Paris exposition was no coincidence and emphasized the contrasts between the two concerns. An article in the *American Art Annual* (1900–1901) illustrated the *Adams Vase*, the gold and bejeweled spectacle of Tiffany & Co.'s booth, alongside the *Lava Punchbowl*, Louis Tiffany's masterpiece of Favrile glass and the centerpiece of his booth.[6] No greater metaphor could have existed for the collision of styles that typified the turn of the century: historicism and tradition versus early modernism and reform.[7]

Trained as a painter, Louis Tiffany developed his artistic vision in order to create a world separate from his father's, but their careers were inextricably linked. His father's success enabled Louis Tiffany to attend art schools and take extended trips abroad for inspiration and education. Charles Tiffany provided much of the capital for launching young Louis's experimental efforts in the 1870s and later invested more heavily in his company. Never in competition, their ventures only served to establish the Tiffany name as the source for everything luxurious—a classic exercise in name recognition and branding that ultimately benefited the larger commercial enterprise of Tiffany & Co., which by the time of the 1900 Exposition Universelle in Paris was probably the most recognizable luxury brand in America.

Certainly, Louis Tiffany enjoyed rare opportunities to experiment in glass and other media as a result of his father's financial support. However, these achievements would have been short-lived if not for the business strategies that Louis adopted for his company. Much like his father, he achieved visibility and

This gold and turquoise belt by Tiffany & Co. is a playful concoction of ancient and middle eastern influences (cat. 223).

Tiffany & Co. led the market in the 1880s with wares decorated in the Japanese taste such as the card case at the upper right with its enameled surface typical of Japanese asymmetrical patterning (cat. 234).

Technique as well as decoration distinguished Tiffany & Co.'s work. In the cigarette case at right, the firm's designers have recreated the mottled layering of Japanese mokume metalwork (cat. 237).

fame through advertising, exhibitions, and high-profile commissions that made his works a desirable commodity.

Tiffany & Co.'s achievements at the Paris exposition were a world away from the four dollars and ninety-eight cents that Charles Lewis Tiffany earned on the day in 1837 that he opened the doors of Tiffany & Young, his New York City fancy goods store.[8] The son of a Connecticut mill owner, Charles Tiffany grew up working for his father until he joined his friend John B. Young in their own venture. Charles had displayed no unusual ability aside from business skills learned from his father, but he arrived in New York at a propitious moment, and he took advantage of its rapidly growing economy.

The inexpensive fancy goods that Charles Tiffany sold during the early years of his enterprise soon gave way to finer items that appealed to an increasingly wealthy clientele. As international exhibitions and the development of public collections stimulated private collecting in America, Tiffany developed a strategy of linking his pieces to the quality of work seen in museums, for a time even reproducing Cypriot jewelry from the collection of the Metropolitan Museum of Art.[9] In time, he presented exhibitions of rare and exotic works and developed an exclusive, museum-like atmosphere that rivaled the Metropolitan Museum of Art as a city attraction. In 1873 one critic pointedly omitted mention of the young museum while favorably reviewing Tiffany's quality wares and its gallery setting, observing that Tiffany & Co. offered "some of the most charming articles of *vertu* I have seen outside of the South Kensington Museum in London."[10]

Tiffany & Co. was not the only firm to produce jewelry inspired by ancient forms. Fortunato Pio Castellani & Sons made this necklace with cameos of theatrical masks after ancient sources (cat. 17).

Fig. 86. In 1870, Charles Lewis Tiffany moved the New York showroom from Broadway to Union Square at 15th Street.

Key Figures, Foreign Outposts, and Competitors

Initially, Tiffany & Co. was not so different from firms in New York, Chicago, Philadelphia, and Boston, such as Ball, Black & Co., Theodore Starr, Spaulding & Co., William J. E. Caldwell, or Bigelow, Kennard & Co.[11] All sold imported goods, paintings, and sculpture, along with silver and jewelry by American and European craftsmen. Charles Tiffany was able to distinguish his company from its peers by seeking ever more exotic and desirable wares to attract clientele. He surpassed his rivals by opening a watch factory in Geneva, bringing a new level of precision and accuracy to American timekeeping.[12] Beautifully enameled examples, worn as brooches or chatelaines, became a mainstay of their stock-in-trade. Later, around the turn of the century, the wristwatch was introduced, establishing Tiffany & Co. as the best source for new fashion accessories.

Tiffany also leapt ahead of his competition by promptly establishing outposts in Paris and London, popular with cosmopolitan American travelers.[13] When Charles's partner and by this point his brother-in-law, John Burnett Young, traveled to Paris in 1848 to purchase paste (costume) jewelry, he found a country in crisis after the abdication of Louis-Philippe I.[14] As anxious Parisians in search of hard currency flooded the market with gems and jewelry, Young altered his business plan and returned with a bounty of ornaments. In so doing, he secured the firm's early reputation as a source of quality jewels.[15]

Among the luxurious goods Tiffany & Co. sold were wristwatches, the latest rage in timekeeping (figs. 87, 88). The firm imported its timepieces from Switzerland, where for a period it owned a watch factory in Geneva.

Fig. 89. A view of the workshop of Tiffany & Co.'s Union Square store around 1880.

Sale of the Century: The French Crown Jewels

The sale of the French crown jewels in 1887 inspired the renewed fashion for diamond bowknot brooches. Top: Tiffany & Co. (cat. 224); middle: attributed to Cartier (cat. 308); bottom: Marcus & Co. (cat. 201).

Fig. 90. The bowknot and tassel brooch below, created by François Kramer in 1885, belonged to Empress Eugénie, wife of Napoleon III, the last emperor of France. The box identifies the brooch as part of the French crown jewels. Sold in 1887 to Caroline Astor, this rare surviving ornament has recently been returned to the Louvre.

When a nation dissolves its monarchy, symbols of investiture are done away with, as in 1922 when the Bolsheviks sold the Russian imperial treasures.[1] In that instance, the revolutionaries industriously catalogued and valued every jewel and sold them off, allegedly to raise capital for the fragile government. A few decades before, in 1887, a similar sale had scattered France's crown jewels in a decisive act that had society watching.

As a result of the February Revolution of 1848, King Louis-Philippe I (duc d'Orléans) abdicated after an eighteen-year reign, prompting France's aristocrats to panic and sell their jewels in order to finance escape from an uncertain political climate.[2] Charles Lewis Tiffany was then in partnership with John B. Young and J. L. Ellis. Young and the firm's buyer, Thomas Crane Banks, were in Paris at that momentous time and staked all of Tiffany, Young, and Ellis's available money

into purchasing the jewels. Rumors circulated (largely of the firm's own making) that Tiffany had acquired important pieces, including the infamous necklace at the center of the Affair of the Diamond Necklace.[3] While this assertion that the firm possessed the fallen monarchy's crown jewels was false, Charles Lewis Tiffany became known as "King of Diamonds" on the strength of the rumors alone.

In reality, the French crown jewels that survived the 1792 raid on the royal repository were with the new empress Eugénie, wife of Louis-Napoleon Bonaparte, and she loved them. As the wife of Napoleon III, who became president of the Second Republic at the end of 1848 and went on to restore France's empire, Eugénie was an international fashion plate. She had the jewels reset by Germain Bapst and other eminent French jewelers.[4] Taking eighteenth-century styles as a guide, her pieces included bows, feathers, tassels, flowers, and stars. When images of these jewels circulated in sale catalogues and the press, they amounted to a jeweler's style chart that maintained the "Old Style" right up to the twentieth century. One of Eugénie's most famous jewels was a large diamond belt created by the Parisian jeweler François Kramer in 1855. It was disassembled in 1864, but the centerpiece, the bow, remained, enhanced at the suggestion of the empress with tassels and five *pampilles* that rained down diamonds.

The historic Bapst firm fashioned numerous new pieces and parures for the empress, including seven delicate stars in 1856 and a crescent moon for her hair. Bapst also made large bowknots of diamonds inspired by jewels from Marie-

DIAMANTS
DE
LA COURONNE
DE
FRANCE

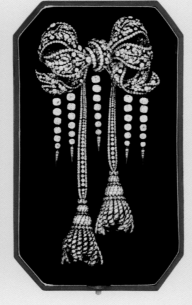

Antoinette's era. Created in 1863 by Alfred Bapst, these jewels held the empress Eugénie's court mantle. A year later, Bapst joined the collar of four necklaces to the bows, their 222 brilliant-cut diamonds draped between the bows in four *rivières*.[5]

Napoleon and Eugénie's Second Empire ended with France's 1870 defeat in the Franco-Prussian War. Alfred Bapst, whose family had been associated closely with the jewels for decades, was instrumental in securing the crown jewels' safety; they were secreted away in the Banque de France in August 1870. The jewels were taken out again in 1878 and put on view in the Exposition Universelle of that year as a testament to the art of the French jeweler. After a century of governmental fits and starts, however, the newest parliamentary republic wanted to thwart any further monarchist uprisings. In 1886, the heir of the French royal Orléans family was forbidden to enter France, and in December, Jules Grévy, president of the republic, signed a law to sell the crown jewels. Député Meullon's report was read aloud in the National Assembly on 7 December 1886:

> [a] democracy that is sure of itself and confident in the future has a duty to rid itself of these objects of luxury, devoid of usefulness and moral worth, and to ensure that such considerable assets are not left lying idle in some cellar. Moreover, many pretenders to the royal title themselves understand this, and . . . they shall have the opportunity, to this great advantage, of competing with each other for the jewels, on the battleground of the auction rooms.[6]

Once decreed, the sale hurtled forward.

In 1887, England was preparing for Queen Victoria's jubilee celebrating fifty years of her reign.[7] Across the channel in France, however, official white posters appeared announcing the sale of the French crown jewels.[8] A correspondent for the *New York Times* wrote, "It is the final liquidation of royalty, a sort of sale after decease, when the auctioneer's mallet will ring on the tables of the Hôtel Drouot like the hammer of the undertaker on a coffin lid."[9]

French jewelers were dismayed with the potential loss of France's artistic heritage. In order to placate them, the government ordered the photographer Berthaud to photograph the entire collection for historical record. His images appeared in the auction catalogues and sale promotions as well, putting the sympathetic gesture in question. To those in the jewelry profession, it was a shameless flaunting, for commercial purposes, of once sanctified jewels and tantamount to publishing state secrets.

The Musée du Louvre displayed the jewels one last time in the Pavilion de Flore but, as in a national mourning, let viewers only pass by and not linger. Those regarded as serious buyers might ask for private viewings, and many of these requests came from wives of American senators.[10] The *New York Times* claimed that the collection

Fig. 91. This page from the official sale catalogue includes Kramer's famous stomach brooch as well as two bow brooches that once held Empress Eugénie's mantle. They were purchased by a member of the banished House of Orléans.

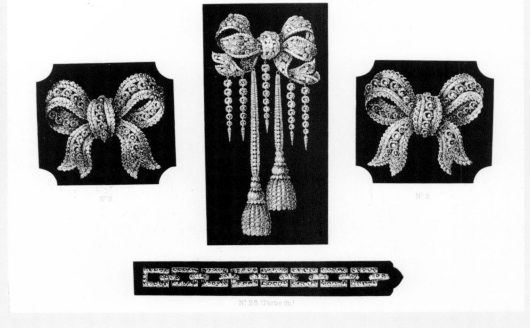

was "more estimable for the memories which are attached to it than for its intrinsic market value" and eulogized the crown jewels with a history lesson.[11] The collection began with Francis I's marriage to Eleanor of Austria, sister of Holy Roman Emperor Charles V, in 1530. The French king created a permanent treasure of national jewels with the "obligation to keep them for the crown forever."[12] Successive rulers added to the collection over the centuries.

The most significant works included the eighteen large Mazarin diamonds named for Cardinal Mazarin (1602–1661), minister to Louis XIV's mother during the youth's regency. Mazarin donated his gems to the national collection, including the Sancy and the Mirror of Portugal diamonds, formerly among England's crown jewels. The Mazarins disappeared during the Revolution but some were retrieved. Of these, the Grand Mazarin was the glory.[13] Colored diamonds were particularly beloved among France's crown jewels. The French Blue (from which the Hope diamond was cut) is probably now the most famous, but inventory records also took note of rose-colored, yellow, and cinnamon-brown diamonds.

A small group of jewels was kept out of the 1887 sale. The famous Regent diamond, which alone was purported to be worth two-thirds of the crown jewels' total value, went to the Louvre. A slave from India allegedly carried this jewel inside his wounded leg and gave it to an English skipper as trade for safe passage to freedom. The untrustworthy skipper threw the man overboard, sold the jewel, spent the money, and then hung himself.[14] A Madras governor, Sir Thomas Pitt, purchased the diamond and took it to England where a jeweler cut it into a brilliant, shaving it down from 410 to 136 carats.[15] Pitt sold the stone, which had caused him to live in constant fear of robbery, to the duc d'Orléans in 1717. It then disappeared in 1792 only to reemerge a year later in a Paris attic.[16]

Other pieces were saved for posterity and donated to the Louvre, including Charles X's coronation sword with 1,576 brilliant-cut diamonds (stolen in 1976) and the Chimera jewel of pearl and enamel to which Louis XIV attributed fetishistic powers.[17] A number of loose gems, such as the Louis XVIII opal, Marie-Louise's portrait diamond, and numerous amethysts, rubies, pearls, turquoises, pink topaz, and emeralds, went to the Musée National d'Histoire Naturelle. A final small group of emeralds and diamonds went to the School of Mines in Paris.

With these notable exceptions, the rest of the jewels were separated, some broken up, and others put on the auction block. The *New York Times* reported that it was mostly "foreigners or *petits bourgeois*" who went to ogle them.[18] Jewelry firms drove up the prices and handily outbid the superficially curious. Boucheron took Lot 48 of sundry precious stones and pearls, as well as the Grand Mazarin. Tiffany & Co. took four other alleged Mazarins.[19] Louis Aucoc, Henri Vever, and Van Cleef and Arpels each had small successes. Other very spirited buyers included Germain Bapst, whose family had been the court's jewelers for nine generations.

Governments from all over the world sent representatives, and the banished Orléans family reclaimed some of its family jewels through dealer Alfred Doutrelon, who bid particularly well.[20] Among his purchases were a 9-carat solitaire once set in a garland of currant leaves, two hairpins paved in brilliants, and the two shoulder knots designed by Alfred Bapst in 1863 for the empress's court mantle.[21] American R. H. Macy purchased a diadem and put it on view in New York. Made of diamonds and turquoises, the diadem had been worn by Empress Eugénie before it sat on a purple velvet display in Macy & Co.'s department store.[22]

Just as he had in 1848, C. L. Tiffany sought to corner the market. "Our house was the largest buyer at the sale of the French Crown Jewels," a representative told the *New York Times* and reported an outlay of $487,956 in a show of bravado meant to give the impression of market prowess.[23]

Their successes included rows of pearls and numerous loose diamonds, the Mirror of Portugal diamond bought by Napoleon I for Marie-Louise's diadem, the famous four-strand diamond collar, and a suite of currant-leaf breast ornaments (Bapst 1855), which were taken to New York.[24]

Contrary to popular perception, Tiffany & Co. said it would be selling the objects without regard to their past worth, arguing that the oldest and most historically valuable stones were cut before the jeweler's art had reached its peak, and therefore more modern additions to the crown jewels would have the most value in their sales.[25] The firm offered a movable feast of luxury to Americans vacationing in Paris; by buying abroad they saved the ten percent import duty they would have been charged on their return. Tiffany & Co. therefore succeeded in selling most of the pieces from Europe, apparently finding buyers for many right away. The firm offered anonymity to buyers, though some, Kate Pulitzer for example, immediately wore their new jewels to parties.[26]

Fig. 92. The garland of currant leaves at the top, made by Bapst in 1856, could be disassembled into sixteen parts, each including a brooch and three pendants. Auctioneers sold the piece in eight separate lots, two of which went to Tiffany & Co.

Fig. 93. Charles Lewis Tiffany was poised to capture a large portion of the European luxury market when he and his partners opened a Paris branch in the rue de Richelieu in 1850. Tiffany & Co. moved its showroom, pictured here, to the fashionable rue de l'Opéra in 1910.

George F. Kunz wrote on the fate of various collections for *Mineral Resources of the United States* (1888). Interestingly, he never mentioned Tiffany & Co. by name (he said merely "a single American firm, the largest buyer at the sale") or lamented the breaking up and sale of the crown jewels as he did the Hope gem collection in the same report. Perhaps he had conflicting emotions about his association with Tiffany & Co.'s profiteering, but if so, he masked it by lauding the taste of American buyers: "In its way this sale did more than anything that had before occurred to establish a reputation abroad for American taste, wealth, and enterprise."[27]

Catherine Walworth

1. What was unexpected was the behavior of the Russian emissaries to the Hague who purchased bicycles, smart clothes, and generally spent lavishly when they were supposed to be frugal and concentrate on raising money for Russia. With wariness as to how the men were to pay their bills, the Hague burgomaster issued an order that no more collections for famine relief were to be taken up by the delegation. The film *Ninotchka* (1939) has a similar plot line.

2. John Loring, *Tiffany Diamonds* (New York: Abrams, 2005), 7–8.

3. This infamous scandal caused the increasingly detested Marie Antoinette to be dragged into court to defend herself against allegations of diamond gluttony. For the story and its place in Marie Antoinette's sartorial and political history, see Caroline Weber, *Queen of Fashion: What Marie Antoinette Wore to the Revolution* (New York: Henry Holt, 2006).

4. Penny Proddow and Marion Fasel, *Diamonds: A Century of Spectacular Jewels* (New York: Abrams, 1996), 15.

5. For these and other details of the French crown jewels, see the well-researched work by Bernard Morel, *The French Crown Jewels* (Antwerp: Fonds Mercator, 1988).

6. Député Meullon, as quoted in ibid., 369.

7. Queen Victoria's so-called Diamond Jubilee was celebrated in 1897, making her the longest reigning monarch in England's history. A planned gift of a 245-carat, cushion-shaped diamond was named the Jubilee Diamond but never actually given to the queen. Instead, it went on view at the 1900 Paris Exposition Universelle, where it was one of the most popular displays.

8. C.T., "The French Crown Jewels to be Sold at Public Auction on May 12," *New York Times*, 12 April 1887, 10.

9. Ibid.

10. "Crown Jewels for Americans," *New York Times*, 21 April 1887, 1.

11. C.T., "French Crown Jewels to be Sold," 10. The author drew heavily from Germain Bapst, who was writing a history of the crown jewels at the time; see Germain Bapst, *The French Crown Jewels: Histoire des Joyaux de la Couronne de France, d'Apres des Documents Inedits* (Paris: Librairie Hachette, 1891).

12. C.T., "French Crown Jewels to be Sold," 10.

13. Edward Francis Twining, *History of the Crown Jewels of Europe* (London: Batsford, 1960), 246. According to Lord Twining, when the Grand Mazarin (no. 8) reappeared it no longer matched the previous inventory in weight or color.

14. H. D. Crider, "The Story of the Diamond," *American Midland Naturalist* 9, no. 4 (July 1924): 183–84.

15. Ibid.

16. Twining, *History of the Crown Jewels of Europe*, 263.

17. Ibid., 274–75.

18. "The French Crown Jewels: Opening of the Auction Sale in Paris," *New York Times*, 13 May 1887, 1.

19. "The Mazarins Sold: Tiffany secures Four of the Famous Diamonds," *New York Times*, 22 May 1887, 1.

20. Doutrelon reportedly won Lots 1, 2, 6, and 8 out of ten lots on 12 May, according to the *New York Times*, 13 May 1887, 1.

21. Twining, *History of the Crown Jewels of Europe*, 282.

22. "Ablaze with Diamonds: R. H. Macy & Co. Exhibit one of the French Crown Jewels," *New York Times*, 12 October 1887, 8.

23. "The Crown Jewel Sale Ended: More Purchases by New-Yorkers—The Criers Dissatisfied," *New York Times* (Paris), 23 May 1887, 1.

24. Morel, *French Crown Jewels*, 380.

25. Ibid., 380.

26. Loring, *Tiffany Diamonds*, 43. When Kate Pulitzer's husband, New York *World* publisher Joseph Pulitzer, purchased the famous *collier aux quatre rivières*, she wore it to a party in Paris the very next day.

27. George F. Kunz, "Collections of Jewels and Precious Stones," excerpted in "Scientific News in Washington," *Science* 11, no. 278 (1 June 1888): 260.

Sensing new opportunities in Paris, frequently visited by wealthy American travelers, and seeking an international clientele in one of the world's most famous and fashionable cities, Tiffany opened a store in 1850 in the rue Richelieu, a short walk from the Bourse, France's stock market, and near the Louvre. The firm's new partner, Gideon F. T. Reed, in charge of the establishment first called Tiffany, Reed & Co., quickly developed relationships with the city's many talented jewelers. He soon procured ornaments for sale in New York, thus enabling the firm to boast in an early advertisement that the "foreign connections of which their Paris house is the focal center, gives them extraordinary facilities for the selection of their general stock and the execution of special orders."[16]

The retail relationship between Tiffany & Co. and foreign jewelers continued for decades, during which the firm sold handsome adornments and accessories by René Lalique, Henri Husson, Henri Vever, and Georges le Saché, among others. Tiffany & Co.'s rapid success in selling to wealthy American visitors in Europe likely provided the impetus for opening another branch, this time in London in 1872. As in Paris, the company engaged local goldsmiths to produce accessories that were sold in its London shop as well as in New York.[17] This arrangement and the cachet it provided for the firm appears to have been unique among American jewelry houses until 1890, when Chicago's Spaulding & Co. established a shop in the same building as Tiffany's later Paris location at 36 avenue de l'Opéra.[18] By that time, however, Tiffany's dominance in the jewelry and luxury goods market over its American competitors was all but complete.

Meanwhile, Tiffany's advances in jewelry were matched by similar developments in silver. In 1851 the company engaged John C. Moore & Co., one of New York's leading silver manufacturers, to work exclusively for the firm, and adopted the English sterling standard, an internationally recognized index of the amount of pure silver in an alloy. While other U.S. firms observed the sterling standard, the American silversmithing industry was without a tradition of alloy control. Charles Tiffany's decision to publicly adopt this standard, at a time when silver content was confused by many items marked "coin silver," was a brilliant marketing strategy because it placed the name of Tiffany at the forefront of quality control. By employing Moore's services, the firm also gained, with minimal effort, a reputable in-house provider of fine silver—Moore's talented son, Edward C. Moore, who was soon engaged as Tiffany's artistic director.[19] In 1867 his designs for silver won the firm its first international award, a bronze medal at the Paris Exposition Universelle, in the face of strong French competition.

Above: Cross pendant watch, marked by Parisian jeweler Verger, for Tiffany & Co. (cat. 241).

Center: Inkwell by Georges le Saché for Tiffany & Co.'s Paris showroom (cat. 249).

Left: Small box, probably by a French enameler, retailed by Tiffany & Co. in Paris (cat. 227).

Many private jewelers and artisans worked independently in Paris as suppliers for more public firms, such as Tiffany & Co. Georges le Saché was a source for many of the luxurious accessories sold in Tiffany's Paris showroom, such as the tortoiseshell and enameled cigar cutter at right, which is unmarked but most likely from Le Saché (cat. 236).

This fair undoubtedly convinced Charles Tiffany of the advantages to be gained through international competitions. At the Vienna exposition in 1873, when he served as jewelry specialist for the United States "advisory committee of citizens," he had an excellent opportunity to study the sizable English and Continental displays of jewelry, as well as those at the Japanese installation. Not a single American jeweler or silversmith was represented at the exhibition, a fact that could not have escaped his attention, and a situation he rectified in 1876 with Tiffany's participation in the Philadelphia Centennial Exposition.[20]

In 1879, Charles Tiffany made important additions to his staff. The brilliant gemologist George Frederick Kunz, who had focused on minerals from an early age, had caught Tiffany's attention in 1876 by bringing him a sparkling green tourmaline. Throughout his long career Kunz secured dazzling stones for all manner of Tiffany & Co. jewelry, hollowware, and accessories, a role he continued with Louis Comfort Tiffany well into the twentieth century. Thanks to Kunz's efforts Tiffany rivaled the great firms of Europe for the size, color, and rarity of the stones they set. Kunz joined Tiffany & Co. the same year as the talented designer George Paulding Farnham, whose work would have perhaps the most impact on Tiffany & Co.'s reputation leading up to the turn of the century.

Farnham's arrival at Tiffany & Co. was not coincidental; his uncle was Charles Thomas Cook, vice president and later president of the firm. He began by enrolling in the so-called Tiffany School taught by Edward C. Moore to train young designers for places within the company.[21] Students prepared studies from nature, illustrations in the company's growing design library, and artifacts from the Near and Far East in a collection that Moore maintained at the firm's Union Square store.[22] In 1885, at the age of twenty-four, Farnham completed his preparatory work and was accepted as a "general assistant" to Moore.[23]

Recognizing the attraction of novelty for a luxury-loving clientele, Charles Tiffany saw potential in importing European goods to augment the firm's own designs. Tiffany's first major venture in retailing foreign goods was the sale of Russian silver. In 1876, the Russians had exhibited traditional trompe l'oeil damask-draped trays at the Philadelphia centennial that were copied by Gorham, Whiting, and other American firms. Instead of following suit, however, Tiffany chose to import enameled accessories from Russia in charming folk designs and historic forms such as the *kovsh* (a boat-shaped cup). Ethnically based works were popular in Russia

Fig. 94. The scent bottle at right, by the House of Fabergé around 1905, is one of a pair retailed by Tiffany & Co. in London.

The aquamarine and diamond brooch above by Tiffany & Co. demonstrates the fashion for single large colored gemstones surrounded by diamonds, an eighteenth-century taste revived by royalty in the nineteenth century and also promoted by Fabergé (cat. 229).

Tsar Nicholas II's sister, Grand Duchess Xenia Alexandrovna, and her husband, Grand Duke Alexander Mikhailovich, purchased this Fabergé bellpush from Tiffany & Co. in London in December 1902 (cat. 26).

The use of hardstones, particularly jade, in luxury wares was often associated with Russian taste around 1900 when Tiffany & Co. made this gold and nephrite coffee (cabaret) set (cat. 239).

With its colorful enameled and gemstone-set surface, the box below was likely made by one of the Russian firms whose wares were sold by Tiffany & Co. in New York during the 1880s and 1890s (cat. 226).

beginning in the mid nineteenth century, when publications of archaeological drawings on Russian subjects, supported by Nicholas I, led to a revival of historic ornament called Ruuskii stil'.[24]

The sale of Russian enamels began in earnest during the 1880s when New York–born Henry Winans Hiller, a pioneer in the Russo-American trade, was engaged as an agent for Tiffany & Co.[25] Hiller had served as the U.S. consular agent for Eastern Siberia under Lincoln's administration and upon his return to the United States was among the first to import Russian jewelry and enameled wares. In 1883 he was hired by Tiffany & Co. to procure Russian goods for sale, and an abundance of pieces followed, many in cloisonné enamel, by Antip Kuzmichev and Gustav Klingert of Moscow, in particular. Hiller mounted a selection of these items for Tiffany & Co. in December 1887.[26]

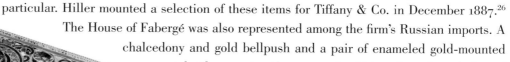

The House of Fabergé was also represented among the firm's Russian imports. A chalcedony and gold bellpush and a pair of enameled gold-mounted scent bottles survive that carry the Fabergé mark and that of Tiffany & Co. in London. While the date is not known precisely, this retail arrangement could have been established around 1903, when the Russian firm opened its own London shop.[27]

American visitors to Europe often frequented Tiffany & Co.'s London or Paris showrooms where they could find all manner of expensive luxury accessories, such as the domino set at left in ivory with gold and enameled decoration, probably supplied by Parisian jeweler Georges le Saché (cat. 246).

Above: Group of timepieces by Tiffany & Co. (two at right, cats. 252, 253) and their chief rival in the jewelry trade, Marcus & Co. (two at left, cats. 203, 206). An upside-down face enabled the wearer to tell the time correctly when looking down.

Among Tiffany & Co.'s chief American competitors, the German émigré Herman Marcus had been a court jeweler in Dresden before arriving in New York in 1850.[28] After working for almost fifteen years for other jewelry retailers, he and Theodore B. Starr became partners in 1863. Starr & Marcus was celebrated for having the "largest stocks of high-class jewelry and gold and silver ware on this side of the Atlantic [and concentrating on] the development of art and artistic taste."[29] Starr & Marcus dissolved in 1877, and Marcus joined Tiffany & Co., where he had worked decades before. In 1884 he left that firm to join Marcus & Co., a company his sons George and William had founded. Ornaments designed by George maintained the respect accorded the Marcus name. Some notable examples were set with cabochon and carved opals, longtime favorites of Herman Marcus.

Marcus & Co.: An American Competitor

On a summer day in New York in 1893, a "shabbily-dressed" man threw a brick into the display window of Marcus & Co., grabbed two watches worth $950 and $225, and took off toward Fifth Avenue. Apprehended by a patrolman, the thief explained that he was homeless, penniless, and had only recently arrived from Pittsburgh.[1] The Marcus window, with such expensive pieces on display, must have been designed to tempt. The store not only attracted customers of great means but apparently also the occasional thief. Despite the pitched contrast between luxurious items in the window and the poverty of the man in this scene, Marcus & Co. was more than simply a purveyor of exclusive goods. This family firm was also part of a late-nineteenth-century trend to bring craftsmanship, artistry, and relative affordability of sumptuous items to the middle classes.[2] In contrast to the costly works handcrafted by Arts and Crafts jewelers, larger firms such as Marcus & Co. were in a position to make luxury relatively accessible to more than just Mrs. Astor's elite guest list of four hundred New Yorkers.

Herman Marcus, an independent craftsman and patriarch of Marcus & Co., had trained in Dresden, a city whose jewelers and clockmakers drew inspiration from the bejeweled oddities and treasures in the Green Vaults, an eighteenth-century palace museum. Dresden and its collections were also a training ground for Peter Carl Fabergé and his brother Agathon. The prevalence of carved gemstones in Marcus jewelry from the earliest beginnings to the later work suggests that Herman gained experience in this specialty while working for the court jeweler in Dresden.

Marcus immigrated to America in 1850 and soon found work in New York with Tiffany & Co. and joined Ball, Black & Co. in 1855. After fourteen years of working for others, he and fellow entrepreneur and jeweler Theodore B. Starr formed their own company in 1864. Like Tiffany & Co. at the time, the firm sold jewelry, particularly hardstone cameos, along with silver and other fine household objects, clocks, and decorative bronze sculptures. Evidence of Marcus's lapidary training in Dresden was alluded to in a review in the *New York Times* in 1872:

> To the lover of all that is beautiful and valuable in art, a visit to the ware-rooms of Starr & Marcus ... is something to be long remembered, for there can be found specimens of the lapidary skill to be seen, probably, nowhere else in the country. We

In contrast to the intricately detailed and very expensive orchid brooches of Tiffany & Co., this one in the form of lady slipper blossoms used less expensive colored glass and simple enameling techniques (cat. 202).

Herman Marcus followed the taste for jewelry set with gemstones and natural pearls, as in the necklace at right (cat. 204).

[examined] their stock of precious stones and rich jewelry until the sense of sight was bewildered, for their attendants were true artists in their work of exhibiting the goods.[3]

That same year, Starr & Marcus produced a showy diamond pendant, *Aurora,* aptly named for the magnificent displays of light to be seen

priced at $65,000.[5] The firm was establishing a pattern of creating newsworthy jewels, a successful marketing device because *Harper's Weekly* illustrated Starr & Marcus work alongside that of Boucheron of Paris and Tiffany & Co.[6]

While extravagant goods made news, Marcus wisely offered jewelry acessible to the rising middle class. Publications such as *House Beautiful*

on starry nights in the northernmost part of the hemisphere. This lavish jewel was intended for the Vienna world's fair of 1873, although apparently the partnership did not participate.[4] However, Starr & Marcus did exhibit at the 1876 Centennial Exhibition in Philadelphia, where American firms first significantly challenged European leadership. The display concentrated on diamonds, the favorite jewel of the era, and included a spectacular necklace and pendant

devoted pages to educating the public's artistic taste, creating a groundswell of knowledgeable consumers. One example of goods that might reach this wider audience included the firm's line of "Roman gold." A reporter who visited Starr & Marcus in 1873 said that the quiet luster of this burnished gold made it less likely to compete with the brilliancy of enamel, jewels, or miniatures set against it. In fact, some jewelry could be attractive for the gold alone.[7]

Like many jewelry firms, Starr & Marcus retailed goods by other luxury firms in addition to its own wares and sterling silver by the Gorham Mfg. Co. Advertisements noted Gorham's standard English sterling, quality design and workmanship, advantageous price, and Starr & Marcus's promise never to sell the wares in electroplate.[8] While electroplating would have reduced the price even more, in 1872 the process was a matter of debate and, in some circles, comparable to counterfeiting quality silver objects. In reality, America's more affordable, factory-made metal wares had a democratic effect that was becoming acceptable in all but society's highest echelons. Horace Greeley, editor of the New York *Herald Tribune*, reviewing America's industrial products twenty years earlier at the 1853 Crystal Palace exhibition in New York, wrote: "Our vases and cups may not be more exquisitely wrought than the vases and cups of Benvenuto Cellini, but they are wrought, not like his, for Popes and Emperors, but for Smith and Jones."[9]

Marcus & Co. was one of the few jewelry firms to participate in the inaugural exhibition sponsored by the Society of Arts and Crafts, Boston, in 1897.[10] Luxury firms among the sea of independent makers had to follow the same strict standards and credit each designer's name beside that of the manufacturer. Despite the exhibition coordinators' intent to spotlight independent artists, Marcus & Co.'s display dominated the front page of the *Jewelers' Circular*, a journal for tradesmen. Evoking goods at an exotic bazaar, the reporter listed Marcus & Co.'s jeweled delicacies for three running columns, including:

> brooch, Hindu workmanship, set with pearls, olivines and diamonds . . . brooch, tibula, set with pearl and sapphires, made after Algerian model . . . brooch, turquoises and diamonds, set in Pompeian style . . . necklace, old Indian cut briolet diamonds hanging from small diamond ornaments and fine gold open work . . . antique Chinese snuff bottle, with top of Pompeian workmanship, set with small rubies and diamonds.[11]

The list mentions star sapphires, enamel flowers, pearl drops, and diamonds, concluding by crediting George Elder Marcus, one of Herman's sons, with much of the design work. By exhibiting in Arts and Crafts expositions, such firms as Marcus & Co. and Gorham Mfg. Co. were announcing artistic standards that could compete with those of craftsmen who made each piece from start to finish.

In 1899, a reviewer of Boston's Arts and Crafts exhibition pointed out the positive role played by commercial firms:

> If the movement towards increase of beauty in things of everyday use is to reach the mass of us who have only moderate means it must come through the recognized channels of trade. . . . It is

Marcus & Co., noted for making jewels in a style evoking the Near East, displayed such finery at the 1897 inaugural exhibition of the Society of Arts and Crafts in Boston (cat. 205).

The elaborate lapel watch at right by Marcus incorporates rare opals still within their original matrix or as-found state, a subtle nod to the trend toward gem collecting in the period (cat. 203).

handwritten notice of his arrival signed by the jeweler was sent to special clients.[14] He was soon dispatched to Paris as Tiffany's representative during the 1878 Exposition Universelle. Tiffany & Co. made sure to advertise Marcus's talents, and he remained with the firm until 1884.[15] Despite the advantages of working for a large company like Tiffany & Co., Marcus may have preferred to help his sons build a family enterprise. At that time, Herman joined son William Elder Marcus's jewelry firm, a partnership with George B. Jacques known as Jacques and Marcus. According to jewelry historian Janet Zapata, Herman's other son, George, most likely joined the growing firm in 1890. When Jacques, the only non-Marcus firm member, retired in 1892, the business name changed to Marcus & Co.

Marcus & Co. jewelry began to achieve a distinctive look after this point, displaying a robust, eclectic decoration that incorporated a range of styles. Influences likely included both Tiffany firms, René Lalique, and even the House of Fabergé.[16] Eastern revivalism was popular, as described in the 1897 Arts and Crafts exhibition review, but so too were various historicist styles and Art Nouveau. Marcus & Co. pieces also featured a range of stones, including fiery opals and uneven baroque and "blister" pearls, artistic materials favored by avant-garde jewelers from the British Guild of Handicraft to René Lalique.

While diamonds still dominated the market for formal jewelry, the new family firm carried on Jacques and Marcus's legacy of using semiprecious gemstones. Herman Marcus would likely have shared this interest after working with Tiffany & Co.'s gemologist George F. Kunz.[17] The use of lesser gems certainly broadened the firm's prices and artistic designs. Some notable examples were set with cabochon and carved opals, a longtime favorite practice of Herman Marcus that required the same lapidary skills first reported in 1872 about Starr & Marcus ornaments.[18]

Marcus & Co. was one of the few American concerns to create jewelry that featured

encouraging that these firms have reached such artistic excellence and equally so that the public are beginning to appreciate it.[12]

In his short list of "these firms," the reviewer names both Marcus & Co. and Tiffany Glass and Decorating Company. The size and quality of larger firms also assured that Boston's exhibition, which focused on independent craftsmen and smaller names, did not suffer from lack of public interest.[13]

When Starr & Marcus dissolved in 1877, Herman Marcus rejoined Tiffany & Co., where he had first worked in the diamond department; the following year he moved to the watch and jewelry division. Marcus must have been considered an important asset to the company since a

plique-à-jour, an enameling technique favored by European craftsmen. The firm's skills in enameling over machine-engraved decoration (*guilloché*) were on par stylistically with those produced by Tiffany & Co., the House of Fabergé, and French makers Husson and Le Saché, who provided Tiffany with such goods. Marcus & Co.'s execution of this type of enameling, however, often fell short of the technical prowess of rivals who were more experienced in this delicate technique. The company's sphere of commerce was limited to America, whether by design or necessity, and to boost its reputation among the American buying public, generally confined its exhibitions to regional fairs rather than large international expositions. As an example, the cost of travel and shipping prevented Marcus & Co.'s participation in the Vienna exposition of 1873 and may also have played a part in its absence from the 1900 Exhibition Universelle; it was the only notable competitor of Tiffany & Co. that was not represented in Paris.

Herman Marcus died in 1899, and his sons moved the business to a new location at 544 Fifth Avenue, an area populated by luxury retailers. With larger, more spacious premises, a silver department was added. Marcus & Co.'s inkwells, porringers, and smoking sets demonstrate the influence of British Arts and Crafts designers such as Charles Robert Ashbee and Archibald Knox.[19] The company is also known to have competed with Tiffany & Co. by selling Japanese-inspired mokume metalwork as well as goods decorated with Native American motifs.[20]

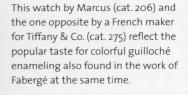

This watch by Marcus (cat. 206) and the one opposite by a French maker for Tiffany & Co. (cat. 275) reflect the popular taste for colorful guilloché enameling also found in the work of Fabergé at the same time.

A mainstay of Marcus & Co.'s stock-in-trade was formal diamond and pearl jewelry in historicist styles (cat. 201), just as it was for competitors such as Tiffany & Co.

The Boston Arts and Crafts exhibition continued to promote the individual craftsman well into the twentieth century. At its tenth exhibition, Favrile glass vases were credited to Louis C. Tiffany rather than Tiffany Studios. Lalique exhibited a floral bracelet and critics hailed him as a leader in the independent art jewelry movement, despite begrudging his so-called barbarity.[21] With sons William and George at the helm, Marcus & Co. was still competing as a top American jewelry firm well into the twentieth century. Yet the impending war and a luxury tax signed by President Franklin D. Roosevelt signaled a death knell for the firm and many others like it that catered to clients conscious of their spending. Grandson William Marcus Jr. sold the firm to Gimbel Brothers department store in 1941. Just as Louis Tiffany's reputation experienced resurgence in the late twentieth century, a renewed scholarly and collecting interest in Marcus & Co. has ensured that the firm will once again take its historical place among the most well-respected American jewelers and purveyors of luxury goods.

Catherine Walworth

1. "Many People Saw Him Steal," *New York Times*, 2 July 1893, 14.

2. Many thanks to Janet Zapata, whose recent articles on Marcus & Co. are the most thorough examinations of the firm to date, and to Jeannine Falino, who inspired much of this vignette.

3. "Rich and Rare Jewels, a Visit to the Store of Starr & Marcus: What is to be Seen There," *New York Times*, 18 December 1872, 5.

4. Ibid.

5. For a discussion of this diamond jewelry set and other goods exhibited at the centennial, see Janet Zapata, "The Legacy of Herman Marcus and Marcus and Company, part 1, The Early Years 1850–1892" *Antiques* 172, no. 2 (2007): 68–77.

6. "The Centennial Diamonds and Jewelry," *Harper's Weekly* (2 December 1976): 968.

7. "Roman Gold," *New York Times*, 16 May 1873, 5.

8. Display ad, *New York Times*, 1 November 1872, 8.

9. As quoted in Julie Wosk, *Breaking the Frame: Technology and the Visual Arts in the Nineteenth Century* (New Brunswick, N.J.: Rutgers University Press, 1992), 129.

10. Their sizable display of forty-five examples of jewelry was designed by George Elder Marcus. *First Exhibition of the Arts and Crafts, Copley Hall, April 5–16, 1897*, exh. cat. (Boston, 1897), 15 cat. 205.1–44.

11. "Features of the Arts and Crafts Exhibition," *Jewelers' Circular* 34, no. 12 (21 April 1897): 1–2. Marcus & Co.'s jewelry display was followed by a description of Gorham Mfg. Co's metalwork by W. C. Codman, Goodnow & Jenks's colonial-inspired goods, and a very brief description of George P. Kendrick's works.

12. Charles H. Caffin, ed., *Artist* (May-June 1899): i–ii.

13. Ibid.

14. Undated, handwritten announcement noting that "the facilities of this representative house [Tiffany & Co.] are of such as I have never before had at my command and warrant me in promising you more thorough service than has hitherto been in my power to render." Tiffany Archives clipping book, 1878. Courtesy of Tiffany Archives.

15. Zapata, "The Legacy of Herman Marcus and Marcus and Company, part 1," 72.

16. Janet Zapata, "The Legacy of Herman Marcus and Marcus and Company, part 2, The Marcus and Company Years, 1892–1941," *Antiques* 172, no. 2 (2007): 88.

17. Charlotte Gere and Geoffrey C. Munn assert that there may be a direct link between Edward Colonna and Tiffany Studios. Marcus & Co. seems to have made jewelry from Tiffany Studios' designs that are close to Colonna's jewelry for Bing's L'Art Nouveau in Paris. Charlotte Gere and Geoffrey C. Munn, *Artists' Jewellery: Pre-Raphaelite to Arts and Crafts* (London: Antique Collectors' Club, 1989), 190.

18. For a poem entitled "The Birth of the Opal" written by Ella Wheeler and used by Herman Marcus, see *Yenowine's Illustrated News* (Milwaukee) 308 (15 February 1891): 6.

19. Zapata, "The Legacy of Herman Marcus and Marcus and Company, Part 2," cites W. Scott Braznell, "The Influence of C. R. Ashbee and His Guild of Handicraft on American Silver, Other Metalwork, and Jewelry," in *The Substance of Style: Perspectives on the American Arts and Crafts Movement*, ed. Bert Kenker (Winterthur, Del.: Henry Francis du Pont Winterthur Museum, 1996), 42.

20. Zapata, "The Legacy of Herman Marcus and Marcus and Company, part 2," 87.

21. "Notable Arts and Crafts Exhibition," *Brush and Pencil* 19 (January–June 1907): 78.

Fame and Fortune: Clients for Tiffany Luxury Goods

Charles Lewis Tiffany grasped the value of free publicity associated with wealthy patrons who visited his store, including royalty, dignitaries, and popular entertainers. The activities of these notables generated newspaper reports that, in turn, fueled public interest in his company. Among the celebrated persons who crossed the Tiffany threshold were Queen Kapiolani of Hawaii and her royal party, who visited the store in 1887, and the English actress Lillie Langtry, who stopped by in 1889 to "invest . . . a few spare thousands in the black pearls."[30] Similarly, the American opera singer Lillian Nordica, the youthful "Yankee Diva," received a diamond coronet in 1896 from a group of her admirers "among the box and seat owners of the Metropolitan Opera." Set in platinum with 233 diamonds with a total weight of 30 carats, it was a gift fit for an operatic queen.[31] Taken as a group, these press appearances suggest that Charles Tiffany, and in all likelihood his publicist, George Frederic Heydt, planted such stories in the press to raise the company's profile and heighten excitement about their celebrity clientele.

Some patrons hailed from old monied families, while others were newly rich industrialists or businessmen whose acquisitions, sales, and mergers were the topics of newspaper stories. The private lives and public activities of this social set, coined the "Four Hundred" for the number of guests accommodated in the large but exclusive ballroom of Mrs. William Backhouse Astor Jr., fascinated the public.[32] The press eagerly covered their weddings and debutante balls, the gifts they gave, descriptions of their yachts, their homes, and their seasonal travels to Newport, London, and Paris.

Anna Gould, daughter of New York financier George Jay Gould, was already a social celebrity when she married Count Paul Ernest Boniface de Castellane in 1895. Her marriage, with all its associated gifts, was extensively covered by the New York papers. Among the most notable of her wedding presents was the famed Esterhazy jewels, which she received from her sister Helen, who had purchased the gems from Tiffany & Co.[33] The royal Esterhazy family of Hungary was renowned in the eighteenth century for the diamond jewels first assembled by Prince Nicholas and worn as part of his

Fig. 95. In this photograph American opera singer Lillian Nordica wears the diamond tiara given her by a group of admirers among the box-seat set at the Metropolitan Opera in 1896.

Jeptha H. Wade II had these beautifully matched pink tourmalines set by Tiffany & Co. for his wife, Ellen Garretson Wade (cat. 255).

Elaborate garland-style diamond necklaces recall jewels and lace from the age of Louis XVI. Tiffany & Co. supplied this quintessential example to Jeptha H. Wade II for his wife around 1900 (cat. 274).

officer's dress. After profligate spending forced the family to declare bankruptcy in 1866, Tiffany & Co. purchased $100,000 worth of the jewelry at an auction held in the following year.[34] The sale of the Esterhazy diamonds to the Goulds offered ideal press coverage that conferred both royal and high-society links to the Tiffany name.

Longtime Tiffany clients Jeptha Homer Wade II of Cleveland, Ohio, named for a grandfather who had founded the Western Union Telegraph Co. in 1856, and his wife, Ellen Garretson Wade, were also prominent collectors of gems and jewelry. Knowledgeable and sophisticated collectors who traveled extensively, the Wades acquired precious objects in places as far flung as London, Paris, Berlin, and Rome as well as Constantinople, Bombay, Tokyo, Bangkok, and St. Petersburg.[35] At the World's Columbian Exposition of 1893 in Chicago they acquired an enameled and jeweled bracelet with pierced figures from French jeweler Henri Vever. In the next year and a half, the couple met

with gem dealers and jewelers that included Marcus & Co. and, from whom they bought an enameled scent bottle (*vinaigrette*) with jeweled lid, a turquoise ring, and a figured brooch in gold—all made by René Lalique.[36] The Wades probably engaged Tiffany to mount some of the gems purchased during their travels, as in the case of a group of emeralds purchased in Delhi, which the firm set in 1894.[37] The Wades bought many items at Tiffany's London shop, including a tortoiseshell and linen fan, a diamond bowknot brooch, and a hat pin set with sapphires and diamonds. Tiffany also created a richly colored pink tourmaline and diamond necklace with stones either collected by the Wades or supplied by Kunz, and a necklace of diamond brilliants in the Belle Époque style. These two remarkable necklaces show the prowess of Tiffany & Co. in traditional compositions of extraordinary gems, featuring the stones in symmetrical, garland-style settings inspired by eighteenth-century ornament. Such jewelry became identified with Tiffany, which rivaled the great firms of Europe for the size, color, and quantity of the stones they would set. Formal, historicist jewelry was absolutely essential for women in the highest echelons of society, such as Anna Gould and Elizabeth Wade, especially those who were presented at court in London or who regularly attended the opening nights of operas around the world.

A review of the Wades' acquisitions and an address list of their favorite shops suggest that the couple began their gem and jewelry collection by purchasing items from Cleveland retailer Cowell & Hubbard, but soon they were buying gems and jewelry on their travels. They made visits in New York to silversmiths Howard & Co., jewelers Dreicer & Son, and Japanese art importer Yamanaka & Co. In Philadelphia, they purchased from Bailey Banks & Biddle, and Caldwell & Co. In London, they visited art dealers Thos. Agnew & Son and silversmiths Hukin and Heath, and in Paris, Spaulding &

Wade purchased this ornamental comb from Lalique's shop after admiring his work at the 1900 Exposition Universelle in Paris (cat. 162). The delicate lily of the valley was a common Art Nouveau motif and also used extensively by Fabergé in his flower studies (cat. 72).

Fig. 96. The group of invoices at right shows jewelry purchased by Wade from several different sources.

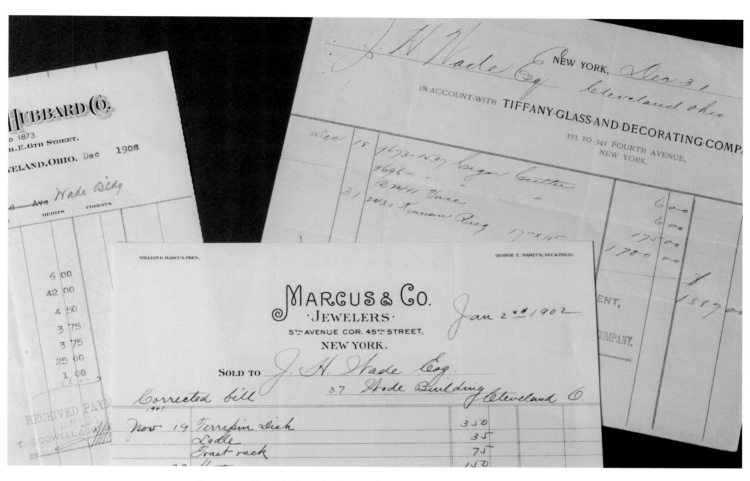

Co., as well as Tiffany & Co. In the Paris atelier of René Lalique they purchased a hair comb decorated with lilies of the valley, now in the Cleveland Museum of Art.

The Wades were also a client of Louis Tiffany's firm, Tiffany Studios, having commissioned two mosaic walls and an important stained-glass window for the burial vault of Mr. Wade's grandfather in Cleveland just before 1900.[38] This window was considered so spectacular that Tiffany requested it for his display at the Paris Exposition of that year. It was one of four such windows in the United States pavilion at the fair. Afterward, the window came back to Cleveland to be installed in the remarkable chapel interior in Lake View Cemetery.

The purchases of Jeptha and Ellie Wade offer a rare insight into the challenges faced by jewelers in attracting and retaining wealthy customers. In the late nineteenth century, although most American manufacturers had achieved industrial parity with their English and Continental counterparts, the public perception of American inferiority remained, and Americans frequently returned from their travels with furnishings, clothing, and jewelry. Tiffany combated this potential loss of revenue by opening stores in Paris and London where foreign wares were sold alongside those of the firm, making it "European" by association.

Eclectic in buying from many vendors, the Wades were selective in building a quality collection of gems and ornaments, invariably concentrating on the rarity of the gems and the luxury of their settings. Their repeated visits to Marcus & Co. demonstrates that Herman Marcus and his sons were significant competition for Tiffany & Co., which provided custom settings for the precious gems the couple purchased elsewhere.

Emerald Parks and Diamond Necklaces: The Wade Family Legacy in Cleveland

During the Gilded Age, Cleveland's oil magnates, inventors, and captains of industry lived side by side on Euclid Avenue, known as "Millionaires' Row." Euclid was one of the most beautiful streets in America. French actress Sarah Bernhardt performed in Cleveland's theaters on her American tours, and local firms such as such as Potter & Mellen and Cowell & Hubbard sold luxurious accessories, including bejeweled parasol handles, snuffboxes, lorgnettes, and silver serving pieces that gilded an era of prosperity. On the corner of Euclid and Case Avenues, not far from the grand home of John D. Rockefeller, lived Jeptha Homer Wade (1811–1890), founder of Western Union Telegraph Company.

The year before he died, Wade wrote out his life's story for his grandson, Jeptha Wade II (1857–1926). The account is a nineteenth-century rags-to-riches tale. Born in New York State and entering the trades at the age of twelve, Wade learned leather tanning and shoemaking, brickmaking, and carpentry. As a young man, he befriended a portrait painter, Randall Palmer, who shared Wade's love of music. During one of their discussions, Palmer handed Wade a brush and a canvas and encouraged him to paint. The experiment worked, and Wade became an itinerant portrait painter for hire like Palmer. Jeptha married Rebecca Loueza Facer in 1832, and in 1835 the couple had a son whom they named Randall

(1835–1876) after their friend. Wade described the challenges of life as a painter:

> I made out to support myself and family with my brushes till forced by ill health to quit painting in 1845. . . . Good paints, brushes, etc., were hard, and sometimes impossible, to get in the country and I was sometimes obliged to make, and always to grind and prepare all the paints myself, and was without access to good works of art from which to learn, or I might say any works of art.[1]

Jeptha's financial fortunes improved dramatically in the 1850s. He found work as a subcontractor putting up telegraph lines across the Midwest. Recognizing enormous opportunity in the technology, Wade consolidated his lines with those of thirteen other companies to create the Western Union Telegraph Company. After establishing other Morse system outposts in Ohio, Wade moved his family to Cleveland in 1856.

In this era of early photography and bodiless voices over gramophones and telephone wires, occult spiritualism was gaining popularity. Perhaps Wade's understanding of telegraphic communication made mental telepathy seem particularly feasible; he was a devoted attendee at local séances. The Wade family papers at the Western Reserve Historical Society in Cleveland contain a lively correspondence between Jeptha and his first wife and son, both before and after

Fig. 97. Before founding the Western Union Telegraph Co., young Jeptha H. Wade made a living as an itinerant portrait painter. He painted this portrait of Nathaniel Olds in 1837.

Fig. 98. In 1896 Jeptha Wade II and his wife traveled to Russia where they purchased jewelry and luxury goods from several makers, all revealed within their extensive travel journals. The receipt pictured at right is from the St. Petersburg shop of a Mr. Jakobson.

their untimely deaths, such as this note from 11 February 1882 to his deceased son:

> My Dear Randall
> Is Mrs. Cristie on the Crawford Road an honest Medium? Write me fully about that and anything else you wish. Give my love, thanks and a kiss to your Angel Mother for her last letter and ask her to write me again.
> Yours Affectionately,
> J. H. Wade[2]

For Wade, life continued after death, and this belief would later inform one of the family's most important artistic commissions.

Randall's son, Jeptha II, inherited his family's sense of adventure. In the 1880s, traffic stopped on Euclid Avenue to watch the young man pass by on his new high-wheeled bicycle, riding toward Public Square.[3] Like his philanthropic grandfather, Jeptha II supported worthy charities, including the Children's Fresh Air Camp and the Protestant Orphan Society. As a park commissioner, Jeptha II fought against city apathy to create Cleveland's Metroparks system, called the Emerald Necklace, perhaps after

Frederick Law Olmsted's series of green spaces in and around Boston.

Jeptha II married Ellen Garretson in 1878 and the two traveled around the world as art and gem collectors. Journals capture the daily activities of two young socialites in cities as far away as Cairo and New Delhi. Their address books contain pages of gemological notes, art purchases, and the addresses of the finest art dealers, jewelers, and fashion houses along their routes.

In 1896, the Wades traveled to Russia on the heels of an historic event: the 26 May coronation in Moscow of the last tsar, Nicholas II, and his wife, Alexandra Feodorovna, which was marred by tragedy. At a banquet provided for Moscow's citizens, rumors that free beer and souvenir enameled cups were in short supply caused the crowd to surge forward, crushing thousands of people. Despite his desire not to attend the French embassy ball the following evening, Nicholas II's uncles persuaded him that it would be a political misstep not to go, a decision the tsar's subjects never forgave. Wade's journal entry from 2 July 1896 reveals the tension and anxiety in Moscow just weeks after the fateful events:

> The emperor is now living a few miles out of the City. The line to St. Petersburg we found patrolled the entire distance by soldiers as the Emperor leaves for that city in a few days. . . . Drove out to the plain near Petrovsky palace where recently 4,000 were killed & 4,000 wounded in the stampede. The chief cause of the disaster was a trench a 1000 feet long & 5 feet deep into which they fell & were trampled to death.[4]

Despite the tragic scene he related, Wade and his wife went on to marvel at the opulence of the Russian state. The couple visited the Kremlin Armory, Tsarskoe Selo, Sts. Peter and Paul Cathedral, and various bazaars and expositions in Moscow and St. Petersburg. At the Hermitage Museum they marveled at the "most superb collection of boxes, watches, & jeweled ornaments I ever saw."[5] The Wades collected examples of

Russian fans, lace, and other luxury goods on this Russian tour, some of which are now in the collection of the Cleveland Museum of Art.

Following their return to Cleveland, planning began on a memorial to Jeptha H. Wade in Lake View Cemetery, whose plots were marketed to high society as an idyllic final resting place away from the pollution of downtown. In 1881, the cemetery's prestige rose when President James Garfield was interred in a towering monument.[6] Because the park was outgrowing its facilities, the Wade Memorial Chapel was commissioned as a new receiving vault and chapel.[7] Jeptha II chose Hubbell & Benes architects to create an intimate neoclassical temple. This same firm would later design the Cleveland Museum of Art (1913–16) along similar lines. When ground broke for the chapel in 1900, stonemasons arrived from Italy to cut the quarried stone, and many settled permanently on the nearby slope in what is today Little Italy.

Jeptha II also commissioned Louis Comfort Tiffany, the most important American designer of the era, to decorate the interior. Tiffany's windows had been installed in several Cleveland churches, office buildings, and private homes since the 1880s, proving him to be a fashionable choice. His firm, the Tiffany Glass & Decorating Co., had effectively showcased its large-scale ecclesiastical work at the 1893 Columbian Exposition in Chicago with a mosaic chapel interior with bronze fittings.

Frederick Wilson, an English artist who specialized in ecclesiastical work for Tiffany and was "second only to Tiffany himself among Tiffany Studio's artists," designed the mosaic panels that span each side wall.[8] The Women's Glass Cutting Department executed them in New York.[9] On the west wall seven Old Testament prophets strain at their oars, with Death symbolically surmounting the barge; the east wall presents figures from the New Testament. Religious symbolism is heavy throughout Wilson's scenes, but the chapel's

interior is ecumenical in its design. The wave pattern on the floor, tiled like an ancient Roman bath, carries the aquatic theme from wall to wall. The white alabaster and gilt-bronze lamp fixtures, in Moorish style with Egyptian motifs, are some of the earliest electric lights in Cleveland.

The interior's crowning gem, however, is the window above the altar, *The Flight of the Soul*, designed by Tiffany himself.[10] It features the apotheosis of Jesus into heaven amid a rainbow-arced sky, with a field of poppies (symbolizing sleep) parted by lilies (denoting rebirth). In its middle section, horizontal striations of Tiffany's celebrated Favrile glass depict "the sea of crystal described in the Apocalyptic vision as flowing before the throne of heaven."[11] This theme of rebirth suggests Jeptha's private belief in an afterlife, which also included the spirit world:

> I have always felt surer that my intellect and reason were given me for use by my Creator, who will hold me responsible, than I am that he wrote any book. I have listened a good deal, and reflected upon Orthodox preaching, and have also been an honest and somewhat thorough searcher for proof touching the question of our future existence. And while the church never gave me any satisfactory proof of it, I have found elsewhere what is

Fig. 99. Wade commissioned a window, *The Flight of the Soul*, from Louis Comfort Tiffany for the family chapel and mausoleum at Lake View Cemetery in Cleveland. Tiffany regarded the final product so highly that he asked to show it in the United States Palace of the Liberal Arts at the 1900 Exposition Universelle in Paris. Unfortunately, when Wade saw the window installed there, he complained that it was "dimly lit."

Fig. 100. *The Flight of the Soul*, designed by Louis Comfort Tiffany around 1899.

Addresses

[handwritten address book page showing European jewelers and silversmiths]

to me conclusive proof that life is continuous and that our departed friends are not absent from us after death, but are about us, invisible, and can under favorable circumstances, and sometimes do, communicate with us.[12]

Considered in these terms, the chapel dedicated to Jeptha H. Wade by his grandson reflects a varied system of spiritual beliefs. It may have meant something very personal to Jeptha II as well because his father's death had largely spurred his grandfather to try communicating with loved ones by transcendental means.

For his part, Louis Comfort Tiffany considered the chapel's seven-by-nine foot window as one of his finest ecclesiastical windows and asked Wade if he could include it in the firm's display at the 1900 Exposition Universelle before installing it in Cleveland. Jeptha II and Ellen traveled to the exposition, where they saw their window prominently displayed in the United States pavilion.

The Wades visited the finest luxury purveyors, both at the fair and in the chic shopping districts of Paris. Their address book includes René Lalique's studio in the rue Thérèse as well as Tiffany & Co.'s Paris and London branch stores, along with impressions of both: "Visited Lalique's shop and was much interested in his

artistic designs in jewelry."[13] More than just curious, the Wades purchased a beautiful hair comb of carved horn and enameled lilies of the valley now in the collection of the Cleveland Museum of Art. A lyrical expression of Art Nouveau, such a comb was still wearable for a lady of society in comparison to the massive sculptural ornaments Lalique designed for leading stage actresses.

At the exposition, the critical reception of their Tiffany window was favorable, although Jeptha II did not think very highly of the installation: "At L. C. Tiffany's our chapel window has not enough light & looks dull & grey. Their glass is fine but has insufficient light to show it."[14] The window returned to Cleveland after the fair ended in November and was fitted into the chapel wall above the altar, where shifting light continually transforms the piece throughout the day.

When a group of wealthy Cleveland citizens came together in the 1890s to plan the city's first art museum, Jeptha II had the opportunity to fulfill another of his grandfather's wishes, by donating the land upon which the new museum would sit. The museum founders hired Wade Chapel architects Hubbell & Benes in 1906 to design

Fig. 101. The page at left from Wade's address book gives the locations of European jewelers and silversmiths, including Spaulding & Co., Tiffany & Co., and Lalique in Paris as well as the Arts and Crafts purveyors Hukin & Heath in London.

Fig. 102. This rear view of the Wade Chapel in Lake View Cemetery around 1905 shows the window, *The Flight of the Soul,* installed at the north end.

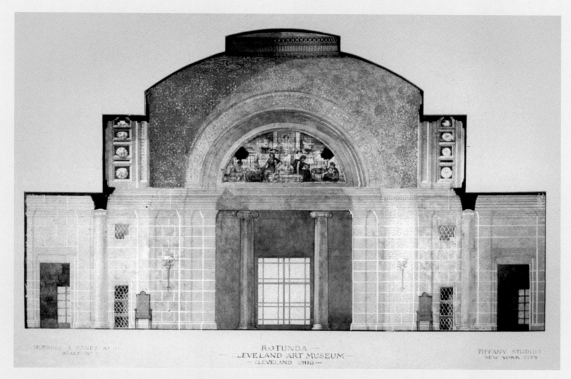

Fig. 103. This unrealized decorative scheme of around 1915 by Tiffany Studios was meant for the rotunda of the Cleveland Museum of Art.

the building; the architects, in turn, asked Louis Comfort Tiffany to submit ideas for decorating the dome and lunettes in the museum's grand rotunda. Although his mosaic designs were never realized, Tiffany's bronze lighting standards were executed and installed. Jeptha II served as the museum's first vice president when it opened in 1916. He also donated vast amounts of his family collections to the museum and other Cleveland cultural institutions, providing the city with a rich legacy of Gilded Age collecting.

Catherine Walworth

1. J. H. Wade, "Sketch of the Life of J. H. Wade from 1811 to about 1867" (unpublished manuscript, July 1889), container 3, folder 19, Jeptha Homer Wade Family Papers (hereafter Wade Family Papers), Western Reserve Historical Society, Cleveland.

2. Wade, MS 3292, container 2, folder 16, Wade Family Papers.

3. William Ganson Rose, *Cleveland: The Making of a City* (Kent, Ohio: Kent State University Press, 1990), 434.

4. J. H. Wade II, journal "Russia, Germany, Switzerland" (June to September 1896), MS3292, container 6, folder 45, Wade Family Papers.

5. Ibid.

6. "The Final Resting Place: The Beautiful Place Selected for the Grave—The Scenes along the Avenue to the Cemetery," *New York Times*, 26 September 1881, 1.

7. Diana Tittle, *The Jeptha Wade Memorial Chapel* (Cleveland: Lake View Cemetery Association, 2003), unpaginated.

8. Pamphlet, "In Memory of Jeptha Wade" (1901), unpaginated, Western Reserve Historical Society.

9. Martin Eidelberg et al., *A New Light on Tiffany: Clara Driscoll and the Tiffany Girls*, exh. cat. (New York: New York Historical Society, 2007), 35.

10. This is the title used in period publications: "Tiffany-Gläser auf der Pariser Welt-Ausstellung 1900," *Deutsche Kunst und Dekoration* 7 (October 1900-March 1901), 92, and "Les Vitraux à L'Exposition de 1900," *Revue des Arts Décoratifs* 20 (1900), 276.

11. Ibid.

12. J. H. Wade, "Sketch of the Life of J. H. Wade," Wade Family Papers.

13. J. H. Wade II, journal, "Paris and England (June to September 1900)," MS 3292, container 6, folder 46, Wade Family Papers.

14. Ibid.

While the patronage of nationally significant wealthy families was crucial to the reputation of the Tiffany name, the firm also sought and received important commissions from politicians that were widely reported in the popular press, bringing instant recognition to both Tiffany & Co. and the new firm of Louis Comfort Tiffany. Weddings in the families of two American presidents produced a flood of luxury gifts, both domestic and foreign, for presidential daughters. When Julia D. Grant, the granddaughter of Ulysses S. Grant, married Prince Cantacuzene of Russia in 1899, she received from her father-in-law, Grand Duke Vladimir, several works by Lalique: a large corsage ornament of diamonds and enamel, a very long necklace of pearls with enamel and diamond drops (*sautoir*), and a corsage ornament featuring a cabochon sapphire.

Fig. 104. Martin Johnson Heade's evocative and scientifically detailed paintings of orchids reflect the late-nineteenth-century obsession with cultivating this seductive flower.

From her American guests, Julia Grant received dozens of gifts made of silver and gold, but in press accounts almost none were identified by maker except "Tiffany," possibly Louis Comfort Tiffany, in five separate gifts of glass, one with a silver jar.[39] Their friend, the Baltimore collector Henry Walters, conveyed the newlyweds from Newport to New York on his yacht, the *Narada*. When Walters visited the couple two years later at their home in St. Petersburg, they visited the newly opened House of Fabergé on Morskaya Street, where Walters purchased parasol handles ornamented with enamel and jewels, and hardstone animal sculptures.[40]

The 1906 wedding of Theodore Roosevelt's oldest daughter, Alice, to Nicholas Longworth, the U.S. Representative from Ohio, yielded similar costly goods. Gifts from friends and heads of state included rich-cut glass, a jeweled fan from Tiffany & Co., a silver-mounted Favrile vessel, and seven dozen Favrile glasses by Tiffany Studios. In addition, Rookwood ceramics were given by Longworth's family, who were related to members of Cincinnati pottery studio. Two unnamed Providence, Rhode Island, silversmithing firms, one of which was almost certainly Gorham, produced a ninety-piece silver service for the newlyweds.[41] Exhaustively covered in the newspapers, such events offered ordinary readers a voyeuristic view into the lives of the rich and famous. The highly publicized lists of wedding gifts were a form of product placement that gave young brides ideas for their own trousseaus and which Tiffany & Co. and Tiffany Studios fulfilled at a wide range of prices. In this manner, the Tiffany name conjured up simultaneous notions of exclusivity and affordability that was the secret of its great success.

Orchid brooches were the stars of the 1889 Exposition Universelle in Paris, where they were shown by many firms, not just Tiffany & Co., reflecting the international popularity for realistic interpretations of nature. This example at left is probably from the Paris workshop of Georges Duval and Julien Le Turcq (cat. 315).

The large orchid brooch at right retains its original snakeskin presentation case, marked for the Paris showroom of Tiffany & Co. Precisely rendered orchid jewels such as this one were designed by Paulding Farnham after actual specimen orchids (cat. 262).

Tiffany at International and National Expositions

Ever since the New York Crystal Palace Exhibition of 1853, Charles Lewis Tiffany had appreciated the visibility that international events offered his firm. As each successive show brought greater accolades to Tiffany & Co., it was clear that such fairs provided an unparalleled platform to market their goods.[42] When C. L. Tiffany and Edward C. Moore chose Paulding Farnham to design works for the 1889 Exposition Universelle in Paris, they ushered in a great age of jewelry for the company. Farnham designed magnificent gem-set jewelry along with a sensational display of twenty-four orchids based on individual species of the exotic flowers.

The attraction of orchids in the nineteenth century was due in part to their rarity. Plucked from the wild in remote areas of South

America, orchids were acquired at great prices early in the century by horticulturists. Obsessed with the flowers, the New York financier Jay Gould was said to lavish hundreds of thousands of dollars on the plants and a greenhouse for their cultivation. American painter Martin Johnson Heade furthered the craze by traveling to South America in 1866, where he began to paint orchids and hummingbirds. Orchids became more accessible to the general public as better methods of transport and care were devised. In 1885 a single orchid plant cost fifty dollars and required a greenhouse for proper care, but by 1899, one author proclaimed that "the cultivation of orchidaceous plants is no longer the privilege of the few ... where there were once hundreds there are now thousands who fairly worship these aerial beauties."[43]

Tiffany jewelers achieved remarkably naturalistic effects in the orchid series. Surviving sketches demonstrate that the artists prepared for their task by closely examining orchids from life and from botanical references. Subtly shifting leaves, seductive coloring, and alternating shiny and matte enameled surfaces of the flowers reveal the jewelers' painstaking efforts in fabrication and enameling. Gem-set stems added sparkle and winking pendant diamonds conveyed the flash of a sparkling dewdrop.

When the enameled and gem-set orchids were briefly placed on view in New York before the 1889 exposition, the ornaments were greeted warmly by critics who described "stems made green with emeralds." In Paris, the orchids were considered "so faithfully reproduced that one would almost doubt that they are enamel, so well do they simulate the real flowers."[44] In this, his first exposition, Farnham demonstrated his facility for designing in a range of styles. He devised large, formal diamond-set corsages and necklaces as well as a series of brooches with Native American designs drawn from Zuni pottery, Sitka basketwork, and Sioux war shields.[45] These were Farnham's first efforts in working with Native American motifs, which complemented the engraved scenes of an Indian buffalo hunt that adorned a humidor shown by the firm.

For the first time, Tiffany & Co. staked its claim to the all-American quality of its designs, materials, and labor, a theme it would reinforce at future expositions. A windfall of honors included the grand prize for silverware, five gold medals for jewelry as well as Kunz's collection of North American pearls and precious stones, and other awards for achievements in leather, engraving, and printing.

Tiffany & Co. and Gorham Mfg. Co. enjoyed a prominent location at the Chicago world's fair in 1893, opposite the clock tower of the Manufacturing Building. Slightly smaller and adjacent to Tiffany & Co. was the Tiffany Glass & Decorating Co. This location was no doubt arranged with the elder

With its scenes of buffalo hunting, tobogganing, and other outdoor pursuits, not to mention its distinctive bison finial, this humidor by Tiffany & Co. represented the optimism and national pride reflected in the American West (cat. 248). It was presented as a gift from one of America's foremost industrialists, August Belmont, to the heir of one of Europe's greatest fortunes, Lionel Walter Rothschild, in 1889.

Fig. 105. Tiffany & Co.'s booth was situated next to that of Gorham Mfg. Co., its chief American rival, at the 1893 World's Columbian Exposition in Chicago.

Fig 106. The August 1893 issue of *Godey's Magazine* included an essay by Tiffany & Co. publicist George Frederic Heydt on the firm's exhibit at the Chicago world's fair. The design for the title (below) shows how important big gems were to Tiffany's stock-in-trade.

Tiffany's cooperation, if not encouragement, to benefit his son's growing enterprise. Together, Gorham and the two Tiffany firms constituted the most sizable installations within their division at the fair.

With the death in 1891 of Edward C. Moore, Tiffany & Co. had lost the firm's first and foremost hollowware and jewelry designer. Fortunately, two talented men were ready to step into his shoes. Paulding Farnham had proved himself as a jewelry designer at the 1889 Paris exposition and was appointed head of this division in 1891; another Moore protégé, John C. Curran, became head of hollowware. Both men were well prepared to create a memorable display for the 1893 exposition, designed as a grand neoclassical city that proudly welcomed the world.

Tiffany & Co. featured an impressive quantity of hollowware that included large and ambitious vessels in an array of historical styles. Of them, forms based on Viking, pre-Columbian, and Native American designs were notable. The company also borrowed back from various owners a collection of their yachting trophies of impressive size and sculptural form. The many outstanding works included giant tankards, punch bowls, chargers, love cups, and a table, all of silver and many adorned with elephant tusks, mother-of pearl, turquoise, and rare woods that demonstrated the firm's myriad skills

in the mounting and inlay of exotic materials. Smaller fancy works such as canes, boxes, chatelaine bags, and bonbonnières abounded, each unique in concept and execution.

Perhaps more remarkable than the display of hollowware was the firm's "million dollar" installation of jewelry.[46] Most of the jewelry designed under Farnham's direction was, like the hollowware, intended to emulate styles and refer to costumes from around the world. By comparison, his ethereal Cupid and dove pendant watch hints at experimentation with new designs in jewelry. While the subjects are ancient, the playful entrapment of the dove, arranged in a vertical composition of carved moonstone and diamond-set gold ribbons, is a tribute to both designer and lapidary.

The 1893 Chicago exposition was a turning point for Tiffany & Co. Not only did it garner the greatest acclaim to date, but it was also the first serious debut of Charles Tiffany's son in the public arena. Born scarcely twelve years after his father went into business, Louis Comfort Tiffany grew up in a prosperous family, but this advantage did not inhibit his desire to do something significant with his life. Influenced by the jewelry, decorative arts, and sculptures sold at his father's store, he pursued academic training in painting in 1866 at the National Academy of Design, including studies of antique casts. Two years later in Paris, Tiffany worked in the studio of Léon Bailly and pursued informal lessons with his friend, the American painter Samuel Colman. In 1870, he traveled to North Africa, painting along the way with Robert Swain Gifford.[47] The exotic imagery of the region left an indelible impression on Tiffany; he frequently revisited it in his paintings, and from that time forward it colored his approach to decorative arts.

Far left: Fig.107. Some of Tiffany's "million dollar" jewels displayed at the 1893 World's Columbian Exposition were shown on the smiling bust of a woman.

Left: Exoticism popularized at the 1893 world's fair endured long enough as a successful motif to resurface at later expositions. The eclectic ornamental tankard at left made from an elephant tusk was a feature of Tiffany's booth at the Paris exposition of 1900 (cat. 272).

The revival of historical styles reached the apex of popularity after 1890. The Renaissance-style dog collar (above, cat. 245) and carved moonstone pendant watch in the Louis XVI style (right, cat. 242), the latter designed by Paulding Farnham for Tiffany & Co.'s display at the 1893 world's fair in Chicago.

Louis Tiffany's education was also advanced by his association with his father's firm. At the Philadelphia Centennial of 1876, where Tiffany & Co. exhibited several of his North African paintings, the young Tiffany was exposed to the highly popular Japanese pavilion and its quantities of goods.[48] Through his father, he likely also met English botanist and designer Christopher Dresser, who visited the exposition on his way to Japan.[49] Louis may also have seen examples of East Indian jewelry displayed by London's India Museum in the centennial's main building, an influence that would remain a strong current throughout his design career.[50] Other American jewelers designed in this style, including Marcus & Co.

Charles Tiffany was supporting his son as late as 1878, when the commercial credit reporting agency R. G. Dun & Co. reported that the twenty-nine-year-old Louis Tiffany was "a young [married] man of fair ability & no means whatever," aside from funds provided by his father.[51] Two years later, the Dun report noted that Louis Tiffany's venture with Candace Wheeler, called Tiffany & Wheeler, was underwritten by his father, and recognized the patronage that their "influential circle of friends & acquaintances" could provide.[52] It is evident that Charles Tiffany's support was a critical source of strength that freed his son to realize his own commercial goals. These funds provided Louis with the financial, and ultimately artistic, control that he sought in his various partnerships, Louis C.

An early interest in motifs associated with the Near East surfaced in all aspects of Louis Comfort Tiffany's design, including jewelry such as this opal and gemstone brooch suggestive of early moghul jewels from India (cat. 283).

Marcus & Co., Tiffany's great rival in the New York jewelry trade around 1900, also produced work inspired by the Near East (detail, cat. 205).

Fig. 108. Louis Tiffany traveled extensively in North Africa and the Near East, painting along the way with his friend the American artist Robert Swain Gifford. This painting, *Moroccan Interior*, reflects Tiffany's interest in the design motifs of the region.

Fig. 109. Louis Tiffany's career in design began in 1878 with his firm Associated Artists, which worked on the interiors for noted social families, and culminated in his enhancement of the White House under President Chester A. Arthur in 1881. Tiffany described his stained-glass screen in the entrance hall as having "a motif of eagles and flags, interlaced in the Arabian method."

Interests in interior design and glass-making were interwoven in Louis Tiffany's ornamental windows for domestic spaces such as this window for a house in Cleveland, in which he created a veritable "painting" in glass of an idyllic outdoor scene (cat. 285).

Tiffany & Co. and Associated Artists, which at various times included Wheeler, Lockwood de Forest, the painter Samuel Colman, and others who participated as partners or contracted artists.[53] These fruitful ventures channeled the skills cultivated by his art education toward the more practical and commercially viable interior design business. No doubt the reputation of Tiffany & Co. helped Louis and his partners obtain important commissions, though his first major work was one actually created for himself.

Louis first turned his hand seriously to interior decoration in 1878, when he designed his own residence, the Bella Apartments at 48 East 26th Street in New York. The bold eclecticism he achieved by combining exotic motifs brought him important commissions executed alone or with others throughout the 1880s. In 1890 Tiffany and his partner, Samuel Colman, received perhaps their most important and ultimately most significant commission, the interior of Henry O. and Louisine Havemeyer's home at Fifth Avenue and 66th Street in New York. For this project, which is clearly his most original expression, Tiffany created rich textures and layers of Near and Far Eastern decoration.

The Havemeyer interior also served as a proving ground for some of Louis Tiffany's later work in stained glass, blown glass, and jewelry. His designs for a desk lamp and chandeliers in the residence presage his interest in lighting well before any examples of his celebrated table and floor lamps were publicly exhibited.[54] Moreover, his use of emerald-like glass and smooth beach stones amid a delicate wrought-iron setting foreshadowed his compositions in jewelry.[55] The Havemeyer commission was thought to have been initiated by Colman,[56] but many others—such as the Fifth Avenue residences of George Kemp and Cornelius Vanderbilt, the Seventh Regiment Armory, and the White House's magnificent stained-glass screen and redecoration under Chester A. Arthur—were secured largely by Tiffany himself, based on his family connections and his ability to marshal large forces of talented decorators and artisans.

Louis Comfort Tiffany, Artist in Glass

As early as 1873, Louis Comfort Tiffany had been busily exploring the physical properties of colored glass and later took out three patents: for iridescent glass tesserae, or tiles; for plating glass panels together; and for the use of oxides to create iridescence on window glass. Like his rival John La Farge, who was ten years his senior, Tiffany rejected the painted glass windows that had become standard by the mid nineteenth century. The efforts of the two artists to "paint" with pure, unadulterated, colored glass led each to work closely with craftsmen to develop special glass for this purpose. Each artist developed more refined leading to avoid the obstruction of structural horizontal bars. Both focused on creating volume and atmosphere by layering and using opalescent glass, a new kind of glass that La Farge may have first attempted as early as 1876 and patented in 1879.

In 1885, Louis Tiffany had established the Tiffany Glass Company at 333 Fourth Avenue, while continuing his work as a decorator. In that same year he took on the first of several commissions for three members of the Garrett family in Baltimore, interior decoration projects that kept him and his partner Lockwood de Forest occupied for several years. Tiffany produced some of his most important and early stained-glass compositions for the Garretts while de Forest designed some rooms in the East Indian style in which he had become fluent.[57]

Shortly after the 1889 exposition, perhaps in response to La Farge's success, Tiffany was studying stained glass in European churches. During this period he also visited Émile Gallé's famed glass workshops in Nancy, where he may have begun to consider the possibilities of blown glass.[58] Louis Tiffany had commenced a new chapter in his long and creative life. He established Tiffany Glass & Decorating Co. in 1892 and opened furnaces in nearby Corona, Long Island, from which blown-glass vessels and leaded-glass lamps soon emerged.

Louis Comfort Tiffany always took primary credit for the designs and products of his firm, despite the assistance of many craftsmen and designers required by the scale and number of his projects. A few stained-glass designers were marginally known to the public, such as Frederick Wilson, a figurative specialist, and Agnes Northrop, a floral designer. Louis Tiffany valued the women in the glass-

Fig. 110. Workers at Tiffany Studios assemble glass for windows and lamps around 1913.

Louis Tiffany presented a line of enameled wares at the 1900 Paris world's fair to great acclaim. With their deep, rich colors and naturalistic motifs, these works evoked an ethereal aesthetic well at home with his other Art Nouveau creations (cat. 240).

Tiffany used Favrile glass in many applications including mosaics such as this dragonfly trivet, poppy wall plaque, and water lilies paperweight (above, cat. 298) and, as unfinished pieces (below cat. 297), in clocks, tiles, mantels, and windows.

One type of Favrile glass by Tiffany was called "paperweight" because the designs encapsulated small bits of formed glass in the manner of Venetian glass paperweights, as in the narcissus vase at left (cat. 289). Émile Gallé employed the same technique in his inlaid glass works called *marqueterie de verre.*

cutting department for their sensitivity to the nuances of color and their skill in handling glass, but these very skills created tensions with the male staff, who were concerned with job stability.[59]

Clara Driscoll's role within the firm as glass-cutting designer and department manager grew in responsibility and creative scope because of her access to Tiffany, who was receptive to her designs and authorized many for production.[60] She is credited with introducing mosaic tiles for use on lamp bases that until then were made solely in metal or glass. Though Driscoll was known only as the designer of the dragonfly lamp, recently discovered letters document her many contributions to Tiffany's highly regarded series in this genre, including the wisteria, peony, poppy, and swirling butterfly lamps.[61]

The familiarity of Tiffany & Co.'s retail business enhanced recognition of Louis Comfort Tiffany's products, but to prevent confusion between the two firms his name was prominently featured on all advertisements and brochures, and newspaper coverage invariably referred to Louis Comfort Tiffany, with rare mention of other designers or individuals. His initials or full name were also often

engraved on the works, further negating the contribution of others in the fabrication. Promotional materials often included the phrase that work was made "under the personal supervision of Louis Comfort Tiffany," despite the fact that the business had grown beyond the supervision of one man.[62] Such language reinforced the image of a single artist who led a many-faceted enterprise, but did little to advance his staff. Tiffany's dominance led to grumbling among the ranks, especially in later years by Arthur J. Nash, an English craftsman formerly in the employ of Thomas Webb, and his son Leslie H. Nash, who were key figures in the development of Favrile glass.[63]

By the time of the 1893 exhibition, Tiffany had already begun to produce glass vessels at his new glasshouse in Corona, New York, although he did not show them publicly until a year later. Working privately in his studio with the help of a Dr. Doremus, who assisted him on at least one occasion in creating colored glass, and in the Corona glasshouse with Arthur Nash, he began to see gratifying results. In April 1894, examples were shipped to the Parisian gallery of Siegfried Bing, where they soon found their way into public collections. By the next month these experiments were also on view in the firm's workshops on Fourth Avenue, near 24th Street, and in June of the same year at the Boston painting gallery of Williams & Everett. One American reviewer, undecided about the startling new shapes, colors, and finishes in the New York exhibition, nevertheless declared, "but the series is an interesting one, and will repay a visit, even if merely a visit of curiosity, to see the beginnings of a new industry, for such it may well become under the auspices of the Tiffany Glass Company."[64]

The initial years of glassblowing produced a thrilling range of forms, colors, and techniques that hint at the many ideas with which Tiffany and his staff experimented. These richly colored vessels, some with irregular contours and others with undulating forms derived from plant forms and gourds, are among the best of his career. His patrons Henry O. and Louisine Havemeyer purchased many of these early pieces and gave fifty-six of them to the Metropolitan Museum of Art in 1896, scarcely two years after the first vessels were exhibited.[65] Louis Tiffany and Samuel Colman installed the glass at Havemeyer's request, which provided an excellent public relations opportunity for the company. That same year the Smithsonian acquired a substantial group, as did the Cincinnati Art Museum in 1897 and 1898. In time the need to create a profitable line moved Tiffany toward a more formulaic approach to shapes and iridescent finishes adapted for tableware.

The success of Favrile glass prompted Louis Tiffany to create an arresting display at the 1893 Chicago fair, the centerpiece of

Because of its glorious iridescent tail feathers, the peacock was a common motif in Art Nouveau work such as Louis Tiffany's enameled medallion (left, cat. 293) as well as in more conventional treatments such as the small powder compact sold by Tiffany & Co. (below, cat. 266).

Right, top: Mosaic work was a stunning feature of Louis Tiffany's display at the 1893 world's fair, particularly in his Byzantine-style chapel (fig. 111, facing page, left) and garden court fountain (fig. 112, facing page, right).

Right, bottom: The mosaic inkwell by Tiffany Studios incorporates more than 800 tiny pieces of Favrile glass (cat. 284).

Overleaf: Favrile glass was produced in both subtle and vibrant opaque colors with exotic swirling patterns or delicately carved surfaces in the manner of French glass artist Émile Gallé (left, cat. 303; right, cat. 301).

which was a full-scale mockup of a Byzantine-style chapel.[66] Mosaic decoration adorned the columns, stairs, baptismal font, and altar. A large electrolier in the shape of a cross dominated the center. Set with shades of green glass and delicate wirework, it foreshadowed his later jewelry designs. Hubert Bancroft, who reviewed the exposition in his mammoth *Book of the Fair*, found the whole "grouped with a view to symphony of color, the effect of which is further increased by rays of gold and emerald reflected from the ceiling."[67] In an adjacent room, a circular fountain flowed over a series of rounded steps, while in each corner, large, elliptical leaded glass globes were suspended from above. The triumph achieved in these dramatic spaces attested to Louis Tiffany's genius in interior design, and as a colorist, using the mosaic, glass, and metalwork that had become a hallmark of his company.

The installation won Louis Comfort Tiffany admirers from Europe who were visiting the Chicago fair, among them two museum directors from Berlin: Wilhelm Bode of the Gemäldegalerie and Julius Lessing of the Kunstgewerbemuseum. Lessing purchased a stained-glass window, lamps, and vessels, and thus his museum became the first in Europe to acquire glass produced under the direction of Louis Comfort Tiffany. Other visitors at the fair, the painter Hans Christiansen and glass artist Karl Engelbrecht, members of the Hamburg Chamber of Commerce, found themselves deeply attracted to the glass and also returned with examples. These men were the first to bring examples of Tiffany glass to Europe. Soon they and others would acquire even more for private and public collections, and Continental stained-glass artists would purchase sheets of Louis Comfort Tiffany's marvelously undulating and ever-changing iridescent glass for use in their own window designs.[68]

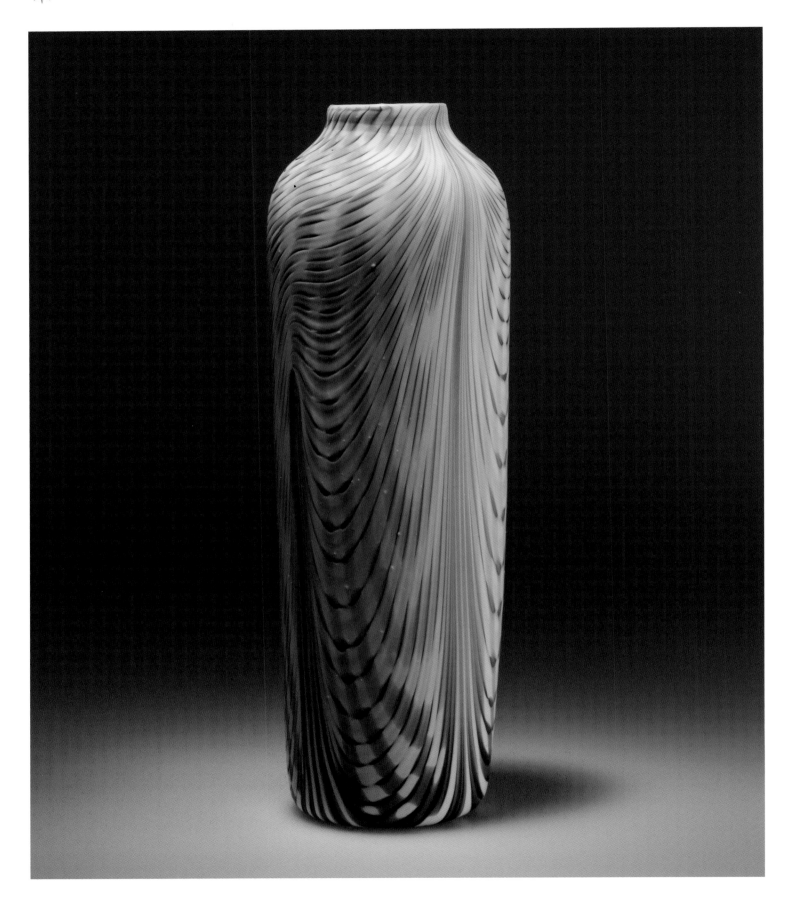

Siegfried Bing and the Marketing of Tiffany Glass

As the Chicago fair spread word of Tiffany in the United States and abroad, the Parisian art dealer Siegfried Bing played a central role in placing important works in European museums and private collections.[69] Bing was a refined art critic, dealer, and advocate of Japanese art, the founder of the gallery L'Art Nouveau, and an indefatigable advocate for Tiffany. Bing's promotional efforts were so successful that countless European imitators began to spring up whose work was generically dubbed "Tiffany" glass, proving his dominance in the market.

That Bing and Tiffany would meet was inevitable, although the exact nature and moment of their acquaintance is unknown. Both were products of merchant families that sold decorative arts; Bing's family sold Japanese wares as well as European works during the same period that Tiffany & Co. was a purveyor of jewelry, hollowware, and imported luxury goods.[70] Moreover, Bing maintained an office in New York as early as 1887. Their business relationship, which lasted approximately six years, began in 1894, when Bing traveled to the United States at the urging of Henri Roujon, director of the Société des Beaux-Arts, who was concerned about American advances in the decorative arts.

This Tiffany Favrile glass vase with French silver-gilt mounts was sold by Siegfried Bing in his Paris shop L'Art Nouveau (cat. 300).

Fig. 113. The stained-glass panel at right by Louis Tiffany, after a design by French artist Henri de Toulouse-Lautrec, *Au Nouveau Cirque: The Female Penguin and the Five Clowns (Papa Chrysanthème)*, 1894–95, is now in the collection of the Musée d'Orsay in Paris.

Fig. 114. Bing promoted Louis Tiffany's work in the major capitals of Europe through gallery exhibitions and advertisements in major art periodicals.

Bing also made the voyage in order to reach a wider audience for the Japanese art that he sold and passionately collected. In a report of the trip published in 1895 he revealed considerable knowledge of developments in American painting, sculpture, architecture, and especially the decorative arts, an area in which he was particularly interested. Tiffany was featured in this section, along with Edward C. Moore and John La Farge. Bing's chief observation was that the French could learn from American artists, who, unshackled by tradition, were willing to create imaginative works and use new techniques to make them.[71] It seems almost certain that Bing met Louis Comfort Tiffany and saw his glassmaking enterprise during this 1894 trip because of the remarkable commission that followed. One month after Bing's return to Paris, he showed samples of Tiffany's glass to members of the Nabis, a small band of French Post-Impressionist painters, and soon planned for their designs to be transformed by Tiffany into stained-glass windows.[72]

The seeds of this idea were related in a letter sent in 1894 by Édouard Vuillard to a fellow Nabi, Maurice Denis, regarding a discussion between printmaker Henri Ibels and Bing:

Here is a proposition that comes from Ibels. He has made the acquaintance of Bing, the merchant of curios who would like to present, in France, with the help of artist/decorators, a special type of colored glass where one can achieve all kinds of color, including gradations in the same color while the glass remains transparent. He has, at his home, samples of this type of glass and samples by artists of the country (who are Americans). Ibels has told him about all of us and Bing is waiting to show us samples. He would take it upon himself to have our sketches executed because the fabrication itself is a secret which they would not divulge . . . it should interest you and Bonnard most of all.[73]

Until this time, it appears the Nabis were unaware of Bing's interests in contemporary decorative arts, as indicated by Vuillard's deprecating reference to the "merchant of curios." Nevertheless, Vuillard's curiosity was aroused and the group eventually participated in Bing's project to translate their designs into Tiffany's revolutionary form of stained glass. The surviving windows validate Bing's vision, for the flat expanses of color preferred by the Nabis were a fine match for Tiffany's richly figured and opalescent glass. Bing was ahead of his time, however, and the windows, shown at the Salon of the Societé Nationale de Beaux-Arts on the Champs de Mars, did not receive the warm response that he hoped for.

Bing understood the influence that museum collections had upon collectors, however, and moved quickly to find institutions that would be receptive to Tiffany glass. With skills honed through his representation of Japanese art to patrons and museums, Bing followed a straightforward plan, holding exhibitions in a series of European cities. At each venue, he met with museum staff and usually convinced them to acquire Tiffany glass for their collection. The result was a runaway triumph: between 1894 and 1901 Bing placed works with twenty-nine museums in Great Britain, France, Germany, Austria, Sweden, and Denmark.[74]

Having shown Tiffany's work in a number of European venues, Bing turned his attention to London, where in 1899 he arranged an exhibition featuring Tiffany glass at the Grafton Galleries.[75]

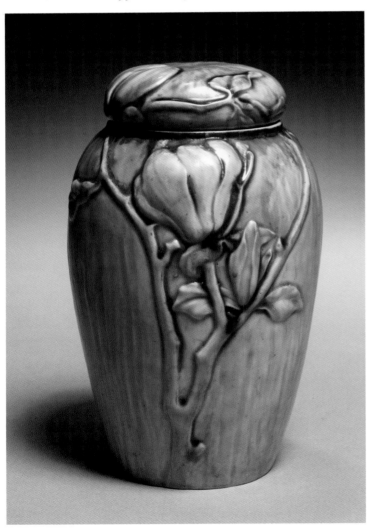

The influence of Japanese aesthetics can be seen in the asymmetrical placement of branch and blossoms on this ginger jar by Tiffany Studios (cat. 286). Ceramic production never challenged the overwhelming success of Louis Tiffany's Favrile glass, which explains the rarity of surviving pieces.

The glass was shown with "artistic jewels" designed by Edward Colonna, a talented German-born designer who had worked in the United States and Canada before his association with Bing's L'Art Nouveau workshop.[76] In addition, Bing showed "antique Japanese prints and Indo-Persian miniatures," his earlier stock-in-trade, which probably reduced the financial risk of mounting the exhibition. For the catalogue accompanying the show Bing wrote an essay introducing Louis Comfort Tiffany to a British audience. He reviewed Tiffany's early experiments in stained glass and his later achievements in opalescent and iridescent glass. Some poetic passages in the text offer insights into Bing's deep appreciation for the works on display. He found in Tiffany's glass a "nacreous richness over which played, according to the breaking of the light, an infinite variety of tones, and wherein were opalised [sic] radiations, so subtle, delicate, and mysterious, that the water of an exquisite pearl can alone be compared to them."[77] His rhapsodic language testified to Tiffany's skill in evoking and, in Bing's eyes, even surpassing the radiance of nature.

A number of electric lamps were shown in the Grafton exhibition, including one with a real nautilus shell and another with a leaded glass shade of a similar shape. This appears to be the first time that Louis Comfort Tiffany displayed domestically scaled examples of lighting in leaded glass, having moved from the large electrolier in his Columbian chapel to the "writing" lamps or "reading" and "student" lamps with shades of leaded glass intended for residential use.[78]

Eugène Feuillâtre, master enamelist, worked in Paris both independently and in the workshop of René Lalique. Feuillâtre's delicately styled pastille (hard candy) boxes, such as the one above from around 1912, were sold by Tiffany & Co., among other firms (cat. 228).

Fig. 115. This Favrile glass vase, with a gilt-metal mount adorned with plique-à-jour enamel peacock feathers, may have been shown at the 1899 exhibition at the Grafton Galleries in London. The metal armature was probably designed by Bing collaborator Edward Colonna; the enamel was executed by Feuillâtre.

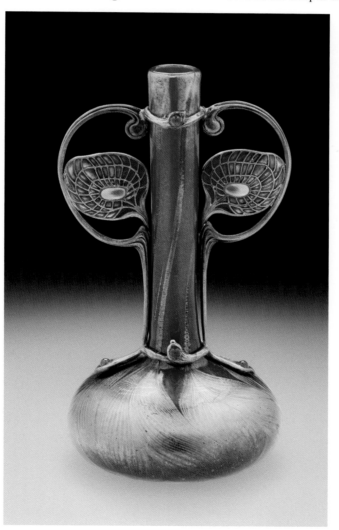

One Favrile vessel illustrated in the Grafton catalogue displayed an unusual gilt-metal, enameled, and ruby-set mount. Although the catalogue listed no designer for the vase aside from Tiffany, the metalwork's peacock motif was the work of Colonna, whose jewelry and graphic designs were characterized by a sinuous line evident in the vase. It may have been the second time that Colonna worked for Tiffany, since he claimed a brief engagement early in his career with Associated Artists.[79] The enamelwork in the vessel can be attributed to Eugène Feuillâtre, a talented French artist who worked both independently and as chief enameler in the workshop of René Lalique. Feuillâtre's own delicately enameled covered boxes were sold in the Tiffany & Co. showrooms as well.[80]

Louis Comfort Tiffany and the 1900 Exposition Universelle in Paris

For the Paris exposition of 1900, the firm's chief work of blown glass was a punch bowl in a chased, gilt-metal framework that appeared as "breaking waves" to one reviewer, having "foaming crests [from which] spring six arms of peacock-hued Favrile glass, they in turn support the uprights of the frame, becoming a richly ornamental band at the top."[81] The punch bowl shared the dynamic movement and color of other Art Nouveau displays, such as the dances of Loïe Fuller as she swirled hundreds of yards of shimmering fabric beneath chromatic stage lights or the "changing lights and pulsing waves of color" seen at night at the Palais de l'Electricité.[82]

The punch bowl was surrounded by four large cases containing blown glass forms, each one dominated by a different color, some with peacock feather designs and others with plant forms. In New York, before the fair, one critic had likened the assembled vases to an Easter display of flowers conjured by petal-like textures and freely shaped forms found in nature,[83] in sharp contrast to a display in 1889 by Tiffany & Co., whose orchid jewelry shown prior to the Paris exposition was praised for its botanical precision.

Stained glass was displayed in an octagonal gallery that visitors "approached by four corridors, which are shaded so that the light is gradually cut off, and the room itself is lit only through the four screens of stained glass which form its walls."[84] The dramatic, darkened space also featured windows by John La Farge, the Tiffany Glass & Decorating Co., J. and R. Lamb, and Maitland, Armstrong & Co. It was here that Louis Comfort Tiffany displayed his large *Four Seasons* window, as well as another majestic religious window entitled *The Flight of the Soul*, which was described as "cold, sad, and dark, in spite of a slightly iridescent white tonality!"[85] Smaller, but equally impressive windows in the fair included the *Magnolia*, designed by Agnes Northrop, who specialized in floral

Left: Louis Tiffany showed Favrile vases of this type at the 1900 world's fair in Paris (left, cat. 294; center, cat. 295; right, cat. 305). The attenuated shapes of his vases perfectly suited the abstracted floral motifs achieved by his talented glass blowers.

This stained-glass window of magnolia blossoms (cat. 287) was shown at the 1900 Exposition Universelle in Paris and purchased from Bing's L'Art Nouveau gallery for the Baron Stieglitz Museum of Decorative and Applied Arts in St. Petersburg. After the Russian Revolution, the window was transferred to the Hermitage Museum, where it has rested in storage until recently.

Left: Favrile glass lamp with peacock decoration by Tiffany Studios from around 1900 at the cusp of the change from oil lighting to electric (cat. 292). Tiffany provided both types of mechanisms so that his lamps could be converted easily to either purpose.

Table and floor lamps became the perfect vehicle for Tiffany's Favrile glass because the concentration of light brought out the special visual effects that could be achieved with his color formulas. As a result, the stylistic possibilities were endless, from florals to geometrics, such as the Indian basket motif for a desk lamp at right (cat. 278).

designs; she was a colleague of Clara Driscoll, who managed the women's glass-cutting operation for Louis Comfort Tiffany. The subtly nuanced blushes of pink, green, and ivory glass chosen for the petals and leaves of the magnolia blossoms demonstrate a refined sensibility in color selection, offering proof of Tiffany's well-founded admiration for Driscoll and her "Tiffany girls."[86] The *Magnolia* window was purchased a year after its exhibition in Paris by the Stieglitz Museum of Decorative and Applied Arts, founded in St. Petersburg by Baron Alexander von Stieglitz, a proponent of craft education.

Leaded-glass lamps were featured prominently in the firm's exhibit, and here Tiffany built upon his efforts at the Grafton Galleries exhibition by showing many forms and designs. These lamps marked a change from the simple blown-glass shades that typified fuel and electric lamps up to that time and which Tiffany continued to show even at the Paris fair.[87] The varying requirements of natural light, oil lamps, and the light bulb offered a constant source of interest and experimentation for Tiffany, who had grasped the dramatic possibilities of light and dark in his earlier career as an interior designer.

Tiffany first actively used light as a design element in January 1897, with an ambitious, sixty-foot illuminated tower for an exhibition held by the Gas Industries Company at Madison Square Garden. Employing a combination of gas, water, steam, and some 3,000 lights, he created a wonderland of water jets, fountains, and clouds of steam for the incredulous visitors. He refined these ideas for the 1901 Pan American exposition in Buffalo, where he reprised the cascading glass fountain he had made for the 1893 Chicago fair. For the Buffalo exposition, he placed a more imposing Favrile glass fountain within a darkened room, delighting visitors with a play of light that came from within.[88]

Left: The *Adams Vase* of 1893–95 was designed by Paulding Farnham of Tiffany & Co. and created from American gold, gemstones, and mineral specimens provided by gemologist George Frederick Kunz (cat. 222). Presented as the crowning achievement of its production, Tiffany & Co. displayed the vase at the 1900 Paris world's fair.

Fig. 116. Paulding Farnham, seen at the height of his career as chief designer of Tiffany & Co., around 1900.

Farnham's brooch of Montana sapphires, diamonds, and pearls at right was exhibited at the 1900 Paris Exposition among other traditional designs (cat. 230).

Paris 1900: Tiffany & Co. and the Adams Vase

Altogether, the irrepressibly varying forms and ingenious use of materials found in the works of Tiffany Glass & Decorating Co. was in marked contrast to that of Tiffany & Co., whose rich materials and meticulous craftsmanship served an increasingly historicized and traditional style. The massive ivory tankard made from a single intricately carved elephant tusk shown at the 1900 fair typifies this "robber-baron" style reflective of a clientele familiar with hunts and safaris.

Similarly historical in style, the *Adams Vase* was ornamented throughout with chased flowers and delicately articulated figures in gold set with gems. One of Tiffany & Co.'s most celebrated works at the Paris exposition, this masterpiece of design and execution is comparable in technique and ambition to the work of Renaissance goldsmiths and the ingenious eggs created for the Russian imperial family by the House of Fabergé shown at the fair. The vase celebrated a hero of the modern business world, the banker Edward Dean Adams, a talented financier who successfully guided the American Cotton Oil Company out of a troubled period into an era of prosperity.[89] In 1891 company stockholders formally resolved to honor Adams for his contributions and commissioned Tiffany & Co. to devise a suitable presentation piece made entirely of American materials. Paulding Farnham chose the cotton flower as the primary motif because it was the source of the company's production, and produced watercolor sketches of cotton plants at various stages of growth in preparation for his design. These drawings were translated by the goldsmiths into chased floral elements that adorned the entire vessel. Farnham's narrative scheme featured Modesty on one side of the elliptical form and Genius on the other, honoring Adams's unselfish work on behalf of the firm. The historical design was in keeping with the tradition of presentation silver, but the choice of lavish materials and the unique concentration of talents involved in its creation were intended to elevate it to new heights.

Nearly twenty-three troy pounds of gold were used in the production of the vase, which was delicately repousséed with figurative reliefs, occasionally finished in the round.[90] The gold was enhanced with large mineral specimens that included gold-bearing quartz, rock crystal, and petrified wood. Pearls, amethysts, spessartites (garnets), and tourmalines also adorned the vessel.[91] The gold and minerals secured by George Kunz especially for this commission were mined in the United States, a feature that Tiffany & Co. had begun to emphasize as early as 1889. Such unusual materials and extraordinary technique confirmed the company's belief that the *Adams Vase* qualified as a work of great importance. Their favorable opinion of their own vase was cleverly published in a handsome book that Tiffany & Co. produced for its presentation, and in the smaller publication that was issued for the Paris exposition.[92]

George F. Kunz: Tiffany's Celebrity Gemologist

In 1902, a mysterious, rough gemstone turned up in an abandoned mine at California's Pala Mountain. The pink tourmaline with a lilac cast then arrived, with a letter, at Tiffany & Co. in New York on the desk of Tiffany's gem man, George Frederick Kunz. Thunderstruck, Kunz realized he was looking at a mineral assumed to be extinct. After Kunz identified the stone and its characteristics, including its rare ability to store light and glow in the dark, it was subsequently given the name "kunzite."[1]

Kunz valued each stone's intrinsic beauty and strongly promoted America's vast mineral wealth. In his influential role as Tiffany & Co.'s celebrity gem specialist, he helped broaden taste in an era when high society preferred diamonds, emeralds, rubies, and sapphires. In the 1890s he boasted, "No lady with a quarter yard of diamond and emerald bracelets up her arms or three yards of Oriental pearls around her neck now scorns a star sapphire or beryl bracelet for less formal moments."[2] At the turn of the century, increased prices for gems such as rubies and emeralds also encouraged the demand for other, more affordable stones. Kunz's authoritative writings in books and newspapers, and his influential position with the most famous American jewelry store, certainly helped fuel trends.

Kunz was born in 1856, and his interests developed alongside America's growing interest in natural history and its preservation. The Industrial Age brought with it progress as well as the less palatable effects of rapid change to a once pristine landscape. Sewer construction and projects such as the Bergen Hill Tunnel overturned the land around his childhood home in Hoboken,

New Jersey, revealing many specimens to catch a boy's eye. He became a prodigious collector who corresponded with museums at age fourteen; by twenty he was a respected gemologist with a penchant for America's overlooked and semiprecious stones. In 1879, after a year of selling such rocks independently to Tiffany & Co., he was hired by Charles Tiffany as a gem specialist and later made a vice president at just twenty-three. Kunz had turned his passion into a powerful position within America's greatest jewelry firm.

With Tiffany's lucrative backing, the young specialist could now train his eye on the world, overturning stones in the ground from Montana's riverbeds to Russia's Ural Mountains.[3] His scientific fame translated into connoisseurship and fashionable tastemaking. Soon he not only found gems firsthand in Brazil's diamond mines but also simply by opening his mail. Anyone hoping

Fig. 117. George Frederick Kunz became the celebrity explorer of his day, procuring rare mineral specimens and gemstones for use by Tiffany & Co. as well as for private and institutional collectors. Here he is seen examining kunzite, a mineral named for him.

The refractive quality of kunzite allows it to appear pink, purple, or even colorless depending on the angle from which it is viewed (cat. 231).

to sell his or her family jewels or a rough gem unearthed in the yard might write a letter to George F. Kunz, Esq., care of Tiffany & Co. He thus had a singular hold on the flow of gems into and out of personal collections.[4]

Kunz represented New York's American Museum of Natural History at the 1876 Centennial Exposition in Philadelphia, but it was in 1889 when the world converged on Paris for the Exposition Universelle that he made his presence truly felt. The United States display mirrored the fair's overall theme of national innovation and abundance. Kunz was in charge of the Mining Department's exposition area, but he also took an active part in Tiffany & Co.'s display.[5] He sent two bushels of pearls from Little Miami Valley, Ohio, to illustrate America as virtually

tripping over its own mineral wealth. Tiffany & Co.'s exhibit also included Kunz's dazzling collection of American stones—both rough and cut—representing eleven states and territories.

Corporate financier, and loyal Tiffany & Co. customer, J. Pierpont Morgan purchased Kunz's 382-piece American gem collection intact from the fair. He did so in order to donate it to the American Museum of Natural History, of which he was a trustee, as the Tiffany-Morgan Collection of Gems.[6] Tiffany & Co. exhibited a second Morgan collection, also assembled by Kunz, at the 1900 Paris Exposition Universelle. Rather than solely American stones, this second group had been chosen from sites around the world.[7] Morgan donated this second collection to the American Museum of Natural History. The conjoined

Fig. 118. American financier and philanthropist J. P. Morgan was one of George Kunz's most avid gem collectors, purchasing multiple complete collections to donate to museums in New York and Paris. Kunz honored his loyal customer by naming a newly discovered mineral morganite.

This bodice ornament of rare conch pearls, c. 1890–1900, by Tiffany & Co. (cat. 225), is shown with an abalone shell jewelry box from Tiffany's Paris showroom, a honeymoon gift to the Countess Beulah d'Etchegoyan in 1892 (cat. 251). Conch pearls were especially favored in Europe, considered exotic and chic because they came from the Caribbean.

collections along with their elaborate ebony display case, white velvet backings, and labels "printed in red and black on slips of celluloid" made the front page of the *Jewelers' Circular* in 1901.[8] This lavish visual display helped separate the distinct quality of the Morgan stones from the museum's other mineral collections, attesting to Kunz's connoisseurship.

To Kunz, gems were more than simply luxurious adornment, they embodied an ancient symbolic history. His award-winning writings propagated a mood in some circles of America that reflected the popularity of occultism the world over.[9] The era's new fashion for collecting birthstones attests to the impact of Kunz's

writings. The fad was mentioned often in the *Jewelers' Circular*, a trade journal that associated the trend with "the superstitious side of human nature."[10] The chapter headings in his popular book *The Curious Lore of Precious Stones* (1913), such as "On Ominous and Luminous Stones," "On Crystal Balls and Crystal Gazing," and "Planetary and Astral Influences of Precious Stones," blend two strains of late-nineteenth-century thought, namely science and spiritualism. Kunz's gemological folklore might be compared to Lalique's unconventional materials and symbolic use of flowers. Lalique drew inspiration from Decadent poets such as Charles Baudelaire and Robert de Montesquiou, whose work helped

Tiffany & Co. promoted the wearing of rare, multicolored gemstones as an alternative to diamonds and pearls at the turn of the century with designs such as this bodice ornament of gold, diamonds, and various gemstones (cat. 267).

George Kunz supplied the pink conch pearl for use in Tiffany & Co.'s egg-shaped design at right (cat. 265) similar to pendants popularized by Fabergé, such as the one below surmounted by the Russian imperial crown (cat. 83).

popularize myth, occultism, and symbolism—subjects similar to Kunz's interests.[11] With this in mind, perhaps Lalique and others were attracted not only by the fiery iridescence of opals but by their temptingly sinister associations as well.

Although not everyone at Tiffany & Co. would have been as well versed in folklore, Kunz's material influence lurked behind every design. Paulding Farnham's *Adams Vase*, a cornucopia of American minerals, is encrusted with Kunz's gems. Conch pearls appear as timeless blossoms in Farnham's floral jewelry designs. Evoking the bejeweled world of the legendary Hindu Kalpa Tree, Kunz might have been describing a Tiffany display case:

> Pearls hung from its boughs and beautiful emeralds from its shoots; the tender young leaves were corals and the ripe fruit consisted of rubies. The roots were of sapphire; the base of the trunk of diamond, the uppermost part of cat's-eye, while the section between was of topaz. The foliage (except the young leaves) was entirely formed of zircons.[12]

Unlike nacreous pearls, with their milky surfaces, conch pearls had been popular only since the 1850s. Their saturated color appears to burn with an effect known as "chatoyancy" from the French *chat oeil* (cat's eye). Evoking the pearl's marine formation, its striated surface resembles the waves of a light-reflective sea. The celebrated American collector Henry Walters purchased a single pink conch pearl from Kunz set in a cage of diamonds by Tiffany & Co. It is now in the Walters Art Museum in Baltimore. The design is reminiscent of Japanese traditions that celebrate singular natural forms, and Kunz would also have known of the penchant for single egg-shaped pendants made popular by Russian jewelers, most notably Fabergé.

The adventuring, globetrotting gemologist Kunz was a sympathetic peer to America's president and former Rough Rider, Theodore Roosevelt, and his conservation efforts at home. In 1908, Kunz delivered a paper at the White House called "The Preservation of Scenic Beauty" for the Conference on the Conservation of Natural Resources. In it, he powerfully describes all landscape as the product of mineral wealth pushing upward. His heartfelt proposal called for a cooperative spirit of industrial progress that took nature's interest into consideration.

A self-made man, Kunz was a scientific celebrity in the Gilded Age. His long life and career was full of awards, honorary degrees and positions at major institutions, and even foreign knighthoods such as France's Legion of Honor, Norway's Knight of the Order of St. Olaf, and Japan's Officer of the Rising Sun. During the 1920s, he spun yarns of global adventure for the *Saturday Evening Post* and in 1923 married his second wife, named Opal, a young aviator and spitfire in her own right. Throughout his fifty-three-year career, Kunz rejected permanent posts with leading museums and universities in order to remain with Tiffany & Co. His personal fame enabled the firm, in large part, to succeed in capturing the attention of the world's wealthiest collectors.

Catherine Walworth

1. For a discussion of the controversy surrounding the discovery and naming of kunzite, see Lawrence H. Conklin, "Kunz and Kunzite," *Mineralogical Record* 18 (1987): 369–72.

2. As quoted in Joseph Purtell, *The Tiffany Touch* (New York: Random House, 1971), 64.

3. In 1893, Kunz lent not just gemological expertise to the World's Columbian Exposition in Chicago but also his collection of Russian icons to the fair's religious object display; see *Annual Report of the Board of Regents of the Smithsonian Institution* (Washington, D.C.: Government Printing Office, 1895), 114. These icons may have been collected during his various research trips to Russia and reveal some of the breadth of his collecting interests.

4. Examples of these personal letters can be found in the George F. Kunz Papers at the National Museum of Natural History, Smithsonian Institution, Washington. They show a lively, personal interchange with scientists and private collectors looking for specimens and thanking Kunz for sending samples, telling him they dropped specimens off at his office, or trying to sell family pearls.

5. Kunz is recorded as returning from Europe on board the *St. Louis,* accompanied by his wife and family, the last week of November 1900. "Trans-Atlantic Voyagers," *Jewelers' Circular* (5 December 1900): 39.

6. Kunz was an honorary curator of the museum from 1904 to 1918.

7. Displaying a bit of nepotism toward his employer and best customer, Kunz named other previously unidentified stones "tiffanyite" and "morganite."

8. "The Morgan Gems," *Jewelers' Circular* (25 September 1901): 1, 7.

9. Kunz received a gold medal for his writings on gems, as well as a bronze medal for gem folklore in 1900.

10. Elsie Bee, "Fall Fashions in Jewelry, Silverware and Art Goods," *Jewelers' Circular* (28 October 1896): 10.

11. See K. A. Citroen, "Lalique et Baudelaire: Quelques Réflexions sur un Bijou Art Nouveau," *Simiolus: Netherlands Quarterly for the History of Art* 1, no. 3 (1966–67): 153–56.

12. George F. Kunz, *Curious Lore of Precious Stones* (Philadelphia/London: J. B. Lippincott, 1913), 238.

Louis Tiffany collaborated with Paulding Farnham on the creation of jeweled perfume flacons for Tiffany & Co., such as these examples probably made after 1900 when the series was first presented at the Paris world's fair (above, cat. 269; right, with gold stopper, cat. 270; right, cat. 271). Tiffany provided the Favrile glass bottles, and Farnham designed the jeweled and enameled tops.

The desk set below in glass, enamel, and silver gilt was retailed by Tiffany & Co. (cat. 244).

Yet, according to at least two stinging reviews, the French critics did not share Tiffany & Co.'s sentiments about the *Adams Vase*. Both authors recounted the design, materials, and labor involved in its creation but were not impressed by the overall effect. One reviewer admitted the vase represented perfection in handcraftsmanship but did not achieve a satisfactory result; rather, the author found the forms imprecise and the details tiresome.[93] Similar observations were made by the judges, who noted that all of Tiffany's efforts and ingenuity only succeeded in producing a poorly designed work that in the final analysis was not truly artistic. For these reasons, the judges conferred upon Tiffany & Co. a second-place grand prix award, just as it had received in the Paris exhibition of 1889.[94]

Paulding Farnham and Louis Comfort Tiffany collaborated for the 1900 Paris exposition on a series of scent bottles. These delicate and marvelously crafted works represented a high point for the firm and a singular moment in which Farnham's jeweled and enameled mounts, in designs of Near Eastern flavor, crowned slender, iridescent Favrile vessels. This Near Eastern aesthetic was pronounced in Farnham's work, appearing time and again in designs for hollowware and jewelry. A

spectacular silver-gilt and enameled coffee set adorned with amethysts survives from about 1904, with its original case and a card inside indicating it was bought in Paris for delivery to a client in Monte Carlo.

Farnham's taste for the exotic, as found in cultures both near and far, was evident in his series of silver bowls based on Native American baskets and pottery. From Tiffany's display, echoing the United States pavilion's exhibition of actual American Indian artifacts, clients could buy their own luxurious versions in inlaid silver studded with turquoise and other jewels. This Native American motif was popular with those who may have patronized the American firm Joseph Heinrichs.[95] Makers of hotel and domestic wares in copper, Heinrichs included among his line a group of designs featuring Native American arrowheads. At about the same period, Louis Tiffany designed lamps and hanging ceiling shades with Indian basketry motifs for collectors of genuine Native American artifacts.[96] Depicted in paintings, recorded in photographs, painted on Rookwood pottery vases, and made larger than life in the great camps of the Adirondacks and the Rockies, Native American imagery conjured visions of the untamed frontier that was already a memory, eroded by the railroad's advance and the settlers who followed in its wake. These sentiments for a vanishing native culture were paralleled in Europe and Russia, where expressions of regional and national folk traditions resulted, for example, in designs by Fabergé depicting Cossacks and enamelwork in the Pan-Slavic taste, or Lalique with his evocations of medieval French characters. Traditional folk styles were much present at the 1900 Paris exposition, and their impact can be seen in these designs.

Above: Among the fashion for exotic motifs at the end of the nineteenth century was the craze for designs inspired by Native American objects. Joseph Heinrichs, a New York manufacturer of hotel plate as well as finer objects in mixed metal that he sold to retailers including Tiffany & Co., likely made this punch bowl decorated with arrowheads (cat. 115).

Left: Farnham was well known for his designs in exotic motifs, such as the black coffee set in the Moorish taste of silver gilt enhanced with elaborate enameling and cabochon amethysts (cat. 238). This set survives in its original case with a calling card, revealing that it was sold from the Paris showroom of Tiffany & Co. to a client in Monte Carlo.

Right: A rarefied specialty line of mixed-metal and jeweled vessels mimicking Native American pottery and woven grass baskets was among Tiffany & Co.'s designs celebrating America's cultures and mineral wealth (cat. 276).

Farnham was adept at designing in a wide vocabulary of styles from Native American to the more conservative historical styles of the Italian Renaissance, such as this line presented by Tiffany & Co. at the 1900 Paris exposition (cat. 235).

It was not unusual for Louis Tiffany's small vases and tableware to be enhanced by other firms. The Favrile glass miniature vase or salt cellar below (cat. 254) displays mounts by the House of Fabergé. The same form can be seen in the photograph at below right showing a French mount by Maurice Dufrène in the manner of C. R. Ashbee (fig. 119).

Perhaps the only significant competition for Tiffany in the realm of silversmithing was the Gorham Mfg. Co. The 1900 Paris exposition represented an opportunity for Gorham to display works created for an international market in its Art Nouveau line called Martelé, meaning hand-hammered.[97] Gorham was represented in Paris by Chicago's Spaulding & Co., located at 36 avenue de l'Opéra, in the same building as Tiffany & Co. Spaulding was the only other American luxury firm to be located in Paris at this desirable address, which was conveniently located near the American consular office and the *New York Herald*, both frequented by Americans. This location also proved ideal for jewelry collectors, as the elite shops of French jewelers Cartier, Vever, and Mellerio were steps away on avenue de la Paix.[98]

Like Tiffany & Co., Gorham produced silver in historical styles, and works in the Renaissance, Jacobean, Oriental, and Greek fashions were included in the Paris exposition. However, it was Martelé, loosely based upon the sinuous lines of Art Nouveau, that invariably received the greatest acclaim. For this occasion, the firm developed special designs in the Martelé style called *Night and Day*, in which they produced a vanity table, chair, toilet accessories, and candelabra. Gorham won a grand prix and gold medal for its silverwares. Previous collaborations with Rookwood pottery, whose celebrated Black Iris glaze had won a gold medal at the fair, had yielded a fine body of silver-deposit wares that enhanced their painted decorations by the Cincinnati firm. Gorham's exposition catalogue even included an illustration of a liqueur service in silver-mounted Favrile glass, apparently in the Merovingian line, indicating a brief collaboration between Gorham Mfg. Co. and Tiffany Glass & Decorating Co.[99]

The earthenware vase with silver mounts above was shown at the 1900 Exposition Universelle in Paris (cat. 216). It was made by Rookwood Pottery, a Cincinnati firm that won a grand prix for its black iris glaze.

In another curious pairing, a few vessels of Tiffany Favrile glass were mounted in silver by the House of Fabergé. Perhaps these vessels were purchased at a small exposition of decorative arts in St. Petersburg in 1901 in which Louis Comfort Tiffany exhibited, and then taken by their owners to Fabergé to be embellished. Organized under the patronage of Grand Duchess Elizabeth Mavrikievna, this fair was limited to ceramics and glass from foreign countries.[100] Russian firms apparently did not participate, although information on this exhibition is spotty at best. The existence of a design drawing for a small Favrile glass vase may suggest that Tiffany had works mounted by Fabergé especially for the exhibition. Fabergé continued this luxury tradition with mounts for Gallé glass, Royal Doulton ceramics, and Rörstrand porcelain[101] as well as Tiffany vessels with French mounts. With each successive exhibition and advertisement Favrile glass grew in popularity. The very word, coined by Louis Comfort Tiffany from "fabrilis, Latin for 'craftsmanlike,'" was for a time so well known that it was commemorated in a painting by the same name.[102] Having triumphed at international exhibitions, and as wedding gifts for the children of presidents, the glass was first sold in New York as early as 1896 by Tiffany & Co, and then concurrently by Tiffany Studios.[103]

As waves of iridescent glass entered the marketplace in the wake of Favrile's popularity,

company advertisements pressed buyers to consider the monetary and artistic value of the original. Tiffany Studios was among the first firms to educate shoppers about the value of maker's marks, noting in 1900 that "every piece of the Tiffany Favrile Glass is signed; the larger pieces by the full name Louis C. Tiffany; the smaller pieces by the initials L.C.T."[104] In other cases, buyers were candidly warned that "so called Favrile Glass which hasn't the Louis C. Tiffany mark is like counterfeit money—and whoever infringes will be prosecuted."[105]

Advertising was one method Tiffany used to guard against encroachment from competitors. He sued glass artist Frederick Carder in 1913 for the similarity between Favrile and Carder's golden Aurene iridescent glass, a suit that was eventually dropped. Quezal Art Glass and Decorating Company was established in Queens, New York, in 1902 with a few former Tiffany staff, which also served a luxury-minded clientele. Carder and Quezal were only two of many firms that sought to capture a segment of the luxury market for these goods. Firms across Europe, especially in Germany and Austria, also produced glass with iridescent surfaces and hand-blown forms. Though loosely referred to as "Tiffany" glass, the usually harsh and incongruous color palettes betrayed their makers. This glass did little, though, to cut into the popularity of Tiffany's originals. Indeed, the proliferation of iridescent glass in the wake of Tiffany's consistent showings at international expositions suggests that by 1910 Tiffany had made a significant impact in Europe, enhancing his reputation as an artist.

Fig. 120. After 1900, Louis Comfort Tiffany expanded his business and increased production of Favrile glass for use in stained-glass windows and lamps, a genre he promoted through evocative advertisements markedly different from the conservative ads run by Tiffany & Co.

Depending on the mood of light intended, Tiffany lamps often employed three types of Favrile glass: fully blown shapes for an ethereal look, such as in the mushroom lamp at right (cat. 288); geometric shapes for a regular rhythmic pattern, as in the web-like spider lamp (overleaf, left, cat. 299); or irregular colored pieces for dynamic floral effects, as in the poppy lamp (overleaf, right, cat. 291).

Following his father's emphasis on exclusivity as an attraction for prospective buyers, early advertisements declared Tiffany & Co. and Tiffany Studios as the only source for these exclusive goods, warning: "Readers are asked to remember that there is only one maker of Tiffany Favrile glass and only two places in New York where it may be bought."[106] However, it was not long before Louis Comfort Tiffany broke with his father's methods and made Favrile glass available to retail establishments around the country, each with so-called exclusive arrangements for sale in their region. Some of these retailers' advertisements focused on the unique qualities of Tiffany glass and the engraved "L.C.T." marks, while others boasted of the international awards received. Prices for these works ranged from one to fifty dollars, following Charles Lewis Tiffany's lead in appealing to all customers in search of quality goods.

Retailers from such diverse locations as Portland (Oregon), Macon (Georgia), Lexington (Kentucky), Chicago, and Salt Lake City featured Tiffany Favrile glass in their advertisements, which probably accounts for its presence in virtually every historic house and historical society in the United States.[107] Such widespread availability must have contributed to the overexposure that probably faded the novelty of Favrile glass and its many competitors before World War I.

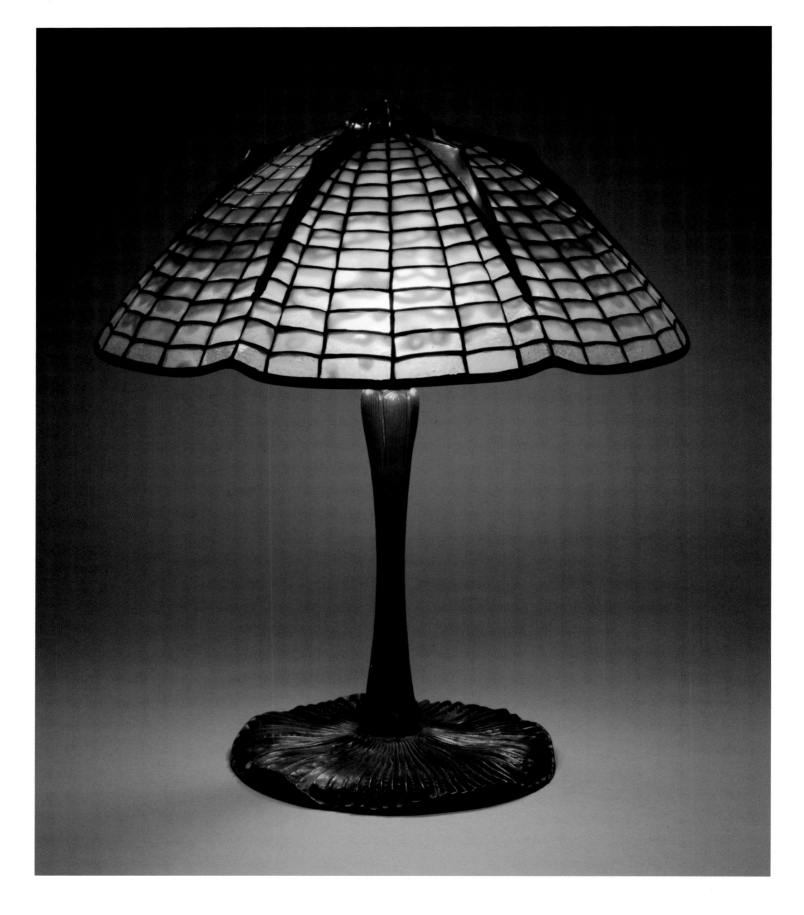

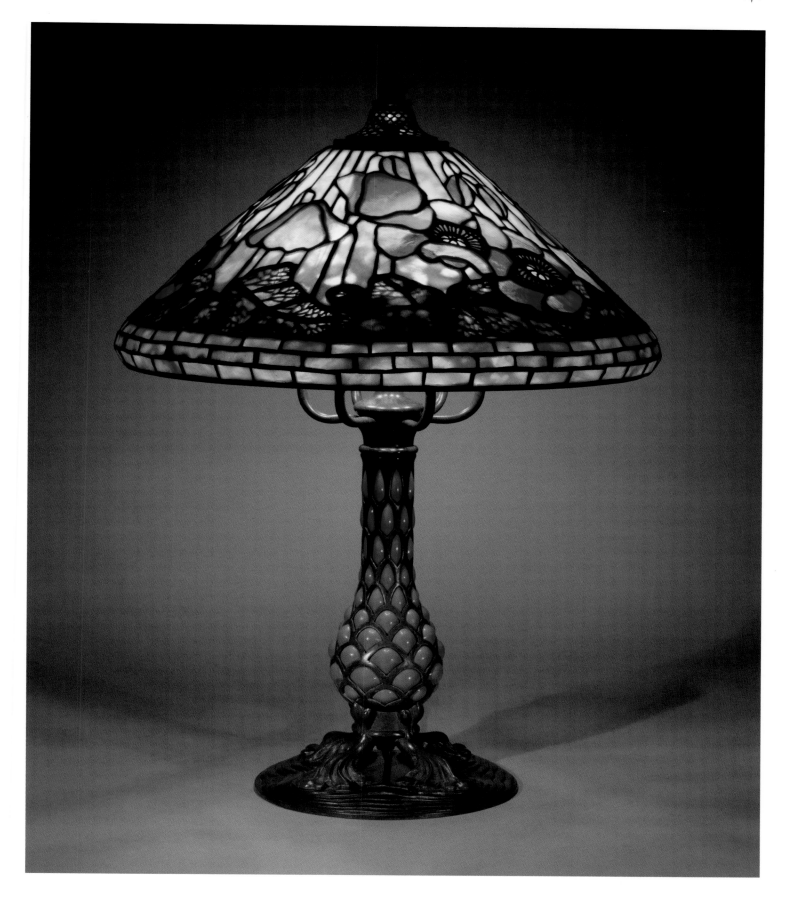

Tiffany Studios

In 1902, Louis Comfort Tiffany purchased the Knickerbocker Athletic Club, where for the first time he was able to display the many facets of his business to the public.[108] Located at Madison Avenue and 45th Street, the new building was intended as a showroom for all aspects of his interior design services, including the sale of fabrics, wallpaper, leaded-glass windows, mosaic work, lighting, and imported oriental rugs. One could also shop for stylish furniture. New York furniture makers Schmitt Brothers had joined with Tiffany Studios in 1902, producing furniture under Tiffany designs and managing the

Fig. 121. This interior view of the Tiffany Studios showroom on Madison Avenue around 1905 shows the eclectic nature of Tiffany's offerings.

Fig. 122. Tiffany Studios provided every interior design service imaginable, including rug repair, as seen here in this view of the rug repairing department around 1913.

Fig. 123. Not to be eclipsed by other more traditional design firms, Tiffany Studios worked in conservative colonial revival styles as adeptly as it did creating exotic motifs.

"old furniture, curios, and bric-a-brac," while also maintaining a separate shop next door on Madison Avenue. Here, Schmitt Brothers sold a "comprehensive collection of antiques and reproductions" that complemented the Tiffany offerings.[109]

The new building was occasionally adapted to other purposes, such as the sale at auction of the celebrated architect Stanford White's collection in 1907.[110] In time Tiffany's emporium became known for one-stop shopping for interior furnishings and decorations. To guide his clients Tiffany published promotional booklets that contributed to the aura of the merchandise, boosting confidence that it was the ultimate in good taste. The booklet "Character and Individuality in Decorations and Furnishings," published in 1913, featured the interiors of the Madison Avenue building and illustrated not only model interiors decorated in predictable colonial revival styles, but also the wide variety of workshops and showrooms filled with paintings, marble garden furniture, lamps of all sizes, desk accessories, and even a rug repair shop. The furniture was probably designed and made by Schmitt Brothers, with the agreement of Louis Tiffany, and little resembled the early achievements of his career as a decorator to the very wealthy. But a different strategy was at work: the new products were intended to appeal to comfortable middle- and upper-class homes where design reform was unknown, but the Tiffany name and the reputation of Tiffany Studios were familiar. The new strategy was to provide decorating services for affluent consumers who were moving into Manhattan at a rapid pace.[111]

Louis Comfort Tiffany and Tiffany & Co.

The year 1902 became momentous for Louis Tiffany as well as for Tiffany & Co. when Charles Lewis Tiffany died, leaving the company that he had founded sixty-five years earlier at a crossroads. Charles Tiffany had kept a tight rein on the family firm, imprinting it deeply with a vision and style perfectly articulated by his chief designer, Paulding Farnham, who had helped make lavish gemstones in expensive settings synonymous with the Tiffany name throughout the nineteenth century. But in the new century fresh artistic ideas dominated the press of the day. In a move that was both bold and protective, Charles Cook, the former vice president of the company, was named president, providing administrative continuity, and Louis Comfort Tiffany was named first vice president and head of design, opening the door to more design innovation.

Louis wasted no time assuming leadership of the design department. He and Farnham had collaborated earlier when Farnham had designed jeweled mounts for Tiffany's Favrile glass perfume bottles. While the company's stock-in-trade of glittering jewels in designs of flora and fauna continued apace, presumably under Farnham's direction, Louis Tiffany began creating his own designs for jewelry with his chief assistant from the Tiffany Furnaces, Julia Munson. It was there that his reliable metalworkers and enamelers were already located and where he produced his first designs for public display, unveiled at the 1904 St. Louis world's fair. Significantly, though Farnham was amply represented by silver and gold hollowware at the St.

After the death of his father in 1902, Louis Tiffany took over the design department at Tiffany & Co. He oversaw the continued production of jewels and luxury goods epitomizing conservative taste, while introducing his own line of jewelry featuring great stones set in more abstract motifs. Tiffany Studios artisans created brooches such as the one above featuring deep blue opals surrounded by enameled gold (cat. 233).

Tiffany's naturalistic designs in multi-colored gemstones evoke the color of his famous Favrile glass, as in the brooch and earrings at right (cat. 243; the inset shows the backs of the earrings). He also set rare stones such as Montana sapphires and apatites in more conventional settings (left, cat. 258).

Overleaf: The grapevine necklace of jade and gold (left, cat. 257) and the necklace of pale aquamarines and peridots set in platinum resembling a Mughal Indian pendant (right, cat. 260) demonstrate the diversity of motifs throughout Tiffany's work.

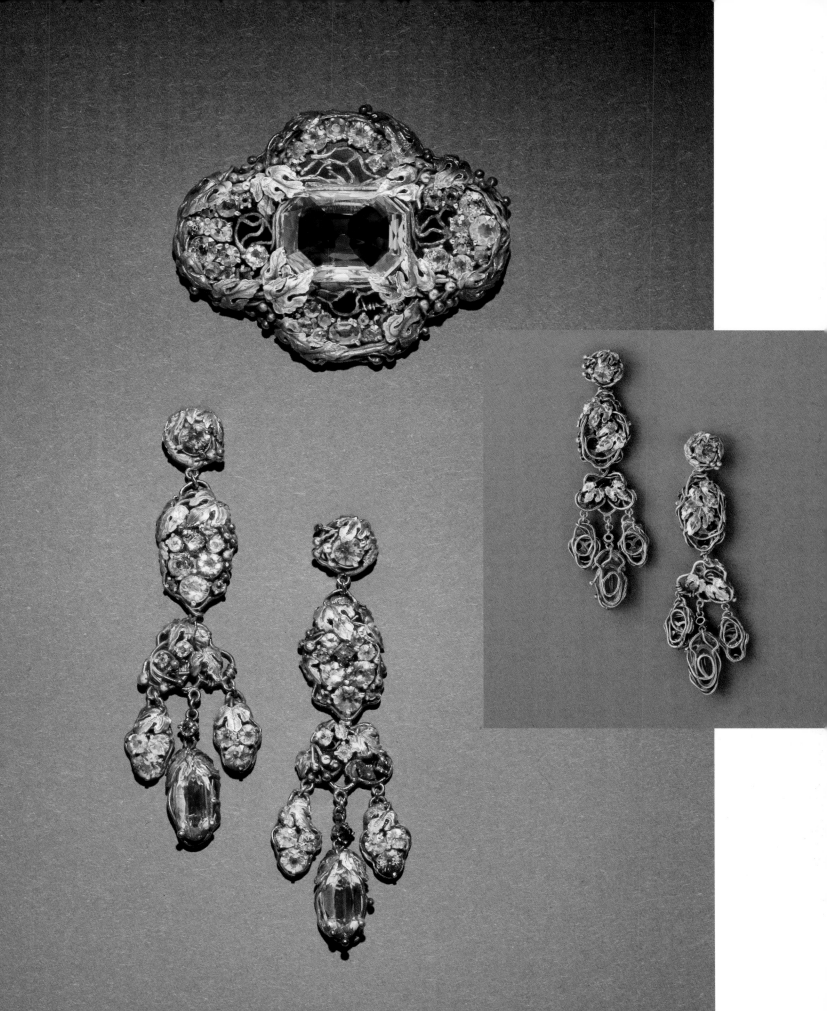

Louis fair, only one of his jewelry designs was taken, a far cry from his lavish displays that had won the firm numerous prizes and medals at the 1900 Paris and 1901 Buffalo expositions.[112] The difference between the design approaches of Farnham and Tiffany could not have been more striking than in the works brought to Buffalo, where Farnham's pendant necklace in the Renaissance style confronted Tiffany's numerous naturalistic and avant-garde works. Louis Tiffany was taking the firm in a new direction; it was only a matter of time before Paulding Farnham would resign, leaving the firm in 1908.

Tiffany's early designs for jewelry drew inspiration from natural subjects, most frequently the humble wildflowers and grasses found along any country road, rather than the predictable "floral aristocracy," as one reveiwer put it in Gustav Stickley's *Craftsman*.[113] The similarity with the approach of René Lalique was not lost on Tiffany's admirers, even as they marveled at his execution and design. In comparing the two, the same reviewer wrote that Tiffany "is much less radical, less original, and far more conventional than the distinguished French artist."[114] In jewelry, Tiffany's signal achievement— with his associate Julia Munson—was the color palettes, at once soothing and provocative, which attracted the notice of critics who immediately began to term his work artistic. In an effort to exploit the commercial potential of this perception, Tiffany's work was set apart from the more conventional work of Tiffany & Co., and termed "Tiffany Art Jewelry" in the 1909 Tiffany Blue Book. It was also said that each piece was "designed and made under the personal supervision of Louis C. Tiffany," giving the impression that the client was purchasing the work of an artist personally involved in its creation.[115]

Just as Tiffany's forms derived from nature, so did his palette, reflecting the luscious hues of autumn leaves, the bright blues and greens of the sky and grass, and the iridescence of insect wings, all depicted with a combination of exquisite enamel and multi-colored semiprecious stones. In elaborate gold-wire or platinum settings created by Munson and later Meta Overbeck, Tiffany deployed the exotic stones procured by George F. Kunz as if they were stained glass. He even designed a soaring two-tiered setting of gold and emeralds to accompany an extraordinary marquise-cut, fancy yellow diamond, a stone for which Tiffany & Co. had become famous since the mesmerizing display of yellow diamonds at the 1893 Chicago fair. The combination of moonstones alternating with light blue Montana sapphires is found in many of Overbeck's works from Tiffany's studio during this period.[116] The result is a glittering contrast between opaque and sparkle, while yet another necklace might pit blue beryls against yellow ones for a distinctive color pairing.

It was perhaps in these geometric arrangements of colored gemstones that Tiffany began to lift out of a purely Art Nouveau aesthetic to reflect other early modern movements in Europe. An amethyst necklace from Tiffany's studio recalls the arrangement and delicate rhythm of Austrian Secessionist works from this period, as do his multicolored palettes. While there are no documented associations between Tiffany and any of the Secessionist architects or designers, his extensive travels throughout Europe must have acquainted him with their work. He would have no

Right: With their luminescent quality, cabochon moonstones became a popular gemstone in early modern jewelry design, especially in the work introduced by Tiffany & Co. after 1903 under the creative helm of Louis Comfort Tiffany (cat. 259).

Fig. 124. Meta Overbeck's jewelry designs for Tiffany Studios featured colored gemstones in gold or platinum settings.

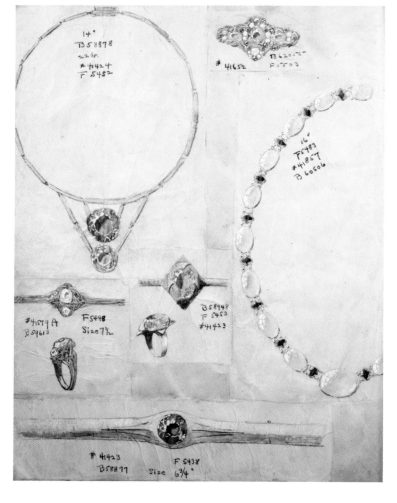

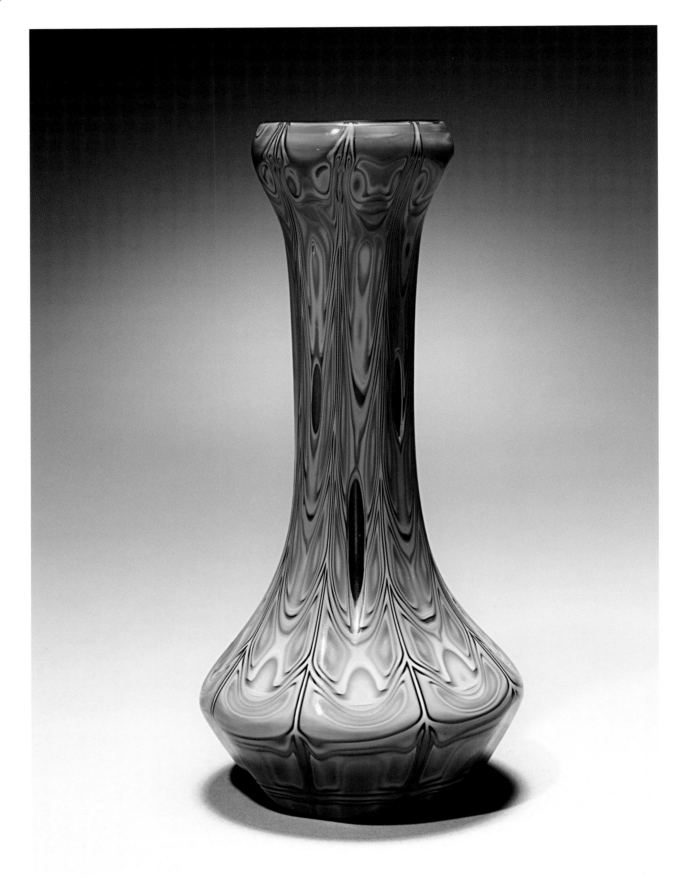

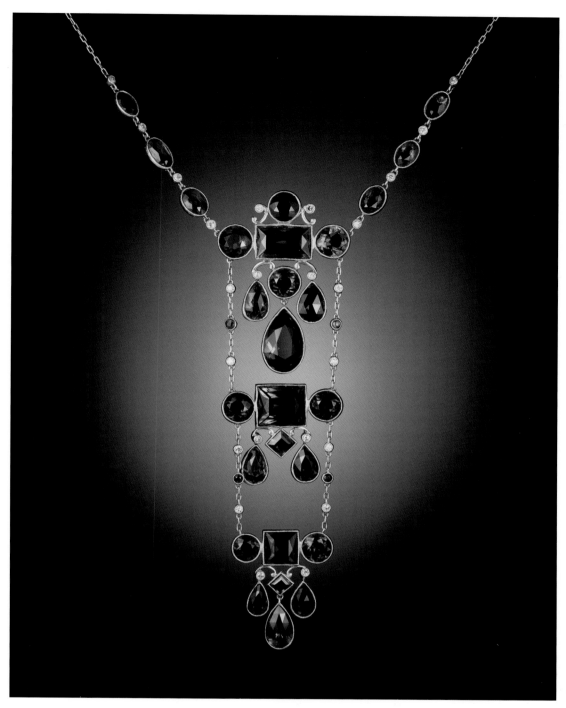

The influence of Austrian early modernism can clearly be seen in Tiffany's glass and jewelry from around 1910, such as the vase at left (cat. 277), recalling the panel-cut designs of Josef Hoffmann and Kolomon Moser, and the delicate amethyst, diamond, and platinum necklace at right (cat. 256), by Tiffany Studios for Tiffany & Co., in the geometric patterning typical of Secessionist jewelry of this period.

doubt seen the glass with broadly faceted surfaces designed by Josef Hoffmann and Kolomon Moser. This aesthetic is repeated in Tiffany's *Agate* vases, made around the time of the First World War.

While Tiffany may have been preoccupied as head of design for Tiffany & Co., his Tiffany Studios were flourishing. The stained-glass business had grown exponentially as a result of notable religious commissions and extensive but discreet marketing. Most sizable American towns could boast a Tiffany window in at least one of their prominent churches by the 1920s, and the Favrile glass lamp business was also in its prime during this period. The decade from 1910 to 1920 saw perhaps the most productive period in Tiffany's career. He exhibited in the prestigious Paris Salon of 1910,

winning a gold medal and proving once again his respectability among the French, from whom he had long sought recognition.

Despite such prodigious growth, change was in the air by 1913, the year of the groundbreaking Armory Show in New York, in which modern art first burst on the American scene. The exhibition took place in the National Guard's Sixty-ninth Regiment Armory, which coincidentally was also the site of Tiffany's magnificent, but by this point unfashionable, Associated Artists interior of 1879–80. Tiffany was now in his mid sixties and perhaps unwilling to alter his aesthetics to embrace these new, more radical expressions of art. A self-published biography written by Charles de Kay in 1914, *The Art Work of Louis C. Tiffany*, continued to promote his status as an artist, a sentiment echoed in the popular press of the day: "There is one artist who makes the luminists and the Post-Impressionists look like gropers in the murk. . . . The unique artist alluded to is Louis Comfort Tiffany of New York, and his medium is the now world-famous Tiffany Favrile glass."[117] Tiffany continued to exhibit in Paris in both 1914 and 1921, but his appeal was never as great as before. His final exhibition in America was the Panama-Pacific Exposition in 1915 in San Francisco, where he won his final gold medal and the long-sought honor of exhibiting amid fine arts participants. Tiffany Studios' extraordinary mosaic mural, the *Dream Garden*, exhibited at the Pan-Pacific fair, was not even his own design, but that of Maxfield Parrish. A large covered cup by Tiffany with an enameled frieze echoed the heroic classical panoply in the Parrish mural. Stark in form, indicative of the change in taste by the First World War, its enameled panel is among the finest ever produced by the firm.

After his retirement from Tiffany & Co. in 1918, Louis Tiffany, by then a wealthy man, set up the Louis Comfort Tiffany Foundation to aid gifted young artists. Tiffany brought these artists to Laurelton Hall, his home on Long Island and his final and perhaps greatest masterpiece as it was filled with his own collections as well as new works and examples from previous expositions, all laid out with sensitivity to the quality of light and land on its commanding site. But time was running out for him; his beloved Tiffany Studios, the atelier reminiscent of European guilds from which he discovered, created, and promoted an aesthetic much copied and emulated, declared bankruptcy in 1932, a casualty of the Great Depression, and Louis Tiffany died a year later

The precipitous fall from grace the Tiffany Studios suffered in the ensuing years was not shared by his father's firm. Indeed, despite the absence of either father or son at the helm, Tiffany & Co. survived the early years of the twentieth century and by the 1950s had found a renewed sense of prestige in the American luxury goods market that continues to this day.

Tiffany & Co.'s presentation vase for the 1915 Pan-Pacific Exposition in San Francisco reflects a refined modern aesthetic in its austere form, delicate rhythmical border pattern, and the richly enameled but nonetheless rigidly controlled, allegorical frieze (cat. 273).

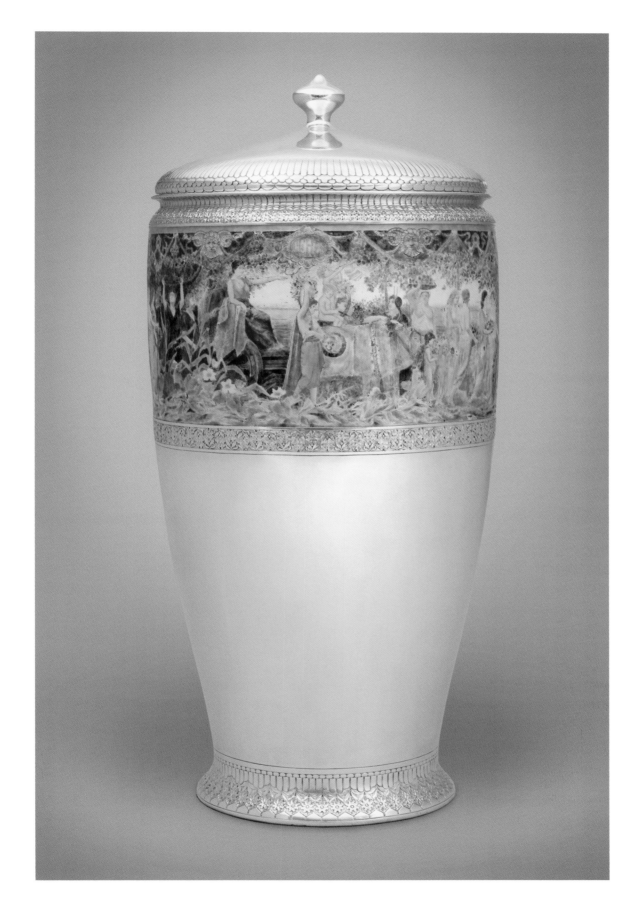

1. Tiffany & Co. received three grand prizes for work in gold, silver, and leather; three gold medals for stationery and printing; three silver medals for hunting outfits and cutlery; "Americans as Art Workmen, Substantial Recognition Shown by Paris Exposition Judges to Two New York Concerns," *New York Times*, 18 September 1900, 11. Tiffany Glass & Decorating Co. received two grand prizes (for both Louis Comfort Tiffany and Arthur J. Nash), two gold medals, and one bronze medal; "Paris Exposition Awards," *Jewelers' Circular* 41, no. 6 (5 September 1900): 10–11.

2. "Prizes at the Paris Exposition," *Jewelers' Circular* 41, no. 3 (15 August 1900): 27.

3. "Modern Jewellery at the Paris Exhibition," *Artist* (London) 29 (October 1900–January 1901): 191–93.

4. See Martin Eidelberg and Nancy A. McClelland, eds., *Behind the Scenes of Tiffany Glassmaking: The Nash Notebooks* (New York: St. Martin's Press, 2001).

5. Lewis F. Day, "Favrile Glass," *Magazine of Art* 25 (1901): 541–44.

6. *American Art Annual* 3 (1900–1901): 21, ill. p. 33.

7. Commissioned by Henry O. Havemeyer; see Alice Cooney Frelinghuysen et al. *Splendid Legacy: The Havemeyer Collection*, exh. cat. (New York: Metropolitan Museum of Art, 1993), 124.

8. The firm went through several name changes in the early years and with several partners before Charles Lewis Tiffany assumed full control in 1853. For more details on the early years of the firm and Tiffany's early merchandising activities, which fall outside the scope of this essay, see Jeannine Falino and Yvonne Markowitz, eds., *American Luxury: Jewels from the House of Tiffany* (Suffolk: Antique Collectors' Club, 2008), and Claire Phillips, ed., *Bejewelled by Tiffany 1837–1987*, exh. cat., Gilbert Collection (New Haven/London: Yale University Press/Gilbert Collection Trust/Tiffany & Co., 2006).

9. See Jeannine Falino and Yvonne Markowitz, "The Cesnola Collection of Cypriot Jewels and Charles Louis [sic] Tiffany," *Minerva* 17, no. 3 (May/June 2006): 36–39.

10. C.E.P., "A Visit to Two Art Galleries," *Boston Daily Globe*, 21 January 1873, 2. The Metropolitan Museum of Art was founded in 1870.

11. For a brief survey of American jewelry firms and retailers of the nineteenth and early twentieth centuries, see Penny Proddow and Debra Healy, *American Jewelry: Glamour and Tradition* (New York: Rizzoli, 1987), 11–25. Despite the fact that silver produced by the Gorham Mfg. Co. was on a par with that produced by Tiffany & Co., direct comparison is difficult because Gorham retailed its wares through other firms.

12. The Geneva watch factory was advertised in the *Baltimore American, Boston Post, Chicago Daily Tribune, Cleveland Daily Herald, Indianapolis Daily Journal*, and *Philadelphia Evening Transcript* between 10 and 22 May 1875. Clipping files, Tiffany & Co. Archives, Parsippany, N.J.

13. The first office in Paris opened in 1850 as Tiffany, Reed & Co. at 79 rue de Richelieu, with a later shop in 1868 established at 57 rue de Chateaudun. In 1872, Tiffany, Reed opened an office in London at 29 Argyll Street, moved to 5 Argyll Street in 1883, and opened a grand store at 221 Regent Street in 1892. For more information on Tiffany's European branches, see Katherine Purcell, "Tiffany and Paris, 1850–1910," in Phillips, *Bejewelled by Tiffany 1837–1987*.

14. Young's purchases are recorded in George Frederic Heydt, *Charles L. Tiffany and the History of Tiffany & Co.* (New York: Tiffany & Co., 1893). Louis-Philippe I ruled France from 1830 until 1848.

15. See Purcell, "Tiffany and Paris: 1850–1910," 26–45.

16. Advertisement in *Bigelow's Illustrated Annual, History of Prominent Mercantile and Manufacturing Firms in the United States* (Boston: D. Bigelow, 1857), 6:16.

17. For an 1889 parasol with watch bearing the marks of the Stockbridge, England, firm of S. Fox & Co., see Phillips, *Bejewelled by Tiffany 1837–1987*, 188–89.

18. Henry A. Spaulding was employed by Tiffany & Co. beginning in the early 1870s. He began working at the Paris branch soon after, staying until the late 1880s; he opened Spaulding & Co. in Chicago in 1888.

19. Tiffany acquired Moore's firm in 1869; Charles L. Venable et al., *Silver in America 1840–1940: A Century of Splendor* (Dallas: Dallas Museum of Art, 1994), 320.

20. W. C. Aitken, *Report presented to the Council of the Birmingham Chamber of Commerce* (Birmingham, 1873), 36–37; Robert H. Thurston, ed., *Reports of the Commissioners to the International Exhibition held at Vienna, 1873* (Washington, D.C.: Government Printing Office, 1876), 1:159.

21. Phillips, *Bejewelled by Tiffany 1837–1987*, 237.

22. John Loring, *Paulding Farnham: Tiffany's Lost Genius* (New York: Abrams, 2000), 13.

23. Ibid., 8.

24. Anne Odom, "Russkii stil': The Russian Style for Export—Hillwood Museum and Gardens," *Antiques* 163 (March 2003): 102–7.

25. "H. W. Hiller Dead; Pioneer Importer," *New York Times*, 21 January 1926, 21; Henry Winans Hiller Papers, Collection 77, box 2, volume 7, Mystic (Connecticut) Seaport Museum. Hiller was also responsible for the Tiffany installation at the 1889 Exposition Universelle in Paris, although his personal correspondence indicates that he clashed with company gemologist George Frederick Kunz.

26. For examples by Kuzmichev, see Christie's (New York), lot 253, sale no. 1821, lot 253 (18 April 2007); Christie's (London), lot 678, sale no. 5261 (10 July 2007); and Christie's (London), lot 149, sale no. 7307 (29 November 2006). For Klingert, see Odom, "Russkii stil': The Russian Style for Export."

27. Christie's (London), lot 121, sale no. 9626 (29 November 2006). Kieran McCarthy, "Fabergé in London," *Apollo* 165 (July 2006): 34–39.

28. The information on Marcus is drawn from Janet Zapata, "The Legacy of Herman Marcus and Marcus and Company, Part I," *Antiques* 172 (August 2007): 68–77, and Zapata, "The Legacy of Herman Marcus and Marcus and Company, Part II," *Antiques* 172 (September 2007): 84–93.

29. "Starr & Marcus," *New York Times*, 17 December 1874, 8.

30. "Queen Kapiolani," *New York Post*, 20 May 1887, clipping files, Tiffany Archives; "Fortunes in Jewels," *Philadelphia Inquirer*, 18 April 1899, 4.

31. "The coronet for Mme. Nordica," *New York Times*, 12 April 1896, 11. The coronet was designed, as many were, with detachable elements. The central floral spray could be combined with a comb in the coronet and used as a smaller hair ornament.

32. The phrase was first used by Samuel Ward McAllister, the self-appointed "kingmaker" of New York society. See his memoirs, entitled *Society as I have Found It* (New York: Cassell Publishing, 1890).

33. "To be a Countess Today, Final Preparations for the Marriage of Miss Anna Gould," *New York Times*, 4 March 1895, 8.

34. J. Leander Bishop, *History of American Manufacturers from 1608 to 1860* (Philadelphia: Edward Young, 1868), 1:187.

35. Jeptha H. Wade II was an avid collector of gem specimens, many of which were given to the Cleveland Museum of Natural History in 1924.

36. The details about Wade's Lalique purchases are from manuscript collection no. 3292, Jeptha Homer Wade Family Papers (hereafter Wade Family Papers), Western Reserve Historical Society, Cleveland.

37. Ibid.

38. Receipt to J. H. Wade, Esq. from Tiffany Glass & Decorating Co., 31 December 1901, included the sale of two cigar cutters (9673–1537 and 9696–1537). The date of purchase suggests they were intended as gifts. Whether these items were made or retailed by the firm is not known. Folder 41, container 5, Wade Family Papers.

39. "Showered with Gifts, Society Gets a Glimpse of the Wedding Presents," *Boston Daily Globe*, 12 September 1899, 2; "Grant Wedding Presents," *New York Times*, 12 September 1899, 7.

40. William R. Johnston, *William and Henry Walters, the Reticent Collectors* (Baltimore/London: Johns Hopkins University Press in association with the Walters Art Gallery, 1999), 119–20.

41. "Silver and Gold/Rich Gifts Being Made for Miss Alice/Providence Concerns Turning Out Two Splendid Services," *Boston Daily Globe*, 28 January 1906, 7; "Won't Show Bridal Gifts/Miss Roosevelt to Keep Them from Public Inspection," *New York Times*, 7 February 1906, 9; "Potpourri of Gifts for the Happy Bride," *Washington Times*, 17 February 1906, 2; "Never a Gift Array Like It," *Boston Daily Globe*, 18 February 1906, 10. "Tiffany Favrile Glass For Table Use," in *Tiffany Favrile Glass/Made at the Tiffany Furnaces Corona Long Island New York/Legion D'Honneur–Grand Prix–Paris 1900* (Corona, New York: Tiffany Furnaces, 1905), 5–13.

42. Up to this time, Tiffany & Co. had participated in the New York Crystal Palace Exhibition (1853), the New York Sanitary Fair (1865), the Philadelphia Centennial (1876), and the Paris Exposition Universelle (1878); see Jeannine Falino, "Unsurpassed in Splendor: Exhibitions and Expositions by Tiffany & Co.," in Falino and Markowitz, *American Luxury*.

43. "Howard's Letter, Fads for Everybody the World Over," *Boston Daily Globe*, 17 June 1872, 28; "In the Floral World, the Demand for Nature's Choicest Handiwork," *New York Times*, 24 May 1885, 3; "Reign of the Orchid," *Boston Daily Globe*, 19 March 1899, 40.

44. *New York Herald* (Paris), 30 September 1889, as cited in John Loring, "Putting the Metal to the Petal," *Garden Design* 19, no. 8 (December 2000–January 2001): 89–92.

45. *Jewelers' Weekly* 8, no. 6 (6 June 1889): 39.

46. "The Tiffany Exhibit," *Independent* (New York), 13 April 1893.

47. Marilynn A. Johnson, *Louis Comfort Tiffany, Artist for the Ages*, exh. cat., Seattle Art Museum and tour (London: Scala, 2005), 23.

48. James D. McCabe, *The Illustrated History of the Centennial Exhibition, Philadelphia 1876* (Philadelphia: J. R. Jones, 1876; repr. Philadelphia: National Publishing Company, 1976), 192.

49. Dresser was later engaged by Charles Tiffany to purchase wares in Japan for sale in the Tiffany & Co. store.

50. The chased gold and silver Indian jewelry "not surpassed by any in the exhibition" was shown by importers Watson & Co. of Bombay and may have been included within the India Museum installation; J. S. Ingram, *The Centennial Exposition* (Philadelphia: Hubbard Bros., 1876), 592–93.

51. The Dun quotation was cited by Roberta A. Mayer and Carolyn K. Lane, "Disassociating the 'Associated Artists': The Early Business Ventures of Louis C. Tiffany, Candace T. Wheeler, and Lockwood de Forest," *Studies in the Decorative Arts* 8, no. 2 (Spring–Summer 2001), 6.

52. R. G. Dun & Co. Collection, Historical Collections, Baker Library, Harvard University Graduate School of Business Administration, Cambridge, as cited in Mayer and Lane, "Disassociating the 'Associated Artists'," 33n18.

53. For a full discussion of Louis Comfort Tiffany's various interior decorating firms see Mayer and Lane, "Disassociating the 'Associated Artists,' " 2–36. For an excellent chronology of the various L. C. Tiffany businesses, see Eidelberg and McClelland, *Behind the Scenes of Tiffany Glassmaking*, xiii–xvi.

54. There is no record of any of his lamps being publicly displayed until 1896.

55. Frelinghuysen, *Splendid Legacy*, 183–84.

56. Ibid., 176.

57. Tiffany's activities with glass during the period and his work for the Garretts have been drawn from Johnson 2005, 36–40.

58. Therese Charpentier, "La Clientèle Etrangère de Gallé," *21st International Congress of the History of Art* (Berlin, 1967), 1:259, 261–62, as cited by Martin Eidelberg, "Tiffany and the Cult of Nature," in Alastair Duncan et al., *Masterworks of Louis Comfort Tiffany*, exh. cat., Renwick Gallery (New York: Abrams, 1989), 94n43.

59. Established in 1892, with six women, the department soon came into conflict with the men's union. It was agreed that the women's department, which was not unionized, would not grow beyond thirty-five members. Martin Eidelberg et al., *A New Light on Tiffany, Clara Driscoll and the Tiffany Girls* (New York: New York Historical Society, in association with D. Gilles Limited, 2007), 30.

60. Driscoll began work for Tiffany in June 1888; ibid., 14.

61. Driscoll's work on the dragonfly lamp first came to light in an article entitled "Women Who Make $10,000 a Year or More," *New York Daily News*, 17 April 1904, as cited in Eidelberg, *New Light on Tiffany*, 12. The discovery and analysis of her letters is fully detailed in Eidelberg's book; for the Brittany voyage, see ibid., 152.

62. See an advertisement by Tiffany Glass & Decorating Co., originally published in *Art Interchange* (February 1896) in which Tiffany Favrile glass is stated as "made by special processes under the personal supervision of Mr. Louis C. Tiffany"; Martin Eidelberg, "Tiffany's Early Glass Vessels," *Antiques* 137, no. 2 (February 1990): fig. 1.

63. Eidelberg and McClelland, *Behind the Scenes of Tiffany Glassmaking*, 3–9.

64. "Pots and Flasks of Many Hues, L. C. Tiffany and Dr. Doremus Try for Colored Blown Glass," *New York Times*, 20 May 1894, 17; "Art Exhibition of New Tiffany Glassware," *American Architect and Building News*, 2 June 1894, 4.

65. Frelinghuysen, *Splendid Legacy*, 123.

66. Originally installed after the fair in the Cathedral of St. John the Divine in New York, the chapel's interior is now on view at the Morse Museum of American Art, Winter Park, Florida.

67. Hubert Howe Bancroft, *The Book of the Fair* (Chicago: Bancroft Co., 1893), 150.

68. Johnson, *Louis Comfort Tiffany*, 78–79.

69. Siegfried Bing has been the subject of intense scholarly interest in recent years. For an excellent overview with bibliography, see Gabriel P. Weisberg et al., eds., *The Origins of L'Art Nouveau: The Bing Empire*, exh. cat. (Amsterdam/Paris/Antwerp: Van Gogh Museum/Musée des Arts Décoratifs/Mercatorfonds, 2005).

70. Tiffany and Bing may have encountered one another through their connection to collector Henry O. Havemeyer, who was a client of both men. Bing described Louis Tiffany's design for the Havemeyer home (unnamed as such) in his article for Roujon. Chief Tiffany & Co. designer Edward C. Moore may have purchased some of his own Japanese objects from Bing, either in Paris or through Bing's New York office, which opened its doors in 1887. Moore could have exerted an artistic influence over Louis Comfort Tiffany because of his long association with the firm; see Martin Eidelberg, "S. Bing and L. C. Tiffany: Entrepreneurs of Style," *Nineteenth-Century Art Worldwide* 4, no. 2 (Summer 2005), http://www.19thc-artworldwide.org/summer_05/articles/eide.shtml. Exactly how Moore assembled his collection has not been determined, but because of his interest in Japanese art, he would likely have known of Bing, who exhibited Asian decorative arts at the Paris Exposition of 1878 and opened a sales room at 220 Fifth Avenue in New York in 1887; Weisberg, *Origins of L'Art Nouveau*, 77. "Priceless Works of Art, The Moore Collection Opened at the Metropolitan Museum," *New York World*, clipping files, Tiffany Archives.

71. Samuel Bing, "La Culture Artistique en Amerique," translated by Benita Eisler, in *Artistic America, Tiffany Glass, and Art Nouveau* (Cambridge: MIT Press, 1970), 1–193.

72. With Paul Sérusier, as head and originator of their name, Les Nabis, or prophets, were progressive members of the Académie Julian who strove to create art that combined a response to nature with personal symbolism, a stance that eventually led toward the nonrepresentational art of the twentieth century. Influenced by Paul Gauguin, and loosely related to the Symbolists, members of the Nabis included Maurice Denis, Pierre Bonnard, Édouard Vuillard, Ker-Xavier Roussel, Paul Ranson, Henri-Gabriel Ibels, and Félix Vallotton, among others. Their effort to integrate art with daily life was consistent with the Arts and Crafts theories then prevalent.

73. Letter from Édouard Vuillard to Maurice Denis, 30 May 1894, as cited in Gabriel Weisberg, *Art Nouveau Bing: Paris Style*, exh. cat. (New York/Washington, D.C.: Abrams, in association with the Smithsonian Institution Traveling Exhibition Service, 1986), 49n6.

74. Johnson, *Louis Comfort Tiffany: Artist for the Ages*, 88. For a more detailed list of Tiffany exhibitions that Bing held in Europe and the museums that acquired his work, see Eidelberg, *Origins of L'Art Nouveau*.

75. The *New York Times* quoted an unnamed London critic who was well disposed to the exhibition. Similarly, a favorable review in the *Collector* mentioned the *London Times*, *Builder*, *Daily News*, *Daily Chronicle*, and *Gentlewoman* was also appreciative; a review by the *Pall Mall Gazette* was the sole negative example cited. "The Collector," *Art Amateur, Devoted to Art in the Household* 41, no. 3 (August 1899): 51; "Art at Home and Abroad," *New York Times*, 17 June 1899, BR400. For a long and detailed review focused on Tiffany glass and Colonna's designs, see also Horace Townsend, "American and French Applied Art at the Grafton Galleries," *International Studio* 8 (1899): 39–44.

76. For a detailed biography of Colonna, see Martin Eidelberg, *E. Colonna*, exh. cat. (Dayton: Dayton Art Institute, 1983).

77. "Exhibition of L'Art Nouveau, S. Bing, Paris, May–July 1899" (London: Grafton Galleries, 1899), 18. Martin Eidelberg notes that this article was an English translation of one Bing had published anonymously in *Kunst and Kunsthandwerk* 1 (1898): 105–11 as "Die Kunstgläser von Louis C. Tiffany." For an accessible analysis of the relationship between Bing and Louis Comfort Tiffany, see Eidelberg, "S. Bing and L. C. Tiffany: Entrepreneurs of Style."

78. "Exhibition of L'Art Nouveau, S. Bing," 22, nos. 1–30.

79. For an illustration of a Tiffany vase shown at the Grafton Galleries labeled "monture de vase, E. Colonna," see "Les Objects d'Art des Salons," *Art et Décoration* 5 (January–June 1899): 6. Colonna apparently worked for Louis C. Tiffany, de Forest, Colman, and Wheeler on the decoration of the Ogden Goelet residence. See Eidelberg, *E. Colonna*, 7nn16–17.

80. Ibid., 7n16. René Haase, who worked with Bing and succeeded him, identified Feuillâtre and Colonna as collaborating on a Tiffany vase in *Les Renouvateurs de l'Art Appliqué 1890–1910* (Paris, Musée Galliera, 1925), 12, no. 259, as cited in Eidelberg, *E. Colonna*, 77n103. The example now in the Corning Museum of Glass (2006.4.161) may indeed be the same one shown at the Grafton Galleries exhibition.

81. *American Art Annual* 3 (1900–1901): 21, 33.

82. Burton Holmes (1901), quoted in David Park Curry, "Tiffany's Golden Bowl," *Antiques* 151, no. 1 (January 1997): 244–47n13.

83. "Display of Favrile Glass at Tiffany's," *New-York Tribune*, 12 March 1900, 4.

84. R. R., "The Paris Exposition, I. Some American Exhibits," *Art Amateur* 42, no. 5 (April 1900): 4.

85. Éd[ouard] Didron, "Les Vitraux a l'Exposition de 1900," *Revue des Arts Décoratifs* 20 (1900): 176.

86. Eidelberg, *New Light on Tiffany*, 184. An illustration of the window and its Northrop attribution appeared in *Brush and Pencil*, along with photographs of "The Seasons" (the four seasons), the dandelion lamp, and a covered enameled vessel in Gardner Teall, "Artistic American Wares at Expositions," *Brush and Pencil* 6, no. 4 (1900): 176. Thanks to Emmanuel Ducamp for providing information about the Stieglitz purchase.

87. For an example of these early glass shades, see Dr. Walter Gensel, "Tiffany-Gläser auf der Pariser Welt-Ausstellung 1900," *Deutche Kunst und Dekoration* 7 (October 1900–March 1901): 90–96, illus. 90.

88. "The Tiffany Glass at the Pan American," *Keramic Studio* 3, no. 2 (June 1901): 30–31. The source of light may have been similar to the rotating color wheel that was used on the fountain in Laurelton Hall, c. 1904–10. Alice Cooney Frelinghuysen, *Louis Comfort Tiffany and Laurelton Hall: An Artist's Country Estate*, exh. cat. (New York/New Haven: Metropolitan Museum of Art/Yale University Press, 2006), fig. 135.

89. Adams was a man of considerable influence who worked quietly in the background for big business. He played a key role in the adoption of alternating current over direct current electricity, reorganized the New York, West Shore, and Buffalo Railroads, and helped J. P. Morgan prevent the Panic of 1896. "Golden Jubilee," *Time* 13, no. 21 (27 May 1929), http://205.188.238.109/time/magazine/article/0,9171,927947-2,00.html.

90. Troy pounds were used primarily to measure precious metals. A troy pound (5,760 grains) is divided into twelve ounces of 480 grains each.

91. *The Adams Gold Vase* (New York: Tiffany & Co., 1896), 30.

92. According to Tiffany & Co., three draftsmen, fifteen modelers, eighteen goldsmiths, twenty-one chasers, twelve finishers, four molders, three turners, two enamelers, three stonecutters, and two lapidaries were engaged at various stages of production; their combined efforts equaled 2,420 days of labor; *The Adams Gold Vase* (New York: Tiffany & Co., Exposition Universelle, 1900).

93. Paraphrase of the original text by the author. [Oculi], "L'Orfèverie étranger à L'Exposition de 1900," *Revue de la Bijouterie, Joaillerie, Orfèverie* 6 (October 1900): 54.

94. The French awarded different degrees of grand prix awards. Paraphrasing of the original text by the author. Jury international, Exposition Universelle internationale de 1900, *Rapports du jury international* (Paris: Imprimerie Nationale, 1902–6), Groupe 15, Industries diverses, classes 92–97, 314.

95. The spelling of Joseph Heinrichs's name was mistakenly recorded as "Heinrich" without the "s" in Charles Venable's *Silver in America* and subsequently published incorrectly by auction houses and other authors. However, the correct spelling, as it appears on patent records and in period references should be "Heinrichs." In addition, his wares were most often stamped "Jos. Heinrichs/Paris + New York," though some works have also surfaced with retail marks instead of his own. A newly discovered trade pamphlet from around 1900 refers to the name of his company as the Bi-Metal and French Steam Coffee Pot Co., a name that does, in fact, appear in period references. He also lists his address at "948 Broadway, Between 22nd and 23rd Streets," in New York and indicates that in addition to Paris, his works could be purchased in London. The pamphlet also proudly proclaims that his goods have been "adopted by the principal Courts and Embassies of Europe: by the aristocracy and the very best hotels and restaurants of Paris, London, and New York." Despite these promotional claims, there is no proof, as yet, that Heinrichs actually sold his wares outside the United States. *Bi-Metal and French Steam Coffee Pot Co.: Inventors and Manufacturers of the Best Coffee Pot in Existence* (New York: Jos. Heinrichs, n.d.), unpaginated. I am grateful to Melissa D. Buchanan (Rhode Island School of Design Museum, Providence) for sharing her research and to Stephen Harrison for providing the trade pamphlet.

96. In 1899 Robert and Emily de Forest commissioned Louis Comfort Tiffany to design an Indian basket hanging lampshade for their Long Island home, where their collection of baskets was displayed. For a discussion of the de Forest commission and Tiffany's own collecting activities in this area, see Elizabeth Hutchinson, "Native American Art at Laurelton Hall," in Frelinghuysen, *Louis Comfort Tiffany and Laurelton Hall*, 177–89, fig. 299.

97. "A Revival of Art," *New York Observer and Chronicle*, 1 March 1900, 280.

98. Phillips, *Bejewelled by Tiffany 1837–1987*, 34, 41–42.

99. "The Gorham Manufacturing Co. Orfèvres, New York, Représentée à Paris par Spaulding & Co., 36 Avenue de l'Opéra" (New York, 1900), in *Gorham Design Library*, electronic resource (Cranston, R.I.: Owl at the Bridge, 2003), disk 6.

100. "Studio-Talk," *Studio* 12, no. 45 (November 1900): 137.

101. J. Alastair Duncan, "The Jewelry of Louis Comfort Tiffany and Carl Fabergé: A Comparative Study," in Géza von Habsburg et al., *Fabergé, Imperial Craftsman and His World*, exh. cat. (London: Booth-Clibborn Editions, 2000), 352.

102. For a discussion of the term "Favrile," see Martin Eidelberg, "Tiffany's Early Glass Vessels," *Antiques* 137 (February 1990): 502–15. The painting *Favrile* by Elliot Daingerfield depicts a woman in profile who holds a Favrile vase in her hand. "Lotos Club Exhibition," *New York Sun*, 27 February 1903, 6.

103. Tiffany & Co., advertisement, *Illustrated American* 19, no. 324 (25 April 1896). The advertisement offered "Tiffany Favrille [sic] Glass."

104. "Tiffany Favrile Glass," Tiffany Studios and Tiffany & Co., advertisement, *New-York Tribune*, 31 October 1900, 6.

105. Ibid., 21 November 1900, 2.

106. Ibid., 18 November 1900, 6. It should be noted that Tiffany & Co. maintained only one location in the United States until 1963, when branches were opened in San Francisco and Houston.

107. O'Brien's Art Galleries (Chicago), advertisement, *House Beautiful* 7, no. 1 (December 1899): xviii; Leyson's Jewelers, advertisement, *Deseret Evening News* (Salt Lake City), 12 April 1904, 8; Brower's Art Gallery, advertisement, *Lexington* (Kentucky) *Bourbon News*, 20 November 1908; Sylvan Bros., Jewelers, advertisement, *State* (Columbia, South Carolina), 20 September 1919; W. A. Doody, advertisement *Macon* (Georgia) *Weekly Telegraph*, 11 June 1921; A. & C. Feldenheimer, advertisement, *Portland Oregonian*, 22 December 1922, 2.

108. The firm was reorganized in 1900 as Tiffany Studios. "First Club, then Art Shop, Evolution of an Athletic Club into a Haunt of Artisans," *New York Times*, 21 October 1905, 9.

109. Schmitt Brothers advertised under their own name and maintained two locations: 40 East 23rd Street and 343–345 Madison Avenue *New York Sun*, 13 December 1907, 3; 15 November 1908, 9; 16 May 1909, 9.

110. It is possible that Tiffany Studios served as an overflow location for auctions by the American Art Association. "Stained glass sells high, a day of lively bidding at the White sale," *New York Sun*, 28 November 1907, 5. [Tiffany Studios], "Illustrated catalogue of a notable collection of beautiful English furniture of the XVII and XVIII centuries, the collection formed by Mr. Thomas B. Clarke and acquired by the Tiffany Studios, for whose account the collection will be sold at unrestricted public sale on the dates herein stated [1–3 December 1910] catalogued by Luke Vincent Lockwood; the sale will be conducted by Mr. Thomas E. Kirby, of the American Art Association, managers" (New York: Press of the Lent & Graff Company, 1910).

111. [Tiffany Studios], *Character and Individuality in Decorations and Furnishings* (New York: Tiffany Studios, 1913).

112. *Official catalogue of exhibitors, Universal Exposition, St. Louis, U.S.A. 1904, Division of exhibits, Department B, Art* (St. Louis: Official Catalogue Company, 1904), nos. 154–66, 756–80, 781–835.

113. "Tiffany and Company, at the Saint Louis Exposition," *Craftsman* 7, no. 2 (November 1904): 169–83.

114. Ibid., 181.

115. For excellent survey of Louis Comfort Tiffany's jewelry production, see the pioneering work of Janet Zapata, *The Jewelry and Enamels of Louis Comfort Tiffany* (New York: Abrams, 1993), and Alice Cooney Frelinghuysen, "'Nature Studies': The Art Jewelry of Louis Comfort Tiffany," in Phillips, *Bejewelled by Tiffany 1837–1987*, 64–81.

116. For examples of designing in moonstone and sapphire, see Phillips, *Bejewelled by Tiffany 1837–1987*, 246–47.

117. "New York Art Exhibitions and Gallery News," *Christian Science Monitor*, 14 July 1916, in Louis Comfort Tiffany scrapbook, 1902–18, Archives of American Art, Smithsonian Institution, Washington, D.C.

Catalogue of the Exhibition

Dimensions, as provided by lenders, are given in centimeters (cm), height (h.) preceding width (w.) (or length [l.]) and depth (d.) (or diameter [diam.]). The numbers in parentheses after each catalogue number indicate the page(s) on which the object (or its caption) appear.

Louis Aucoc Fils (French, Paris, established 1877)
Casimir Aucoc established a silversmith shop in Paris in 1821. His son, Louis Aucoc Aîné, ran a goldsmith's firm at 6 rue de la Paix and was later joined by his two sons, Louis and André. In 1877, Louis Aucoc took over the Maison Lobjois and added jewelry design and retail to the family firm's services, continuing until after 1900. René Lalique was apprenticed to the firm from 1876 to 1878; Louis designed in the "Genre Lalique"-style from 1899 to 1900 and applied Art Nouveau influences to his jewelry. In 1900, André began management of the family firm. Louis served on the international jury for the Bijouterie-Joaillerie division of the 1898 and 1900 Paris Expositions Universelle, acted as president of the Chambre Syndicale de la Bijouterie-Joaillerie-Orfèvrerie from 1895 to 1908, and participated in the 1906 International Exhibition in Milan.

Cat. 1 (p. 85). *Dog Collar Plaque*, c. 1900. Designer: Louis Aucoc. Gold, platinum, diamonds, enamel; 4.4 x 7.6 cm. The Newark Museum, Gift of Herman A. E. and Paul C. Jaehne, 1941, 41.725.

Cat. 2 (p. 204). *Kettle on Stand with Tray*, 1911. Designer: André Aucoc. Silver. Kettle: 36.4 x 30 x 22 cm; stand: 16.2 x 36.2 x 22.8 cm; tray: 93 x 56.5 cm. Calouste Gulbenkian Foundation/Calouste Gulbenkian Museum, 1286 A/B/C.

Edmond-Henri Becker (French, Paris, active c. 1900)
Producing Art Nouveau metalwork and sculptural wood objects such as parasol handles and inkwells, Becker worked primarily for Boucheron and also produced models for Louis Aucoc. An exhibitor at the 1900 Exposition in Paris, Becker also created medallions for the costume jewelers Savard.

Cat. 3 (p. 130). *Pendant "Belle de Nuit,"* c. 1900. Ivory by Edmond Becker. Ivory, plique-à-jour enamel, diamonds, platinum; 10 x 11 cm. Private collection.

Maison Boucheron (French, Paris, est. 1858)
Instituted in 1858 in the Place du Palais Royal in Paris by Frédéric Boucheron, a student of Jules Chaise, the firm gained recognition for his extravagant diamond jewelry designs, notably at the 1867 Exposition Universelle in Paris, where he was awarded a gold medal. The firm also exhibited at the 1900 Paris Exposition Universelle. Jules Brateau, Jules Debut, Lucien Hirtz, Octave Loeuillard, and Louis Rault were all employed at the firm at various points, each bringing his own style to enhance the diversity of the firm's work. Using innovative techniques, Boucheron designed for clients with extravagant tastes. In 1893, the firm relocated to the Place Vendôme,

opening branches in Moscow around the turn of the century and London in 1903, and a company in New York in 1903. In 1902, Louis Boucheron took over the business after his father's death.

Cat. 4 (p. 163). *Eagles Brooch*, 1903. Designer: Lucien Hirtz. Gold, olivines, peridots, old-cut diamonds; 8.4 x 6.8 cm. Boucheron Collection, Paris.

Cat. 5 (p. 173). *Iris Vase*, 1905. Workmaster: J. A. Martel. Glass, silver gilt; h. 53 cm. Boucheron Collection, Paris.

Cat. 6 (p. 97). *Necklace*, 1890. Blue-tinted steel, diamonds, zircons, pearls; w. 5.3 cm. Boucheron Collection, Paris.

Félix Bracquemond (French, Paris, 1833–1914)
Trained as a painter under Joseph Guichard, Bracquemond exhibited at various Salons from 1852 until he gave up painting after 1869. Studying printmaking around 1849, Bracquemond produced nearly 900 prints and founded the Société des Aquafortistes in 1862. Bracquemond exhibited at the 1855 Exposition Universelle, the 1863 Salon des Refusés, and the Impressionist exhibitions of 1874, 1879, and 1880, all held in Paris. Producing ceramics and etchings in the early 1860s, Bracquemond was influenced by Japanese ukiyo-e prints, especially the designs in Hokusai's *Manga* sketchbook. Interested in the theory of the art of relief and the role of color in design work, he published *Du dessin et de la couleur* in 1885. A member of the Société des Artistes Français and the Société Nationale des Beaux-Arts, he founded the Société des Peintres-Graveurs Français in 1890. Bracquemond was awarded first prize for his etchings at the 1900 Exposition Universelle in Paris and went on to produce jewelry, table services, and furniture, which he exhibited at the Salon of 1902.

Cat. 7 (not illustrated). *Design for Hand Mirror*, 1900–1902. Ink on paper; 62 x 45 cm. Private collection.

Cat. 8 (p. 133). *Hand Mirror*, 1900–1902. Relief: Auguste Rodin; enamel: Alexandre Riquet; goldsmith: Falize Frères. Gold, enamel, ivory; 32.2 x 16.1 x 1.2 cm. The Cleveland Museum of Art, Gift of Ralph King, by exchange, 1978.43.

Carlo Bugatti (Italian, 1856–1940)
Educated at the Accademia di Belli Arti di Brera in Milan and the École des Beaux-Arts in Paris, Bugatti completed paintings and architectural drawings early in his career. Influenced by Japanese, Islamic, and Romanesque design, he exhibited furniture at the 1888 Italian Exhibition at Earl's Court, London. Bugatti exhibited his Snail Room at the 1902 First International Exposition of Modern Decorative Arts in Turin. In 1904, Bugatti sold his business to the De Vecchi firm and launched his silversmithing career in Paris. Still influenced by Art Nouveau, Bugatti used hybrid creatures, grotesque, fantastic, and surrealistic subject matter to decorate his objects, which were sold through Adrien Hébrard's firm in Paris. By 1910, Bugatti was near retirement and focused on portrait painting.

Cat. 9 (pp. 37, 57). *Table*, c. 1907. Inlaid wood, cast and gilded bronze mounts, inlays of ivory or bone, metal, mother-of-pearl; 71.5 x 67.1 x 41.3 cm. The Cleveland Museum of Art, Leonard C. Hanna Jr. Fund, 1991.45.

Cat. 10 (pp. 37, 57). *Tea and Coffee Service with Salver*, 1907. Maker: A. A. Hébrard Firm. Raised silver vessels, hammered tray, cast and chased decoration, gilded, ivory handles. Tray, cream pitcher, covered sugar bowl, tea pot, hot water pot. Hot water pot: 18.4 x 15.3 x 9.7 cm, and various dimensions for other pieces. The Cleveland Museum of Art, The Thomas L. Fawick Memorial Collection, 1980.74.1–5; salver: Leonard C. Hanna Jr. Fund, 1991.46.

Firm of Paul (Pavel) Buhre (Swiss, active Russia, 1815–1917?)
Swiss watchmaker Paul Léopold Buhre opened his shop in St. Petersburg in 1815, which his son, Pavel, later managed. Buhre received the Imperial Warrant in 1899 and established a firm in Switzerland with branches in Moscow and St. Petersburg. Producing jeweled watches for the tsar's cabinet, Buhre also served as supplier to the Imperial Court and produced gold watches for the actors of the Imperial Mariinski Theater. From 1880, Paul Girard directed the workshop, known for gold watches, which closed in 1917.

Cat. 11 (p. 222). *Pendant Watch*, 1901. Gold, diamonds, enamel; 8.7 x 0.9 cm. Hillwood Estate, Museum & Gardens, Bequest of Marjorie Merriweather Post, 1973, 16.18.1–2.

Maison Cardeilhac (French, Paris, 1802–1951)
Founded in 1802 in Paris by Vital Antoine Cardeilhac, the firm specialized in trading and silversmithing. In 1850, Vital's son Édouard took over the business, managed by Ernest Cardeilhac after 1860. Producing silver in the Art Nouveau style, the firm exhibited at the 1900 Paris Exposition Universelle and featured the design work of Lucien Bonvallet. Jacques and Pierre Cardeilhac, Ernest's sons, directed the firm together from 1927 until 1944, when Jacques assumed the directorship after Pierre's death. Maison Cardeilhac joined L'Orfèvrerie Christofle in Paris in 1951.

Cat. 12 (p. 75). *Chocolate Pot*, 1895–1900. Designer: Lucien Bonvallet. Silver, ivory, wood; h. 21.2 cm. Rijksmuseum, Amsterdam, BK-1976-17ab.

Maison Cartier (French, Paris, est. 1847)
Established in Paris by Louis François Cartier in 1847, the firm gained acclaim by designing jewelry for Empress Eugénie and Princess Mathilde Bonaparte, Napoleon III's cousin. L. F. Cartier's son, Alfred, who had been associated with the business for ten years, replaced his father in 1874. By the turn of the century the firm had begun its ascent to becoming one of the most recognized names in jewelry and luxury goods in the world. When the firm transitioned to management by a new generation, L. F. Cartier's grandsons, Louis, Pierre, and Jacques, relocated the shop to the rue de la Paix in 1899. Cartier established retail shops in London in 1902, St. Petersburg in 1908, and New York in 1909. Louis renamed the firm Cartier Frères in 1906, while Jacques took over the London branch in the same year. Around 1910, Louis Cartier, allegedly inspired by the Ballet Russes production of *Shéhérazade*, changed the firm's design standards and began using new color and gem combinations as well as Asian-inspired and geometric designs. The Cartier family maintained control of the business until 1964.

Cat. 13 (p. 165). *Cigarette Case*, 1900–1905. Enamel, gold; 9.5 x 6.3 cm. Collection of Neil Lane.

Cat. 14 (p. 164). *Imperial Egg*, 1906. Designers: Picq, Césard, and Guesdon. Gold, fluorite, diamonds, pearls, enamel; h. (with base) 11.6 cm. The Metropolitan Museum of Art, New York, Bequest of Laird Shields Goldsborough, 1951 (51.91.1).

Cat. 15 (p. 185). *Miniature Japanese Apple Blossom*, 1907. Workmaster: Henri Lavabre. Ivory, quartz, glass, diamonds, gold, wood; h. 15 cm. Musée des Arts Décoratifs, Paris, 36247.70.

Cat. 16 (p. 165). *Pair of Kangaroos*, 1905. Workmaster: Henri Lavabre. Agate, nephrite, diamonds; 9 x 7.5 cm. Musée des Arts Décoratifs, Paris, 36247.64–65.

Fortunato Pio Castellani & Sons (Italian, active Rome, Paris, 1814–1927)
Fortunato Pio Castellani began his career in 1814, opening a workshop in Rome on the Via del Corso. He and Michelangelo Caetani became partners, and after 1826 Castellani began to feature imitations of ancient goldwork design in his pieces, eventually producing "Etruscan"-style jewelry. His relationship with Caetani also led to an international, aristocratic clientele. Continuing the legacy of archaeological-style jewelry, his sons, Alessandro and Augusto, were trained in antique and classical jewelry techniques, primarily producing design work and eventually their renowned "Italian Archaeological Jewelry." After exposure to the Campana jewels collection, the Castellani firm began featuring Baroque, medieval, Renaissance, and Roman influences in their pieces. In 1860, after being exiled from Rome in 1859, Alessandro opened a shop in Paris as well as a firm in London, with Carlo Giuliano. Three years later, Alessandro established a shop in Naples. The brothers met with success in 1861 in Florence at the International Exhibition and later in 1862 when they exhibited their Etruscan-style jewelry at the International Exhibition in London. In 1865, after Fortunato Pio's death, the brothers assumed a professional division when Augusto reopened the firm as "A. Castellani," and Alessandro established himself as an art dealer. Returning to Rome in 1870, Alessandro established a gallery at Via Poli and exhibited at the 1876 exposition in Philadelphia, while Augusto participated in exhibitions in Vienna in 1873 and Paris in 1878. Although serving fewer clients, Augusto continued to fulfill royal commissions until the 1890s. After his death in 1914, his son Alfredo, known for his *ciste*, or cylindrical caskets, oversaw the business until closing it in 1927.

Cat. 17 (p. 236). *Necklace with Cameos of Theatrical Masks*, 1880–1900. Gold, enamel, emeralds, pearls; 39.9 x 3.4 x 1 cm. Cooper-Hewitt, National Design Museum, Smithsonian Institution, museum purchase through gifts of various donors in memory of Annie Schermerhorn Kane and Susan Dwight Bliss, 1969-40-16.

Louis Chalon (French, Paris, 1866–1940)
Trained in the art of painting by Gustave Boulanger and Jules-Joseph Lefebvre, Chalon exhibited in the Salons of the Société des Artistes Français and illustrated for *Le Figaro* as well as editions of Rabelais and Balzac. After experimenting with waxed forms for a still life, he began producing other works to be cast in bronze including portrait busts, inkwells, vases, and lighting fixtures, which were known for their *femme-fleur* motifs.

Cat. 18 (p. 121). *Bouquet Nouveau (New Bouquet) Perfume Bottles* (with original box), c. 1900. Perfumer: Roger & Gallet. Molded green glass, brass, wood, cardboard, paper; h. 10.7 cm. Christie Mayer Lefkowith Collection.

Gaston Chopard (French, Paris, 1883–1942)

Cat. 19 (p. 117). *Comb with Cicadas*, 1902. Tortoiseshell, gold, pearl, enamel; 15.1 x 9.5 cm. Musée des Arts Décoratifs, Paris, 37 291.

Edward Colonna (American, New York, Paris, 1862–1948)
Trained as an architect in Brussels from 1877 to 1882, Colonna acquired an impressive résumé after immigrating to America in 1882 and establishing himself as an interior designer with Associated Artists, founded by Louis Comfort Tiffany. In 1885 he moved to Dayton, Ohio, where he worked as chief designer at Barney & Smith Manufacturing Company, during which time he also published his *Essay on Broom Corn*, expressing his Art Nouveau designs. Moving to Paris in 1898 to work for Siegfried Bing, Colonna began designing jewelry and furniture for the Maison de l'Art Nouveau. In 1899, he participated in the Salon des Artistes Français and the International Exhibition of the Munich Secession. Along with Georges de Feure and Eugène Gaillard, his work was met with popular acclaim at Bing's pavilion at the 1900 Paris exposition. Colonna returned to America around 1902 after Bing's shop closed, producing designs for Brainerd B. Thresher and Marcus & Co.

Cat. 20 (p. 81). *Buckle*, c. 1900. Retailer: L'Art Nouveau. Gold, opals, pearls, garnets; 6 x 8 cm. Cooper-Hewitt, National Design Museum, Smithsonian Institution, Gift of Mr. and Mrs. Maxime Hermanos, 1967-88-3.

Lionel-Aristide Le Couteux (French, Paris, 1847–1909?)

Cat. 21 (p. 111). *Ornamental Comb with Lily Pads*, c. 1900. Tortoiseshell, gold; 12.8 x 1.8 x 7.8 cm. Collection of Robert A. Zehil.

Wilhelm Lucas von Cranach (German, Berlin, 1861–1918)
Trained in France, von Cranach began work as a landscape and portrait painter in Berlin in 1893. Earning a gold medal at the 1900 Paris world's fair and noted for his participation in the 1906 Berlin Secession exhibition, he applied French and Belgian influences in creating his jewelry designs, which often featured Art Nouveau motifs and mythical subjects. Noteworthy among his work is a 335-piece silver dinner service, designed for the Duke of Saxe-Weimar's wedding.

Cat. 22 (p. 16). *Butterfly and Octopus Brooch*, c. 1900. Maker: Louis Werner. Gold, pearls, diamonds, rubies, amethysts, topaz, enamel; 9.8 x 8.3 cm. Schmuckmuseum Pforzheim, Germany, 197916.

Auguste Delaherche (French, Paris, 1857–1940)
Ceramist Auguste Delaherche, born in 1857, was dubbed "the poet of stoneware" in his native France. As a boy, Delaherche became interested in pottery, likely influenced by his uncle Alexandre's immense collection. Delaherche studied at the Paris École des Arts Décoratifs and in 1887 replaced Ernest Chaplet in the Parisian studio formerly owned by Haviland & Co. In 1889 he was awarded a gold medal at the Exposition Universelle in Paris, and he participated in the 1893 World's Columbian Exposition in Chicago, where the American potter William Henry Grueby first became influenced by his work. Living into his eighties, Delaherche's oeuvre spans various styles. He worked exclusively in stoneware, an unpopular clay in France at the time, with decorative motifs ranging from organic or Persian to minimalist. As a potter, he is particularly known for his handmade glazes resulting from his obsessive experimentation with kiln techniques. As time went on, he began to produce work with simpler forms to highlight the glaze as a medium unto itself. Around 1900, Delaherche began to work almost exclusively in porcelain, and after 1910 his ceramics reveal an indebtedness to Chinese Fukien ware.

Cat. 23 (p. 76). *Vase*, 1895. Stoneware, silver, glass; 19.6 x 7.7 cm. The Cleveland Museum of Art, Gift of Henry H. Hawley, 1997.288.

Pierre-Georges Deraisme (French, Paris, 1859–1932)
Deraisme was born on 24 May 1859 in Paris and later entered the jewelry field as a modeler and chaser. By 1889 he had become established and soon began collaborating with René Lalique. Deraisme was active in two areas: luxurious accessories and jewelry. As a silversmith he drew inspiration from historicism, particularly the Renaissance and Rococo eras. He distinguished himself from Lalique in his interpretation of the eighteenth century. Deraisme also created work for the French crystal manufactory Baccarat.

Cat. 24 (p. 124). *Nelly Flacon (Perfume Bottle)*, 1913. Perfumer: D'Orsay. Molded clear glass, charcoal gray patina, perfume; h. 6.5 cm. Manufacturer: Baccarat. Christie Mayer Lefkowith Collection.

Peter Carl Fabergé (Russian, St. Petersburg, 1846–1920)
House of Fabergé (Russian, 1842–1918)
After training in Frankfurt and St. Petersburg under Peter Heskias Pendin, a goldsmith from his father's firm, in 1870 Fabergé took over the House of Fabergé, which had been founded by his father, Carl Gustav Fabergé, in 1842. Until 1881 the firm manufactured jewelry and in 1885 began producing its presentation Easter eggs by commission from Tsar Alexander III. Agathon, Peter Carl's brother, joined the firm in 1883, after which they produced luxurious accessories and hardstone sculptures. Their workmasters used guilloché enamel, Russian-style filigree, and cloisonné techniques in their pieces, including flower studies, cigarette cases, desk accessories,

and other novelty items. At one time employing around 300 workers, Fabergé also employed twenty-two workmasters, including Mikhail Perkhin and Henrik Wigström. Fabergé was awarded gold medals at the 1882 Pan-Russian Exhibition in Moscow, the 1885 International Goldsmiths' Exhibition in Nuremburg, the 1896 Pan-Russian Exhibition in Nizhny Novgorod, and the 1899 Munich Secession Exhibition, later receiving the Legion of Honor at the 1900 Paris Exposition Universelle. A branch of the firm opened in Moscow in 1887, specializing in "Old Russian"-style jewelry, while branch openings were to follow in Kiev, London, and Odessa, as well as new premises in St. Petersburg. At the onset of the Russian Revolution, Fabergé fled the country and his firm was nationalized by the Bolsheviks in 1918.

Cat. 25 (p. 202). *Barometer*, 1896–1908. Workmaster: Johan Viktor Aarne. Palisander wood, silver gilt, garnet, glass; 14 x 12.5 cm. The Cleveland Museum of Art, The India Early Minshall Collection, 1966.484 (not in the exhibition).

Cat. 26 (p. 246). *Bellpush*, c. 1900. Retailer: Tiffany & Co. Hardstone, gold, ruby; 4 x 6 x 3.3 cm. Wartski, London.

Cat. 27 (p. 84). *Bellpush with Two Elephants*, 1896–1908. Workmaster: Henrik Wigström. Enamel, onyx, amazonite, rock crystal, gold. Bellpush: 4.1 x 24.3 x 4.1 cm; case: 5.4 x 12.4 x 6.4 cm. Cincinnati Art Museum, the Bayard Livingston Kilgour, Jr., and Katie Gray Kilgour Collection of Icons and Other Russian Objects, 2000.91.a.

Cat. 28 (p. 196). *Box*, 1903. Silver, gold, amethyst, chrysoprase, pearl; 15.5 x 44.5 x 30.5 cm. Kunstgewerbemuseum, Berlin, W–1962.7.

Cat. 29 (p. 16). *Brooch*, 1894. Workmaster: Henrik Wigström. Gold, Siberian aquamarine, diamonds; 3.5 x 3.9 x 1.5 cm. Private collection, courtesy of Wartski, London.

Cat. 30 (p. 217). *Brooch*, 1899–1908. Workmaster: Albert Holmström. Diamonds, pink mecca stones (cabochon chalcedony), gold; h. 5 cm. Collection of Joan and Melissa Rivers.

Cat. 31 (p. 216). *Brooch*, c. 1900. Gold, diamonds, star sapphire; h. 3.18 cm. Collection of Joan and Melissa Rivers.

Cat. 32 (p. 216). *Brooch*, 1905–10. Siberian amethyst, diamonds, gold; 5.3 x 5.3 cm. Private collection.

Cat. 33 (p. 184). *Bulldog*, 1890–1917. Amethystine quartz, diamonds; 4.4 x 5.1 x 3.5 cm. The Cleveland Museum of Art, The India Early Minshall Collection, 1966.450.

Cat. 34 (p. 198). *Cameo Box*, 1910. Workmaster: Henrik Wigström. Silver gilt, guilloché enamel, shell, diamonds; 2.5 x 9.5 x 8.3 cm. Cincinnati Art Museum, The Bayard Livingston Kilgour, Jr. and Katie Gray Kilgour Collection of Icons and Other Russian Objects, 2001.1.

Cat. 35 (p. 185). *Cigarette Case*, c. 1885. Workmaster: Eric Kollin. Agate, gold, cabochon sapphire; 9.5 x 6. 7 cm. Private collection.

Cat. 36 (p. 202). *Cigarette Case*, 1899–1908. Workmaster: August Hollming. Gold, sapphires, cotton; 9.7 x 6.2 cm. Musée des Arts Décoratifs, Paris, 39443.

Cat. 37 (p. 201). *Cigarette Case*, 1908. Gold, enamel, diamonds; l. 9.4 cm. Lent by Her Majesty Queen Elizabeth II, RCIN 40113.

Cat. 38 (p. 201). *Cigarette Case*, 1908–17. Workmaster: Henrik Wigström. Gold, enamel, diamonds; 1 x 8.6 x 5.6 cm. Collection of Joan and Melissa Rivers.

Cat. 39 (p. 202). *Cigarette Case*, 1908–17. Workmaster: Henrik Wigström. Gold, platinum, diamonds, enamel, cotton; 10 x 6.2 cm. Musée des Arts Décoratifs, Paris, 38343.

Cat. 40 (p. 197). *Cigarette Case*, 1912. Workmaster: Henrik Wigström. Gold, ruby, platinum, cotton; 10.2 x 6.8 cm. Musée des Arts Décoratifs, Paris, 38344.

Cat. 41 (p. 220). *Cloak Clasp*, 1903–8. Workmaster: Henrik Wigström. Aquamarine, pearl bezel, guilloché enamel, silver; 1.3 x 14 x 5.8 cm. Private collection.

Cat. 42 (p. 26). *Clock*, 1896–1908. Workmaster: Julius Rappoport. Clockworks: H. Moser & Cie. Silver gilt, bowenite, ivory, gemstones, pearls; 28.6 x 10.2 cm. Hillwood Estate, Museum and Gardens, Bequest of Marjorie Merriweather Post, 1973, 12.155.

Cat. 43 (pp. 180–81). *Cottage Rose*, 1890–1917. Gold, silver, enamel, diamonds, jade, rock crystal; 10.2 x 4.5 cm. The Cleveland Museum of Art, The India Early Minshall Collection, 1966.440.

Cat. 44 (pp. 180–81). *Cranberry*, 1890–1917. Chalcedony, gold, jade, rock crystal; 11.5 x 4.8 cm. The Cleveland Museum of Art, The India Early Minshall Collection, 1966.446.

Cat. 45 (p. 186). *Daisy Frame*, c. 1900. Enamel, rose-cut diamonds, gold; 12 x 8 x 1.5 cm. Collection of Joan and Melissa Rivers.

Cat. 46 (p. 183). *Dandelion*, 1870–1920. Asbestos fiber, diamonds, gold, nephrite, rock crystal; h. 18.4 cm. The Brooklyn Museum, Bequest of Helen B. Sanders, 79.129.17a–c.

Cat. 47 (p. 203). *Design for Vase with Serpent Mounts*, 1908–17. Ink on paper, framed; 25.7 x 19.7 cm. The Forbes Collection, New York, FAB89003.

Cat. 48 (p. 38). *Desk Clock*, 1886–1918. Lapis lazuli, jade, diamonds; 7 x 5.1 x 2.5 cm. The Brooklyn Museum, Bequest of Helen B. Sanders, 78.129.1.

Cat. 49 (p. 39). *Desk Clock*, 1903. Workmaster: Henrik Wigström. Rhodonite, silver, enamel, diamonds; 5.3 x 5 x 2.9 cm. The Cleveland Museum of Art, The India Early Minshall Collection, 1966.476.

Cat. 50 (p. 39). *Desk Clock*, 1908–17. Workmaster: Henrik Wigström. Jade, gold, enamel, diamonds; 7.9 x 3.4 x 2.5 cm. The Cleveland Museum of Art, The India Early Minshall Collection, 1966.475.

Cat. 51 (p. 175). *Egg*, 1890–1917. Lapis lazuli, gold, pearls, rubies, diamonds, enamel; 5.9 x 4.5 cm. The Cleveland Museum of Art, The India Early Minshall Collection, 1966.436.

Cat. 52 (pp. 180–81). *Forget-Me-Nots*, 1890–1917. Turquoise, diamonds, silver gilt, rock crystal; 8.9 x 3.1 cm. The Cleveland Museum of Art, The India Early Minshall Collection, 1966.444.

Cat. 53 (p. 200). *Frame (Tenth Anniversary)*, 1901. Workmaster: Viktor Aarne. Gilded silver, guilloché enamel; 19.1 x 13 cm. Courtesy of A La Vieille Russie, New York.

Cat. 54 (p. 184). *Gypsy Singer Vara Panina*, 1900–1910. Aventurine quartz, jasper, quartz, purpurine, calcite, other Russian hardstones, diamonds, gold, silver; h. 17 cm. Courtesy of A La Vieille Russie, New York.

Cat. 55 (p. 65). *Ice Pendant*, 1910. Workmaster: August Holmström; designer: Alma Pihl. Rock crystal, diamonds, platinum; 6.4 x 2.5 x 1.3 cm. Middlebury College Museum of Art, Vermont, Gift of Nancy and Edward Wynkoop, 2001.021.

Cat. 56 (p. 176). *Imperial Blue Serpent Egg*, 1887. Workmaster: Mikhail Perkhin. Gold, blue guilloché enamel, opalescent white enamel, diamonds, sapphires. Clock, h. 11.7; base, 6.8 x 6 cm. Lent by His Serene Highness Prince Albert II of Monaco.

Cat. 57 (p. 210). *Imperial Bridal Fan*, 1901. Workmaster: Mikhail Perkhin; miniaturist: Sergei Solomko. Polychromed parchment, nacre, guilloché enamel, yellow and rose gold, rose- and briolette-cut diamonds; 35.6 x 67.6 cm. Cheekwood Botanical Garden and Museum of Art, Nashville, on loan from the Matilda Geddings Gray Foundation.

Cat. 58 (pp. 24–25). *Imperial Danish Palaces Egg*, 1895. Workmaster: Mikhail Perkhin; miniaturist: Konstantin Krijitski. Green, rose, and four-colored gold guilloché enamel, star sapphire, cabochon emerald, rose-cut diamond; 10.2 x 6.7 cm. Cheekwood Botanical Garden & Museum of Art, Nashville, on loan from the Matilda Geddings Gray Foundation.

Cat. 59 (p. 178). *Imperial Framed Miniature*, 1896. Workmaster: Mikhail Perkhin. Gold, jade, rubies, gouache, ivory, glass; 15.3 x 5 x 5 cm. The Cleveland Museum of Art, The India Early Minshall Collection, 1966.458.1.

Cat. 60 (p. 182). *Imperial Lilies of the Valley Basket*, 1896. Attributed to August Holmström. Yellow and green gold, silver, nephrite, pearl, rose-cut diamonds; 19.1 x 21.6 x 15 cm. Cheekwood Botanical Garden and Museum of Art, Nashville, on loan from the Matilda Geddings Gray Foundation.

Cat. 61 (p. 23). *Imperial Pansy Egg*, 1899. Workmaster: Mikhail Perkhin; miniaturist: Sergei Solomko. Nephrite, silver gilt, enamel, rose-cut diamonds; h. 14.6 cm. Private collection.

Cat. 62 (pp. 55, 177). *Imperial Red Cross Egg*, 1915. Workmaster: Henrik Wigström; miniaturist: Adrian Prachov. Gold, silver, enamel, glass; 8.6 x 6.4 cm. The Cleveland Museum of Art, The India Early Minshall Collection, 1963.673.

Cat. 63 (p. 179). *Imperial Rose Trellis Egg*, 1907. Workmaster: Henrik Wigström. Gold, enamel, diamonds; 7.7 x 5.9 cm. The Walters Art Museum, Baltimore, 44.501.

Cat. 64 (p. 66). *Kelch Bonbonnière Egg*, 1903. Workmaster: attributed to Mikhail Perkhin. Egg: rose-cut diamonds, chalcedony, paillons, demantoid garnets, seed pearls, translucent white enamel, velvet lining; miniature box: agate, portrait diamond, white enamel, cabochon

rubies; miniature pendant: gold, colored enamels; h. 12.7 cm. Private collection.

Cat. 65 (p. 66). *Kelch Rocaille Egg*, 1902. Varicolored gold, platinum, rose-cut diamonds, translucent enamel, silk lining; 12 x 14.2 cm. Collection of Diane B. Wilsey.

Cat. 66 (p. 187). *Kovsh (Cup)*, 1906. Workmaster: Mikhail Perkhin. Nephrite, gold, enamel, diamonds; 25 x 13.5 cm. Musée des Arts Décoratifs, Paris, 25990.

Cat. 67 (p. 214). *Kovsh (Cup) with Bogatyrs*, 1908. Silver, precious stones; 54 x 60 x 32 cm. Musée National de la Marine, Paris, MnM7S035.

Cat. 68 (pp. 153, 213). *Kremlin Tower Clock*, 1913. Rhodonite, silver, enamel, emeralds, sapphires; 29 x 14.6 cm. The Cleveland Museum of Art, The India Early Minshall Collection, 1966.477.

Cat. 69 (pp. 180–81). *Ladybug Pill Box*, 1896–1908. Workmaster: Mikhail Perkhin. Gold, enamel, diamonds; 2.1 x 5 x 3.5 cm. The Cleveland Museum of Art, The India Early Minshall Collection, 1966.465.

Cat. 70 (p. 187). *Leaf-shaped Box*, 1896–1908. Gold, bloodstone, diamonds; 3 x 6.5 cm. Hillwood Estate, Museum & Gardens, Bequest of Marjorie Merriweather Post, 1973, 11.219.1–2.

Cat. 71 (p. 215). *Letter Opener*, 1899–1908. Silver, bear claw, garnet; 1.3 x 17 x 2.5 cm. Private collection.

Cat. 72 (pp. 180–81, 258). *Lily of the Valley*, 1890–1917. Pearls, silver, diamonds, gold, jade, rock crystal; 12.1 x 3.1 cm. The Cleveland Museum of Art, The India Early Minshall Collection, 1966.443.

Cat. 73 (pp. 180–81). *Lily of the Valley*, 1890–1917. Pearls, jade, gold, rock crystal; 5.1 x 2.3 cm. The Cleveland Museum of Art, The India Early Minshall Collection, 1966.445.

Cat. 74 (p. 199). *Miniature Bidet*, 1908–17. Workmaster: Henrik Wigström. Gold, jade, enamel, pearls; 8.3 x 3.5 x 4.5 cm. The Cleveland Museum of Art, The India Early Minshall Collection, 1966.455.

Cat. 75 (p. 199). *Miniature Chair*, 1896–1908. Gold, silver gilt, enamel, rubies, diamonds; 10.5 x 5.3 x 4.8 cm. The Cleveland Museum of Art, The India Early Minshall Collection, 1966.454.

Cat. 76 (p. 21). *Miniature Shoe*, 1903. Workmaster: Mikhail Perkhin. Bloodstone, gold, diamonds, silver; 7.2 x 8.9 x 3.4 cm. The Cleveland Museum of Art, The India Early Minshall Collection, 1966.482.

Cat. 77 (p. 199). *Miniature Table with Compass*, 1896. Workmaster: Mikhail Perkhin. Gold, enamel, glass, steel; 5.6 x 4.2 cm. The Cleveland Museum of Art, The India Early Minshall Collection, 1966.480.

Cat. 78 (p. 27). *Necklace*, 1895–1900. Siberian amethysts, diamonds, gold, platinum, demantoid garnets; 43 x 2 x 1.5 cm. Collection of Neil Lane.

Cat. 79 (p. 206). *Pair of Candelabra*, 1887–90. Workmaster: Julius Rappoport. Silver; 28.5 x 25.1 x 12 cm. The Cleveland Museum of Art, The India Early Minshall Collection, 1966.494.1–2.

Cat. 80 (p. 170). *Pair of Decanters*, 1896. Glass, silver; 15.8 x 10 x 12 cm. Lent by Her Majesty Queen Elizabeth II, RCIN 100337.

Cat. 81 (pp. 180–81). *Pansy*, 1890–1917. Gold, jade, enamel, rock crystal; 11.8 x 4.8 cm. The Cleveland Museum of Art, The India Early Minshall Collection, 1966.438.

Cat. 82 (p. 185). *Parrot*, 1896–1908. Workmaster: Mikhail Perkhin. Silver, enamel, jasper, agate, emeralds; 15.3 x 7.4 cm. The Cleveland Museum of Art, The India Early Minshall Collection, 1966.447.

Cat. 83 (p. 297). *Pendant*, c. 1900. Silver, diamonds, gold; l. 3 cm. Private collection.

Cat. 84 (p. 191). *Pendant*, 1908–17. Designer: Gaston Lafitte. Gold, silver, diamonds, enamel; 6.5 x 8.4 cm. State Historical Museum, Moscow, 104464-OK22733.

Cat. 85 (p. 185). *Puppies on a Mat*, 1890–1917. Agate, chalcedony, marble; 2.9 x 11.7 x 9.9 cm. The Cleveland Museum of Art, The India Early Minshall Collection, 1966.451.

Cat. 86 (p. 186). *Rococo Frame*, 1899. Gold, nephrite, diamonds, seed pearls; 12 x 8 x 1.5 cm. Collection of Joan and Melissa Rivers.

Cat. 87 (p. 216). *Rosebud Brooch*, 1899–1908. Workmaster: August Hollming. Gold, diamonds, Siberian aquamarines; l. 5.1 cm. Courtesy of A La Vieille Russie, New York.

Cat. 88 (p. 219). *Sautoir*, 1895–1900. Gold, carnelian, chalcedony; l. 78 cm. Collection of Neil Lane.

Cat. 89 (p. 198). *Series of Incomplete Objects from Henrik Wigström's Workshop*, 1903–18. Various materials: gold, nephrite, lapis lazuli, enamel, moonstone, moss agate. Oval blue picture frame: 16.2 x 10.8 cm, and various dimensions for other pieces. Courtesy of A La Vieille Russie, New York.

Cat. 90 (p. 216). *Snowflake Brooch*, c. 1900. Diamonds, platinum; 2.7 x 2.7 cm. Private collection.

Cat. 91 (pp. 30–31). *Tea Service*, 1896. Silver gilt, opaque cloisonné enamel. Teapot: 12.8 x 17.8 x 10.8 cm, and various dimensions for other pieces. The Cleveland Museum of Art, The India Early Minshall Collection, 1966.500.1–11.

Cat. 92 (p. 205). *Tea Service and Tea Table*, 1896–1908. Workmaster: Julius Rappoport. Tea service: silver, ivory; table: lemonwood, silver and ormolu mounts, Karelian birch veneer. Kettle: h. 34.3, and various dimensions for other pieces; table: 68.6 x 76.2 cm. Fine Arts Museums of San Francisco, gift of Victoria Melita, Grand Duchess Kiril, through Alma de Bretteville Spreckels, 1945.366.1, 1945.355–65.

Cat. 93 (p. 28). *Tiara*, c. 1900. Workmaster: Albert Holmström. Rose- and brilliant-cut diamonds, platinum; 13 x 25 cm. Private collection.

Cat. 94 (p. 207). *Triptych Icon*, 1895. Workmaster: Mikhail Perkhin. Silver gilt, enamel, rubies, emeralds, sapphires, pearls, birch; 10.3 x 32.3 cm. Courtesy of A La Vieille Russie, New York.

Cat. 95 (p. 204). *Vase*, c. 1900. Ceramic, silver gilt; 17.8 x 10.2 cm. Private collection.

Cat. 96 (p. 90). *Vase with Metal Base*, 1896–1908. Workmaster: Mikhail Perkhin. Topaz, gold, wood, velvet, satin, brass; h. 22.54 cm. The Brooklyn Museum, Bequest of Helen B. Sanders, 78.129.18a–b.

Cat. 97 (pp. 180–81). *Violet*, 1890–1917. Enamel, silver gilt, jade, diamonds, rock crystal; 9.9 x 3.7 cm. The Cleveland Museum of Art, The India Early Minshall Collection, 1966.442.

Cat. 98 (pp. 180–81). *Wild Flower*, 1903. Workmaster: Henrik Wigström. White stone, gold, sapphires, jade, rock crystal; 14.3 x 3.9 cm. The Cleveland Museum of Art, The India Early Minshall Collection, 1966.441.

Falize Frères (French, Paris, 1838–1936)
Alexis Falize began his career by training with François Mellerio from 1833 to 1835. By 1838 he had developed a career as an anonymous maker for larger firms such as Boucheron, Mellerio, and eventually Tiffany & Co. in Paris. His focus on cloisonné enamel and neo-Renaissance styles later led to his much celebrated work in the Japanese style. After training in his father's firm beginning in 1856, Lucien took over in 1876; he exhibited in the 1878 Paris Exposition Universelle under his own name. From 1880 to 1892, Germain Bapst joined Lucien, and together they established the firm of Bapst et Falize, producing enameled jewelry in the Japanese style with cloisonné and basse-taille techniques. Lucien was also influenced by Hans Collaert in his neo-Renaissance-style jewelry. Falize's son André, a goldsmith and jeweler in the Art Nouveau tradition, began working alongside his father in 1894. After Lucien's death, André, accompanied by his brothers Jean and Pierre, headed the firm Falize Frères beginning in 1897. Maintaining the design aesthetics of their father and grandfather, they continued to manufacture Renaissance-style works ias well as their signature Japonisme. The brothers were awarded two grand prix for jewelry and goldsmithing at the 1900 Paris Exposition Universelle and participated in the 1904 International Exhibition in St. Petersburg, the 1911 Turin International Exposition, and Salons of the Société des Artistes Français. Among their notable commissions were swords for Académie Française members and Serbian regalia. Sustaining financial strain in its later years, Falize Frères went out of business after André's death in 1936.

Cat. 99 (p. 5). *Dog Collar Necklace*, 1895–1900. Attributed to Falize Frères. Pearls, enamel, lapis lazuli, onyx, gold; 46.5 x 3.5 cm. Collection of Neil Lane.

Cat. 100 (p. 115). *Match Holder and Cigar Cutter*, 1870–8. Unknown maker in the manner of Alexis Falize. Enamel, gold; 6.4 x 2.5 cm. Collection of Neil Lane.

Cat. 101 (p. 100). *Necklace and Bracelet*, c. 1900. Auguste Perrette in the manner of Alexis Falize. Pearls, gold, diamonds, enamel. Bracelet: 19 x 1.3 x 0.6 cm; necklace: 34.9 cm diam. Collection of Neil Lane.

Cat. 102 (p. 193). *Peter the Great Kovsh (Cup)*, 1891–1906. Model: Mark Antokolsky. Silver; 69 x 85 x 45 cm. State Historical Museum, Moscow, 68257/8925.

Paul Follot (French, Paris, 1877–1941)
A designer and sculptor who trained with Eugéne Grasset, Follot began exhibiting in 1904. With influences ranging from Art Nouveau to historicism, Follot designed lighting and domestic accessories for Julius Meier-Graefe's La Maison Moderne beginning in 1901. Producing work in bronze, wood, wrought iron, and stained glass, he exhibited his light fixtures and furniture at the Société des Artistes Décorateurs, the Salon d'Automne, and the 1925 Exposition Internationale des Art Décoratifs et Industriels Moderne in Paris. In 1923, he became the director of Pomone, the studio associated with Bon Marché in Paris and also produced silver designs for Christofle and Lapparra.

Cat. 103 (p. 46). *Pendant*, c. 1900. Gold, enamel, citrine; 9 x 10.2 x 0.6 cm. Collection of Robert A. Zehil.

Georges Fouquet (French, Paris, 1862–1957)
The son of goldsmith Alphonse Fouquet, Georges worked under his father for eleven years before joining the firm as co-owner in 1891, taking over in 1895 after his father's retirement. Initiating his jewelry in the "mil-neuf-cent" (1900) style in 1900, Fouquet transformed the business by focusing on modern production, adapting the Art Nouveau style, and hiring enamelist Étienne Tourette and designer Charles Desrosiers. In 1897, Fouquet exhibited at the Salon de la Société des Artistes Français. He later produced designer Alphonse Mucha's jewelry for Sarah Bernhardt, winning a gold medal at the 1900 Paris Exposition Universelle. Working with indigenous materials and vivid enamels, his designs were influenced by nature and Japonisme; in time, he adopted Egyptian and geometric ornamentation, which gained popularity with the onset of Art Deco. Jean Fouquet joined his father in 1919, six years before Fouquet ended his business venture to focus on his archives.

Cat. 104 (p. 99). *Orchid Brooch*, 1898–1902. Designer: Charles Desrosiers. Gold, enamel, ruby, pearls; 10 x 10.5 x 2.5 cm. The Anderson Collection of Art Nouveau, University of East Anglia, Norwich, UEA21149.

Lucien Gaillard (French, Paris, 1861–1933)
The third generation of Parisian jewelers, Gaillard was a student of the sculptor Henri Louis Levasseur before becoming an apprentice silversmith in his father's workshop in 1878, which had been established by Lucien's grandfather, Amédée, in 1860. Inspired by Japanese mixed-metal techniques, Gaillard's silversmith designs were well received at the 1889 Paris Exposition Universelle, where he won a gold medal. In 1892, he became manager of the family firm after his father's retirement. At the 1900 Paris Exposition Universelle, he won the grand prix for his pieces in the Bijouterie-Joaillerie division. At the turn of the century and persuaded by René Lalique, Gaillard drew his attention to jewelry design, using enamels, ivory, and horn, and began employing craftsmen from Tokyo. Gaillard exhibited at the 1901 Glasgow International Exhibition. His new style was successful, later winning him first prize in jewelry at the 1904 Paris Salon of the Société des Artistes Française, in which he participated from 1901 to 1909.

Cat. 105 (p. 116). *Dragonfly Comb*, 1904. Horn, gold, emerald, diamonds, citrine, enamel; 11.2 x 15.4 cm. Rijksmuseum, Amsterdam, BK–1990–1.

Cat. 106 (p. 37). *Hawthorn Comb* (with original box), 1900–1903. Horn, ivory, gold, diamonds; 14 x 8 cm. Private collection.

Cat. 107 (p. 114). *Moth Pendant* (with original box), c. 1900. Gold, champlevé enamel, citrines, carved horn; 7.6 x 9.2 cm. The Metropolitan Museum of Art, New York, Purchase, Dorothy Merksamer Bequest, in honor of Cynthia Hazen Polsky, 2000 (2000.176.1,2).

Cat. 108 (p. 112). *Necklace with Thistles*, 1900. Enamel, gold, opals, diamonds; l. 35 cm. Collection of Robert A. Zehil.

Émile Gallé (French, Nancy, 1846–1904)
Educated at Weimer and Nancy in art and botany, Gallé trained at the Burgun, Schwerer & Cie glassworks in Meisenthal, later producing faience tableware under the direction of his father. He exhibited at the 1871 London International Exhibition and founded his glassware workshop in 1874 along with a furniture workshop in 1885, both in Nancy. After years of defining his style based on botany and Japonisme, Gallé won a medal at the 1889 Paris exposition for his cameo glassware, which was influenced by Chinese cased glass. Producing works with Art Nouveau motifs, he became well known for his cased-glass technique and his particular style of inlaid glass, called "marqueterie sur verre." By 1900 he employed around 300 workers. A recipient of the French Legion of Honor, Gallé also exhibited his furniture and glass at the 1900 Paris Exposition Universelle and founded the Alliance Provinciale des Industries d'Art (the École de Nancy) in 1901. After Gallé's death in 1904, Jean Prouvé directed the firm until 1913, and production continued until 1931. The shop closed in 1935.

Cat. 109 (p. 110). *Mounted Vase*, c. 1900. Mounts by Bapst and Falize. Glass, bronze; 34.5 x 28 x 14 cm. Collection of Robert A. Zehil.

Goldsmiths' & Silversmiths' Company Ltd. (English, London, 1898–1952)
The company was established as the Manufacturing Goldsmiths and Silversmiths Ltd. by William Gibson and John Langman, and began trading in 1880. They operated in London and had marks at both London and Sheffield Assay Offices. In 1889 they acquired Mappin Brothers, followed in 1893 with the Goldsmiths Alliance (A. B. Savory & Sons). Their interest in Mappin Brothers was later sold to Mappin & Webb in 1903. Goldsmiths' & Silversmiths' Company Ltd. entered the public domain in 1898 in London with a large retail store on Regent Street. The firm produced and sold jewelry along with silver and gold tableware, exhibiting at the 1900 Exposition Universelle in Paris where it won a grand prix for silver. The company later produced designs by Harold Stabler, Bernard Cuzner, S. J. Day, Leslie Durbin, and A. E. Harvey in the 1930s. After merging with Garrard & Co., the company changed its name to Garrard's in 1952. In 1959, Goldsmiths' & Silversmiths' Company Ltd. was taken over by Mappin & Webb.

Cat. 110 (pp. XII, 29). *Centerpiece from the Nereid Service,* 1900. Silver; 66.1 x 97.8 cm. The Cleveland Museum of Art, The Thomas S. Grasselli Memorial Collection, 1943.189.

Gorham Mfg. Co. (American, Providence, est. 1852)
Jabez Gorham and Christopher Burr, George C. Clark, William Hadwin, and Henry Mumford became partners in a jewelry business in Providence, Rhode Island, in 1813. The group disbanded five years later, with Gorham continuing under the name Jabez Gorham, Jeweler. From 1818 to 1831 he produced jewelry in the "French Filigree" style and became known for the Gorham Chain. He began producing spoons and formed Gorham & Webster with Henry L. Webster in 1831. The firm became Gorham, Webster & Price in 1837 when William G. Price joined the company. Gorham sold out to Peter Church and Whitney Metcalf around 1840, forming Gorham & Son with his son John in 1841. After Jabez left the firm, his son John and Gorham Thurber became partners in 1850, working as Gorham & Thurber until 1852. That year their cousin Lewis Dexter Jr. joined the firm, which became Gorham & Co. The firm became Gorham Manufacturing Co. after 1863. Retail store branches opened in New York in 1873 and in Chicago and San Francisco in 1887. William C. Codman became art director in 1891, overseeing the introduction of the hand-hammered Martelé line of silver in 1897. Martelé won a grand prix at the 1900 Paris Exposition Universelle.

Cat. 111 (p. 35). *Martelé Dressing Table and Stool,* 1899. Designer: William C. Codman. Silver, glass, fabric, ivory; 152.4 x 137.2 x 83.8 cm. Dallas Museum of Art, The Eugene and Margaret McDermott Art Fund, Inc., in honor of Dr. Charles L. Venable, 2000.356.A–B. MCD.

Hector Guimard (French, Paris, 1867–1942)
A student of the École des Arts Décoratifs and the École des Beaux-Arts in Paris, Guimard was an influential architect in the Art Nouveau style. Influences from Eugène-Emmanuel Violet-le-Duc appear in his early designs, but Art Nouveau inspirations emerge in his designs of the Castel Beranger block in Paris. Noted for designing the ironwork for the Paris Métro stations in 1900, he continued to design flats and town houses, as well as furniture and gilded-bronze and metal objects, up until shortly after World War I. Guimard ceased building after 1929, and he and his wife immigrated to America in 1939 to escape anti-Semitism and the coming war. He died in New York in 1942.

Cat. 112 (p. 121). *Kantirix Flacon (Perfume Bottle),* 1900. Perfumer: Félix Millot. Molded, gilded clear glass, perfume, paper; h. 39 cm. Christie Mayer Lefkowith Collection.

Marius Hammer (Norwegian, Bergen, 1847–1927)
A prolific manufacturer of filigree silverwork and a leading firm in Norway. Hammer was known for pioneering techniques of intermixing filigree and plique-à-jour enamel in silverwork, especially spoons. Often producing items for royalty, the firm was also known for its enameled Viking ships. After 1905, Emil Hoye began producing silver designs for the firm.

Cat. 113 (p. 208). *Vase,* 1900–1910. Plique-à-jour enamel, silver filigree; h. 21.6 cm. Toledo Museum of Art, Purchased with funds from the Libbey Endowment, gift of Edward Drummond Libbey, 2006.16.

Ferdinand Hauser (Austrian, Vienna, 1864–1919)
Ferdinand Hauser adhered to the principles of Jugendstil, the German form of Art Nouveau around the turn of the nineteenth century, and designed works using abstracted natural motifs. Hauser adopted this style after relocating from Vienna to Munich prior to 1912, combining the Jugendstil design principles with semiprecious and colored materials to attract more avant-garde clients.

Cat. 114 (p. 38). *Brooch,* 1912–13. Gold, enamel, moonstones; 6.4 x 4.1 cm. The Metropolitan Museum of Art, New York, Purchase, Dorothy Merksamer Bequest, in honor of Cynthia Hazen Polsky, 1998 (1998.356).

Joseph Heinrichs (American, New York, 1897–1937)
Employed as a metal molder and finisher in the 1880s, Heinrichs began producing copperware in 1897. Until the late 1920s, he operated a copperware workshop and retail shop established in New York City by 1902. Retailed at Shreve, Crump & Low Co.; Black, Starr & Frost; Tiffany & Co.; and Cowell & Hubbard, Heinrichs's products included pitchers, coffee sets, cooking utensils, and punch bowls, among other silver and copper household accessories. For a while, the company was known as the Bi-Metal and French Steam Coffee Pot Co. After declaring bankruptcy, the company was reorganized by one of the workers, Angelo Scavullo, as Legion Utensils Co., in 1937. Scavullo had been hired by Heinrichs in 1901 as an errand boy. Eventually, the company moved to Waynesboro, Georgia, where it remains in business producing chafing dishes for the restaurant industry.

Cat. 115 (p. 300). *Punch Bowl, Tray, and Ladle,* 1900–1915. Copper, silver with gilt, horn, stone arrowheads. Punch bowl: 34.3 x 60.3 x 45.7 cm; tray: 81 x 58.4 cm; ladle: l. 52.7 cm. Philadelphia Museum of Art, Purchased with the Richardson Fund and the Thomas Skelton Harrison Fund, 1993–65–1, 2, 15.

Imperial Porcelain Factory and Glassworks (Russian, St. Petersburg, est. 1744)
In 1890 the Imperial Porcelain Factory and the Imperial Glassworks merged to become the Imperial Porcelain Factory and Glassworks. After the merger, the factory adopted refined production techniques and manufactured glass exclusively for the Russian imperial court. Before the merger, Imperial Glassworks produced decorative and table glass with Russian and Byzantine influences, but Danish and Art Nouveau motifs appeared in their products after Tsar Alexander III hired Danish craftsmen in 1892. The factory's work was featured at the 1900 Paris Exposition Universelle and later at the 1901 St. Petersburg Ceramics Exhibition. Baron Nicholas de Wolff began his directorship in 1900, succeeded by N. Stroukhov in 1910, who headed the factory until the Russian Revolution in 1917.

Cat. 116 (p. 172). *Vase*, 1914. Glass, one of a pair; h. 58.42 cm. Hillwood Estate, Museum & Gardens, Bequest of Marjorie Merriweather Post, 1973, 23.208.1.

Lucien-Joseph-René Janvier (French, Paris, b. 1878)
A member of the Société des Artistes Français, Janvier specialized in producing miniature sculptural designs, using his reduction technique known as "tour Janvier."

Cat. 117 (p. 32). *Bat Necklace*, 1900. Attributed to Lucien-Joseph-René Janvier. Retailer: Maison Gustave Roger Sandoz. Silver, silver gilt, plique-à-jour enamel, pearls; 31 x 8 x 1 cm. Collection of Neil Lane.

Georg Jensen (Danish, Copenhagen, 1866–1935)
A successful businessman and trained sculptor, Georg Jensen produced women's accessories and household wares. After studying sculpture at the Royal Academy of Fine Arts, he began his career in 1892 as a modeler for Bing & Grøndahl porcelain manufactory. In 1901 he abandoned ceramics and went to work as a journeyman in the studio of master silversmith Mogens Ballin. In 1904, he established his own shop in Copenhagen and made mostly jewelry, turning toward larger works in silver in later years. Jensen's artistic style drew influence from Jugendstil, English Arts and Crafts, and Art Nouveau motifs, while his sculptural jewelry was influenced by René Lalique's designs. Within ten years of opening his firm, Jensen employed more than fifty workers and had opened retail shops in Barcelona, Berlin, London, and Paris.

Cat. 118 (p. 28). *Ornamental Comb*, 1904–8. Tortoiseshell, silver, coral cabochon; 16 x 2 x 11.4 cm. Collection of Robert A. Zehil.

Kalo Shop (American, Chicago, 1900–1970)
The Kalo Shop of Chicago, established by Clara Barck in 1900, employed a diversified staff of silversmiths who produced handcrafted jewelry and household accessories with naturalistic, curvilinear designs in the Arts and Crafts tradition; Prairie school aesthetics appeared later in various forms. Initially established to produce leather goods, Kalo became known for its austere silverworks that sometimes featured semiprecious stones as well as hammered textures and hand-raised silver in its housewares. Also offering classes, the workshop stayed in business until 1970 and featured the work of several well-known silversmiths, including Julius Randall and Emery Todd.

Cat. 119 (p. 5). *Necklace*, 1905. Blister pearls, gold; l. 25.4 cm. Collection of Neil Lane.

Keller Frères (French, Paris, est. 1857)
The firm was founded in 1857 by Gustave Keller in Paris to produce leather dressing cases and other luxurious accessories. In 1878, his two sons, Gustave and Auguste, took over the business as Keller Frères and began to manufacture silver hollowware and toilet accessories. They soon emerged as one of the leading French silversmiths of their day. The firm exhibited at the 1889 Paris world's fair where it

received high accolades. At the 1900 Paris Exposition Universelle, Keller Frères was especially noted for the diversity of its designs, from historicist to early modern. The firm actively exhibited from 1900 to 1937 in exhibitions in France and other countries.

Cat. 120 (p. 35). *Pitcher*, c. 1900. Silver, partially silver gilt; 32 x 18 x 12.5 cm. Musée d'Orsay, Paris, OAO 1284.

Raoul Lachenal (French, Paris, 1885–1956)
Raoul Lachenal worked as a ceramist for his father, Edmond Lachenal, an influential potter. Edmond was crucial to the development of French ceramics in the late 1880s and a frequent exhibitor at salons and international expositions. His work combined motifs from nature and Japanese influences. Turning toward the Art Nouveau style, Edmond continued to exhibit in the early 1900s and welcomed sons Raoul and Jean-Jacques into the pottery firm at Châtillon. Raoul took over the business in 1904 and created both unique art pottery and production ware. He left to form his own pottery firm at Boulogne-sur-Seine in 1911, to which he added production in earthenware and stoneware. He experimented with motifs such as the whiplash line of Art Nouveau and the delicate glazes of Japanese Oribe ware. Raoul exhibited at the 1911 Salon of the Société des Artistes Français and the Salon of the Société des Artistes-Décorateurs in 1912, 1913, and 1914. Both brothers were conscripted into World War I. Upon his return, Raoul began using enamels and geometric designs, while Jean-Jacques, who taught pottery as occupational therapy at a military hospital, reopened the pottery firm at Châtillon, hiring wounded soliders as assistants.

Cat. 121 (p. 20). *Dormouse Necklace*, c. 1905–11. Raoul Lachenal and Sergei Solomko. Ceramic, silver; 6.4 x 6.4 cm. Collection of Neil Lane.

René Lalique (French, Paris, 1860–1945)
Lalique was first trained at the Lycée Turgot near Vincennes and from 1876 to 1878 he attended the École des Arts Décoratifs and was apprenticed to Louis Aucoc. In 1880, he returned to Paris from London after attending Sydenham College and worked for Auguste Petit Fils and as a designer for the Boucheron and Maison Cartier. Lalique also submitted designs to *Le Bijou* magazine and in the early 1880s produced designs for household objects and studied sculpting under Justin Lequien at the École Bernard Palissy. In 1885, Jules Destape sold his jewelry studio to Lalique, which he eventually expanded to larger facilities. By 1894, he had designed stage jewelry for Sarah Bernhardt, exhibited under his own name, and began participating at the Salon de la Société des Artistes Française, which he continued to do until 1910. Two years later, Lalique began work on the 100-piece series he exhibited at the 1900 Exposition Universelle in Paris, where he won a grand prix and the Order of the Legion of Honor. He exhibited at international exhibitions in Brussels (1897), Munich (1899), Turin (1902, 1911), Berlin (1903), London (1903, 1905), St. Louis (1904), and Liège (1905). For seventeen years, ending in 1912, Lalique designed a 145-piece series, which is now mostly in the Calouste Gulbenkian Museum in Lisbon. A key figure in the

Art Nouveau movement, Lalique was known for his sensitivity to the design and craft aspects before the material, for using of plique-à-jour enamels, horn, and ivory, and for combining precious and nonprecious materials. Lalique created jewelry, ornamental combs, collars, buckles, metalwork daggers and inkwells, and tableware. In 1898, he founded a glass workshop in Clairfontaine and a shop on the Place Vendôme in 1905. He then rented a workshop in Combs-la-Ville in 1909, the same year he produced his first perfume bottles for Coty. Alexandre Millerand helped Lalique obtain a new site for glass production in Wingen-sur-Moder, Alsace, between 1918 and 1919. Later in his career, Lalique focused on producing glassware in the Art Deco style, including vases and perfume bottles, as well as household accessories. In 1925, Lalique exhibited in his own pavilion at the Exposition Internationale des Arts Décoratifs in Paris. In the 1930s, Lalique focused on religious art, designing panels and chapel interiors.

Cat. 122 (p. 132). *Abduction of Deïanira Inkwell*, 1903. Silver, glass; 20 x 58 x 38 cm. Calouste Gulbenkian Foundation/Calouste Gulbenkian Museum, 1190.

Cat. 123 (p. 144). *Abduction Pendant*, 1900–1902. Ivory, gold, enamel, sapphire; 8 x 6.7 cm. Calouste Gulbenkian Foundation/Calouste Gulbenkian Museum, 1173.

Cat. 124 (p. 143). *Angel Comb*, c. 1900. Horn, glass, sapphire; 14.6 x 2.9 cm. Cincinnati Art Museum, Gift of Mrs. James Leonard, Mrs. Harry Mackoy, Mrs. Samuel Bailey, Mr. John Warrington in memory of their mother, Mrs. Elsie Holmes Warrington, 1940.2.

Cat. 125 (p. 70). *Architectural Panels*, 1914. Molded glass with mirrored backplate; h. 28 cm. Collection of Mr. and Mrs. Craig Castilla.

Cat. 126 (p. 125). *Bouchon Eucalyptus Flacon (Eucalyptus Stopper Perfume Bottle)*, 1919. Molded clear glass, partially frosted, greenish-gray patina; h. 13.5 cm. Christie Mayer Lefkowith Collection.

Cat. 127 (p. 151). *Box (Monnaie du Pape)*, 1914. Wood, bombé glass panels with gray patina, metal key; 12 x 31.5 x 19.5 cm. Collection of Mr. and Mrs. Craig Castilla.

Cat. 128 (p. 20). *Brooch*, c. 1900. Gold, painted enamel; 5.1 x 5.7 cm. Collection of Eric Streiner.

Cat. 129 (pp. 20, 131). *Brooch*, c. 1900. Gold, enamel, baroque pearl; 6.4 x 5.1 cm. Collection of Eric Streiner.

Cat. 130 (p. 40). *Brooch*, 1902–4. Glass, moonstones, enamel, gold; 3.8 x 10.1 cm. Schmuckmuseum Pforzheim, Germany, 197519.

Cat. 131 (p. 136). *Butterflies Comb*, 1904–5. Horn, gold, enamel; 9.7 x 10 cm. Musée des Arts Décoratifs, Paris, 12901.

Cat. 132 (p. 147). *Cattleya Orchid Hair Ornament*, 1903–4. Carved ivory, horn, gold, enamel on gold, diamonds; 11.8 x 20.5 cm. Private collection.

Cat. 133 (p. 142). *Chalice*, c. 1900. Cire perdue, blown glass, enameled silver; 19.5 x 12 x 12 cm. Private collection.

Cat. 134 (p. 120). *Chardon Flacon (Perfume Bottle)*, c. 1900. Horn, mold-pressed glass; 8 x 5 cm. Kunstgewerbemuseum, Berlin, 1900.602.

Cat. 135 (p. 140). *Chrysanthemum Pendant Brooch*, c. 1900. Gold, glass, gray pearls, opalescent glass with dark blue patina, plique-à-jour enamel, in original case; 7.9 x 6 cm. The Richard H. Driehaus Museum, Chicago, 120085.

Cat. 136 (p. 122). *Cigalia Flacon (Perfume Bottle), Soap, and Perfume Suite* (each with original box), 1910. Perfumer: Roger & Gallet. Molded clear glass with green-gray patina, perfume, soap, cardboard, paper, textile; h. 13.2 cm. Christie Mayer Lefkowith Collection.

Cat. 137 (p. 127). *Cigar Case*, 1900–1910. Gold, glass, plique-à-jour enamel, sapphire; 14 x 3.8 x 1.9 cm. Cincinnati Art Museum, Gift of Mrs. James Leonard, Mrs. Harry Mackoy, Mrs. Samuel Bailey, Mr. John Warrington in memory of their mother, Mrs. Elsie Holmes Warrington, 1940.1.

Cat. 138 (p. 132). *Cockerel Brooch*, c. 1900. Shell, gold, natural pearl; w. 5.2 cm. Wartski, London.

Cat. 139 (p. 134). *Comb with Figures from the Middle Ages*, 1897–1901. Horn, gold, enamel, sapphires; 132 x 10 cm. Calouste Gulbenkian Foundation/Calouste Gulbenkian Museum, 1153.

Cat. 140 (p. 144). *Comb with Three Bretonnes*, 1900–1902. Horn, silver, ivory; 10.1 x 10.9 cm. Calouste Gulbenkian Foundation/Calouste Gulbenkian Museum, 1174.

Cat. 141 (p. 122). *Cyclamen Flacon (Perfume Bottle)* (with original box), 1909. Perfumer: Coty. Molded clear glass with green with green patina, cardboard, leather, textile; h. 13.5 cm. Christie Mayer Lefkowith Collection.

Cat. 142 (p. 86). *Diadem*, 1899. Aluminum, ivory, garnets; 27 x 35 x 37 cm. Musée Lambinet, Versailles, 1724.

Cat. 143 (p. 148). *Dog Collar Necklace*, 1897. Pearls, opal, enamel, gold, diamonds. Plaque: 9 x 5 cm; necklace: circumference 33.5 cm. Faerber Collection, 10544.

Cat. 144 (p. 48). *Dragonflies and Ferns Necklace*, 1902–4. Carved ivory, horn, gold, enamel on gold, diamonds; 16.7 x 21.8 cm. Private collection.

Cat. 145 (p. 117). *Dragonflies Bandeau (Headband)*, 1904–5. Gold, steel, plique-à-jour enamel, molded glass cabochons, diamonds; 2.4 x 35.5 cm. Private collection.

Cat. 146 (p. 45). *Fallen Rose Petals Vanity Set*, 1904–6. Silver, molded and carved glass. Rectangular box: 7.1 x 22.8 x 8.9 cm, and various dimensions for other pieces. Private collection.

Cat. 147 (pp. 118–19). *Fan*, c. 1900. Mother-of-pearl; 21.5 x 37 x 1.8 cm (open). Collection of Robert A. Zehil.

Cat. 148 (p. 123). *Fougères (Ferns) Flacon (Perfume Bottle)*, 1912. Molded blue glass with gray patina; h. 9.5 cm. Christie Mayer Lefkowith Collection.

Cat. 149 (p. 69). *Four Scarabs Vase*, 1911. Mold-blown black glass, red glass powdered glaze, wheel engraved; 25 x 27 cm. Musée des Arts Décoratifs, Paris, 18223.

Cat. 150 (p. 166). *Franco-Russian Portrait Brooch*, 1897. Gold, enamel; 4.1 x 4.1 cm. Faerber Collection, 10894.

Cat. 151 (p. 44). *Frogs and Lily Pads (Grenouilles et Nénuphars) Vase*, c. 1909–12. Glass; 21 x 29.8 cm. The Cleveland Museum of Art, John L. Severance Fund, 2007.180.

Cat. 152 (p. 49). *Frog Necklace*, 1902–3. Gold, enamel, glass, diamonds; 16.7 x 21.8 cm. Private collection.

Cat. 153 (p. 41). *Glass (Bague Chiens) (Ring of Dogs)*, c. 1912–13. Clear glass with brown patina; h. 11 cm. Collection of Mr. and Mrs. Craig Castilla.

Cat. 154 (p. 41). *Glass (Frise Personnages) (Frieze of Figures)*, 1912–13. Clear glass with brown patina; h. 14.7 cm. Collection of Mr. and Mrs. Craig Castilla.

Cat. 155 (p. 84). *Hair Ornament*, 1903. Horn, enamel, mother-of-pearl, topaz; 19.4 x 16.5 cm. Siegelson, New York.

Cat. 156 (p. 137). *Hair Ornament*, 1902–3. Horn, gold, diamonds; 15.5 x 7.6 cm. Rijksmuseum, Amsterdam, BK-1987-2.

Cat. 157 (p. 33). *Handbag*, 1901–3. Silver, moonstones, suede; 18 x 18 cm. Siegelson, New York.

Cat. 158 (pp. 130, 131). *Hand Mirror*, 1898–1900. Mirror, bronze; h. 34.8 cm. Private collection.

Cat. 159 (p. 148). *Inkwell*, c. 1900. Gold, enamel, opal; 6.4 x 3.8 cm. Private collection.

Cat. 160 (p. 41). *Inkwell (Biches) (Deer)*, c. 1913. Clear glass with brown patina; base: 15 x 15 cm. Collection of Mr. and Mrs. Craig Castilla.

Cat. 161 (p. 147). *Iris Bracelet*, c. 1897. Gold, enamel, opals; 17.2 x 4.9 cm. Private collection.

Cat. 162 (p. 258). *Lily of the Valley Comb*, c. 1900. Horn, enamel, gold; 15.4 x 9.4 x 3 cm. The Cleveland Museum of Art, Gift of Mrs. A. Dean Perry, 1981.49.

Cat. 163 (p. 124). *Misti Flacon (Perfume Bottle)* (with original box), 1913. Perfumer: L. T. Piver. Molded glass with partially frosted sienna patina, perfume, paper, cardboard, textile; h. 5 cm. Christie Mayer Lefkowith Collection.

Cat. 164 (p. 147). *Necklace with Insect Women and Black Swans*, c. 1900. Chased gold, enamel on gold, plique-à-jour enamel, Australian opal, Siberian amethyst; diam. 24.1 cm. The Metropolitan Museum of Art, New York, Gift of Lillian Nassau, 1985 (1985.114).

Cat. 165 (p. 138). *Nesting Swallows Ornamental Comb*, 1906–8. Carved horn, gold, diamonds; 16.7 x 21.8 cm. Private collection.

Cat. 166 (p. 115). *Night Butterfly Clip*, c. 1900. Gold, cloisonné and painted enamel, diamonds, platinum clips; 4.9 x 9.7 cm. Private collection.

Cat. 167 (p. 114). *Orchid Hair Ornament*, 1902. Gold, horn, glass, enamel; 19 x 9 x 6 cm. The Anderson Collection of Art Nouveau, University of East Anglia, Norwich, UEA21125.

Cat. 168 (p. 69). *Pansies Bandeau (Headband)*, 1904–5. Gold, steel, enamel, molded glass cabochons, diamonds; 1.7 x 35.5 cm. Private collection.

Cat. 169 (p. 136). *Pansy Pendant Brooch*, c. 1900. Gold, enamel, diamonds, pearl; l. 9 cm. Bayerisches Nationalmuseum, Munich.

Cat. 170 (p. 123). *Pavot (Poppy) Flacon (Perfume Bottle)*, 1910. Molded clear and red glass with black patina; h. 7 cm. Christie Mayer Lefkowith Collection.

Cat. 171 (p. 154). *Pendant with Serpents*, 1901. Gold, pearls, enamel; l. 11.7 cm. The State Hermitage Museum, St. Petersburg, E-15364.

Cat. 172 (p. 145). *Phryne Cameo Brooch*, 1900–1902. Gold, enamel, ivory, enameled glass; 9 x 12 cm. Private collection.

Cat. 173 (p. 144). *Pilgrim Flask*, c. 1900. Ivory, silver; 20 x 15 x 6.5 cm. Private collection.

Cat. 174 (p. 109). *Pocket Watch*, c. 1900. Gold, enamel, precious and semiprecious stones; 5 x 3.5 x 1.3 cm. Collection of Robert A. Zehil.

Cat. 175 (p. 85). *Poppies Dog Collar Plaque*, c. 1900. Gold, enamel, diamonds; 5.1 x 7.5 cm. Private collection.

Cat. 176 (p. 141). *Poppy Necklace*, 1900–1903. Patinated glass, enamel, gold, rose-cut diamonds. Pendant: 7.3 cm, chain: 57 cm. Toledo Museum of Art, Mr. and Mrs. George M. Jones, Jr. Fund, 1995.13.

Cat. 177 (p. 87). *Purse with Two Serpents*, 1901–3. Gold, silver, antelope skin, silver thread; 23.1 x 17.9 cm. Private collection.

Cat. 178 (p. 127). *Railing*, c. 1900. Bronze; 99 x 101.5 x 35 cm. Section A: Kunstgewerbemuseum, Berlin, 1901.111. Sections B and C: Private collection.

Cat. 179 (p. 46). *Rose Brooch*, 1910–15. Pewter, half baroque natural pearl; 0.5 x 0.5 cm. Private collection.

Cat. 180 (not illustrated). *Rooster Collarette*, 1906. Suede, silk embroidery, gold, enamel, crystal, citrine; w. 41 cm. Private collection.

Cat. 181 (p. 120). *Serpent Flacon (Perfume Bottle)*, 1898–99. Chased and gilt silver, polished jasper; 6 x 4.5 x 3.9 cm. Musée des Arts Décoratifs, Paris, 24508.

Cat. 182 (p. 73). *Serpents Sugar Bowl*, c. 1897–1900. Blown glass, silver; 22 x 29 x 17.6 cm. Calouste Gulbenkian Museum, Lisbon, 1162.

Cat. 183 (p. 122). *Set of Twelve Tester Flacons (Perfume Bottles)* (with original case), 1912. Perfumer: Coty. Molded glass, paper, wood, brass; h. 5.7 cm. Christie Mayer Lefkowith Collection.

Cat. 184 (pp. 75, 149). *Sheaves of Wheat (Épis de Blé) Chalice*, 1900–1902. Transparent blown glass, aluminum; h. 14.5 cm. Private collection, courtesy of Gallery Moderne-Le Style Lalique Ltd.

Cat. 185 (p. 41). *Sirens and Frogs (Sirènes et Grenouilles) Carafe*, 1917. Glass; 39.7 x 16.9 cm. Cincinnati Art Museum, W. W. Taylor Fund, 1917.3–4.

Cat. 186 (p. 41). *Tall Goblet (Vigne) (Vines)*, c. 1912–13. Clear glass with brown patina; h. 20 cm. Collection of Mr. and Mrs. Craig Castilla.

Cat. 187 (p. 113). *Thistle Necklace, Brooch, and Pendant*, 1903–5. Gold, enamel, diamonds, star sapphires, glass. Necklace: 5 x 37 cm; brooch: 5 x 5 cm; bracelet: 5 x 17 cm. Private collection.

Cat. 188 (p. 70). *Thorns (Épines) Box*, 1911. Glass, silvered bronze; 8.5 x 18 x 8.5 cm. Private collection.

Cat. 189 (p. 4). *Three Cockerels Dish Model*, 1898–1900. Terracotta; diam. 19.9 cm. Private collection.

Cat. 190 (p. 109). *Trumpets of Fame Pendant*, c. 1900. Gold, pâte-de-verre, enamel; 10.2 x 5 x 1.3 cm. Collection of Robert A. Zehil.

Cat. 191 (p. 41). *Two Dancers (Deux Danseuses) Carafe*, 1913. Glass; h. 34.5 cm, diam. 17.8 cm. Cincinnati Art Museum, Museum Purchase, 1913.10.

Cat. 192 (p. 140). *Two Revelers Dog Collar Plaque*, 1898–1900. Gold, enamel, milkglass; 5.4 x 7.6 cm. Private collection.

Cat. 193 (not illustrated). *Unfinished Parts of Jewels*, c. 1900. Ivory, horn, glass, mother-of-pearl, opal. Private collection.

Cat. 194 (p. 149). *Wheat Cup and Saucer*, 1904–5. Silver, enamel. Cup: 5 x 9.6 x 0.7 cm, saucer: 1.4 x 15.7 cm. Private collection.

Cat. 195 (p. 159). *Winter Woodland Pendant*, 1898–1900. Gold, enamel, plique-à-jour enamel, sapphires; 9.4 x 6.2 cm. Museum für Kunst und Gewerbe Hamburg, 1900.451.

Cat. 196 (p. 101). *Wisteria Lorgnette and Chain*, c. 1900. Gold, enamel, diamonds, jade, glass. Double chain, l. 85.1 cm; total l. 101.6 cm. The Metropolitan Museum of Art, New York, Gift of Mrs. J. G. Phelps Stokes (née Lettice L. Sands), 1965 (65.154ab).

F. Walter Lawrence (American, New York, 1864–1929)

Beginning his training in design and jewelry production in 1880, Lawrence apprenticed at Durand and Company, Howard and Company, and Jacques and Marcus. By 1889, he founded his own firm in Newark, later moving the business to New York City in 1894. In 1898, he founded F. Walter Lawrence, a jewelry salon at Union Square, relocating to Fifth Avenue in 1905. Producing jewelry in an American Art Nouveau style with an emphasis on nature and sculptural designs, Lawrence exhibited at the 1903 Arts and Crafts Exhibition in Syracuse and Rochester; the 1904 St. Louis world's fair, in which he exhibited twenty-seven pieces of gold jewelry, including fragments of Cyprian glass; and the 1914 Arts and Crafts Exhibition at the Art Institute of Chicago. In 1913, the F. Walter Lawrence firm was incorporated; by the 1920s, Lawrence was producing Art Deco designs and created the catalogue *Unusual Jewelry Silverware and Bronzes*. The business closed in 1975.

Cat. 197 (p. 233). *Hair Ornament*, c. 1900. Gold, ancient glass, gemstones, tortoiseshell; 14.3 x 5.8 x 1.9 cm. The Cleveland Museum of Art, Gift of the Trideca Society, 2001.106.

Liberty & Co. (English, London, est. 1875)

Established in 1875 by Arthur Lasenby Liberty, the firm used his business contacts and experience with oriental ware to start East India House, a business that imported Indian enamels and Japanese metalwork. A Paris shop opened in 1890, becoming known for its use of the Celtic interlace pattern. In 1899, influenced by the Arts and Crafts movement, Liberty appointed English designers, including Arthur Gaskin and Archibald Knox, to produce silver and pewter ware and began what has been called the Liberty "cymric" jewelry venture, a break with traditional design. Some of Liberty's jewelry and silverwork was produced by other Birmingham firms: W. H. Haseler and Son; Murrle, Bennett; and a firm with the mark L. C. & Co. Liberty & Co. had commercial success with its synthesis of Art Nouveau and Arts and Crafts motifs.

Cat. 198 (p. 75). *Barley Corn Diadem*, c. 1900. Designer: Fred Partridge. Horn, moonstones; 8.9 x 14 cm. The Richard H. Driehaus Museum, Chicago, 120148.

Cat. 199 (p. 79). *Pendant*, 1900. Designer: Archibald Knox. Enamel, diamonds, gold, pearls, platinum, opals; 8.9 x 27.9 cm. Collection of Neil Lane.

Firm of Fedor Lorié (Russian, active Moscow, 1871–1916)

The Lorié firm, which began in 1871, was often associated with the Moscow branch of the House of Fabergé. Both companies shared storage in the same building of the Merchants Society at Kuznetsky Bridge, Moscow's "Diamond Street." The Lorié firm crafted silver and gold jewelry. The firm's work was noticed at various art and industrial exhibitions and shows, including the first international art and industrial exhibition of metal and stone art objects (1904, St. Petersburg). Lorié received a silver medal at the exhibition, while the gold medal was given to the famous courtier firm F. Kekhli. Just after the reorganization of the company in 1913, a fastidious cigar case was made using two types of gold and decorated with a clamp adorned with small roses. The firm finally closed just before the Russian Revolution in 1916.

Cat. 200 (p. 224). *Pendant*, c. 1899–1908. Gold, opaque enamel, diamonds, pearls, cabochon sapphires; 6 x 8 cm. Private collection.

Marcus & Co. (American, active New York, 1892–1941)

Beginning as Jacques and Marcus, the firm was renamed Marcus & Co. in 1892 by Herman Marcus, with his partners-sons William Elder and George Elder, after George B. Jacques' retirement. Based in New York, Marcus & Co. produced jewelry with both Arts and Crafts and Art Nouveau styles, eventually producing Egyptian and Renaissance revival motifs in the early twentieth century. In 1897, the firm exhibited a diverse display of jewelry and accessories at the First Exhibition of the Arts and Crafts in Boston, later participating in an exhibition at the Rhode Island School of Design in 1916. After Herman Marcus died in 1899, the sons relocated the business to Fifth Avenue and began producing silverware objects. The firm became known for its plique-à-jour enameling resulting from George

Marcus's innovation, which he produced until his death in 1917. In 1920, William Marcus retired, and upon his death in 1925, his sons William and Chapin took over the business, later establishing branches in Bombay, London, and Paris. Because of William Marcus Jr.'s different interests in materials, the firm's work began to feature pearls, emeralds, and black opals, and became known for Art Deco floral motifs. In the 1930s, Marcus & Co. published a series of five books on pearls and gemstones, later exhibiting at the New York World's Fair in 1939. William Marcus Jr. sold the company to the Gimbel Brothers Department Store in 1941.

Cat. 201 (p. 239, 254). *Bodice Ornament,* c. 1905–15. Platinum, diamonds, natural pearls; 10.2 x 8.9 cm. Primavera Gallery, New York.

Cat. 202 (p. 250). *Brooch,* c. 1895–1900. Glass, enamel, gold, diamond; 10 x 6 x 3.5 cm. Private collection.

Cat. 203 (p. 249, 253). *Lapel Watch,* c. 1900. Gold, opals, demantoid garnets; 6.9 x 3.2 cm. Collection of Eric Streiner.

Cat. 204 (p. 251). *Necklace,* c. 1900. Gold, baroque pearls, diamonds, demantoid garnets, zircons, other precious stones; 5.1 x 5.7 cm. Collection of Eric Streiner.

Cat. 205 (p. 252, 273). *Necklace,* c. 1900–1905. Gold, rubies, pearls; l. 25 cm. Collection of Neil Lane.

Cat. 206 (p. 249, 254). *Pendant Watch,* 1905. Gold, enamel, sapphires, diamonds; 38.1 x 3.18 cm. Collection of Eric Streiner.

Lluís Masriera (Catalan, Barcelona, 1872–1958)

Lluís and his brother inherited the family firm, which had been established by their grandfather in 1839 and produced conventional Spanish decorations. Trained under the enamelist Frank-Edouart Lossier, Lluís studied at the School of Art in Geneva. In 1900, after attending the Exposition Universelle in Paris, he began creating a whole new line of jewelry in the Art Nouveau style reflecting the influence of the circle of René Lalique. His translucent enamel technique and new style brought fame to the family firm, as he was awarded the grand prize for jewelry at the 1908 International Exhibition of Zaragoza and at Ghent in 1913. The firm continues to produce jewelry in Barcelona under the name Bagués-Masriera.

Cat. 207 (p. 103). *Carnation Brooch,* 1904. Gold, diamonds, rubies, enamel; 12.2 x 5.2 cm. Private collection.

Cat. 208 (p. 104). *Dragonfly Dog Collar Plaque,* 1903–6. Silver, gold, diamonds, plique-à-jour enamel, emeralds, rubies; 4.5 x 7 cm. Bagués-Masriera.

Cat. 209a (p. 104). *Folio from Design Book Number 3: Study for a Dragonfly Brooch;* cat. 209b (p. 103): *Folio from Design Book Number 83: Study for a Flower Brooch,* c. 1900–1910. Paper, ink, leather binding; 14.5 x 12.5 cm. Bagués-Masriera.

Cat. 210 (p. 106). *Necklace,* 1909–16. Gold, platinum, ivory, diamonds, sapphires; 3.9 x 12.5 cm. Bagués-Masriera.

Mellerio dits Meller (French, Paris, est. c. 1613)

The Mellerio family was established as goldsmiths in France by 1613. In 1815, the firm moved to the rue de la Paix and was selected as Bijoutier de Madame la Duchesse d'Orléans. It also produced wares in later years for the royal house and commissions for Charles X, Emperor Napoleon III and Empress Eugènie, Princess Mathilde, and Queen Isabella II of Spain. After Francois Mellerio's death in 1843, Jean-François Mellerio managed the firm. By 1848, Jean-François established a branch of the firm in Madrid, while his brother, Joseph, started a business on the Boulevard des Italians in Paris. The Mellerio firm participated in the 1855 Paris and 1862 London world's fairs, later receiving a gold medal at the 1867 Paris Exposition Universelle. After the firm received the Grand Diploma of Honor at the 1873 Vienna fair, it received more business from the French, Russian, and Polish aristocracies. Participating in the 1878 and 1900 Paris expositions, the firm also expanded its Madrid branch and established branches in Baden-Baden and Biarritz in 1879, specializing in traditional court jewelry of diamonds and pearls.

Cat. 211 (p. 60). *Peacock Feather Dog Collar Necklace,* c. 1900. Gold, enamel, diamonds; 6 x 11.1 cm. Smithsonian American Art Museum, gift of Laura Dreyfus Barney and Natalie Clifford Barney in memory of their mother, Alice Pike Barney, 1964.25.1.

P. I. Olovianishnikov & Sons (Russian, Moscow, active 1776–1917)

Established in 1776, the Olovianishnikov firm is one of the oldest in Russia. Much of the firm's early twentieth-century work was influenced by its artistic director, Sergei Vashkov, who focused on Christian symbolism. As a result, the firm mainly produced liturgical items as well as some decorative household wares.

Cat. 212 (p. 208). *Chalice,* 1908–17. Designer: Sergei Vashkov. Silver, glass, enamel, ivory, semiprecious stones; 19.1 x 13.7 cm. Hillwood Estate, Museum & Gardens, Bequest of Marjorie Merriweather Post, 1973, 12.614.

Plisson & Hartz (French, Paris, 1872–1904)

A Parisian firm specializing in jewelry with naturalistic motifs, Plisson & Hartz was among the first to produce jewelry designs with chimera or scary dragon-like creatures as the featured element. The firm's *broches chimères* (chimera brooches) depicted two intertwined mythical beasts and became popular around the turn of the century. Hartz & Cie succeeded Plisson & Hartz in 1904.

Cat. 213 (p. 135). *Pendant,* c. 1900. Gold, diamonds, baroque pearl, enamel; 6 x 4.1 cm. The Metropolitan Museum of Art, New York, purchase, Gift of Mrs. Mercedes Meyerhof in memory of Mrs. Hedwig Hallgarten, 1968 (68.35).

Potter & Mellen (American, Cleveland, est. 1899)

Alumnus of the Cleveland School of Art, Horace E. Potter was a jewelry and silverware designer who ran the Potter Studio, a small jewelry design firm he founded in 1899. After hiring Louis Mellen in 1921 and becoming partners with Guerdon W. Bentley, a printmaker and bronzier in 1928, the shop became Potter Bentley Studios, Inc. After Bentley left the firm in 1933, the shop became Potter & Mellen, Inc. and included a newly expanded facility as well as fine china and glassware in its salesroom. Potter died in 1948, but Mellen stayed with the firm until 1967 after selling it to Frederick Miller and Jack Schlundt.

Cat. 214 (p. x). *Pendant Brooch*, 1905. Enamel, gold, citrines; 7 x 4.2 x 0.5 cm. Private collection.

Rookwood Pottery Co. (American, Cincinnati, 1880–1967)
Originating from the Cincinnati Pottery Club, Rookwood Pottery of Cincinnati was founded by Maria Longworth Nichols in 1880 and renamed the Rookwood Pottery Co. one year later. William Watts Taylor became director in 1883, and Nichols gave the business to him in 1890. Criticized as a "feminine endeavor," the firm used purely native resources for its designs, clay, and staff. The decorating department was established in 1881, and by the 1890s the firm was producing roughly 10,000 ceramic pieces per year. Keeping on top of market demand and current trends, artists worked in a broad spectrum of designs and techniques, the chemist Karl Langenbeck was hired to produce innovative glazes, and Rookwood developed ceramic pieces electroplated with silver overlays. The company exhibited extensively around the turn of the twentieth century and was awarded a first prize gold medal at the 1889 Exhibition of American Art Industry at the Pennsylvania Museum, a gold medal at the 1889 Paris Exposition Universelle, grand prizes at the 1893 World's Columbian Exposition and the 1900 Paris Exposition Universelle, and a grand prix at its last exhibition at the Alaska-Yukon Pacific Exposition in Seattle. After filing for bankruptcy in 1941, the business went through four ownerships in eighteen years. In 1960 the company relocated to Starkville, Mississippi, and ceased production seven years later.

Cat. 215 (not illustrated). *Grand Prize Medal* (awarded to Rookwood Pottery Co., Universal Exposition), 1900. Bronze; 5.1 cm. The Rookwood Pottery Company, Cincinnati, L34.2002.

Cat. 216 (p. 303). *Vase*, c. 1900. Designer: Matthew Daly. Black iris glaze line (stoneware) with copper and silver electrodeposit; 36.8 x 22.9 cm. Cincinnati Art Museum, Museum Purchase: Lawrence Archer Wachs Trust and a generous gift from Judge and Mrs. Norman A. Murdock, 2004.68.

Fedor I. Rückert (Russian, Moscow, active 1887–1917)
From around 1890 until the Russian Revolution, Rückert produced jewelry reminiscent of seventeenth-century design, using filigree, painted enamels, and the Russian *skan* technique. Rückert's workshop was well known for its traditional "Old Russian"-style jewelry, which was later influenced by Art Nouveau. His pieces illustrate a synthesis of cloisonné and enamel painted en plein, with heavy gilt or silver on the cloisons. Fabergé's Moscow branch opened in 1887 and acquired a division of Rückert's firm, and he became the sole workmaster for cloisonné for Fabergé.

Cat. 217 (p. 196). *Kovsh (Cup)*, 1896–1906. Silver gilt, enamel, gemstones; 8.6 x 20.5 x 13.2 cm. The Cleveland Museum of Art, The India Early Minshall Collection, 1966.496.

Anton Seder (German, Munich, 1850–1916?)
Producing paintings and designs in the Art Nouveau style, Seder also served as director of the École Supérieure des Arts Décoratifs from 1890 to 1920. A co-editor of the magazine *Das Kunstgewerbe in Elsass-Lothringen (The Arts and Crafts in Alsace-Lorraine)*, he also produced two collections of prints, *Die Pflanze in Kunst und Gewerbe (The Plant in Art and Trade)* and *Das Their In Der Decorativen Kunst (Animals in Decorative Art)*, which supplemented source materials to manufacturing companies.

Cat. 218 (p. 29). *Holy Grail Centerpiece*, c. 1900. Goldsmith: Theodor Heiden. Gold, silver gilt, enamel, diamonds, rubies, emeralds, sapphires, nephrite, precious stones; h. 60.7 cm. Bayerisches Nationalmuseum, Munich.

Otto Stüber (German, Hamburg, 1885–1973)
Influenced by the Wiener Werkstätte, Stüber produced functional silver objects, mostly in nickel silver. While in Munich, Stüber was a student of Fritz von Miller and later worked in Scandinavia. In 1910, along with Christoph Kay, he established a workshop in Hamburg.

Cat. 219 (p. 52). *Cup*, 1910–14. Designer: Christopher Kay. Silver, opals; h. 16.7 cm. Museum für Kunst und Gewerbe Hamburg, 1991.63.

Henri Téterger (French, Paris, b. 1862)
Trained by his father, Hippolyte, Henri became director of the family firm, Henri Téterger Fils, which was known for manufacturing fashionable jewelry during the mid to late nineteenth century in Paris. Adopting Art Nouveau designs, the firm displayed its new creations at the 1900 Paris Exposition Universelle to great acclaim.

Cat. 220 (p. 97). *Jewelry Box*, 1895–1905. Agate, silver gilt, silk; 10.2 x 8.9 cm. Collection of Neil Lane.

André Fernand Thesmar (French, Paris, 1843–1912)
An established painter of flowers, Thesmar began working with the Parisian bronze maker Ferdinand Barbedienne in 1872. Working with metal and enamels, and inspired by the Henri Cernuschi collection of Asian art, Thesmar embellished his works with cloisonné enamels while working at the porcelain factory in Sèvres in 1882. From the 1890s on, he used filigree and plique-à-jour techniques combined with Persian motifs and vivid colors. Well received at the 1900 Paris Exposition Universelle, Thesmar was also awarded the Legion of Honor in 1893.

Cat. 221 (p. 208). *Bowl with Anemones*, c. 1900. Plique-à-jour enamel, gold; 5 x 9.1 cm. Toledo Museum of Art, Mr. and Mrs. George M. Jones, Jr. Fund, 2005.43.

Tiffany & Co. (American, New York, est. 1837)
Established as Tiffany & Young in 1837 by Charles Lewis Tiffany and his brother-in-law, John B. Young, the firm was incorporated in 1868 and by the end of the nineteenth century was worth more than $10 million, with showrooms in New York, Paris, and London, and employed more than 1,000 people. Under the direction of chief designer Paulding Farnham, Tiffany & Co. achieved success at the 1900 Paris Exposition Universelle, receiving the grand prize for jewelry and silverware, six gold medals, two silver medals, and one bronze medal. Upon the death of his father in 1902, Louis Comfort Tiffany became the artistic director of the jewelry and silverware divisions, exhibiting examples of his enameled jewelry at the 1904 Louisiana Purchase Exposition in St. Louis. In 1905, the firm relocated to a new showroom designed by Stanford White on Fifth Avenue and 37th Street, later moving to Fifth Avenue and 57th Street in 1940, and eventually establishing retail stores throughout the world.

Cat. 222 (p. 292). *The Adams Vase*, 1893–95. Designer: Paulding Farnham. Gold, amethysts, quartz, spessartites, tourmalines, freshwater pearls, enamel; 49.4 x 30.5 x 23.5 cm. The Metropolitan Museum of Art, New York, Gift of Edward D. Adams, 1904 (04.1).

Cat. 223 (p. 235). *Belt*, 1880–1900. Turquoise, gold; 76.2 x 5.1 cm. Collection of Neil Lane.

Cat. 224 (p. 239). *Bodice Ornament*, 1890–95. Designer: Paulding Farnham. Diamonds, gold, platinum; 6.4 x 16.5 cm. Collection of Neil Lane.

Cat. 225 (p. 296). *Bodice Ornament*, c. 1890–95. Designer: Paulding Farnham. Diamonds, conch pearls, silver, gold; 11.4 x 2.5 cm. Collection of Neil Lane.

Cat. 226 (p. 246). *Box*, 1895–1905. Maker: probably Russian. Silver, gold, enamel, pink tourmalines, demantoid garnets; 2.5 x 8.9 x 5.1 cm. Tiffany & Co. Archives, B2001.13.

Cat. 227 (p. 244). *Box with Lid*, c. 1895–1905. Maker: probably French. Gold, enamel; h. 2 cm, diam. 5 cm. Tiffany & Co. Archives, B2000.08.

Cat. 228 (p. 287). *Box with Lid*, 1912. Designer: Eugène Feuillâtre. Silver gilt, enamel; 2 x 7 cm. Tiffany & Co. Archives, B2003.21.

Cat. 229 (p. 246). *Brooch*, 1895–1900. Aquamarine, platinum, diamonds; 3 x 3.8 x 2.8 cm. Tiffany & Co. Archives, A1999.20.

Cat. 230. *Brooch*, 1900. Designer: Paulding Farnham. Diamonds, pearls, Montana sapphires, enamel, platinum, gold; 5.7 x 5.4 x 1.6 cm. Tiffany & Co. Archives, A1993.01.

Cat. 231 (p. 295). *Brooch*, c. 1902–5. Kunzite, gold, diamonds, platinum; 6.4 x 6.4 cm. Collection of Neil Lane.

Cat. 232 (p. 53). *Brooch*, c. 1915–20. Designer: Julia Munson. Maker: Tiffany Studios. Platinum, moonstones, sapphires; 2.9 x 7.9 cm. Collection of Eric Streiner.

Cat. 233 (p. 310). *Brooch and Pendant*, 1918. Designer: Meta Overbeck. Gold, enamel, opal, flannel; 6 x 3.5 cm. Collection of the Newark Museum, Purchase 2005 Helen McMahon Brady Cutting Fund, 2005.7.2A–C.

Cat. 234 (p. 235). *Card Case*, 1895–1905. Silver, enamel; 26.5 x 6.8 x 0.8 cm. Tiffany & Co. Archives, B2006.05.

Cat. 235 (p. 302). *Centerpiece*, 1900. Designer: Paulding Farnham. Silver; 48.3 x 81.4 cm. Dallas Museum of Art, gift of Michael L. Rosenberg, 1998.13.

Cat. 236 (p. 245). *Cigar Cutter*, 1890–1900. Maker: possibly Georges le Saché. Carved amber, enamel, gold, gilt bronze; 13.3 x 2.5 cm. Collection of Eric Streiner.

Cat. 237 (p. 235). *Cigarette Case*, 1890–1900. Gold, marbleized alloy; 7.6 x 6. x 1.4 cm. The Metropolitan Museum of Art, New York, Gift of Susan Dwight Bliss, 1941 (41.140.2).

Cat. 238 (p. 301). *Coffee Set*, 1902–3. Designer: Paulding Farnham. Silver gilt, enamel, amethysts, ivory. Coffeepot: 27.3 x 15.2 x 10.8 cm, and various dimensions for other pieces. High Museum of Art, Atlanta, Virginia Carroll Crawford Collection, 1984.168.1–5.

Cat. 239 (p. 247). *Coffee Service with Tray*, 1900–1910. Designer: Albert Southwick. Gold, nephrite, citrines. Coffee pot: h. 22.9 cm, and various dimensions for other pieces. Tiffany & Co. Archives, B1999.24.01–05.

Cat. 240 (p. 277). *Covered Jar*, 1898–1907. Enamel on copper; h. 24.8 cm. The Walters Art Museum, Baltimore, 44.589.

Cat. 241 (p. 244). *Cross Pendant Watch*, c. 1900. Maker: Verger Frères. Enamel, glass, platinum, rose-cut diamonds, brilliant-cut diamonds; 4.5 x 2.5 cm. Private collection.

Cat. 242 (p. 271). *Cupid Watch*, 1893. Moonstone, gold, diamonds; 7.7 x 3 x 1.5 cm. Collection of Neil Lane.

Cat. 243 (p. 310). *Demi-Parure* (with original case), 1910–20. Designer: probably Louis Comfort Tiffany. Maker: Tiffany Studios. Gold, topaz, precious gemstones. Brooch: 3.8 x 5.1 cm; earrings: 6.4 x 1.9 cm. Collection of Eric Streiner.

Cat. 244. *Desk Set*, 1895–1905. Glass, enamel, silver gilt. Inkstand: 10.5 x 17.5 cm; blotter: 5.5 x 9.5 x 6.7 cm; pen tray: 1.5 x 23.4 x 8.4 cm; box: 4 x 14.5 x 5.8 cm. Tiffany & Co. Archives, B2003.02.01–04.

Cat. 245 (p. 271). *Dog Collar Necklace*, 1893. Gold, enamel, turquoise, pearls, diamonds; 36.2 x 3.2 cm. Tiffany & Co. Archives, A1999.51.01.

Cat. 246 (p. 249). *Domino Set*, c. 1900. Maker: probably Georges le Saché Ivory, gold, enamel; 21.5 x 20.5 x 2.5 cm. Private collection.

Cat. 247 (p. 59). *Frog*, c. 1900. Jade; h. 22.2 cm. The Walters Art Museum, Baltimore, 44.288.

Cat. 248 (p. 268). *Humidor*, 1889. Designer: Robert Francis Hunter. Sterling silver, cast and acid-etched; 23.5 x 32.4 x 20.6 cm. Dallas Museum of Art, Foundation for the Arts Collection, Mrs. John B. O'Hara Fund, 1993.69.1.A–E.FA.

Cat. 249 (p. 244). *Inkwell*, 1895–1905. Designer: Georges le Saché. Glass, gold, enamel, rubies, sapphire; h. 9.5 cm, diam. 10 cm. Tiffany & Co. Archives, I1999.07.

Cat. 250 (p. 17). *Iris Brooch*, c. 1900–1901. Designer: Paulding Farnham. Pink tourmalines, demantoid garnets, platinum; 13.3 x 4.4 x 0.6 cm. Primavera Gallery, New York.

Cat. 251 (p. 296). *Jewelry Box*, c. 1900. Abalone shell, silver gilt, silk; 20 x 11 x 14 cm. Collection of Neil Lane.

Cat. 252 (p. 249). *Lapel Watch*, c. 1895. Pink enamel, gold; 4.5 x 2.7 cm. Collection of Eric Streiner.

Cat. 253 (p. 249). *Lapel Watch*, c. 1895. Red guilloché enamel, gold; 6 cm. Collection of Eric Streiner.

Cat. 254 (p. 302). *Miniature Vase* or *Salt Cellar*, c. 1900. Mounts: House of Fabergé. Favrile glass, bronze; w. 7.6 cm. Collection of Eric Streiner.

Cat. 255 (p. 256). *Necklace*, 1885–95. Diamonds, tourmalines, platinum, yellow gold. Necklace circumference 34.5 cm; pendant h. 4 cm. The Cleveland Museum of Natural History, 1991–20.

Cat. 256 (p. 317). *Necklace*, 1905–15. Designer: probably Meta Overbeck. Amethysts, diamonds, platinum; 27.9 x 3 cm. Collection of Neil Lane.

Cat. 257 (p. 312). *Necklace*, 1912. Designer: Louis Comfort Tiffany. Maker: Tiffany Studios. Gold, nephrite; 34.2 x 8.6 cm. Toledo Museum of Art, Purchased with funds given by Rita Barbour Kern, 1996.1.

Cat. 258 (p. 310). *Necklace*, 1907–14. Designer: Louis Comfort Tiffany. Maker: Tiffany Studios. Apatites, Montana sapphires, gold; 26.7 x 4.5 cm. Collection of Eric Streiner.

Cat. 259 (p. 315). *Necklace*, 1915. Designer: Louis Comfort Tiffany. Platinum, moonstone, Montana sapphires; l. 50.8 cm. Collection of Eric Streiner.

Cat. 260 (p. 313). *Necklace*, 1916. Maker: Tiffany Studios. Platinum, peridots, aquamarines, chrysoberyl, gold; 28 x 3.5 cm. Collection of Neil Lane.

Cat. 261 (p. 3). *Opera Glasses*, c. 1900. Designer: Georges le Saché. Retailer: possibly Tiffany & Co. Gold, ivory, enamel; 10 x 5.72 cm. Private collection.

Cat. 262 (p. 267). *Orchid Brooch* (with original case), 1889. Designer: Paulding Farnham. Enamel, gold, diamonds; 8 x 7.4 cm. Private collection.

Cat. 263 (p. 5). *Parasol Handle*, 1895–1905. Jade, gold, sapphire; 8 x 4 cm. Private collection.

Cat. 264 (p. 59). *Pearl Collection* (with original case), 1890–1900. Freshwater pearls, box lined in velvet. Box: 16.2 x 16.4 x 3.5 cm. The Cleveland Museum of Natural History, 1975–45.

Cat. 265 (p. 297). *Pearl Pendant*, 1900–1910. Pearl, platinum, diamond. Pendant: 1.6 x 1.5 x 1.3 cm. The Walters Art Museum, Baltimore, Gift of Miss Laura F. Delano, 1977, 57.2034.

Cat. 266 (p. 280). *Powder Case*, 1890. Gold, enamel, feathers, silk. Body: 9 x 1 cm; chain handle: h. 18.4 cm. Cincinnati Art Museum, gift of Gates T. and Margaret K. Richards, 2006.137.

Cat. 267 (p. 297). *Renaissance-style Bodice Ornament*, c. 1893. Designer: Paulding Farnham. Gold, diamonds, gemstones; 8.9 x 3.8 cm. Collection of Neil Lane.

Cat. 268 (p. 231). *Ring*, c. 1905–15. Designer: Louis Comfort Tiffany. Yellow diamond, emeralds, gold; 2.3 x 3 x 2 cm. Collection of Neil Lane.

Cat. 269 (p. 299). *Scent Bottle*, c. 1900–1908. Designer: Paulding Farnham. Glass, enamel, diamonds, demantoid garnet; 11.4 x 3.5 cm. Primavera Gallery, New York.

Cat. 270 (p. 299). *Scent Bottle*, c. 1900–1908. Designer: bottle, Louis Comfort Tiffany; mount, Paulding Farnham. Favrile glass, gold, circular-cut diamonds, brown diamond finial; h. 12.1 cm. Collection of Eric Streiner.

Cat. 271 (p. 299). *Scent Bottle*, c. 1900–1908. Designer: Louis Comfort Tiffany. Favrile glass, silver, opal; h. 14.9 cm. Collection of Eric Streiner.

Cat. 272 (p. 270). *Tankard*, c. 1900. Silver gilt, ivory; 69.9 x 29.2 x 33.7 cm. Tiffany & Co. Archives, B2001.06.

Cat. 273 (p. 319). *Triumph of Spring Vase*, 1915. Designer: Louis Comfort Tiffany. Sterling silver, enamel; 55.9 x 27.3 cm. Allentown Art Museum, Gift of Bethlehem Steel Co., 1985, 1985.25a,b.

Cat. 274 (p. 257). *Wade Necklace*, c. 1900. Gold, platinum, diamonds; 36 x 8.5 cm. Tiffany & Co. Archives, A1999.49.01.

Cat. 275 (p. 255). *Watch*, c. 1900. Gold, enamel, diamonds; h. 4.5 cm. Private collection.

Cat. 276 (p. 301). *Zuni Bowl*, c. 1900. Designer: Paulding Farnham. Sterling silver, turquoise, inlaid with niello and copper; 8.6 x 29.8 cm. Private collection.

Louis Comfort Tiffany (American, New York, 1848–1933)
Tiffany Glass & Decorating Co.
Tiffany Studios
Trained as a landscape painter in the 1860s in New York and Paris under Léon Bailly, Tiffany was the son of Charles Lewis Tiffany, a prominent New York silversmith, jeweler, and founder of Tiffany & Co. Louis Tiffany established the society of American Artists with John La Farge among others in 1877; within two years, he established his interior design firm, Louis C. Tiffany and Associated Artists, designing opulent interiors with Samuel Colman, Lockwood de Forest, and Candace Wheeler. After 1885, Tiffany focused on his stained-glass windows and lamps, forming the Tiffany Glass & Decorating Co. in 1892, and patenting his line of handmade Favrile glass in 1894. The company became Tiffany Studios in 1900, a few years before Louis became artistic director of Tiffany & Co., after his father's death in 1902. Tiffany Studios took advantage of industrial technology and economic prosperity to produce and sell its glass, ceramics, enamels, and lamps. Tiffany also produced interior furnishings, windows, and lighting fixtures for churches. He participated in many international exhibitions but was most noted for having shown at the 1893 World's Columbian Exposition in Chicago and the 1900 Paris Exposition Universelle. Tiffany Studios filed for bankruptcy in 1932.

Cat. 277 (pp. 8, 316). *Agate Vase*, 1909. Tiffany Studios. Favrile glass; 22.3 x 11 cm. Private collection.

Cat. 278 (p. 291). *American Indian Basket Desk Lamp*, 1900–1910. Tiffany Studios. Favrile glass, bronze; h. 30.5 cm. Private collection.

Cat. 279 (p. 50). *Autumn Leaf Globe Lamp*, 1900–1910. Tiffany Studios. Favrile glass, gilt bronze; h. 79.4 cm. Private collection.

Cat. 280 (p. 8). *Bowl*, c. 1895–1900. Favrile glass; 18 x 25 cm. Collection of Clare and Harold Sam Minoff.

Cat. 281 (p. 50). *Box*, 1905–15. Patinated brass, bone; 10.2 x 15.2 x 15.2 cm. Collection of Neil Lane.

Cat. 282 (p. 53). *Brooch*, 1895. Designer: probably C. R. Ashbee. Opal, gold, enamel; 4.3 x 1.5 cm. Private collection.

Cat. 283 (p. 272). *Indian-style Pendant*, c. 1915–20. Designer: probably Louis Comfort Tiffany. Maker: Tiffany Studios. Australian opals, sapphires, topaz, demantoid garnets, pearls, chrysoberyl, gold; l. 4.5 cm. American Museum of Natural History, New York, gift of Lilian Betts, 1934, 42795.

Cat. 284 (p. 281). *Inkwell*, 1898–1906. Maker: Tiffany Glass & Decorating Co. Retailer: Tiffany Studios. Favrile glass mosaic, bronze; 8 x 10.5 cm. Private collection.

Cat. 285 (p. 275). *Landscape with a Greek Temple*, c. 1900. Tiffany Studios. Stained glass; 227.3 x 114.3 cm. The Cleveland Museum of Art, Gift of Mrs. Robert M. Fallon, 1966.432.

Cat. 286 (p. 286). *Magnolia Jar*, 1901. Tiffany Studios. Pottery; 23.5 x 13 cm. Private collection.

Cat. 287 (p. 289). *Magnolia Window*, c. 1900. Designer: Agnes Northrop. Stained glass; 133.5 x 76.5 cm. The State Hermitage Museum, St. Petersburg, B-349.

Cat. 288 (p. 305). *Mushroom Night Lamp*, 1896–1902. Tiffany Glass & Decorating Co. Favrile glass; h. 12.7 cm. Private collection.

Cat. 289 (pp. 8, 279). *Narcissus Paperweight-style Vase*, 1909. Tiffany Studios. Favrile glass; 32.2 x 12.5 cm. Private collection.

Cat. 290 (p. VII). *Nymph and Butterfly Lamp Pendant*, c. 1900. Designer: Alphonse Mucha. Leaded glass, bronze; 22 x 28 x 4 cm. Collection of Mr. and Mrs. Robert Sage.

Cat. 291 (p. 307). *Oriental Poppy Lamp*, 1900–1910. Tiffany Studios. Favrile glass; h. 40.6 cm. Private collection.

Cat. 292 (p. 290). *Peacock Lamp*, 1898–1906. Tiffany Glass & Decorating Co. Favrile glass, bronze; h. 45.7 cm. Private collection.

Cat. 293 (p. 280). *Peacock Medallion*, 1906. Tiffany Studios. Copper, enamel, gilt bronze; 14.3 x 0.9 cm. Private collection.

Cat. 294 (p. 288). *Peacock Vase*, c. 1913. Favrile glass; 59.8 x 17.5 cm. Dallas Museum of Art, gift of Mr. and Mrs. Nelson Waggener, 1983.27.

Cat. 295 (p. 288). *Peacock Vase*, c. 1900. Favrile glass; 33.7 x 25 x 14 cm. Cooper-Hewitt, National Design Museum, Smithsonian Institution, Gift of Stanley Siegel, from the Stanley Siegel Collection, 1975-32-11.

Cat. 296 (p. 233). *Perfume Bottle*, c. 1900. Tiffany Studios. Retailer: Tiffany & Co. Favrile glass with gilt-metal cover; h. 13.4 cm. The Cleveland Museum of Art, Gift of Ellen Wade Chinn, Elizabeth Wade Sedgwick, and J. H. Wade III in memory of their mother, Irene Love Wade, 1966.379.

Cat. 297 (p. 279). *Set of Unfinished Glass Pieces*, 1900–1905. Tiffany Studios. Glass; various dimensions. Favrile glass; various dimensions. Private collection.

Cat. 298 (p. 279). *Set of Three Mosaics: Dragonfly Trivet, Poppy Plaque, Water Lilies Paperweight*, 1900–1910. Favrile glass mosaic. Dragonfly: 6.2 x 6.2 x 2.5 cm; poppy: 27.4 x 12 x 1.5 cm; water lilies: 23.3 x 9.5 x 1.5 cm. Private collection.

Cat. 299 (p. 306). *Spider Lamp*, 1900–1910. Tiffany Studios. Favrile glass, bronze; h. 38.1 cm. Private collection.

Cat. 300 (pp. 8, 284). *Vase*, 1896–1900. Tiffany Glass & Decorating Co. Retailer: L'Art Nouveau. Favrile glass, gilt-silver mount; 12.2 x 11.5 x 8 cm. Private collection.

Cat. 301 (p. 283). *Vase*, 1896. Tiffany Glass & Decorating Co. Designer: Louis Comfort Tiffany. Glass; 7.6 x 6.4 cm. Philadelphia Museum of Art, Gift of Lydia Thompson Morris, 1925, 1925–27–97.

Cat. 302 (p. 233). *Vase*, 1897. Tiffany Glass & Decorating Co. Favrile glass; 47 x 19.1 cm. Cincinnati Art Museum, gift of A. T. Goshorn, 1897.121.

Cat. 303 (p. 282). *Vase*, 1897. Tiffany Glass & Decorating Co. Favrile glass; 30.5 x 9.5 cm. Cincinnati Art Museum, gift of A. T. Goshorn, 1897.132.

Cat. 304 (pp. 82–83). *Vase*, c. 1900. Tiffany Studios. Favrile glass; h. 14.5 cm, diam. 10 cm. Kunstgewerbemuseum, Berlin, 1900.594.

Cat. 305 (p. 288). *Vase*, 1907. Glass; 46 x 12.2 cm. Cooper-Hewitt, National Design Museum, Smithsonian Institution, Gift of Stanley Siegel, from the Stanley Siegel Collection, 1975–32–13.

Cat. 306 (p. 8). *Vase*, c. 1914–18. Favrile glass; 19.4 x 14.3 cm. The Cleveland Museum of Art, Norman O. Stone and Ella A. Stone Memorial Fund, 1970.126.

Cat. 307 (p. 203). *Vase with Serpent Mounts*, 1908–17. Mounts: House of Fabergé. Workmaster: Viktor Aarne. Silver gilt, glass; h. 16.2 cm. The Forbes Collection, New York, FAB88013.

Unknown Maker

Cat. 308 (p. 239). *Bodice Ornament*, 1895–1905. French, possibly Maison Cartier. Diamonds, platinum, pearls; 12.1 x 5.1 cm. Collection of Neil Lane.

Cat. 309 (p. 101). *Butterfly Brooch*, 1895–1905. French. Diamonds, silver, gold; w. approximately 12 cm. Collection of Neil Lane.

Cat. 310 (p. 219). *Butterfly Brooch*, c. 1900. French. Gold, enamel, rubies, diamonds; 7 x 4 x 1 cm. Private collection.

Cat. 311 (p. 219). *Butterfly Brooch*, 1908. Probably Russian. Gold, enamel, diamonds, sapphires, rubies; 6.5 x 4.3 x 1.5 cm. Private collection.

Cat. 312 (p. 2). *Dragonfly Brooch*, 1895–1905. Probably French or German. Diamonds, demantoid garnets, other precious stones, platinum; 9.7 x 8 x 1.5 cm. Private collection.

Cat. 313 (p. 233). *Goblet*, c. 2nd–3rd century AD. Roman. Glass; h. 9 cm. The Cleveland Museum of Art, Gift of J. H. Wade, 1923.953.

Cat. 314 (pp. 180–81). *Large Pansy*, before 1919. French. Gold, jade, diamonds, enamel, rock crystal; 14 x 5.1 cm. The Cleveland Museum of Art, The India Early Minshall Collection, 1966.439.

Cat. 315 (p. 266). *Orchid Brooch*, 1890–1900. French, possibly the workshop of Georges Duval and Julien Le Turcq. Enamel, gold, diamonds; 6.5 x 5 x 3 cm. Private collection.

Cat. 316 (p. 174). *Snuffbox in the Form of a Horse Head*, c. 1750. Probably German. Hardstone, opal, gold, diamonds, rubies; h. 7 cm. Private collection.

Henry Van de Velde (Belgian, Brussels, Berlin, 1863–1957)
Van de Velde was schooled in architecture and painting in Paris under Carolus-Duran and at the Antwerp Academy. He began his painting career in 1889 and was associated with Les XX, a Brussels avant-garde group. By the 1890s, he was designing with Victor Horta in Belgium and later, interiors for Siegfried Bing in Paris. In 1894–95, Van de Velde began design work for furniture and for his own house, Bloemenwerf; the furniture went on to influence contemporaneous design. He designed three rooms for the inauguration of Bing's L'Art Nouveau gallery in 1895 and decorated Julius Meier-Graefe's La Maison Moderne in 1899. Van de Velde cofounded the Deutsche Werkbund in 1907, and his linear design work was popular in Germany, where he designed the Werkbund theater for the 1914 Cologne exhibition. He founded the École des Beaux-Arts de la Chambre and directed it until 1938.

Cat. 317 (p. 78). *Necklace*, 1902. Gold, blue sapphires, green amethysts; 7 x 11 cm. Die Neue Sammlung/State Museum of Applied Arts and Design, Design in the Pinakothek der Moderne, Munich, 116/62.

Maison Vever (French, Paris, 1821–1982)
Founded by Pierre Paul Vever in Metz in 1821, Maison Vever moved to Paris in 1870 under the directorship of Ernest Vever, who succeeded his father in 1848. Paul and Henri Vever partnered with their father, Ernest, in 1874, creating jewelry, belt buckles, combs, and other accessories in the Art Nouveau taste and with Asian and Renaissance influences. Lucien Gautrait, Eugène Grasset, and Tourette were employed at the firm as was Paul Grandhomme, who painted medallions in the Limoges school revival method. In 1878, Ernest served as a member of the jury at the Paris Exposition Universelle, where the firm also exhibited. In 1881, he passed his business on to his sons. The firm received grand prix at the 1889 and 1900 Paris world's fairs and exhibited at the 1891 Exposition Française in Moscow. Between 1906 and 1908, Henri Vever produced a catalogue of nineteenth-century Paris jewelers titled *La Bijouterie Française au XIXe Siècle*. In 1921, Henri relinquished the business to his nephews, André and Pierre.

Cat. 318 (p. 99). *Bodice Ornament*, c. 1900. Dogtooth pearls, plique-à-jour enamel, diamonds; 18 x 13 cm. Faerber Collection, 9423.

Cat. 319 (p. 99). *Bretonne Pendant*, 1899–1900. Gold, diamonds, opal, amethyst, enamel; 11.9 x 5.3 cm. Private collection.

Cat. 320 (p. 12). *Brooch*, 1890–95. Designer: René Lalique. Enamel, gold, diamonds; 11 x 4.5 x 1.5 cm. Private collection.

Julien Viard (French, Paris, 1883–1938)
The son of sculptor Clovis Viard, Julien produced designs for perfume bottles with figural and decorative stoppers, the first of which was trademarked in 1914. After World War I, father and son established a workshop that cold-finished high-temperature-fired glassworks. He designed bottles for Baccarat, Choisy-le-Roi, Cristalleries de Nancy, Dépinoix, Leune, and Pochet & du Courval, creating delicate flacons and stoppers featuring butterflies, flowers, insects, and reclining female nudes, all reminiscent of the work of René Lalique. During his Art Deco phase, Viard produced commissions with Spanish-influenced designs for Myrurgia and Cortes Hermanos, both of Barcelona. Throughout the 1920s, his work featured geometric forms with floral designs and eventually incorporated landscapes and bas-reliefs.

Cat. 321 (p. 125). *D'ara Perfume Bottle* (with original box), 1914. Perfumer: Tokalon. Molded clear glass, partially frosted, charcoal gray patina, perfume, paper, cardboard, leather, textile; h. 9.5 cm. Christie Mayer Lefkowith Collection.

Philippe Wolfers (Belgian, Brussels, 1858–1929)
Trained as a draftsman at the Académie Royale des Beaux-Arts in Brussels and a pupil of the sculptor Isidor de Rudder, Wolfers joined his father's business in 1875. Louis Wolfers was the director of Wolfers Frères, founded in 1812. Philippe applied Rococo, then naturalism and Japanese influences to his pieces. He became art director of the family firm, which he ran, along with his two brothers, after their father's death in 1892. Around the turn of the century, Wolfers Frères produced Art Nouveau pieces with Belgian influences. In 1899, Philippe established an Art Nouveau villa in La Hulpe, Belgium, and later a workshop in the Square Marie Louise. He worked in sculpture after 1908, following years of exhibiting. He participated in the 1889 Paris exposition, the 1894 Antwerp international exhibition, the 1897 International Exhibition in Brussels, the 1898 and 1899 Munich Secession exhibitions, and the 1902 First International Exposition of Modern Decorative Arts in Turin. Wolfers worked in neoclassical and "Gioconda-Art Décoratif" designs in the 1920s and displayed a room of household furnishings at the 1925

Cat. 322 (p. 147). *Butterfly Brooch*, 1906. Gold, enamel, opals, brilliants; 9.5 x 10.5 x 2.4 cm. The Anderson Collection of Art Nouveau, University of East Anglia, Norwich, UEA 21150.

Select Bibliography

Contemporary Publications

Abdy, Jane. "Sarah Bernhardt and Lalique: A Confusion of Evidence." *Apollo* 125 (1987): 325–30.

Agarkova, Galina, and Natalya Petrova. *250 Years of Lomonosov Porcelain Manufacture, St. Petersburg 1774–1994.* Switzerland: Desertina, 1994.

Arwas, Victor. *Art Nouveau from Mackintosh to Liberty: The Birth of a Style.* London: Andreas Papedakis, 2000.

Ashbee, C. R. *Modern English Silverwork: An Essay by C. R. Ashbee.* London: B. Weinreb, 1974.

Badea-Päun, Gabriel. *The Society Portrait: From David to Warhol.* New York: Vendome, 2007.

Bainbridge, H[enry] C[harles]. *Peter Carl Fabergé, Goldsmith and Jeweller to the Russian Imperial Court and the Principal Crowned Heads of Europe. His Life and Work.* London: Batsford, 1949.

Balsan, Consuelo Vanderbilt. *The Glitter and the Gold.* Maidstone, U.K.: George Mann, 1973.

Barten, Sigrid. *René Lalique: Schmuck und Objets d'art, 1890–1910.* Munich: Prestel, 1977.

Bayer, Patricia, and Mark Waller. *The Art of René Lalique.* London: Quintet, 1988.

Becker, Vivian. *The Jewellery of René Lalique.* London: Goldsmith's, 1987.

Beckett, J., and Deborah Cherry, eds. *The Edwardian Era.* Exh. cat., Barbican Art Gallery. London: Phaidon, 1987.

Berlanstein, Lenard R. *Daughters of Eve: A Cultural History of French Theater Women from the Old Regime to the Fin-de-Siècle.* London: Harvard University Press, 2001.

Billcliffe, Roger, and Peter Vergo. "Charles Rennie Mackintosh and the Austrian Art Revival." *Burlington Magazine* 119, no. 896 (1977): 739–46.

Bing, Samuel [Siegfried]. "La Culture Artistique en Amerique." Trans. Benita Eisler. In *Artistic America, Tiffany Glass, and Art Nouveau*, 1–193. Cambridge, Mass.: MIT Press, 1970.

Blades, John M., and John Loring. *Tiffany at the World's Columbian Exposition.* Exh. cat. Palm Beach, Fla.: Henry Morrison Flagler Museum, 2006.

Bolin, Christian, and Pavel Bulatov, eds. *W. A. Bolin: Bolin in Russia, Court Jeweller, Late XIX–Early XX Centuries.* Exh. cat., Kremlin Museums. Moscow: New Hermitage-one, 2001.

Borisova, Elena A., and Grigory Sternin. *Russian Art Nouveau.* Trans. Michael Taylor. New York: Rizzoli, 1987.

Bossaglia, Rossana. *Torino. 1902: Le arti decorative internazionali del nuovo secolo.* Milan: Fabbri, 1994.

Breward, Christopher. "The Case of the Hidden Consumer: Men, Fashion, and Luxury, 1870–1974." In *Representations of Gender from Pre-History to the Present*, ed. Moria Donald and Linda Hurcombe, 183–97. New York: Saint Martin's Press, 2000.

Brumfield, William. "The Decorative Arts in Russian Architecture: 1900–1907." *Journal of Decorative and Propaganda Arts*, no. 5 (1987): 12–27.

Brunhammer, Yvonne, ed. *The Jewels of Lalique.* Exh. cat. Paris/New York: Flammarion, 1998.

———, ed. *René Lalique: Bijoux d'exception 1890–1912.* Exh. cat. Paris: Musée du Luxembourg, 2007. English ed. *René Lalique, Exceptional Jewellery, 1890–1912.* Milan: Skira, 2007.

———, et al. *René Lalique, Bijoux, Verre.* Exh. cat. Paris: Musée des Arts Décoratifs, 1991.

Bullen, J. B. "Louis Comfort Tiffany and Romano-Byzantine Design." *Burlington Magazine* 147 (2005): 390–98.

Burns, Sarah. *Inventing the Modern Artist: Art and Culture in Gilded Age America.* New Haven: Yale University Press, 1996.

Bury, Shirley. *Jewellery, 1789–1910: The International Era.* 2 vols. Woodbridge, U.K.: Antique Collectors' Club, 1991.

Calloway, Stephen, ed. *The House of Liberty: Masters of Style and Decoration.* London: Thames and Hudson, 1992.

Carpenter, Charles H., Jr. *Gorham Silver, 1831–1981.* New York: Dodd, Mead, 1982.

Carpenter, Charles H., Jr., and Janet Zapata. *The Silver of Tiffany and Co., 1850–1987.* Exh. cat. Boston: Museum of Fine Arts, 1987.

Chaille, François. *La Collection Cartier—Joaillerie.* Paris: Flammarion, 2004.

Chazal, Gilles, et al. *L'Art de Cartier.* Exh. cat. Paris: Musée du Petit-Palais, 1989.

———. *Splendeurs de Russie: Mille ans d'orfèvrerie.* Exh. cat. Paris: Musée du Petit Palais, 1993.

Ciofi degli Atti, Fabio. *Fabergé e l'Arte Orafa alla Corte degli Zar.* Genoa: Colombo, 1992.

Citroen, K. A. "Lalique et Baudelaire: Quelques Réflexions sur un bijou art nouveau." *Simiolus: Netherlands Quarterly for the History of Art* 1, no. 3 (1966–67): 153–56.

Clarke, William. *The Lost Fortune of the Tsars.* New York: St. Martin's Press, 1994.

Cologni, Franco, et al. *Cartier: Splendeurs de la Joaillerie.* Lausanne: Bibliothèque des Arts, 1996.

Conklin, Lawrence H. "Kunz and Kunzite." *Mineralogical Record* 18 (1987): 369–72.

Curry, David Park. "Tiffany's Golden Bowl." *Antiques* 151 (January 1997): 244–47n13.

Danziger, Pamela. *Let Them Eat Cake: Marketing Luxury to the Masses as well as the Classes.* Chicago: Dearborn Trade, 2005.

Dawes, Nicholas M., ed. *Lalique: A Century of Glass for a Modern World.* Exh. cat. New York: Paul-Art Press, 1989.

———. *Lalique Glass.* New York: Crown, 1986.

Dell, Simon. "The Consumer and the Making of the Exposition Internationale des Arts Décoratifs et Industriels Modernes, 1907–1925." *Journal of Design History* 12, no. 4 (1999): 311–25.

Dennis, Jessie McNab. "Fabergé's Objects of Fantasy." *Metropolitan Museum of Art Bulletin* 23, no. 7 (1965): 229–42.

Denvir, Bernard. *The Late Victorians: Art, Design and Society, 1852–1910.* London/New York: Longman, 1986.

Dietz, Ulysses Grant, et al. *The Glitter and the Gold: Fashioning America's Jewelry.* Exh. cat. Newark: Newark Museum, 1997.

Duncan, Alastair. *Louis Comfort Tiffany.* New York: Abrams, 1992.

———. *Louis C. Tiffany: The Garden Museum Collection.* Woodbridge, U.K.: Antique Collectors' Club, 2004.

———, et al. *Masterworks of Louis Comfort Tiffany.* Exh. cat., Renwick Gallery. New York: Abrams, 1989.

———. *The Paris Salons, 1895–1914: Jewellery, The Designers A–K.* Woodbridge, U.K.: Antique Collectors' Club, 1994.

———. *The Paris Salons, 1895–1914: Jewellery, The Designers L–Z.* Woodbridge, U.K.: Antique Collectors' Club, 1994.

———. *The Paris Salons, 1895–1914,* vol. 4, *Ceramics and Glass.* Woodbridge, Eng: Antique Collectors' Club, 1998.

———. *The Paris Salons 1895–1914,* vol. 5, *Objets d'art and Metalware.* Woodbridge, U.K.: Antique Collectors' Club, 1999.

———. *Tiffany Lamps and Metalware: An Illustrated Reference to Over 2,000 Models.* Woodbridge, U.K.: Antique Collectors' Club, 2006.

Duncan, Alastair, and Georges de Bartha. *Glass by Gallé.* New York: Abrams, 1984.

Eadie, William. *Movements of Modernity: The Case of Glasgow and Art Nouveau.* London/New York: Routledge, 1990.

Eidelberg, Martin. *E. Colonna.* Exh. cat. Dayton, Ohio: Dayton Art Institute, 1984.

———. "Tiffany's Early Glass Vessels." *Antiques* 137 (February 1990): 500–15.

———, et al. *A New Light on Tiffany: Clara Driscoll and the Tiffany Girls.* Exh. cat. New York: New-York Historical Society in association with D. Giles, 2007.

Eidelberg, Martin, and Nancy A. McClelland, eds. *Behind the Scenes of Tiffany Glassmaking: The Nash Notebooks.* New York: St. Martin's Press, 2001.

Emboden, William. *Sarah Bernhardt.* Macmillan: New York, 1975.

Fabergé, 1846–1920: Goldsmith to the Imperial Court of Russia. Introduction by A. Kenneth Snowman. Exh. cat. London: Debrett's Peerage, in association with the Victoria and Albert Museum, 1977.

Fabergé: The Imperial Eggs. Essays by Christopher Forbes, Johann Georg Prinz von Hohenzollern, and Irina Rodimtseva. Exh. cat., San Diego Museum of Art/Armory Palace, Kremlin Museum, Moscow. Munich: Prestel, 1989.

The Fabergé Menagerie. Exhibition organized by William R. Johnston. Exh. cat., Walters Art Museum, Baltimore, and tour. London: Philip Wilson, 2003.

Fabergé, Tatiana, et al. *The Era of Fabergé.* Moscow: Museum Centre Vapriiki, 2006.

———. *The Fabergé Imperial Easter Eggs.* London: Christie's, 1997.

Falino, Jeannine, and Yvonne Markowitz, eds. *American Luxury: Jewels from the House of Tiffany.* Woodbridge, U.K.: Antique Collectors' Club, 2008.

Feldstein, William, Jr., and Alastair Duncan. *The Lamps of Tiffany Studios.* New York: Abrams, 1983.

Ferreira, Maria Teresa Gomes. *Art Nouveau Jewelry by René Lalique.* Exh. cat. Washington, D.C.: International Exhibitions Foundation, 1985.

Fischer, Diane P., ed. *Paris 1900: The "American School" at the Universal Exposition.* Exh. cat., Montclair Art Museum and tour. New Brunswick, N.J.: Rutgers University Press, 2000.

Forbes, Christopher, and Robyn Tromeur-Brenner. *Fabergé: The Forbes Collection.* New York: Hugh Lauter Levin, 1999.

Francotte-Florence, Jacqueline. *Le Bijou Art Nouveau en Europe.* Paris: La Bibliothèque des Arts, 1998.

Frelinghuysen, Alice Cooney. "The Early Artistic Jewelry of Louis C. Tiffany." *Antiques* 165 (July 2002): 90–95.

———. *Louis Comfort Tiffany and Laurelton Hall: An Artist's Country Estate.* Exh. cat. New York/New Haven/London: Metropolitan Museum of Art/Yale University Press, 2006.

———, et al. *Splendid Legacy: The Havemeyer Collection.* New York: Metropolitan Museum of Art, 1993.

Gary, Marie-Noël de, et al. *Les Fouquet: Bijoutiers et Joailliers à Paris 1860–1960.* Exh. cat. Paris: Musée des Arts Décoratifs, 1983.

Geitner, Amanda, and Emma Hazell. *The Anderson Collection of Art Nouveau.* Norwich, U.K.: Sainsbury Centre for Visual Arts, University of East Anglia, 2003.

Gere, Charlotte. *European and American Jewellery 1830–1914.* London: Heinemann, 1975.

Gere, Charlotte, and Geoffrey C. Munn. *Pre-Raphaelite to Arts and Crafts Jewellery.* Woodbridge, U.K.: Antique Collectors' Club, 1996.

Gilodo, Andrei. *Russian Silver, Mid 19th Century–Beginning of the 20th Century.* Exh. cat., All-Russian Decorative, Applied, and Folk Art Museum. Moscow: Beresta, 1994.

Greenhalgh, Paul, ed. *Art Nouveau: 1890–1914.* Exh. cat. London: Victoria and Albert Museum, 2000.

Guitaut, Caroline de. *Fabergé in the Royal Collection.* London: Royal Collection, 2003.

Habsburg, Géza von. *Fabergé.* Geneva/New York: Habsburg, Feldman Eds./Vendome, 1987. Translation of *Fabergé, Hofjuwelier der Zaren.* Exh. cat., Bavarian National Museum/Kunsthalle der Hypo-Kulturstiftung Munich, 1986.

———, ed. *Fabergé–Cartier, Rivalen am Zarenhof.* Exh. cat., Kunsthalle der Hypo-Kulturstiftung Munich. Hirmer, 2003.

———. *Fabergé: Imperial Craftsman and His World.* Exh. cat., American tour. London: Booth-Clibborn Editions, 2000.

———. *Fabergé in America.* Exh. cat., Fine Arts Museums of San Francisco and tour. London: Thames and Hudson, 1996.

———. *Fabergé: Then and Now.* Munich: Hirmer, 2004.

———. *Fabergé: Treasures of Imperial Russia.* Exh. cat., Armory Palace, Kremlin Museum, Moscow, and tour. Moscow: Sviaz' vremen, 2004.

———. *Fabergé: Treasures of Imperial Russia.* Moscow: Link of Times Foundation, 2005.

Habsburg, Géza von, and Alexander von Solodkoff. *Fabergé: Court Jeweler to the Tsars.* New York: Rizzoli, 1979.

Habsburg, Géza von, and Marina Lopato. *Fabergé: Imperial Jeweller.* Exh. cat., State Hermitage Museum and tour. Alexandria, Va: Art Services International, 1993.

Hatch, Carolyn. "René Lalique and French Modernism in Canada." *Antiques* 170 (October 2006): 98–107.

Hawley, Henry. *Fabergé and His Contemporaries: The India Early Minshall Collection of The Cleveland Museum of Art.* Cleveland: Cleveland Museum of Art, 1967.

Hennessey, William J. *The Havemeyer Tiffany Collection at the University of Michigan Museum of Art.* Ann Arbor: University of Michigan Museum of Art, 1992.

Hill, Gerard, ed. *Fabergé and the Russian Master Goldsmiths.* New York: Macmillan, 1989.

Hillier, Bevis, and Stephen Escritt. *Art Nouveau.* London: Phaidon, 2000.

Hinks, Peter. *Nineteenth Century Jewellery.* London: Faber and Faber, 1975.

———. *Twentieth Century British Jewellery, 1900–1980.* London: Faber and Faber, 1983.

Huey, Michael, ed. *Viennese Silver: Modern Design, 1780–1918.* Exh. cat., Neue Gallery, New York/ Kunsthistorisches Museum Vienna. Ostfildern-Ruit, Ger.: Hatje Cantz, 2003.

Hurel, Roselyne, and Diana Scarisbrick. *Chaumet Paris deux siècles de création.* Exh. cat. Paris: Musée Carnavalet, 1998.

Ivanov, Alexander Nikolaievich. *Unknown Fabergé.* Moscow: Published for the Russian National Museum, 2002.

Janson, Dora Jane. *From Slave to Siren: The Victorian Woman and Her Jewelry from Neoclassic to Art Nouveau.* Exh. cat. Durham, N.C.: Duke University Museum of Art, 1971.

Johnson, Marilynn A. *Louis Comfort Tiffany: Artist for the Ages.* Exh. cat., Seattle Art Museum and tour. London: Scala, 2005.

Johnston, William R. *William and Henry Walters, the Reticent Collectors.* Baltimore/London: Johns Hopkins University Press, in association with the Walters Art Gallery, 1999.

Kaplan, Wendy. *The Arts and Crafts Movement in Europe and America: Design for the Modern World.* Exh. cat. Los Angeles/ London: Los Angeles County Museum of Art/Thames and Hudson, 2004.

———. *"The Art that Is Life": The Arts and Crafts Movement in America, 1875–1920.* Exh. cat. Boston: Museum of Fine Arts, 1987.

Kashey, Elisabeth. *Füssli through Tiffany: Nineteenth- and Early Twentieth-Century Paintings, Drawings and Sculpture.* Exh. cat. New York: Shepherd Gallery, 1987.

Keefe, John Webster. *Masterpieces of Fabergé: The Matilda Geddings Gray Foundation Collection.* New Orleans: New Orleans Museum of Art, 1993.

Kettering, Karen L. "Decoration and Disconnection: The Russkii stil' and Russian Decorative Arts at Nineteenth-Century American World Fairs." In *Russian Art and the West: A Century of Dialogue in Painting, Architecture, and the Decorative Arts,* ed. Rosalind P. Blakesley and Susan E. Reid, 61–85. DeKalb: Northern Illinois University Press, 2007.

———. *Russian Glass at Hillwood.* Washington, D.C.: Hillwood Museum and Gardens, 2001.

Koch, Michael. "The Rediscovery of Lalique's Jewelry." Trans. Rosemary FitzGibbon. *Journal of Decorative and Propaganda Arts,* no. 10 (1988): 28–41.

Koch, Robert. *Louis C. Tiffany's Art Glass.* New York: Crown, 1976.

Krasov, Emma, et al. *Kremlin Gold: 1000 Years of Russian Gems and Jewels.* Exh. cat., Houston Museum of Natural Science/Field Museum, Chicago. New York: Abrams, 2000.

Kratz, Anne. *Le Commerce Franco-Russe: Concurrence & Contrefaçons.* Paris: Les Belles Lettres, 2006.

Krogsgaard, Michael, and Liv Carøe, eds. *The Unknown Georg Jensen.* Exh. cat., Øregaard Museum Denmark: Special-Trykkeriet Viborg, 2004.

Lalique Gallery. Lisbon: Calouste Gulbenkian Museum, 1997.

Landman, Neil H., et al. *Pearls: A Natural History.* New York: Abrams, 2001.

Lehner, Ernst, and Johanna Lehner. *Folklore and Symbolism of Flowers, Plants and Trees.* New York: Tudor, 1960.

Livingstone, Karen, and Linda Parry, eds. *International Arts and Crafts.* Exh. cat. London: Victoria and Albert Museum, 2005.

Loring, John. *Louis Comfort Tiffany at Tiffany & Co.* New York: Abrams, 2002.

———. *Paulding Farnham: Tiffany's Lost Genius.* New York: Abrams, 2000.

Marcilhac, Félix. *Réne Lalique 1860–1945, maître-verrier analyse de l'oeuvre et catalogue raisonné.* Paris: Les Editions de l'Amateur, 1989.

Martin, Steven A., ed. *Archibald Knox.* London: ArtMedia, 2001.

Mayer, A., and Carolyn K. Lane. "Disassociating the 'Associated Artists': The Early Business Ventures of Louis C. Tiffany, Candace T. Wheeler, and Lockwood de Forest." *Studies in the Decorative Arts* 8, no. 2 (2001): 2–36.

McCanless, Christel Ludewig. *Fabergé and His Works: An Annotated Bibliography of the First Century of His Art.* Metuchen, N.J./London: Scarecrow, 1994.

McCarthy, Kieran. "Fabergé in London." *Apollo* 169, no. 533 (2006): 34–39.

McKean, Hugh F. *The "Lost" Treasures of Louis Comfort Tiffany*. Exh. cat., Museum of Science and Industry, Chicago. New York: Doubleday, 1980.

Michael of Greece, Prince. *Jewels of the Tsars: The Romanovs and Imperial Russia*. Trans. Barbara Mellor. New York: Vendome, 2006.

Michman, Ronald, and Edward M. Mazze. *The Affluent Consumer: Marketing and Selling the Luxury Lifestyle*. Westport, Conn.: Praeger, 2006.

Moncrieff, Elspeth. "The Grandest Gift Shop in the World: Fabergé in London, and Wartski's." *Apollo* 136 (1992): 390–92.

Morel, Bernard. *The French Crown Jewels*. Antwerp: Fonds Mercator, 1989.

Mucha, Sarah. *Alphonse Mucha*. London: Mucha Foundation, 2005.

Mukhin, V. V., ed. *The Fabulous Epoch of Fabergé: St. Petersburg–Paris–Moscow*. Exh. cat., Catherine Palace, Tsarskoe Selo. Moscow: Nord, 1992.

Munn, Geoffrey C. *Castellani and Giuliano: Revivalist Jewellers of the Nineteenth-Century*. Exh. cat., Wartski, London. New York: Rizzoli, 1984.

———, et al. *Fabergé and the Russian Jewellers: An Exhibition in Aid of Samaritans*. Exh. cat. London: Wartski, 2006.

———. "The Jewelry of René Lalique." *Antiques* 131 (June 1987): 1288–291.

———. *Tiaras: A History of Splendor*. Woodbridge, U.K.: Antique Collectors' Club, 2001.

———. *Tiaras: Past and Present*. London: V&A Publications, 2002.

———. *The Triumph of Love: Jewelry 1530–1930*. London: Thames and Hudson, 1993.

Muntian, Tatiana, et al. *Fabergé. Joaillier des Romanov*. Exh. cat., Espace Culturel ING. Brussels: Europalia International/Fonds Mercator, 2005.

Murrell, Kathleen Berton. *Moscow Art Nouveau*. London: Philip Wilson, 1996.

Nadelhoffer, Hans. *Cartier: Jewelers Extraordinary*. New York: Abrams, 1984.

Neiswander, Judith A. "Fantastic Malady or Competitive Edge?: English Outrage at Art Nouveau in 1901." *Apollo* 128 (1988): 310–13.

Néret, Gilles. *Boucheron: Four Generations of a World-Renowned Jeweler*. New York: Rizzoli, 1988.

Nunn, Pamela Gerrish. "Fine Art and the Fan, 1860–1930." *Journal of Design History* 17, no. 3 (2004): 251–66.

Ockman, Carol, and Kenneth E. Silver. *Sarah Bernhardt: The Art of High Drama*. Exh. cat., Jewish Museum, New York. New Haven: Yale University Press, 2005.

Odom, Anne, et al. *Fabergé and the Russian Jewellers: An Exhibition in Aid of Samaritans*. Exh. cat. London: Wartski, 2006.

———. *Fabergé at Hillwood*. Washington, D.C.: Hillwood Museum and Gardens, 1996.

———. *Russian Enamels: Kievan Rus to Fabergé*. Exh. cat. London/Baltimore/Washington, D.C.: Philip Wilson/Walters Art Gallery/Hillwood Museum, 1996.

———. "Russkii stil': The Russian Style for Export— Hillwood Museum and Gardens," *Antiques* 163 (March 2003): 102–7.

Odom, Anne, and Jean M. Riddell. *Old Russian Enamels: Nationalism and the Decorative Arts Revival in 19th-Century Moscow*. Exh. cat. Richmond: Virginia Museum of Fine Arts, 1987.

Owen, Nancy E. *Rookwood and the Industry of Art: Women, Culture, and Commerce, 1880–1913*. Athens: Ohio University Press, 2001.

Papi, Stefano, and Alexandra Rhodes. *Famous Jewelry Collectors*. New York: Abrams, 1999.

Parrott, Lindsy Riepma. "The Ceramics of Louis Comfort Tiffany." *Nineteenth Century* 26, no. 1 (2006): 2–11.

Pfeffer, Susanna. *Fabergé Eggs: Masterpieces from Czarist Russia*. Fairfield, Conn.: Hugh Lauter Levin Associates, 1990.

Phillips, Claire, ed. *Bejewelled by Tiffany 1837–1987*. Exh. cat., Gilbert Collection. New Haven/London: Yale University Press/Gilbert Collection Trust/Tiffany & Co., 2006.

———. *Jewels and Jewelry*. New York: Watson-Guptill, 2000.

Possémé, Evelyne. *La Maison Keller*. Paris, 2000.

Price, Joan Elliott. *Louis Comfort Tiffany: The Painting Career of a Colorist*. New York: Peter Lang, 1996.

Proddow, Penny, and Debra Healy. *American Jewelry: Glamour and Tradition*. New York: Rizzoli, 1987.

———. "Tiffany's Orchids of 1889." *Antiques* 133 (April 1988): 900–905.

Prokhorenko, G., and G. Vlasova. *Baron Stieglitz Museum, The Past and the Present*. St. Petersburg: Sezar, 1994.

Purcell, Katherine. *Falize: A Dynasty of Jewelers*. Exh. cat., Wartski, London. London: Thames and Hudson, 1999.

———, trans. *French Jewellery of the Nineteenth Century*. London: Wartski, 2001. Translation of Henri Vever, *La bijouterie française au XIX siècle*. Paris: H. Floury, 1908.

Roberts, Ellen E. "A Marriage of 'The Extreme East and the Extreme West': Japanism and Aestheticism in Louis Comfort Tiffany's Rooms in the Bella Apartments." *Studies in the Decorative Arts* 13, no. 2 (2006): 2–51.

Rodoe, Judy. *Cartier, 1900–1939*. Exh. cat., Metropolitan Museum of Art. New York: Abrams, 1997.

Rosasco, Joan T. "Lalique and the Artistic Jewel." *Antiques* 153 (February 1998): 284–91.

Rydell, Robert W. *The Book of the Fairs: Materials about World's Fairs, 1834–1916, in the Smithsonian Institution Libraries*. Chicago/London: American Library Association, 1992.

———, et al. *Revisiting the White City: American Art at the 1893 World's Fair*. Exh. cat., National Museum of American Art, Smithsonian Institution. Hanover, N.H./London: University Press of New England, 1993.

Saisselin, Rémy G. *The Bourgeois and the Bibelot*. New Brunswick, N.J.: Rutgers University Press, 1984.

Salmond, Wendy R. *Arts and Crafts in Late Imperial Russia: Reviving the Kustar Art Industries, 1870–1917*. New York: Cambridge University Press, 1996.

Scarisbrick, Diana. *Chaumet, joaillier depuis 1780*. Paris: Alain de Gourcuff, 1995.

———, et al. *Jewellery: Makers, Motifs, History, Techniques*. London: Thames and Hudson, 1989.

———. "René Lalique in London: Agnew's 1905." *Apollo* 126 (1987): 16–19.

Schaefer, Herwin. "Tiffany's Fame in Europe." *Art Bulletin* 44, no. 4 (1962): 309–28.

Smorodinova, Galina. "Gold and Silverwork in Moscow at the Turn of the Century." *Journal of Decorative and Propaganda Arts*, no. 11 (1989), 30–49.

Snowman, A. Kenneth. "Carl Fabergé in London." *Nineteenth Century* 3 (Philadelphia), no. 2 (1977): 50–55.

———. *Fabergé, Jeweler to Royalty: From the Collection of Her Majesty Queen Elizabeth II and Other British Lenders*. Exh. cat., Cooper-Hewitt Museum. Washington, D.C.: Smithsonian Institution Press, 1983.

———. *Fabergé: Lost and Found, The Recently Discovered Jewelry Designs for the St. Petersburg Archives*. New York: Abrams, 1993.

———. "Two Books of Revelations: The Fabergé Stock." *Apollo* 126 (1987): 150–61.

Solodkoff, Alexander von. *The Art of Carl Fabergé*. New York: Crown, 1988.

———. *Fabergé Juwelier des Zarenhofes*. Exh. cat. Heidelberg/Hamburg: Edition Braus/Museum fur Kunst und Gewerbe, 1995.

———. "Fabergé's London Branch." *Connoisseur* 209, no. 840 (1982): 102–11.

———. *Masterpieces from the House of Fabergé*. New York: Abrams, 1984.

———. *Russian Gold and Silverwork, 17th–19th Century*. Trans. Christopher Holme. New York/London: Rizzoli/Trefoil Books, 1981.

Soros, Susan Weber, and Stefanie Walker, eds. *Castellani and Italian Archaeological Jewelry*. Exh. cat., Corning Museum of Glass. New Haven: Yale University Press, 2004.

Spillman, Jane Shadel. *Glass from World's Fairs, 1851–1904*. Corning, N.Y.: Corning Museum of Glass, 1986.

Stover, Donald L. *The Art of Louis Comfort Tiffany*. Exh. cat. San Francisco: Fine Arts Museum of San Francisco, 1981.

Stuart, Amanda Mackenzie. *Consuelo and Alva Vanderbilt: The Story of a Daughter and a Mother in the Gilded Age*. New York: Harper Collins, 2005.

Swezey, Marilyn Pfeifer. *Fabergé Flowers*. New York: Abrams, 2004.

Swift, Vivian. "Alma Pihl's Designs for Fabergé." *Antiques* 149 (January 1996): 176–81.

Tarasova, Nina. *Nicholas and Alexandra: The Last Tsar and Tsarina*. Exh. cat., National Museums of Scotland, Edinburgh. Burlington, Vt.: Lund Humphries, 2005.

Taylor, David A., ed. *Georg Jensen Jewelry*. Exh. cat., Bard Center for Studies in the Decorative Arts, Design, and Culture. New Haven/London: Yale University Press, 2005.

Tennenbaum, Suzanne, and Janet Zapata. *The Jeweled Garden*. London: Thames and Hudson, 2006.

———. *The Jeweled Menagerie: The World of Animals in Gems*. London: Thames and Hudson, 2001.

Thiébaut, Philippe. "Le Style Moderne Russe et l'Art Nouveau Européen." In *L'Art Russe dans la Seconde Moitié du XIXe Siècle: en Quête d'Identité*. Paris: Musée d'Orsay, 2005.

———. *René Lalique: Correspondance d'un Bijoutier Art Nouveau, 1890–1908*. Paris: La Bibliothèque des Arts, 2007.

Tillander-Godenhielm, Ulla, et al. *Golden Years of Fabergé*. New York/Paris: A La Vieille Russie/Alain de Gourcuff Editeur, 2000.

Tittle, Diana. *The Jeptha Wade Memorial Chapel*. Cleveland: Lake View Cemetery Association, 2003.

Troy, Nancy, J. *Modernism and the Decorative Arts in France: Art Nouveau to Le Corbusier*. New Haven/London: Yale University Press, 1991.

———. "Towards a Redefinition of Tradition in French Design, 1895 to 1914." *Design Issues* 1, no. 2 (1984): 53–69.

Turner, Eric, et al. *Silver of a New Era: International Highlights of Precious Metalware from 1880–1940*. Exh. cat., Museum Boymans-Van Beuningen, Rotterdam. Seattle: University of Washington Press, 1992.

Valkenier, Elizabeth Kridl. "Opening up to Europe: The Peredvizhniki and the Miriskusniki Respond to the West." In *Russian Art and the West: A Century of Dialogue in Painting, Architecture, and the Decorative Arts*, ed. Rosalind P. Blakesley and Susan E. Reid, 45–60. DeKalb: Northern Illinois University Press, 2007.

Varndoe, Kirk. *Vienna 1900: Art, Architecture & Design*. New York: Museum of Modern Art, 1986.

Vélez, Pilar. *Masriera Jewellery: 200 Years of History*. Trans. Elaine Fradley. Barcelona; Àmbit, 1999.

Venable, Charles, et al. *Silver in America 1840–1940: A Century of Splendor*. Dallas: Dallas Museum of Art, 1994.

Vilinbakhov, George. *Nicholas and Alexandra: The Last Imperial Family of Tsarist Russia*. Exh. cat., State Hermitage Museum. New York: Abrams, 1998.

Viruega, Jacqueline. *La Bijouterie Parisienne 1860–1914: Du Second Empire à la Première Guerre mondiale*. Paris: L'Harmattan, 2004.

Weisberg, Gabriel P. *Art Nouveau Bing: Paris Style 1900*. Exh. cat. New York/Washington, D.C.: Abrams, in association with the Smithsonian Traveling Exhibition Service, 1987.

———. "Italy and France: The Cosmopolitanism of the New Art." *Journal of Decorative and Propaganda Arts*, no. 13, (1989), 110–27.

———. "Lost and Found: S. Bing's Merchandising of Japonisme and Art Nouveau." *Nineteenth-Century Art Worldwide* 4/2, no. 6 (2005). http://www.19thc-artworldwide.org/summer_05/articles/weis.shtml.

———, et al., eds. *The Origins of L'Art Nouveau: The Bing Empire.* Exh. cat. Amsterdam/Paris/Antwerp: Van Gogh Museum/Musée des Arts Décoratifs/Mercatorfonds, 2004.

———. "S. Bing and *La Culture Artistique en Amerique:* A Public Report Reexamined." *Arts Magazine* 61 (1987): 59–63.

———. "S. Bing in America." In *The Documented Image: Visions in Art History,* ed. Gabriel P. Weisberg and Laurinda S. Dixon, 51–68. Syracuse: Syracuse University Press, 1987.

———. "Siegfried Bing and Industry: The Hidden Side of L'Art Nouveau." *Apollo* 128 (1988): 326–29.

Welander-Berggren, Elsebeth, ed. *Carl Fabergé: Goldsmith to the Tsar.* Exh. cat., Nationalmuseum, Stockholm. Arlöv: Berlings Grafiska, 1997.

Williams, Robert C. *Russia Imagined: Art, Culture, and National Identity, 1840–1995.* New York: Peter Lang, 1997.

Wolfers, Marcel. *Philippe Wolfers: Précurseur de l'art nouveau.* Exh. cat., Museum voor Sierkuns, Ghent. Brussels, 1965.

World's Fair of 1900: General Catalogue. New York/London: Garland, 1981.

Yermilova, Larissa. *The Last Tsar.* London: Sirocco, 2002.

Zapata, Janet. "American Plique-à-jour Enameling." *Antiques* 150 (December 1996): 812–21.

———. *The Jewelry and Enamels of Louis Comfort Tiffany.* New York: Abrams, 1993.

———. "The Jewelry and Silver of F. Walter Lawrence." *Antiques* 164 (April 2004): 124–33.

———. "The Legacy of Herman Marcus and Marcus and Company: Part 1, The Early Years, 1850–1892." *Antiques* 172 (August 2007): 68–77.

———. "The Legacy of Herman Marcus and Marcus and Company: Part 2, The Marcus and Company Years, 1892–1941." *Antiques* 172 (September 2007): 92–101.

———. "The Opal: Louis Comfort Tiffany's Lens to a World of Color." *Antiques* 144 (September 1993): 318–27.

———. "The Rediscovery of Paulding Farnham, Tiffany's Designer Extraordinaire: Part 2, Silver." *Antiques* 139 (April 1991): 719–29.

Zeisler, Wilfried. "Fabergé et l'alliance franco-russe." *La revue des musées de France: Revue du Louvre,* no. 3 (2005): 39–45 and 69–75.

Period Publications

The Adams Gold Vase. New York: Tiffany & Co., Exposition Universelle, 1900.

Bancroft, Hubert Howe. *The Book of the Fair.* Chicago: Bancroft, 1893.

Bapst, Germain. *The French Crown Jewels: Histoire des Joyaux de la Couronne de France, d'Apres des Documents Inedits.* Paris: Librairie Hachette et Cie, 1891.

Champier, V. "Introduction" and "The Decorative Arts." In *The Chefs-d'oeuvre: Exposition universelle 1900.* Philadelphia: George Barrie and Son, c. 1902.

Gallé, Émile. *Écrits pour l'Art, floriculture-art décoratif notices d'exposition (1884–1889).* Paris: Librairie Renouard, H. Laurens, 1908.

Geoffroy, Gustave. *Les industries artistiques françaises et étrangères à l'Exposition Universelle de 1900.* Paris: Librairie Centrale des Beaux-Arts, 1900.

Hallays, André. *A travers l'Exposition de 1900.* Paris: Perrin et Cie, 1901.

Heydt, George Frederick. *Charles L. Tiffany and the House of Tiffany and Co.* New York: Tiffany, 1893.

Iribe, Paul. *Défense de Luxe.* Paris, 1902.

King, C. W. *The Natural History, Ancient and Modern, of Precious Stones and Gems, and of Precious Metals.* London: Bell and Daldy, 1865.

Kunz, George F. "American Pearls." *Science* 4, no. 89 (1884): 368.

———. *The Curious Lore of Precious Stones.* Philadelphia/London: J. B. Lippincott, 1913.

———. "International Economic Importance of Precious Stones in Times of War and Revolution." *Scientific Monthly* 12, no. 3 (1921): 239–40.

———. "Review of Gems and Precious Stones of North America." *Science* 16, no. 387 (1890): 11.

———. *Shakespeare and Precious Stones.* Philadelphia/London: J. B. Lippincott, 1916.

Langtry, Lillie. *The Days I Knew.* 2nd ed. London: Hutchinson and Co., 1925.

McAllister, Samuel Ward. *Society as I have Found It.* New York: Cassell Publishing, 1890.

Meier-Graefe, Julius. *Modern Art: Being a Contribution to the New System of Aesthetics.* London: Heinemann, 1908.

"Monograph on the Evolution of Taste in Decorations and Furnishings." In *Character and Individuality of Decorations and Furnishings.* New York: Tiffany Studios, 1913.

Montesquiou, Robert de. *Roseaux Pensants.* Paris: Bibliothèque-Charpentier, 1897.

Nielsen, Laurits C. *George Jensen: Une biographie d'artiste.* Copenhagen, 1920.

"Sentiments and Superstitions in Precious Stones." *Illustrated American* 18, no. 286 (1895): 188.

Velde, Henry Van de. *Déblaiement d'Art.* Brussels, 1894.

Vever, Henri. *La Bijouterie française au XIXe siècle.* Paris: H. Floury, 1908.

Period Journals and Newspapers

American Architect and Building News. Boston

Architectural Review. London

Art Amateur. A Monthly Journal Devoted to Art in the Household. New York

Art and Decoration. New York

Art Collector. New York

Art Décoratif. Revue internationale d'art industriel et de décoration. Paris

Art et Décoration. Paris

Art et la mode. Revue de l'elegance. Paris

Artist: An Illustrated Monthly Record of Arts, Crafts, and Industries. New York

Artist. Journal of Home Culture. London

Art News. New York

Art pour Tous; encyclopedie de l'art industriel et décoratif. Paris

Boston Daily Globe

Brush and Pencil. Chicago

Century Magazine. New York

Christian Science Monitor. Boston

Cleveland Town Topics

Collector. New York

Cosmopolitan: A Monthly Illustrated Magazine. New York

Craftsman. New York

Current Literature

Dress & Vanity Fair. New York

Deutsche Kunst und Dekoration. Darmstadt

Fortune. New York

Gazette des Beaux-Arts. Paris

Gazette du bon ton Paris: Librairie central des Beaux-arts. Paris

Godey's Magazine. Philadelphia

Harper's Bazaar. New York

Harper's Weekly. New York

House Beautiful. New York

Illustrated American. New York

Illustrated London News

International Studio: An Illustrated Magazine of Fine and Applied Art. New York

Jewelers' Circular & Horological Review. Radner, Pa.

Jewelers' Weekly. New York

Journal de l'Exposition Française à Moscou en 1891

Journal of American Folklore. New York

Keramic Studio. Syracuse

La Grande Revue. Paris

La Revue de l'Art Ancien et Moderne. Paris

La Revue des Arts Décoratifs. Paris

L'Art Décoratif. Paris

L'Art Décoratif Moderne. Paris

L'Art Décoratif pour Tous. Paris

L'Art et les Artistes. Paris

Le Figaro. Paris

Le Rire. Paris

Les Arts. Paris

L'Illustration. Paris

London Times

Magazine of Art. Washington, D.C.

Mir Iskusstva. St. Petersburg

Munsey's Magazine. New York

New York Daily News

New York Herald

New York Observer and Chronicle

New York Post

New York Sun

New York Times

New York World

Peterson's Magazine. Philadelphia

Philadelphia Inquirer

Revue de la Bijouterie, Joaillerie, Orfèverie. Paris

Revue Encyclopédique. Paris

Stolitsa i Usadba. St. Petersburg

Starye Gody. St. Petersburg

Studio. London

Times of London

Town & Country. New York

Vanity Fair. New York

Vogue. New York or London

Washington Times

Yenowine's Illustrated News. Milwaukee

Manuscript Collections

Archives Boucheron, Paris

Condé Nast Archives, New York

Henry Winans Hiller Papers, Mystic Seaport Museum, Mystic, Conn.

Jeptha Homer Wade Family Papers, Wester Reserve Historical Society, Cleveland

National Archives of the Russian Federation, Moscow

R. G. Dun & Co. Collection, Historical Collections, Baker Library, Harvard University Graduate School of Business Administration, Cambridge, Mass.

State Hermitage Museum Archives, St. Petersburg

State Russian Historical Archive, St. Petersburg

Tiffany & Co. Archives, Parsippany, N.J.

Comparative Illustrations

Chapter 1, *Artistic Luxury*

Fig. 1. John Singer Sargent, *Lisa Colt Curtis*, 1898, oil on canvas, 219.3 x 104.8 cm. The Cleveland Museum of Art, Leonard C. Hanna Jr. Fund, 1998.168.

Fig. 2. *Grand Staircase of the Paris Opera House*, chromo-lithograph, 35 x 27 cm. Jerome Robbins Dance Division, the New York Public Library for the Performing Arts, Astor, Lenox and Tilden Foundations.

Fig. 3. L'Art Nouveau advertisement, after *Dekorative Kunst* 2 (1898): no page number. Courtesy Cleveland Public Library.

Fig. 4. A boudoir designed by Georges de Feure for Bing's L'Art Nouveau pavilion at the 1900 Paris Exposition Universelle, after *Deutsche Kunst und Dekoration* 12 (April 1903–September 1903): 333. Courtesy Cleveland Public Library.

Fig. 5. The neighboring Tiffany displays at the 1900 Paris Exposition Universelle, 1900. Courtesy Doros Archive Collection.

Fig. 6. René Lalique in his studio, c. 1900. Courtesy Lalique Paris.

Fig. 7. Sir Frank Brangwyn, *L'Art Nouveau S. Bing, Tiffany Art Glass, Meunier Bronzes, Grafton Galleries*, 1890s. Courtesy Corbis Corporation.

Fig. 8. William H. Rau, *Eiffel Tower Illuminated at Night at the 1900 Exposition, Paris*. Courtesy Corbis Corporation.

Fig. 9. The Pavilions of the Nations, III, Exposition Universal, 1900, Paris. Postcard, Detroit Publishing Co. (1905).

Fig. 10. Félix Vallotton, *Lalique's Display Window*, 1901, pl. 3 from the series "Exposition Universelle," woodcut, 12.1 x 16.4 cm. Fine Arts Museums of San Francisco, Achenbach Foundation for Graphic Arts, 1963.30.422.

Fig. 11. Lalique's display window and Maison Vever's display at the 1900 Exposition Universelle. Courtesy Les Arts Décoratifs Paris, Fonds patrimonial Vever. Photographer: Laurent Sully Jaulmes.

Fig. 12. *Miniature Cabinet with Watch*, c. 1770–75, attributed to James Cox (English, active in London), gold, agate, enamel dial, glass. Private collection.

Fig. 13. House of Fabergé's display at the 1900 Paris Exposition Universelle, after Géza von Habsburg and Marina Lopato, *Fabergé: Imperial Jeweller*, exh. cat., State Hermitage Museum, St. Petersburg, and tour (Alexandria, Va: Art Services International, 1993), 117.

Fig. 14. House of Fabergé, Mikhail Perkhin, workmaster, *Imperial Lilies of the Valley Egg*, 1898, gold, ormolu, vermeil, enamel, diamonds, rubies, pearls, rock crystal, h. 20 cm. Collection of Mr. and Mrs. Timothy Forbes, courtesy the Forbes Collection, New York. © All rights reserved. Photographer: Larry Stein.

Fig. 15. René Lalique, *Design for a Clutch Purse with Spiders and Bees*, pencil, india ink, gouache, watercolor, 28 x 22 cm. Courtesy Gallery Moderne, Piermont, New York.

Fig. 16. After William Morris, illustration from *The Wood Beyond the World* (Hammersmith, U.K.: Kelmscott Press, 1894).

Fig. 17. Charles Rennie Mackintosh interior from Windyhill, after *Mir Iskusstva (World of Art)*, no. 12 (1903): no page number.

Fig. 18. Paul Burty Haviland, *Portrait of Suzanne Lalique*, c. 1919, platinum print, 20.7 x 16.2 cm. The Cleveland Museum of Art, Dudley P. Allen Fund, 1995.75.

Fig. 19. Secession Building, Vienna, c. 1905. Courtesy Österreichische Nationalbibliothek Bildarchiv, Vienna.

Fig. 20. Brooch, designed C. R. Ashbee and executed by the Guild of Handicraft (signed by Louis Comfort Tiffany), after *Dekorative Kunst* 2 (1898): 57.

Fig. 21. The grand duchesses Olga and Tatiana dressed as Sisters of Mercy at Tsarskoe Selo, c. 1915. Courtesy Slavic and Baltic Division, the New York Public Library, Astor, Lenox and Tilden Foundations.

Fig. 22. House of Fabergé, *Covered Pot*, 1914, copper, brass, 12.7 x 13.4 cm overall. The Cleveland Museum of Art, The India Early Minshall Collection, 1966.511.a–b.

Fig. 23. Tiffany & Co. advertisement, after *Town & Country* 58 (9 May 1903): 34. Courtesy Cleveland Public Library.

Fig. 24. Tiffany & Co. advertisement, c. 1900 (loose folio, source unknown).

Fig. 25. *Mrs. George Jay Gould*, 1908. Courtesy Corbis Corporation.

Fig. 26. Paul Helleu, *La Duchesse de Marlborough*, c. 1900, after Robert de Montesquiou, *Paul Helleu: Peintre et Graveur* (Paris: H. Floury, 1913), pl. 8.

Fig. 27 "Blenheim Palace" [Charles Spencer-Churchill, ninth Duke of Marlborough], cartoon by "Spy," *Vanity Fair* (22 September 1898). Courtesy Hulton Archive, Getty Images.

Fig. 28. Royal Families; Victoria, Queen of Great Britain, at Balmoral Castle in Scotland, with her son Edward, Prince of Wales (right) and Tsar Nicholas II of Russia (left). Seated on the left is Tsarina Alexandra Feodorovna holding her baby daughter Grand Duchess Tatiana, 1896. Courtesy Hulton Archive, Getty Images.

Fig. 29. The exhibition *Artistic Objects and Miniatures by Fabergé, Von Dervis Mansion*, March 1902. The State Hermitage Museum, St. Petersburg. Photograph © The State Hermitage Museum.

Fig. 30. Ivan Nikolaevic Kramskoj, *Portrait of Maria Fydorovna*, 1882. Courtesy Corbis Corporation. Photographer: Alexander Burkatovski.

Fig. 31. House of Fabergé, *Duchess of Marlborough Egg*, 1902, after Christopher Forbes and Robyn Tromeur-Brenner, *Fabergé: The Forbes Collection* (New York: Hugh Lauter Levin Associates, 1999), 67.

Fig. 32. The Duchess of Marlborough in coronation robes, 1902, after George F. Kunz, *The Book of the Pearl* (New York: Century Company, 1908), 464.

Chapter 2, *France*

Fig. 33. Aubrey Beardsley, *Design for "The Climax from Oscar Wilde's 'Salome'."* Courtesy V & A Images, Victoria and Albert Museum.

Fig. 34. William Morris, *Strawberry Thief*, registered 11 May 1883, plain-weave cotton, discharge printed, 88.3 x 96.1 cm. The Cleveland Museum of Art, Gift of Mrs. Henry Chisholm, 1937.696.

Fig. 35. Liberty & Co., *Petworth*, 1890, roller-printed silk, 93.6 x 67.8 cm. The Cleveland Museum of Art, Gift of Henry Hunt Clark, 1959.120.

Fig. 36. Interior view of L'Art Nouveau exhibition hall, Paris, December 1895. Courtesy Institut Français d'Architecture, fond Louis Bonnier, Paris.

Fig. 37. Manuel Orazi, *La Maison Moderne*, 1900, color lithograph, 83 x 117.5 cm. Les Arts Décoratifs, Musée de la Publicité, Paris. Photographer: Laurent Sully Jaulmes.

Fig. 38. Jewelry by Henri Nocq, after Henri Vever, "Les Bijoux des Salons de 1898," *Art et Décoration* 3 (1898): 175.

Fig. 39. Nawaz, *Sarah Bernhardt*, n.d. Courtesy Billy Rose Theatre Division, the New York Public Library for the Performing Arts, Astor, Lenox and Tilden Foundations.

Fig. 40. Sarah Bernhardt, from cigarette cards, c. 1896. Courtesy George Arents Collection, the New York Public Library, Astor, Lenox and Tilden Foundations.

Fig. 41. Schloss, *Lillian Russell*, 1897. Courtesy Billy Rose Theatre Division, the New York Public Library for the Performing Arts, Astor, Lenox and Tilden Foundations.

Fig. 42. Jeanne Julia Regnault Bartet (Julia Bartet), n.d. Billy Rose Theatre Division, the New York Public Library for the Performing Arts, Astor, Lenox and Tilden Foundations.

Fig. 43. Firm of Chaumet, Design for a large diamond and ruby stomacher. Courtesy Chaumet Collection, Paris.

Fig. 44. Lluís Masriera as a young artist, inside the Masriera workshop, Barcelona, 1904. Courtesy Bagués-Masriera Archives, Barcelona.

Fig. 45. Lluís Masriera, *Pendant of a Woman with Insect Wings*, c. 1916. Courtesy Bagués-Masriera Collection, Barcelona.

Fig. 46. Ink drawing, metal mold, and finished pendant of a design by Lluís Masriera. Courtesy Bagués-Masriera Archives and Collection, Barcelona.

Fig. 47. Robert de Montesquiou, after Robert de Montesquiou, *Paul Helleu: Peintre et Graveur* (1913), pl. 11.

Fig. 48. Exterior of Lalique's display window at the Exposition Universelle of 1900. Musée des Arts Décoratifs Paris, Fonds patrimonial Vever. Photographer: Laurent Sully Jaulmes.

Fig. 49. Sarah Bernhardt as "Théodora," 1890. Courtesy Getty Images. Photographers: W. and D. Downey.

Fig. 50. René Lalique, unrealized design for Sarah Bernhardt's headdress as "Théodora," 1894, after *Art et Décoration* 18 (1905): 187.

Fig. 51. Detail of Lalique's display at the 1902 Turin exposition, after *Deutsche Kunst und Dekoration* 11 (October 1902–March 1903): 172. Courtesy Cleveland Public Library.

Fig. 52. René Lalique, *Kiss Brooch*, 1904–6, pressed glass, silver, 4.9 x 7 cm. Musée des Arts Décoratifs, Paris. Photographer: Laurent Sully Jaulmes.

Fig. 53. René Lalique, *Design for a Swan Pendant*, c. 1898–1900, india ink, gouache, 28 x 22 cm. Courtesy Gallery Moderne, Piermont, N.Y. Photographer: Howard Agriesti.

Fig. 54. René Lalique, *Design for Nesting Swallows Hair Ornament*, c. 1906–8, gouache, 28 x 22 cm. Courtesy Gallery Moderne, Piermont, N.Y. Photographer: Howard Agriesti.

Chapter 3, *Russia*

Fig. 55. *Mir Iskusstva*, nos. 18, 19 (1899), cover by Elena Polenova. Courtesy the Fine Arts Library, Harvard College Library.

Fig. 56. René Lalique, *Design for a Fan Handle, "Grotesque,"* c. 1890–95, crayon, watercolor, gouache. Courtesy Lalique Paris.

Figs. 57a–b. Images of Lalique's work, after " 'L'Art Moderne': enterprise artistique à St. Pétersbourg," *Mir Iskusstva*, nos. 5, 6 (1903): 237, 241–44. Courtesy the Fine Arts Library, Harvard College Library.

Fig. 58. Tsar Nicholas II with his family (left to right): the grand duchesses Olga, Marie, Anastasia; the tsarevitch Alexis; Grand Duchess Tatiana; and Tsarina Alexandra Feodorovna, his wife, n.d. Image © Bettmann/Corbis Corporation.

Fig. 59. Émile Gallé, *Vase Decorated with Flowering Shoots of Clematis*, cast and chased glass, engraved silver, h. 19.8 cm, diam. 9.7 cm. Peter Carl Fabergé workshop. The State Hermitage Museum, St. Petersburg. Photograph © The State Hermitage Museum.

Fig. 60. K. K. Kubesch, *Tsarina Alexandra Feodorovna's Drawing Room*. The State Hermitage Museum, St. Petersburg. Photograph © The State Hermitage Museum.

Fig. 61. After Gustave Keller, Keller Fréres, *Paris 1900, Exposition universelle, cl. 94 et 98* (Paris: Chez Keller), pls. I, II, and IV. Courtesy Wilfried Zeisler, Paris.

Fig. 62. The House of Fabergé at 24 Bolshaia Morskaia Street, St. Petersburg around 1910. Courtesy Wartski, London.

Fig. 63. Jean André Lepaute, *Pendule*, c. 1785, after *Starye Gody* (April–June 1911): no page number.

Fig. 64. House of Fabergé. *Imperial Framed Miniature*, before 1896. Workmaster: Mikhail Perkhin. Gold, jade, rubies, gouache, ivory, glass, 15.3 x 5 x 5 cm. The Cleveland Museum of Art, The India Early Minshall Collection, 1966.458.2.

Fig. 65. K. K. Bulla, *Fabergé Exhibition* at the Von Dervis mansion. The State Hermitage Museum, St. Petersburg. Photograph © The State Hermitage Museum.

Fig. 66. Jérémie Pauzié, *Bouquet of Flowers*, 1740s. The State Hermitage Museum, St. Petersburg. Photograph © The State Hermitage Museum.

Fig. 67. Grand Duchess Maria Pavlovna. Courtesy Chaumet Collection, Paris.

Fig. 68. Boucheron *collier écharpe* (scarf necklace) belonging to Grand Duchess Maria Pavlovna. Courtesy Boucheron Archives, Paris.

Fig. 69. Maria Pavlovna at the 1903 costume ball. Courtesy Hoover Institution Archives, Stanford University, Woronzow-Daschkow (Hilarion) collection, Box B.

Fig. 70. Waterfall tiara similar to the one supplied to Grand Duchess Maria Pavlovna in 1899. Courtesy Chaumet Collection, Paris.

Fig. 71. Firm of Chaumet, Miniature Easter Eggs. Courtesy Chaumet Collection, Paris.

Fig. 72. Firm of Chaumet, *Design for a Stomacher with Double-Headed Eagle*, c. 1902. Courtesy Chaumet Collection, Paris.

Fig. 73. The House of Fabergé design studio on the upper floor at Bolshaia Morskaia Street. Courtesy Wartski, London.

Fig. 74. Detail of a page of drawings for cigarette cases from Henrik Wigström's workshop, 1911, after Ulla Tillander-Godenhielm et al., *Golden Years of Fabergé* (New York/Paris: A La Vieille Russie/Alain de Gourcuff Editeur, 2000). © A La Vieille Russie, reproduced by permission.

Fig. 75. Interior at Talashkino, c. 1900–1905, after Serge Makowsky, "L'Art Décoratif des ateliers de la Princesse Ténichef," in *Talachkino: L'Art Décoratif des ateliers de la Princesse Ténichef* (St. Petersburg: Édition Sodrougestvo, 1906), pl. 85.

Fig. 76. One of the Kremlin Gates in Moscow around 1890. Courtesy Imagno, Austrian Archives; Hulton Archive, Getty Images.

Fig. 77. Tsar Nicholas II and his wife, Alexandra, 1903. Courtesy Hulton Archive, Getty Images.

Fig. 78. Xenia Alexandrovna at the 1903 costume ball. Courtesy Hoover Institution Archives, Stanford University, Woronzow-Daschkow (Hilarion) collection, Box B.

Fig. 79. Russian crown jewels; Soviet officials display the crown jewels which belonged to Russian Royal family, now in the hands of the Soviet government, September 1922. © Hulton-Deutsch Collection/Corbis Corporation.

Fig. 80. Mikhail Vrubel, *Two Hair Comb Designs*, after *Mir Iskusstva*, nos. 13–24 (1899): 85. Courtesy the Fine Arts Library, Harvard College Library.

Chapter 4, *America*

Fig. 81. Tiffany & Co., *Iris Corsage Ornament*, c. 1900, gold, oxidized silver, platinum, sapphires, demantoid garnets, topaz, diamonds, 24.1 x 6.9 cm. Acquired by Henry Walters, 1900. Walters Art Museum, 57.939.

Fig. 82. Tiffany & Co.'s jewel display case at the 1900 Paris Exposition Universelle. Courtesy Tiffany & Co. Archives.

Fig. 83. Display of Tiffany Favrile glass in the United States pavilion at the 1900 Paris Exposition Universelle. Courtesy Alastair Duncan and Antique Collectors' Club.

Fig. 84. After "Tiffany & Co. Exhibits at the Paris Exposition," *American Art Annual* 3 (1900–1901): 33.

Fig. 85. Charles Lewis Tiffany and Charles T. Cook in the ground-floor showroom of the Union Square store, c. 1887. Courtesy Tiffany & Co. Archives.

Fig. 86. Exterior of Tiffany & Co. store on 15th Street at Union Square, built in 1870. Courtesy Tiffany & Co. Archives.

Fig. 87. *Ladies' Wristwatch*, 1900–1910, watch movement by Patek Phillipe, gold, 17.8 x 2.5 cm. Courtesy Neil Lane.

Fig. 88. *Ladies' Wristwatch*, 1890, designer Henri Husson, gold, diamonds, enamel, 17 x 3 cm. Private collection.

Fig. 89. Workshop of Union Square store, c. 1880. Courtesy Tiffany & Co. Archives.

Fig. 90. François Kramer, *Bowknot and Tassel Brooch*, 1885, in its box identifying it as part of the French crown jewels. Photographer: David Behl.

Fig. 91. Lots 2, 5, and part of 28, after *Catalogues de vente des Diamants, perles et pierreries provenant de la collection dite des joyaux de la Couronne* (Paris: Imprimerie Nationale, 1887), pl. 6.

Fig. 92. Lots 3, 8, 11, and 43, after *Catalogues de vente des Diamants, perles et pierreries provenant de la collection dite des joyaux de la Couronne* (Paris: Imprimerie Nationale, 1887), pl. 9.

Fig. 93. Tiffany & Co. Paris store interior. Courtesy Tiffany & Co. Archives.

Fig. 94. House of Fabergé, for Tiffany & Co. (London), *One of a Pair of Jeweled Two-color Gold and Guilloché Enamel Scent Bottles*, c. 1890. Courtesy Christie's (New York).

Fig. 95. Lillian Nordica in diamond tiara, c. 1896. Courtesy Vintage Maine Images.

Fig. 96. Group of invoices from Marcus & Co., Tiffany & Co., and Tiffany Glass & Decorating Co. for jewelry and goods purchased by Jeptha H. Wade II. Wade Family Papers, Western Reserve Historical Society, Cleveland. Photographer: Howard Agriesti.

Fig. 97. Jeptha H. Wade I, *Portrait of Nathaniel Olds*, 1837, oil on canvas, 76.5 x 61.2 cm. The Cleveland Museum of Art, Seventy-fifth anniversary gift of Jeptha Homer Wade III, 1991.134.2.

Fig. 98. Receipt for Russian luxury goods from the shop of Mr. Jakobson, Malaia Morskoia Street and Gorokhovaia Street, St. Petersburg, 16 June 1896, and a travel journal from the Wades' 1896 trip to Russia, Germany, and Switzerland. Wade Family Papers, Western Reserve Historical Society, Cleveland. Photographer: Howard Agriesti.

Fig. 99. V. de Szepessy, Tiffany windows, including *The Flight of the Soul*, in an octagonal room of the United States Palace of the Liberal Arts, 1900, after Samuel [Siegfried] Bing, "La Culture Artistique en Amerique," trans. Benita Eisler, in *Artistic America, Tiffany Glass, and Art Nouveau* (Cambridge, Mass.: MIT Press, 1970), 139.

Fig. 100. Tiffany Studios, designer: Louis Comfort Tiffany, *The Flight of the Soul*, c. 1899. Photographer: Howard Agriesti.

Fig. 101. Page from Jeptha H. Wade II's address book featuring art and luxury goods dealers. Wade Family Papers, Western Reserve Historical Society, Cleveland. Photographer: Howard Agriesti.

Fig. 102. Rear view of the Wade Memorial Chapel in Lake View Cemetery, Cleveland, c. 1905. Wade Memorial Chapel Photographs, 1898–1900, Hubbell & Benes Co. (architects). Courtesy Western Reserve Historical Society, Cleveland.

Fig. 103. Tiffany Studios, *Design for Cleveland Museum of Art's Rotunda Interior Decoration*, c. 1915. Western Reserve Historical Society, Cleveland, 73.122.1.

Fig. 104. Martin Johnson Heade, *Orchid Blossoms*, 1873, oil on canvas, 38.1 x 30.6 cm. The Cleveland Museum of Art, Hinman B. Hurlbut Collection, 461.1915.

Fig. 105. C. D. Arnold and H. D. Higinbotham, *Tiffany and Gorham Exhibits—Manufactures Building* from *Official Views of the World's Columbian Exposition*, c. 1893. The Wolfsonian-Florida International University, Miami Beach, Florida, the Mitchell Wolfson, Jr. Collection, XB1991.19.

Fig. 106. Title page, *A Glimpse of the Tiffany Exhibit at the Columbian Exposition, Chicago (1893)*, after *Godey's Magazine* (August 1893).

Fig. 107. Marble bust from Tiffany & Co.'s display at the 1893 Columbian Exposition, Chicago, from *A Glimpse of the Tiffany Exhibit at the Columbian Exposition, Chicago (1893)*, after *Godey's Magazine* (August 1893).

Fig. 108. Louis Comfort Tiffany, *Moroccan Interior*, 1895, watercolor, 34.3 x 52.1 cm. Collection of Mr. and Mrs. Timothy Forbes, courtesy the Forbes Magazine Collection. Photograph by Erik Landsberg.

Fig. 109. Louis Comfort Tiffany's glass screen in entrance hall of the White House, c. 1893, after Esther Singleton, *The Story of the White House* (New York: McClure Company, 1907), no page number.

Fig. 110. Glass Shop, after *Tiffany Studios, Character and Individuality in Decorations and Furnishings* (New York: Tiffany Studios, 1913). Courtesy the Winterthur Library: Printed Book and Periodical Collection.

Fig. 111. Design for the chapel created by Tiffany Glass & Decorating Co. for the 1893 World's Columbian Exposition, after *The Art Work of Louis Comfort Tiffany* (New York: Doubleday, 1914).

Fig. 112. Tiffany & Co. fountain in the Manufacturers and Liberal Arts Building at the Chicago World's Columbian Exposition of 1893. Courtesy the Chicago History Museum.

Fig. 113. Louis Comfort Tiffany (manufacturer), after Henri de Toulouse-Lautrec, *Au Nouveau Cirque: The Female Penguin and the Five Clowns (Papa Chrysanthème)*, 1894–95, stained-glass window, 120 x 85 cm. Musée d'Orsay, Paris. Courtesy Réunion des Musées Nationaux/Art Resource, N.Y. Photographer Gérard Blot.

Fig. 114. L'Art Nouveau advertisement, after *Art et Décoration* 8 (July–December 1900): unnumbered page.

Fig. 115. Tiffany Studios, *Peacock Vase*, 1898–99, metalwork designer Edward Colonna, enameler Eugène Feuillâttre, translucent reddish glass with applied iridescence, silvergilt mount with plique-à-jour enamel and set rubies, h. 14.1 cm. Corning Museum of Glass, 2006.4.161.

Fig. 116. Paulding Farnham. Courtesy Tiffany & Co. Archives.

Fig. 117. George Frederick Kunz. Humanities and Social Sciences Library, Print Collection, Miriam and Ira D. Wallach Division of Art, Prints and Photographs, the New York Public Library, Astor, Lenox and Tilden Foundations.

Fig. 118. Pach Brothers, *J. Pierpont Morgan*, n.d. The Pageant of America Collection, Photography Collection, Miriam and Ira D. Wallach Division of Art, Prints and Photographs, the New York Public Library, Astor, Lenox and Tilden Foundations.

Fig. 119. Tiffany Favrile "petite coupe," probably a *salière* (salt cellar), metal mount by Maurice Dufrène, after R. Aubry et al., *Reproductions photographiques des principales oeuvres des collaborateurs de La Maison Moderne, Documents sur l'art industriel au vingtième siécle* (Paris: Edition de La Maison Moderne, 1901), 11.

Fig. 120. Tiffany Studios advertisement, after *Town and Country* 58 (12 September 1903–5 March 1904): 51. Courtesy Cleveland Public Library.

Fig. 121. Tiffany Studios interior on Madison Avenue, c. 1905, after *The Art Work of Louis Comfort Tiffany* (New York: Doubleday, 1914), no page number.

Fig. 122. Rug repair department, Tiffany Studios, after *Tiffany Studios, Character and Individuality in Decorations and Furnishings* (New York: Tiffany Studios, 1913). Courtesy the Winterthur Library: Printed Book and Periodical Collection.

Fig. 123. Suggestions for the dining room, after *Tiffany Studios, Character and Individuality in Decorations and Furnishings* (New York: Tiffany Studios, 1913). Courtesy the Winterthur Library: Printed Book and Periodical Collection.

Fig. 124. Meta Overbeck, sheet of studies from design book, 1914–33. The Charles Hosmer Morse Museum of American Art, Winter Park, Fl., gift of Margreta Overbeck, 78-1080. Image © The Charles Hosmer Morse Foundation, Inc.

Image Credits

Images of the works of art in the exhibition were provided by lenders, unless noted otherwise. Objects in the collection of the Cleveland Museum of Art were photographed by museum photographer Howard Agriesti. All the works of art themselves may be protected by copyright in the United States or abroad and may not be reproduced in any form without permission from the copyright holders. The following photographers are acknowledged:

Howard Agriesti, courtesy the Cleveland Museum of Art: pp. vi (cat. 290), x (cat. 214), 2 (cat. 312), 6 (cat. 263), 7 (cat. 99), 8 (cats. 277, 280, 289, 300, 306), 12 (cat. 320), 17 (cat. 250), 20 (cat. 121), 27 (cat. 78), 32 (cat. 117), 37 (cat. 106), 41 (cats. 153, 154, 160, 186), 50 (cat. 281), 51 (cat. 279), 53 (cat. 282), 58 (cat. 264), 71 (cat. 125), 79 (cat. 199), 97 (cat. 220), 100 (cat. 101), 115 (cat. 100), 130 (cat. 3), 149 (cat. 184), 151 (cat. 127), 165 (cat. 13), 174 (cat. 316), 184 (cat. 33), 185 (cat. 35), 218 (cat. 88), 219 (cats. 310, 311), 230 (cat. 268), 238 (cats. 201, 224, 308), 250 (cat. 202), 256 (cat. 255), 266 (cat. 315), 267 (cat. 262), 271 (cat. 242), 273 (cat. 205), 278 (cat. 289) 279 (cats. 297, 298), 280 (cat. 293), 281 (cat. 284), 284 (cat. 300), 286 (cat. 286), 290 (cat. 292), 291 (cat. 278), 295 (cat. 231), 296 (cats. 251, 225), 297 (cat. 83), 305 (cat. 288), 306 (cat. 299) 307 (cat. 291), 316 (cat. 277), 359 (cat. 255)

Ken Burris, courtesy Middlebury College Museum of Art: p. 217 (cat. 55)

Jean Chénel, courtesy H.S.H. Prince Albert II of Monaco: p. 176 (cat. 56)

© Christie Mayer Lefkowith Collection, 2008: pp. 121 (cats. 18, 112), 122 (cats. 136, 141, 183), 123 (cats. 148, 170), 124 (cats. 24, 163), 125 (cats. 126, 321)

Judy Cooper: p. 23 (cat. 61)

Katharina Faerber: pp. 99 (cat. 318), 148 (cat. 143), 166 (cat. 150)

Matt Flynn, courtesy Cooper-Hewitt, National Design Museum: pp. 81 (cat. 20), 236 (cat. 17), 288 (cat. 305)

Toni Marie Gonzalez, courtesy Toledo Museum of Art: p. 208 (cats. 113, 221)

Tino Hammid, courtesy Neil Lane: pp. 297 (cat. 267), 313 (cat. 260), 317 (cat. 256)

Scott Hisey, courtesy Cincinnati Art Museum: pp. 42 (cat. 185), 43 (cat. 191), 127 (cat. 137), 143 (cat. 124), 232 (cat. 302), 280 (cat. 266), 282 (cat. 303), 303 (cat. 216)

Pete Huggins, courtesy the Anderson Collection, University of East Anglia: p. 114 (cat. 167)

Tom Jenkins: p. 301 (cat. 276)

Michael Brandon Jones, courtesy the Anderson Collection, University of East Anglia: pp. 99 (cat. 104), 147 (cat. 322)

Dave King, courtesy Cooper-Hewitt, National Design Museum: p. 288 (cat. 295)

Saturia Linke, courtesy Kunstgewerbemuseum, Berlin: pp. 83 (cat. 304), 120 (cat. 134), 127 (cat. 178), 196 (cat. 28)

© The Metropolitan Museum of Art: pp. 38 (cat. 114), 101 (cat. 196), 114 (cat. 107), 135 (cat. 213), 147 (cat. 164), 164 (cat. 14), 235 (cat. 237), 292 (cat. 222)

Edward Owen, courtesy Hillwood Estate, Museum & Gardens: pp. 26 (cat. 42), 172 (cat. 116), 187 (cat. 70), 209 (cat. 212), 222 (cat. 11)

Richard Pierce, courtesy Tiffany & Co. Archives: p. 247 (cat. 239)

Prudence Cuming Associates: pp. 16 (cat. 29), 28 (cat. 93), 70 (cat. 188), 85 (cat. 175), 132 (cat. 138), 142 (cat. 133), 144 (cat. 173), 148 (cat. 159), 216 (cat. 90), 224 (cat. 200), 246 (cat. 26), 248 (cat. 246)

Doug Rosa, courtesy Siegelson Collection: pp. 33 (cat. 157), 84 (cat. 155)

Royal Collection © 2008 Her Majesty Queen Elizabeth II: pp. 201 (cat. 37), 170 (cat. 80)

Richard Rubins, courtesy Neil Lane: pp. 5 (cat. 119), 101 (cat. 309), 235 (cat. 223)

Michael Sahaida: pp. 204 (cat. 95), 215 (cat. 71), 220 (cat. 41)

David Schlegel, courtesy Joan Rivers: pp. 216 (cat. 31), 186 (cats. 45, 86), 201 (cat. 38), 217 (cat. 30)

David Schlegel, courtesy Eric Streiner: pp. 20 (cats. 128, 129), 53 (cat. 232), 131 (cat. 129), 245 (cat. 236), 249 (cats. 203, 206, 252, 253), 251 (cat. 204), 253 (cat. 203), 254 (cat. 206), 299 (cats. 270, 271), 310 (cat. 258), 311 (cat. 243), 315 (cat. 259)

Andrea Simon, courtesy Philadelphia Museum of Art: p. 283 (cat. 301)

Larry Stein, courtesy the Forbes Collection: p. 203 (cats. 47, 307)

Tim Thayer, courtesy Toledo Museum of Art: pp. 141 (cat. 176), 312 (cat. 257)

Jean Tholance, courtesy Musée des Arts Décoratifs and Les Arts Décoratifs: pp. 69 (cat. 149), 117 (cat. 19), 120 (cat. 181), 136 (cat. 131), 165 (cat. 16), 185 (cat. 15), 187 (cat. 66), 197 (cat. 40), 202 (cats. 36, 39)

© Tiffany & Co. Archives: pp. 235 (cat. 234), 244 (cat. 227), 244 (cat. 249), 246 (cat. 229), 247 (cat. 226), 257 (cat. 274), 270 (cat. 272), 271 (cat. 245), 287 (cat. 228), 293 (cat. 230), 299 (cat. 244)

Tony Walsh, courtesy Cincinnati Art Museum: pp. 184 (cat. 27), 198 (cat. 34)

© The Walters Art Museum: pp. 59 (cat. 247), 179 (cat. 63), 277 (cat. 240), 297 (cat. 265)

Graydon Wood, courtesy Philadelphia Museum of Art: p. 301 (cat. 115)

Paul Wright: p. 67 (cat. 64).

Index

Page numbers in *italic* type refer to illustrations or their captions.

Abramtsevo, 28, 158, 211, 223
Académie des Beaux-Arts, 77
Actresses, 89, 264
  gifts to, 87, 264
Adams Vase, *234*, 234, *293*, 293, 297, 299
Advertising, 235, 304
  and actresses, 91
Aesthetic movement, 80
agate, 97, 168, 175, 183, *184*, 317
Alexander Palace, 169, 215
Alexander III (tsar), 64, 153, 165, 167, 170, 174, 183, 188, 214, 216, 217, 219, 220, 222, 223
Alexandra (Princess of Wales). *See* Alexandra (queen of England)
Alexandra (queen of England), 5, 61, 63, 184, 201
Alexandra Feodorovna (tsarina), 160, *161*, 161, 163, 165, 167, 168, 169, 170, 171, 174, 175, 177, *178*, 178, *183*, 183, 188, 204, *207*
Anichkov Palace, 64, 66, 174, 185
animals, stone, 24, 64, *165*, 165, 183, 184, 187
Antokolsky, Mark, *192*, 194
Art Deco, 40, 46, 68, 70, 103, 107
artist colonies. *See* Abramtsevo; Art Workers' Guild; Darmstadt; Guild of Handicraft; Mir Iskusstva; Roycrofters; Talashkino
Art Nouveau/*moderne*, 4, *16*, 16, *17*, 17, 20, 26, 33, 45, 50, 69, *75*, 77, *77*, 78, 102, 175, 177, 198, 201, 253, 258, 264, 276, *280*, 288, 302
  characteristics of, 80
  critics of, 40, 50
  influence on jewelry, 13, 29, 33, 91, 94
  and Russia, 20, 26, 156, *157*, 158, 165, 166, 171, 174, 189, 208, 212, 223, 224
  and women, 16, 33, 37
Arts and Crafts movement, 76, 80
  development of schools/workshops, 5, 28, 38, 39, 76
Art Workers' Guild, 76
Ashbee, C. R., *53*, 53, 76, 254, *302*
Aucoc, Louis, Fils, *85*, 97, 153, *204*, 204, 241, 324

avant-garde, 38, *39*, 39, 45, 46, 50, 69, 94, 97, *100*, 156, 158, 232, 253, 314
Bagués-Masriera, firm of, 102–7
bandeaux, 116
Ballets Russes, 89
Bapst, firm of, *111*, 239–42, *242*
Bapst & Falize, 155
Bartet, Julia, *86*, 87, 92
Bazanova, Varvara. *See* Kelch, Barbara
Beardsley, Aubrey, 77, 81, 189, 198
Becker, Edmond-Henri, *130*, 324
Belle Époque, 2, *2*, 258
Bénédite, Léonce, 114, 131, 136
Bernhardt, Sarah, 91, 260
  influence of, 63, 89, 91
  and Lalique, 11, 87, 89, 92, *92*
  and jewelry, *89*
  roles of, 87, *89*, 91, *92*, *128*, 128
  Théâtre Sarah Bernhardt, 91
Bing, Siegfried, *80*, *81*, 81, 82, 103, 116, 155, 280, *284*, 286, *287*, 287
  criticism of, 82, 83
  L'Art Nouveau, 3, 5, 8, *9*, 11, 33, 40, *80*, 81, 82, 95, 103, 287, *289*
Blue Serpent Egg (Imperial), 64, *64*, 65, 67, *175*, 177
bolsheviks, selling of imperial treasures, 239
Bolin, firm of, 156, 168, 216, 217, 219
Bonbonnière Egg (Kelch), 67, *67*
Boston Arts and Crafts exhibition, 255
Boucheron, Maison, 5, 11, 17, 54, 86, *97*, 97, 99, 160, *163*, 163, 165, *171*, *173*, *189*, 189, 190, 192, 202, 219, 241, 251, 324
boxes (including snuffboxes), 15, *50*, 50, *59*, 59, 122, 166, 184, 187, 196, *201*, 201, 222, 223, 260, 261, 270, *287*, 287
Bracquemond, Félix, 115, *133*, 324
Bridal Fan (Imperial), 210
brooches, 2, *13*, 17, 20, 26, *38*, 40, 45, *46*, 53, 60, 63, *79*, 87, *89*, 99, *101*, 101, *103*, *104*, 131, 132, *135*, 135, *136*, *144*, 144, *147*, 155, 160, 161, 162, *163*, 163, *166*, 166, 183, 189, 191, 217, 217, *219*, 219, 231, 240, 242, 246, 293
Bugatti, Carlo, 35, *37*, 40, 57, 324
Buhre, Paul (Pavel), firm of, 222, 325
Cardeilhac, Maison, 75, 325
Cartier, Maison, 97, *165*, *185*, 192, 192, 202, 219, 239, 302, 325
  and Russia, 68, 163–65, *165*
Castellani, Fortunato Pio, & Sons, 236, 325

Centennial Exhibition (1876, Philadelphia), 10, 246, 251, 272, 295
Chalon, Louis, 120, *121*, 326
Chanticleer Egg, 67
Charpentier, Alexandre, 132, 135
Chaumet, firm of, 97, 100–101, *101*, 202, 219
  and Russia, 165, *191*, 191, *192*, 192
Chicago world's fair. *See* World's Columbian Exposition (1893, Chicago)
Chopard, Gaston, *117*, 326
cigarette cases, 15, 165, *201*, 201, 202, 202, 222
Cleveland, 91, 92, 259, 260, 261, 262, 264, 265, *274*
  and Jeptha Homer Wade II and Ellen Garretson Wade, *59*, 59, 257, 258, 260–65
  Museum of Art, 40, 175, *177*, 198, 259, 262, 264, *265*
clocks, 21, *21*, 26, *38*, *39*, 64, 67, 132, 187, 250, 279
cloisonné. *See* enameling, cloisonné
collecting, 57, 59, *184*, 235, 252, 255, 265, 296
Colonna, Edward, 5, *81*, *287*, 287, 326
combs, 28, 82, 87, 94, 116, *135*, 135, *136*, 136, *139*, 139, 140, *143*, *144*, 144, 155, 158, 223, *224*
Comédie-Française, 95
Cowell & Hubbard, 258, 260
Craft Guild, 4
craftsmanship, 60, 87, 202, 211, 250, 293
craft tradition, 3, 4, 28
Cranach, Wilhelm Lucas von, *16*, 326
crown jewels
  and France, 239–43
  and Russia, 13, 26, 160, 161, 217, 220
Crystal Palace, 10, 252, 266
Dampt, Jean, 132, 144
Danish Palaces Egg (Imperial), *21*, 26
Darmstadt, 3, 38, *39*, 39, 50
Delaherche, Auguste, *76*, 77, 326
democratization of the arts, 76
Deraisme, Pierre-Georges, *124*, 124, 326
diadems, 26, 75, *86*, 216, 241, 242
dog collar
  necklaces, 5, *104*, *148*, 192, 271
  plaques, *85*, *104*, *140*
Dresden, 39, 174, 175, 249, 250
Dresser, Christopher, 5, 80, 115, 272

Driscoll, Clara, 279, 291

Duchess of Marlborough. *See* Marlborough, Duchess of

Duchess of Marlborough Egg, 65

Earle, Virginia, 89

École des Beaux-Arts, 82

Edward (Prince of Wales). *See* Edward VII (king of England)

Edward VII (king of England), 61, *63*, *65*, 201

enameling
  cloisonné, 132, 144, 196, 208, 247
  guilloché, 20, 175, 177, 196, 198, *199*, 201, 207, *254*, 254
  plique-à-jour, 17, 87, 106, 107, 147, *208*, 208, 254, *287*

Ernst Ludwig. *See* Hesse-Darmstadt, Grand Duke of

Esposizione Internationale (1902, Turin), 13, 35, 40, *128*

Eugénie (empress), 163, 216, *239*, 239, *240*, 240, 241

Exposition Universelle (1889, Paris), 11, *15*, 15, 103, 153, 163, 170, 190, *266*, 266, 268, 269, 276, 288, 295, 299

Exposition Universelle (1900, Paris)
  architecture, 13, *15*, 16, *21*, 33
  and Art Nouveau, 9, 29, 35, 69, 75, 156
  displays at, 5, *9*, *10*, 13, 15, 16, *21*, 29, 59, 60, 163, 169, 231
  and Fabergé, 13, 15, 20, 21, 26, 28, 29, 64, 165, 177, 178, *183*
  historicism, 20, 21, 29, 38, *204*, 204, 208
  and Lalique, 15, *17*, 20, 29, 158, *159*, 160, 162
  and L. C. Tiffany, 5, *9*, *10*, *13*, 15, 231, 232, *293*, 293, 299, *302*, 304, 314
  modernism, 29, 33, 35, *35*, 38
  and Tiffany & Co., *17*, 28, 35, 231
  and Vever, 16, *17*, 29

Fabergé, Agathon, *174*, 174

Fabergé eggs/imperial eggs, 165, 174, *175*, 175, *177*, 177, *178*, 178, 191, 192
  materials used/technique of making, 20, 26, 54, 55, 64, 67, 67
  sentimental value of, 21, 55, 64, 64

Fabergé, Peter Carl, 153–229, 326
  and animal sculptures, 24, 64, 165, 165, 183, 184, 187
  and *Artistic Objects and Miniatures by Fabergé* exhibition, 64, 178, 178

  and Art Nouveau, 5, 16, 20, *26*, 156, *157*, 157, 158, 166, 171, 175, 177, 189, 198, 201, 223, 224
  business strategies of/advertising, 5, 9, 13, 15, 21, 28, 54, 57, 60, 61
  and cigarette cases, 15, 165, *201*, 201, *202*, 202, 222
  and enamel, 20, 26, 28, 29, 64, 65, 174, 175, 177, 183, 198, 199, *201*, 201, *208*, 220
  as goldsmith, 15, 20, 21, *21*, 29, 64
  and jeweled flowers, 64, *178*, 178
  and Russian imperial family, 13, 20, 21, 26, *26*, 55, 60, 61, 62, 64, *67*, 68, 70, 168, 174, 178, *183*, 202, 216
  and Russian nationalism, 13, 26, *26*, 28, 28, 29, 66
  as traditionalist, 20, 21, 28, *28*, 29, 39
  use of materials, 26, 29, 38, *54*, 54, 175, *183*, 183, 187, 201, 202, 215, 223
  and whimsical objects, 21
  works given as gifts by the imperial family, *16*, 91
  See also House of Fabergé; Fabergé eggs

Falize, Alexis, 5, *100*, 100, 132

Falize Frères, 5, *100*, 100, *115*, 116, 329

Falize, Lucien, 86, 166, 167, 192, *193*, 194

Farnham, Paulding, 246, *266*, 266, 269, 271, *293*, 293, 297, *299*, 299, 310, 314

Favrile glass. *See* glass, Favrile

Feuillâtre, Eugène, *148*

flacons, *120*, 120, *121*, 121, 122, 122, 123, 124, *125*, 299

Follot, Paul, 45, *46*, 330

Fouquet, Georges, 5, 95, *99*, 99, 330

Franco-Russian Alliance, 165–66, *166*
  influence in art, 165

French crown jewels, 293–43

Fuller, Löie, 288

Gaillard, Lucien, 5, 17, *37*, 37, *41*, *111*, *114*, 116, 144

Gallé, Émile, 35, 77, 78, 79, 85, 109, *110*, 111, 120, 171, 204, 330
  and Russian imperial family, 35, 155, 158, 165, *166*, 166–68

"Gallé Style," 168

Gatchina Palace Egg (Imperial), 67

Gesamtkunstwerk, 78, 116, 157

Gilded Age, 54, 260, 265, 298

Glasgow school, 35, 38, *50*, 50

Glass, 8, 11, *13*, 13, 35, 39, *41*, 41, *45*, 45, *46*, 46, *70*, 70, 77, *81*, 111, 120, 122, *123*, 123, *124*, 124, *132*, *149*, 153, 155, 158, *166*, 168, *170*, 171, 232, 233, 234, 250, 266, 274, *274*, 276, 279, 280, 281, 284, 287, 288, *289*, 291, 303, 304, 317
  Favrile, 8, *9*, 10, 33, 53, *82*, 155, 202, 232, 233, 234, 255, 262, 266, 279, *280*, 280, *281*, *284*, 286, 287, 288, *289*, 291, 291, 299, *299*, *302*, 302, 303, *304*, 304, *310*, 310, 317, 318
  as material in jewelry, 40, 46, 69, *111*, 120, 132, *135*, 135, 136, 139, *140*, 140, 143, 144, 147
  stained, 82, 83, 155, 223, 232, *232*, 259, *274*, 274, 276, 281, *284*, 284, 286, 287, 288, *289*, *304*, 314, 317

Goldsmiths' & Silversmiths' Company Ltd., 1, 29, *29*, 330

Gorham Mfg. Co., 33, *35*, 252, 268, *269*, 302, 331

Grabar, Igor, 158

Grace (princess), 66

Grafton Galleries, 13, 35, 286, *287*, 291

Great Exhibition (1851, London), 9, 10, 77, 216

"Great War." *See* World War I

Groupe des Cinq (later Groupe des Six), 79, 85

guilloché. *See* enameling, guilloché

Guild of Handicraft, 3, 38, *53*, 53, 76, 253

guilds, 4, 76, 132, 318

Guimard, Hector, *121*, 121, 331

Gulbenkian, Calouste, 60, 144, 160
  foundation, 128
  museum, 135, 155, *161*

Hammer, Marius, *208*, 331

Hauser, Ferdinand, 331

Havemeyer, Henry O., and Louisine, 274, 280

Haviland & Co., 45, 46, 46

Haviland, Paul, 46, 46

Heiden, Theodor, 29

Heinrichs, Joseph, *300*, 301, 331

Hermitage Museum, 155, 160, 165, 171, *175*, 175, *183*, 183, 185, 198, 263, 289

Hesse-Darmstadt, Grand Duke of (Ernst Ludwig), 38

hierarchy of arts, 75, 76, 77, 78, 130, 131

historical styles, 4, 28, 79, 177, *187*, 204, 269, 271, 302, *302*

historicism, *29*, 38, 97, *100*, 196, 234

Hoffmann, Josef, 38, 50, *317*, 317
Hollming, August, 196
Holmström, Albert, 196
Holmström, August, 196, 216
Horta, Victor, 77
House of Fabergé, 5, 13, 16, 20, 60, 62, 64, 66, 67, 68, 91
    See also Fabergé, Peter Carl
Imperial Cabinet, 220–23
    commission of jewelry, 161, 162
    system of awards of purchases, 220–23
    Table of Ranks, 221–22
Imperial Porcelain Factory and Glassworks, 170–74, *172*, 331
    and innovations in glass, 171
    and innovations in porcelain, 171, 174
Imperial Society for the Encouragement of the Arts, 156, 211
industrialization, 9, 62, 107
inkwells, 132, 148, *244*, 254, *280*
International Exhibition of Historical and Modern Costumes and Accessories, 156
international expositions. *See* Esposizione Internationale (1902, Turin); Exposition Universelle (1889, 1900, Paris); Great Exhibition (1851, London); Louisiana Purchase Exhibition (1904, St. Louis); Pan-American Exposition (1901, Buffalo); World's Columbian Exposition (1893, Chicago)
Janvier, Lucien-Joseph-René, *32*, 33, 332
Japonisme, 45
    influence of, 37, 45, *80*, 81, 82, *85*, 100, 114, *115*, 115, *116*, 116, 127, 171, 208, 232, *233*, 235, 254, 272, *286*, 298
Jensen, Georg, *28*, 332
Kalo Shop, 5, 332
Kelch, Barbara, 61, 67, 175
    and charity, 67
    and Fabergé, 62–68
Kelkh, Varvara. *See* Kelch, Barbara
Keller Frères, *35*, 35, *168*, 168, *169*, 332
Keller, Gustave, 168
"Keller Style," 169
Kelly, Grace. *See* Grace (princess)
Khlebnikov, Ivan P., 153, 189, 196, 210, 212
Klimt, Gustav, 38
Knox, Archibald, 5, *79*, 254
kokoshnik, 26, 28, *28*, 191, 192, 216, 217
Korchakov-Sivitsky Firm, 184
kovsh, 28, *187*, 187, *196*, *214*, 215, 223, 246
Kschessinskaia, Mathilda, 89, 91, 95

Kunz, George Frederick, 59, *231*, 243, 246, 253, 258, 268, *293*, 293, 294–98, 314
kunzite, *294*, 294, *295*, 295
Lachenal, Raoul, *20*, 332
Lalique, René, 1, 4, *11*, 11, *13*, 13, 15, *17*, 20, 29, 35, 37, 77, 78–151, 332
    and Art Nouveau, 13, *16*, 16, *17*, 20, 103, 120, 121, 122, 123, 130
    business strategies of/advertising, 9, 60, 89
    criticism of, 4, 5, 17, 45, 87, 92, 94
    and dreams/poetry, 109
    as glassmaker, 41, *45*, 45, 46, *70*, 70, 123
    innovation, 17, 69, 85
    and Japonisme, *85*, 114, 115
    and museums, 57, 60
    and nature, *33*, 40, *101*, 75, *84*, *85*, 111, *115*
    and perfume bottles, 120–25
    praise of, 4, 16, *85*, 86, 109, 131
    and Russia, 154, 155, 158–61, 168
    and sculptural jewelry, 111, *132*, 132–34, *144*, 144
    and Siegfried Bing, 11
    as theatrical designer, 86, 87, 89, 92, 94
    techniques of, 20, 87, 130, *131*, 131, 140
    use of female form, 126–30
    use of materials, 17, *40*, 46, 75, 86, 130, 131, 136–48
Lalique, Suzanne, *46*, 46
Langtry, Lillie, 91, 256
L'Art Nouveau, 3, 11, *13*, *80*, 81, 82, 103, 155, 287
    and Colonna, *81*, 82, 287
    and L. C. Tiffany, 81, *284*, 289
    and Bing, 3, *80*, 81, 82, 103, 284
La Société des Vingt, 78
Lawrence, F. Walter, *233*, 335
Le Couteux, Lionel-Aristide, *111*, 326
Liberty and Co., *75*, 79, *80*, 80, 335
Liberty, Arthur Lasenby. *See* Liberty and Co.
Lilies of the Valley Basket (Imperial), 21, *182*
literature, 109, 128
Lorié, Fedor, firm of, *224*, 335
Louisiana Purchase Exhibition (1904, St. Louis), 13, 35, 37, 69
Louis-Philippe I (king of France), 239
MacDonald, Margaret, 38
Mackintosh, Charles Rennie, 38, *39*
Mackmurdo, A. H., 76
Maison Moderne, La, 3, 5, 33, 40, 81, *82*, 82

Marcus & Co., *239*, *249*, 249, 250–55, 273, 335
    use of materials, 249
Marcus, George, 249
Marcus, Herman, 249
    and Tiffany & Co., *249*
    See also Marcus & Co.
Marcus, William, 249
Maria Feodorovna (dowager empress), 170, 174, 177, 185, 187, 188
Maria Pavlovna (grand duchess), 165, 183, *188*, 188–94, *190*, *191*
marketing techniques, 89, 91
Marlborough, Duchess of (Consuelo Vanderbilt), 61, 62, 65, 62–68
    and charity, 65, 67
    divorce of, 65
    and Fabergé, 64, 65, 67
    and jewelry, 63, 65
    wedding of, 62, 63
marriages
    between European royalty and wealthy Americans, 62, 66, 256, 266
    and luxury goods as wedding presents, 257, 266
Martelé, 33, 35, 302
Marx, Roger, 76, 83, 86, 99, 100, 102, 132
Masriera, firm of (later Masriera y Carreras). *See* Bagués-Masriera, firm of
Masriera, Lluís Rosés, 102–7, 336
    and Bing family, 103
medievalism, 4, 38, 76, 104, *135*, 135
Meier-Graefe, Julius, 78, 81, 82
    La Maison Moderne, 3, 5, 35, 40, 81, *82*
Mellerio dits Meller, *60*, 336
miniatures, *64*, 165, 174, 177, *178*, 178, *191*, 192, 198, 199, 202, 222
Mir Iskusstva, 3, 39, 156, 157
Mir Iskusstva, *39*, 39, *156*, *157*, 157, 159, 160, 161
Modernism, 5, 29, 37–56, *50*, 73, 75, 86, *116*
Modernisme, 102, 104
Molinier, Émile, 83, 85, 86, 87, 109, 130
Moore, Edward C., *244*, 246, 269, 284
Morgan, J. P., 59, *295*, *296*, 296
Morris & Co., 76
Morris, Marshall, & Faulkner. *See* Morris & Co.
Morris, William, 1, 4, *37*, 38, 50, 76, 77
Moscow, 13, 15, 28, 61, 66
    and "Russian Style," 13
    and workshops, 28, *29*, *196*, 196
Moscow Kremlin Armory, 66, 178, 185

Moser, Kolomon, 38, *317*, 317

Mucha, Alphonse, 91, *92*, 95, 99

Munson, Julia, 50, *53*, 310, 314

Musée du Louvre, 83, *239*, 240, 241, 244

museums, 53, 57, 77, 85, 87, 155, 174, 204, 235, 284, 286, 294

Nabis, 284, 286

Napoleon III (emperor), *239*, 239, 240

Nash, Arthur J., 232, 280

nationalism, 223

native traditions, 15, 16, *28*, 28, 29, 156, *157*, *175*, *211*, 215, 254, 268, 269, *301*, 301, *302*

Nereid Service, 1, 29

Nicholas I (tsar), 171, 196, 204, 207, 211, 219, 220, 247

Nicholas II (tsar), 13, 15, *26*, *54*, *55*, 63, 63, 89, 91, 156, 159, 160, *161*, 161, *163*, 163, *165*, 165, 167, *168*, 168, 169, 171, 174, *175*, 175, *177*, *178*, 178, *187*, *188*, 188, *207*, 207, 210, *214*, 215, 217, 220, 222, 246, 261

Nocq, Henry, *84*, 85

occultism, 127, 260, 296, 297

Olovianishnikov, P. I., & Sons, *208*, 208, 336

opera, 2, 3, 63, 223, *256*, 256, 258

ornament, 17, 20, *21*, *38*, 54, 81, *84*, 87, 91, *99*, 100, *115*, 128, 136, *147*, 168, 183, *184*, 216, 219, 231, 233, 236, 239, *242*, 244, 247, 249, 252, 253, 259, 261, 264, 266, 268, *296*, 297

Ovchinnikov, Pavel, firm of, 196, 207, *208*, 208, 210

Overbeck, Meta, *314*, 314

Pan-American Exposition (1901, Buffalo), 35, 291, 314

Pansy Egg (Imperial), 20, 21, 26, 177

pendants, 17, *20*, 20, *46*, 79, 87, 92, *104*, *109*, 115, 130, *135*, *136*, *140*, 144, *155*, 155, 159, 160, *161*, 161, 162, 174, *175*, 175, 190, *191*, 191, 217, 217, 219, 242, 244, 251, 267, 270, *271*, 297, 298, *310*, 314

perfume bottles. *See* flacons

Perkhin, Mikhail, 28, 67, 196

Peter the Great (tsar), *192*, 194, 220, 221

plique-à-jour. *See* enameling, plique-à-jour

Plisson & Hartz, *135*, 336

Plumet, Charles, 87, 128

Polovtsov, Alexander, 155

Potter & Mellen, *x*, 260, 337

Pre-Raphaelites, 79

Providence Stock Co., 91

Rainier III (prince), 66

Red Cross Egg (Imperial), 55, *177*, 177

Rocaille Egg (Kelch), 67

Rookwood Pottery Co., 28, 301, 302, *303*, 337

Rose Trellis Egg (Imperial), 177, *178*

Roycrofters, 3

Rückert, Fedor I., *196*, 196, 337

Ruskin, John, 38, 76, 79, 132

   Stones of Venice, 76

Russell, Lillian ("Diamond Lil"), 91, *92*, 93, 94

Russia

   architecture of, 198, 206, 207, 212

   and imperial family, 153, 156, 160, 161, *163*, 163, 165, 166, 167, 168, 169, 171, 174, 175, *177*, 177, 178, 183, 202, 215, 216, 217, 220, 222

   imperial patronage, 214

   influence of French art in/relationship with France, 153, 155, 165, *166*, 168

   and national pride taken in art, 214

   style *(Russkii stil')*, 191, 196, 207, 211, 212, 214, *215*, 215, 223, 247

   and Western jewelry, 163, 194

Russian Red Cross, 54, 67, *177*, 177 Exhibition, 153, 156

Saché, Georges le, 3, *244*, 244, *249*, 254

salons, France, 3, 11, 17, 60, 82, 86, 87, 109, 130

   Société des Artistes Français, 77, *86*

   Société du Progrès de l'Art Industriel. *See* Union Centrale des Arts Décoratifs

   Société Nationale des Beaux-Arts, 77, 82

Saunier, Charles, 97, 99, 100, 130, 144

Sazikov, Ignati, 207, 208

Scherbatov (prince), 158, 159, *161*

Seder, Anton, 29, *29*, 337

Sèvres Porcelain Factory, 165, 166, 170

Société des Artistes Français. *See* salons, France

Société du Progrès de l'Art Industriel. *See* Union Centrale des Arts Décoratifs

Société Nationale des Beaux-Arts. *See* salons, France

South Kensington Museum (now Victorian and Albert Museum), 35, 40, 155, 235

stained glass. *See* glass, stained

Starr & Marcus, 249, 250–55

Starr, Theodore B., 249

Stieglitz, Alexander von, baron, 35, 155, *289*, 291

   Stieglitz School of Applied Arts, 35, 153, *155*, 155, 156, *159*

St. Louis World's Fair. *See* Louisiana Purchase Exhibition (1904)

Stroganov Academy of Fine and Industrial Arts, 155

Stüber, Otto, *52*, 337

Symbolism, 2, 33, 99, 102, 127, 132, *224*, 224 in jewelry, 99, *109*

Talashkino, 28, *211*, 211

Tassel, Émile, 77

Téterger, Henri, *97*, 97, 337

Theater, 2, 3

   in America, 89, 91, 92, 94, 260

   in France, *86*, 86, 91, 92, 94, 99

Thesmar, André Fernand, *208*, 337

tiaras, 2, 3, 26, 28, 63, 84, 86, 92, *125*, 159, 160, *161*, 163, *191*, 191, 192, 216, 217, 219, 222, 231, 256

Tiffany & Co., 3, 5, *5*, 8, 10, 11, 16, 20, 28, 50, *53*, 54, 61, 63, 69, 70, 82, 148, 230–323, 338

   business strategies of/advertising, 60, 234, 235, 244, 304

   clients of, *59*, 59, 231, 253, 255, 256, 301, 309

   competitors of, 35, *249*

   criticism of, 17, 231, 232

   and exhibitions, 231

   and French crown jewels, 239, 241, 242

   founding of, 235

   and hollowware, 232, 246, 269, 270, 284, 299, 310

   and importing of foreign jewels and precious objects, 236

   and museums, 54, 235

   in Paris, 59, 244, 249

   and Russia, 246, 247, 247, 294, 297

   and silver, 244, 246, 269, 293, 301

   staff of, 246, 279, 280, 286, 304

Tiffany, Charles Lewis, 10, 69, 231, 234, 235, 236, 244, 246, 256, 270, 272, 294, 310

Tiffany Glass & Decorating Co., 10, 16, 231, 232, 262, 268, 276, 288, 293, 302, 339

Tiffany, Louis Comfort, 1, 5, 11, 46, *53*, 230–323, 339

   business strategies of/adverstising, 234, 235

   decline of, 50

   as designer at Tiffany & Co./as jewelry designer, 10, 69

   and Exposition Universelle (1900, Paris), 5, 10, 231, 232

   and glass, 9, 10, 33, 35, 81, 82

   influence, 50

   as interior designer, 232

   and lamps, 232, 274, *276*, 276, 279, 281, 287, *291*, 291, 301, *304*, 309

and museums, 232
and Siegfried Bing, 8, 9, 81
training of/early years of, 10, 11, 13
use of materials, 232, 253, 268, 270, 293, 299
Tiffany school, 246
Tiffany Studios, *50*, 50, *53*, 70, 339
Tsarskoe Selo, *54*, 54, 163, 165, 169, 174, 183, 215
Union Centrale des Arts Décoratifs, 76, 132
Vallotton, Félix, *17*, 17, 82
Vanderbilt, Consuelo. *See* Marlborough, Duchess of
Vekselberg, Viktor, 66
Velde, Henry Van de, *78*, 78, 81, 82, 341
Vessel of Russia, 194
Vever, Henri. *See* Vever, Maison
Vever, Maison, 5, 11, *12*, 16, *17*, 17, 29, 86, 87, 94, 97, *99*, 99, 144, 160, 241, 244, 257, 302, 341

Viard, Julien, 124, *125*, 341
Vienna Secession, 35, 39, *50*, 50, 314, *317*
Vladimir Alexandrovich (grand duke), *91*, 91, 161, 165, 174, *188*, 188, 214, 216
Vladimir Palace, 174, 188
decoration of, 188
Von Dervis mansion, *64*, 64, 67
See also Fabergé, Peter Carl, *Artistic Objects and Miniatures by Fabergé* exhibition
Vrubel, Mikhail A., 39, 223, *224*
Wade, Jeptha Homer, I, *260*, 260, 262
Wade, Jeptha Homer, II, and Ellen Garretson Wade, *59*, 59, *256*, 257–59, *260*–65
Wade Memorial Chapel, 262
Walters, Henry, 35, 60, *231*, 266, 298
watches, *109*
lapel, *249*
pendant, *249*, *252*
wrist, 236, 237
Whiting & Davis, 91

Wigström, Henrik, *196*, 196, *198*, 198, *199*
Winter Palace, *166*, 167, 168, 169, 171, 178, 188, *191*, 191, 210, *215*, 215, *219*, 222, 204
Wolfers, Philippe, 17, *147*, 147, 341
World's Columbian Exposition (1893, Chicago), 10, 11, 16, 28, 50, *82*, 89, 183, 210, 257, 262, 268, *269*, 270, *271*, 271, 280, 281, 284, 291, 314
world's fairs, 1, 10, 120
See also international expositions
World of Art, 39, 156
See also Mir Iskusstva
World War I, 35, 45, *46*, 46, *54*, 54, 55, 63, 68, 69, 192
effects on art, 35, 53
effects on artists, 35, 45, 53, 68, 70, 304
effects on luxury, 35, 45, 318
effects on Russian art world, 55, 192
Xenia Alexandrovna (grand duchess), 156, 184, 217, *219*, 222, *246*
Young, John Burnett, 235, 236, 239

Necklace (cat. 255). Tiffany & Co.